ORGANIC CHEMISTRY

Organic Chemistry

G . H . DAZELEY
M.A., Ph.D., *Rugby School*

 CAMBRIDGE UNIVERSITY PRESS

Published by the Syndics of the Cambridge University Press
Bentley House, 200 Euston Road, London NW1 2DB
American Branch: 32 East 57th Street, New York, N.Y.10022

© Cambridge University Press 1969

Library of Congress Catalogue Card Number: 69-10061

ISBN: 0 521 07171 2

First published 1969
Reprinted with corrections 1972
Reprinted 1974

Printed in Great Britain
at the University Printing House, Cambridge
(Brooke Crutchley, University Printer)

Contents

Contents

Section III

vi

Preface

This book presents a view of organic chemistry which can be appreciated by a student with some knowledge of elementary chemistry, and who is now beginning to study organic chemistry in detail. The basic material covered is that of any intermediate chemistry course, and I have tried to set out this material so that the book can be used as a textbook. Where the book contains a more detailed treatment, the topics chosen for further discussion are those which seem most likely to spring from the student's own curiosity as aroused by his elementary work. Mechanisms of some of the more salient reaction types have been discussed. It is impossible at this level and in a book of this size and scope to give entirely adequate experimental evidence for suggested mechanisms, but I have tried as far as possible to avoid making assertions about reaction mechanisms unless some hint at least of experimental justification can be given.

After the introductory chapters, I have discussed the reactions of each of the most familiar functional groups in turn. I have adopted a unified treatment of aliphatic and aromatic compounds; for example the chemistry of the hydroxyl group in both alcohols and phenols is discussed in chapter 11. Those who prefer the traditional approach of segregating aliphatic and aromatic compounds should find this no obstacle to using the book; it can be a positive advantage to see the subject matter discussed from two different angles. Methods for preparing the various functional types of compound have been given at the ends rather than the beginnings of chapters; this is less likely to distract attention from the study of the functional type itself. The reactions of a number of the more familiar compounds with two or more functional groups are set out in chapter 20.

I have made no attempt to cover the field of organic chemical industry comprehensively. It would have been impossible to produce a worthwhile survey in a book of this size, even if it had been thought desirable. A number of industrial processes are outlined under the appropriate functional group headings. I have included separate chapters on the petroleum industry and on fibres and plastics, partly because they represent very important contributions of organic chemistry to the twentieth century scene, but also because of the interest of the reactions involved. In addition, the discussion of fibres and plastics is a natural extension of the study of bi- and multi-functional compounds. In all cases, I have tried to emphasize the basic physics and chemistry rather than the technological practice of industrial processes.

I have included a comprehensive set of questions with a wide range of difficulty; some of those attached to later chapters inevitably assume a knowledge of the contents of the earlier ones.

I am very greatly indebted to Dr John Biggs of the Chemistry Department of Hull University, who read the whole book in typescript with meticulous attention. Besides correcting my errors, he suggested many improvements in style and treatment which I have gratefully incorporated.

G. H. D.

1972 Reprint

Various misprints and errors have been corrected, and the opportunity has been taken to convert physical quantities to SI units where appropriate.

G. H. D.

1

Introduction

Organic chemistry is the chemistry of the compounds of carbon. This statement immediately poses two questions. Why is the term 'organic' used? Why should the chemistry of one particular element constitute a branch of the science sufficiently self-contained to require a distinctive name?

By the early years of the nineteenth century, chemists had isolated many compounds from living organisms, plant and animal. Unlike the substances obtained in the laboratory from sources which had never been part of a living organism, these compounds seemed at first to require the processes of life for their production. Moreover, many of them were shown by combustion in air or oxygen to contain only the elements carbon, hydrogen and oxygen. Even though other elements, for example nitrogen, were present in some, it seemed an indefinitely large number of compounds, always containing carbon but few other elements, could occur in living organisms. This was in striking contrast with compounds from non-living, or 'in-organic' sources, where the number of different substances obtainable from the same elements—say, hydrogen, nitrogen and oxygen—appeared strictly limited. The two types of substance and their chemistry became known as organic and inorganic respectively. It was widely supposed that some 'vital force' was required for the production of organic substances. It was even doubted whether the laws and principles applying in inorganic chemistry were valid for organic chemistry.

The names have remained, though some of the earlier ideas attached to them proved to be irrelevant. Numerous carbon compounds have been synthesized in the laboratory without using living processes. Although biochemistry, the chemistry of life processes, is not identical in scope with organic chemistry, both are concerned primarily with carbon compounds, mostly of great complexity. It is significant that the known compounds of carbon far outnumber the non-carbon-containing compounds of all the other elements put together. In addition the experimental methods and theories evolved to investigate carbon compounds form a sufficiently extensive and self-contained body of knowledge and method to be regarded as a separate study.

There are a number of reasons for this:

(*a*) Carbon atoms can combine with one another in any number to form stable 'chains' of atoms of any length and complexity. No other element possesses this property of *catenation* in quite the same sense, though several other non-metals in the neighbourhood of carbon in the Periodic Table show similar properties. For example silicon, in the same group as carbon though the next period, has been shown to form chains of up to 5 atoms, and chains of up to eight germanium atoms have been prepared. Longer chains are so unstable that so far they have not been obtained. Some elements, for example silicon and phosphorus, can form complex chain structures with alternate silicon (or phosphorus) and oxygen atoms, thus giving rise to the multifarious silicate and phosphate ions. Even so, the precise structure of all but the simplest of these is not under the control of the laboratory chemist, whereas many carbon structures are.

(*b*) Carbon atoms, whether singly or as part of a chain, form bonds of more or less equal stability with hydrogen, oxygen, nitrogen or the halogens, although hydrogen is electropositive and the rest are electronegative. In extreme contrast with this is the stability of ammonia and water compared with the instability of nitrogen trichloride and oxygen dichloride (chlorine monoxide). Conversely one may compare, say, the relative stability of arsenic trichloride with the easy thermal decomposition of arsine.

With any particular 'skeleton' of carbon atoms, those valency bonds not used to link the carbon atoms of the skeleton may hold atoms of hydrogen, oxygen, chlorine, nitrogen, and so on, in more or less any sequence. We can therefore have not only an indefinitely large number of possible carbon skeletons, but also for each particular skeleton a large number of molecular structures containing other elements derived by varying additions of different atoms to the skeleton.

(*c*) The atomic number of carbon is 6. In addition to the two electrons of the *K* shell, the carbon atom in the ground state has four electrons in the *L* shell out of a maximum of eight. The formation of four covalent bonds therefore leaves no valency electron unshared and at the same time completes the valency shell. Carbon is unique in this respect. Of the other elements in the same period, those preceding carbon (lithium, beryllium and boron) will not complete the group of eight when all their valency electrons are shared.

2

Those succeeding it (nitrogen, oxygen and fluorine) will have one or more unshared (or lone) pairs when the group of eight is completed by covalency formation. In the subsequent periods, the valency shell is not limited to eight electrons. For example the M shell can contain 18 electrons. With carbon alone, therefore, the octet can be completed by forming single covalent bonds and the number of bonds so formed is the covalency maximum of the atom. Compounds in which carbon is covalently linked to four other atoms do not show marked acceptor tendencies (like, say, BF_3 or SiH_4) since there are no spaces in an outer electron shell to accommodate additional electrons. Nor, on the other hand, does it show any donor tendencies (like NH_3 or H_2O) since there are no lone pairs. Therefore these compounds usually show a fairly high degree of what may be called 'chemical inertia'. An attacking reagent can only become attached to the carbon atom if one of the existing covalent bonds to it is 'broken' in some way, either as a preliminary to or simultaneously with the approach of the attacking molecule, ion or radical. It is not surprising that many reactions of organic compounds proceed slowly and reversibly, and that the experimental methods developed to deal with them reflect this point.

Formulae and structure; isomerism

The great majority of organic compounds are non-electrolytes or weak electrolytes. The obvious exceptions to this statement are the salts of organic acids such as acetic acid or of bases such as aniline. In general they are fairly volatile and of comparatively low melting point. However there is no upper limit to melting points or lower limit to volatility. Such familiar substances as methane or calor gas (butane) on the one hand and some of the constituents of tar or pitch on the other, comprise a range within which a very large number of organic compounds would fall. These properties indicate that most organic compounds exist as separate molecules, and not as ionic or macromolecular lattices. The molecular weight of such a compound can be determined by vapour density or colligative property methods. Furthermore, the proportions by weight of the constituent elements can be found. This information combined with a knowledge of the relevant atomic weights enables a formula to be allotted to the compound showing the numbers of each kind of atom constituting the molecule. Such a formula is called the *molecular formula* of the substance (see pp. 33–34).

It soon became obvious that a molecular formula does not give a unique definition of an organic substance. Different substances may have the same molecular formula. For example the formula C_3H_8O applies to three different substances, each having different well-defined physical characteristics (melting point, boiling point, refractive index, etc.) and different chemical properties. Different substances having the same molecular formula are known as *isomers*; a word taken from the Greek, signifying 'the same parts'. Such substances are said to be *isomeric* with one another, or to show *isomerism*. On the other hand, though isomers may differ markedly, substances of different molecular formula may be chemically similar. Thus the chemical behaviour of each isomer of formula C_3H_8O is closely resembled by that of one or more of the isomers of $C_4H_{10}O$.

Clearly then the molecular formula is inadequate to represent the chemical individuality of an organic substance. We need to know not only how many of each kind of atom make up the molecule, but also the way these atoms are put together. This concept, that a molecule has not only a composition but a *molecular structure*, was essential to the great development of organic chemistry in the nineteenth century, and is a major contribution of organic chemistry to chemical thinking.

Each atom is thought of as being linked to other atoms of the molecule by a definite number of *valency bonds*. The number of such bonds formed by each atom corresponds to its elementary numerical valency, defined as the number of hydrogen atoms which combine with a single atom of the element. For example, carbon atoms form four bonds, hydrogen and halogen atoms one, oxygen atoms usually two and nitrogen atoms usually three and so on. An extension of this idea supposes that two atoms can be linked by more than one of their valency bonds, giving the concept of *multiple* (*double and triple*) *bonds* (see chapters 5 and 6).

The development of these ideas by Kekulé and his followers in the 1860s made it possible to allot to the molecules of many substances structures deduced from the molecular formula and chemical behaviour of the substance. It was used in turn to interpret this behaviour, and to account for isomerism, where this was observed. By writing the chemical symbol for each atom and a dash for each valency bond, *graphical formulae* can be written to show molecular structures as in the following illustrations. (The student need not for the moment concern himself with the significance of the names.)

methane	water	ammonia	carbon dioxide

H
|
H—C—O—H
|
H

methyl alcohol

H H H
| | |
H—C—C—C—O—H
| | |
H H H

normal propyl alcohol

H H H
| | |
H—C—C—C—H
| | |
H O H
   |
   H

isopropyl alcohol

H   H H
| | |
H—C—O—C—C—H
| | |
H   H H

methyl ethyl ether

The last three formulae demonstrate the three possible isomers of molecular formula C_3H_8O.

In these formulae, the arrangement of the atomic symbols on the page relative to the atom or atoms to which they are linked is largely conventional. Even in the nineteenth century, however, chemists found it necessary to assume that, when an atom was linked to more than one other, the bonds involved had definite directions in space relative to each other. This meant that there was a definite *bond angle* between any pair of them—and it is an obvious corollary to assume that the bonds are of definite length, although the measurement of bond lengths had to await the development of X-ray crystallography in the twentieth century. In the particular case of the four valencies of a carbon atom attached to four other atoms, the bonds are directed towards the corners of a regular tetrahedron with the carbon atom at its centre, each bond angle therefore being 109° 28'. The classical argument for assuming this is based on the phenomena of optical activity and mirror-image isomerism (see pp. 298–300). Therefore molecules containing carbon atoms bonded in this way are three dimensional. This aspect can only be represented on paper by perspective drawing or by some kind of convention. Graphical formulae such as those given above are liable to mislead the elementary student, who must get a better appreciation of the relative positions of the atoms in space by constructing 'ball-and-spring' models. Springs (e.g. short lengths of expanding curtain-rod) are used to represent the bonds, and spheres with holes drilled towards the centre at the appropriate angles to represent the *centres* of the atoms (though not the space 'filled' by them). A little juggling will show that the graphical formula of dimethyl ether, for example, is a conventionalized projection onto the paper of a suitably oriented three-dimensional model (see Fig. 1).

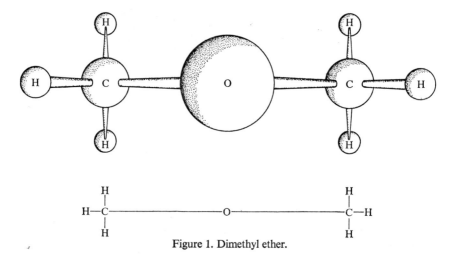

Figure 1. Dimethyl ether.

Formulae such as

$$\underset{\underset{\text{H H H}}{|\ |\ |}}{\overset{\overset{\text{H H H}}{|\ |\ |}}{\text{H—C—C—C—H}}} \qquad \text{and} \qquad \underset{\overset{\text{H}}{\underset{\text{H—C—H}}{|}}}{\overset{\overset{\text{H H}}{|\ |}}{\text{H—C——C—H}}}$$

do *not* represent isomers of C_3H_8, but are simply conventionalized projections on to different planes of one and the same three-dimensional structure.

Bond lengths and bond angles may be changed by distorting forces; that is, by the input of energy in some way. (In these respects, therefore, a spring is qualitatively quite a suitable concrete analogy for the conceptual 'model' of a valency bond). Moreover, it is believed that atoms linked by a single bond can rotate about it as an axis, carrying with them all the other attached atoms. The only exceptions to this occur when the structures of the groups of atoms linked by this axis are such as to cause an overlap which presents a mechanical obstacle to the rotation (see p. 306). This assumption is necessary to account for the fact that no case of isomerism is known which can be attributed simply to a lack of such rotation. There is, for example, only one compound (ethylene dibromide) to which the structure

$$\underset{\underset{\text{H H}}{|\ |}}{\overset{\overset{\text{H H}}{|\ |}}{\text{Br—C—C—Br}}}$$

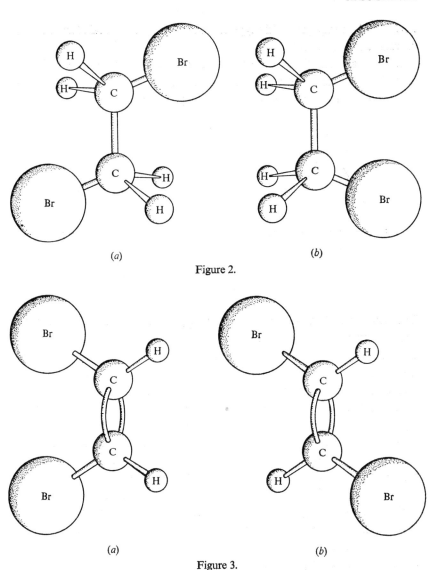

Figure 2.

Figure 3.

can be allotted. The three-dimensional arrangements of Fig. 2(*a*) and (*b*) do not represent different molecules having some degree of permanence, but simply different *conformations* through which the ethylene dibromide molecule passes, at ordinary temperatures, many times per second. Multiple bonds, however, restrict this freedom of rotation, so that the arrangements in Fig. 3(*a*) and (*b*) do represent molecular arrangements of sufficient permanency to give rise to isomeric substances, the so-called *cis-* and *trans*-dibromoethylenes. This type of isomerism (geometrical isomerism) is discussed on pp. 310–14.

It is a characteristic of the regular tetrahedron that, if a different 'label' is applied to each apex, there are two different ways of doing it, yielding figures which are non-identical mirror-images one of the other.

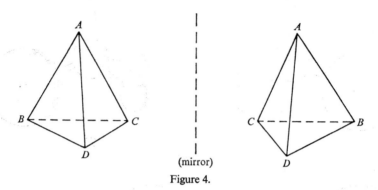

(mirror)

Figure 4.

The tetrahedral distribution of the four carbon valencies therefore leads to 'mirror-image' isomerism when the four valencies are attached to four different groups of atoms. This type of isomerism is discussed in pp. 297 on. Indeed, it was the occurrence of such isomerism which led to the assumption that the four carbon valencies were tetrahedrally distributed.

In the example of isomerism quoted earlier (that of the substances C_3H_8O), to derive one isomeric molecule from another would involve breaking the bonds between two or more atoms in the molecule, and rejoining the bonds so broken to different atoms. For example, to convert the normal propyl alcohol molecule to that of methyl ethyl ether, the oxygen atom would have to be removed from its position between an end carbon and a hydrogen atom and reinserted between two carbon atoms. With geometrical and mirror-image isomers, this is not so. To convert one isomer to another the broken bonds would be rejoined to the *same* atoms, but the spatial arrangements resulting are not identical. By convention the first type is called *structural isomerism*, and the second and third types *stereoisomerism* (that is, spatial isomerism). In the ordinary sense of the word, all isomerism is a matter of differences in molecular structure, and all isomerism involves different spatial arrangements of the same atoms.

The graphical formulae which have just been used (and still more, the perspective drawings of models) are far too clumsy for everyday use, especially with complex molecules. Following the conventions of organic formula-writing certain groups of atoms of frequent occurrence can be written in abbreviated forms without introducing any ambiguities. The formula of isopropyl alcohol (shown graphically on p. 5) can then be written $CH_3.CHOH.CH_3$ or $(CH_3)_2CHOH$. In the first example the carbon atoms of the chain are written in order, and the full-stops indicate the bonds between the carbon atoms.

However, a formula such as $CH_3.CH_3.CHOH$ is wrong since it implies a central carbon atom with a valency of five and a terminal carbon with a valency of three. Any formula adequate to show the structure of a molecule unambiguously is known as a *structural* or *constitutional formula*.

It is essential for those studying organic chemistry to learn the habit of thinking of organic molecules as three-dimensional structures rather than solely in terms of paper formulae. This requires constant effort in the early stages, and the frequent use of molecular models.

Paraffins

A compound of carbon and hydrogen only is known as a *hydrocarbon*. Hydrocarbons in which the carbon atoms are linked by single valency bonds only, to form an open chain as opposed to a closed chain or ring, are known as *paraffins*.

an open chain   a closed chain or ring

Since carbon skeletons can be of any size and complexity, there is a large number of possible paraffin structures. Accordingly, we find a whole series of paraffins, the first few of which are listed below in order of increasing number of carbon atoms in the molecule:

$$CH_4 \qquad \text{methane}$$
$$CH_3.CH_3 \qquad \text{ethane}$$
$$CH_3.CH_2.CH_3 \qquad \text{propane}$$
$$CH_3.CH_2.CH_2.CH_3 \qquad \text{normal-butane}$$
$$\text{(n-butane)} \quad \Big\} \text{ isomers of } C_4H_{10}$$
$$CH_3.CH.CH_3 \qquad \text{isobutane}$$
$$\quad | $$
$$\quad CH_3$$

The prefix 'normal' (abbreviated *n-*) indicates an unbranched chain of carbon atoms; iso- indicates a single branch $\overset{\displaystyle CH_3}{\underset{\displaystyle CH_3}{\diagdown}}$CH— at the end of an otherwise unbranched chain. It will be seen that the molecular formula of any paraffin corresponds to the general formula C_nH_{2n+2} (a consequence of the quadrivalency of carbon and the univalency of hydrogen). Any member of the series can be regarded as formally derived from the preceding member by replacing one hydrogen atom in its molecule by the univalent group of atoms CH_3— (called a *methyl* group—see below). This extends the carbon skeleton at some point by one carbon atom.

Paraffins are comparatively unreactive substances; the name is a concoction from the Latin 'parum affinis', signifying 'having too little affinity'. (Such few reactions of paraffins as are of elementary interest are reviewed in chapter 4).

Functional groups and homologous series

If other atoms or groups of atoms are introduced in place of one or more of the hydrogen atoms of a paraffin molecule, the resulting molecule is usually considerably more reactive than the parent paraffin. Its reactivity is largely confined to the introduced atoms or groups, the 'residue' of the paraffin molecule retaining its original inertness to a large extent. (Exceptions to this statement usually concern those carbon atoms of the paraffin residue to which the introduced atoms are directly attached). We accordingly find that the length and complexity of the paraffin residue to which the other atoms are attached is of small and often negligible importance in determining the reactions of the substance. For example, *n*-propyl alcohol $CH_3 . CH_2 . CH_2OH$ undergoes the same reactions as *n*-butyl alcohol $CH_3 . CH_2 . CH_2 . CH_2OH$ or *n*-dodecyl alcohol $CH_3 . (CH_2)_{11}OH$, the only differences being in the rates of reaction with a given reagent under the same conditions of concentration and temperature. Branching of the chain remote from the attached group is equally of little importance; isobutyl alcohol $(CH_3)_2CH . CH_2OH$ shows the same reactions.

Such molecules are thought of as a more or less inert paraffin residue attached to a reactive atom or group of atoms known as a *functional group*. (A multivalent functional group will, of course, be attached to two or more paraffin residues). Organic chemistry is thus less concerned with the behaviour of individual substances than with the behaviour of whole series of substances containing particular functional groups. As with the paraffins themselves, each member of such a series is formally derived from the preceding member by replacing —H by —CH_3, and all members will conform to a general molecular formula. For the alcohols mentioned above, this is $C_nH_{2n+1}OH$. Such a series of compounds is called a *homologous series*. This may be formally defined as a *series of compounds of the same functional type, in which the molecular formula of any member differs from that of the preceding member by* CH_2. The members of such a series are said to be *homologues* of one another.

As to what atoms constitute the functional group in a molecule, this is to some extent a matter of convenience. Thus all alcohols contain the group —OH. If this is attached to a non-terminal atom of the paraffin chain, certain differences of behaviour appear. It is therefore sometimes convenient to subdivide the homologous series of alcohols into subsidiary series of primary alcohols (functional group —CH_2OH) secondary alcohols (functional group $>CHOH$) and tertiary alcohols (functional group $>COH$).

Many of the most familiar functional groups are univalent. When one such group replaces a hydrogen atom of a paraffin chain, the remaining paraffin residue is a univalent group of atoms of the general formula C_nH_{2n+1}. This is known as an *alkyl* group. The alkyl groups corresponding to the lower paraffins are listed below.

CH_4 methane	CH_3— methyl
$CH_3.CH_3$ ethane	$CH_3.CH_2$—$(C_2H_5$—$)$ ethyl
	$CH_3.CH_2CH_2$— *n*-propyl
$CH_3.CH_2.CH_3$ propane	$\begin{array}{c}CH_3\\ \diagdown\\ CH—\\ \diagup\\ CH_3\end{array}$ isopropyl
	$CH_3.CH_2.CH_2.CH_2$— *n*-butyl
$CH_3.CH_2.CH_2.CH_3$ *n*-butane	$\begin{array}{c}CH_3CH_2\\ \diagdown\\ CH—\\ \diagup\\ CH_3\end{array}$ secondary butyl
$\begin{array}{c}CH_3\\ \diagdown\\ CH.CH_3\\ \diagup\\ CH_3\end{array}$ isobutane	$\begin{array}{c}CH_3\\ \diagdown\\ CH.CH_2—\\ \diagup\\ CH_3\end{array}$ isobutyl
	$\begin{array}{c}CH_3\\ CH_3\diagup\hspace{-4pt}>C—\\ CH_3\end{array}$ tertiary butyl or *t*-butyl

In many formulae, it is convenient to abbreviate CH_3— to Me, C_2H_5— to Et, *n*-C_3H_7— to *n*-Pr and so on. 'Tertiary' is nearly always abbreviated to *t*-, for example *t*-butyl.

Generalizing the relation between the names of the alkyl groups and the parent hydrocarbons, paraffins are now systematically known as alkanes. However, the older name is still widely used.

Functional groups may replace hydrogen atoms in other types of hydrocarbon besides paraffins; thus phenol, C_6H_5OH, is derived from benzene, C_6H_6. The definition of homologues and homologous series remains valid. The next higher homologues of phenol are the cresols, isomers of the formula $CH_3.C_6H_4.OH$.

The group $C_6H_5—$, bearing the same relation to benzene as $CH_3—$ to methane, is known as the *phenyl* group, and is sometimes conveniently abbreviated to Ph, or ϕ.

Compounds whose functional groups are attached to paraffinic residues are known as *aliphatic* (from the Greek ἀλειφή, lard, since fats are compounds of this type). Those containing benzene residues belong to the category known as *aromatic* (see chapters 7 and 8).

In the second section of this book, the chemical behaviour of the functional groups most commonly met with is discussed mainly in terms of the properties and reactions of compounds of single function; that is, compounds whose molecules contain a single functional group attached to residues of hydrocarbons of the paraffin or benzene series.

Since it is impossible to describe the chemistry of one functional group without referring to many others, the earlier chapters must inevitably mention many points whose full implications will only appear in the light of later chapters.

It is best to become familiar with the names and structures of the functional groups as soon as possible. They are set out in the following list in the order in which the groups are dealt with in the chapters of Section II:

Paraffins or alkanes C_nH_{2n+2}; alkyl groups, $C_nH_{2n+1}—$.

The olefinic double bond >C=C< in olefins (alkenes).

The acetylenic triple bond $—C\equiv C—$ in acetylenes (alkynes).

The benzene ring, as in benzene C_6H_6 and its derivatives; the symbol

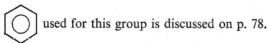 used for this group is discussed on p. 78.

The halide groups $—Cl$, $—Br$, $—I$.

The hydroxyl group $—OH$, in alcohols and phenols.

The ether group $—O—$, where O is bonded to two saturated carbon atoms.

The amino group $—NH_2$ in primary amines and the related groups >NH, >N in secondary and tertiary amines.

The carbonyl group >C=O in aldehydes $(—C\overset{H}{\underset{O}{<}}$, $—CHO)$ and ketones.

The carboxylic acid group (—COOH, —CO$_2$H) and the related groups:

$\quad$—CONH$_2$$\quad$ in amides.

$\quad$—COCl$\quad\quad$ in acyl chlorides.

$\quad$—CO$_2$R$\quad\quad$ in esters (R = alkyl or similar group).

$$\begin{array}{c} -CO \\ \diagdown \\ O \\ \diagup \\ -CO \end{array} \quad \text{in anhydrides.}$$

The cyanide group —C≡N in cyanides (nitriles).

The isocyanide group —N⃗≡C in isocyanides (carbylamines).

The nitro group $-\overset{\oplus}{N}\overset{\diagup O^{\ominus}}{\diagdown O}$ (—NO$_2$) in nitro compounds.

The sulphonic acid group $-\overset{\overset{\displaystyle O}{\parallel}}{\underset{\underset{\displaystyle O}{\parallel}}{S}}-OH$ (—SO$_2$OH, —SO$_3$H)

and the related groups:

$\quad$—SO$_2$NH$_2$$\quad\quad\quad$ in sulphonamides.

$\quad$—SO$_2$Cl$\quad\quad\quad\quad$ in sulphonyl chlorides.

$\quad$—SO$_2$OR(—SO$_3$R)$\quad$ in sulphonic esters.

The diazonium ion group $-\overset{+}{N}≡N$ (—N$_2^{\oplus}$) in aryldiazonium salts.

2

Electronic aspects of structure and reactions

In the nineteenth century organic chemists developed the idea that each atom in a molecule is joined to its neighbours by a characteristic integral number of directed valency bonds. They used this concept to develop ideas of molecular structure so that they could interpret the vast amount of experimental information they had gathered. These ideas had been universally accepted well before the development of the Rutherford–Bohr atom and of electronic theories of the valency bond, and long before twentieth-century physical methods were developed for the more direct investigation of molecular structures. For this reason, the ideas of molecular structure have been set out in the preceding chapter without invoking such theories or methods.

The ideas of atomic structure and electronic valency theory have added greatly to our understanding of bonding in organic molecules. Physical methods such as X-ray and electron diffraction, spectroscopy, electron resonance and nuclear magnetic resonance have enabled us to describe molecular structures in detail unimaginable to the nineteenth century. Here we describe some of the more important applications of electronic valency theory to organic substances and their reactions. It is assumed throughout that the elementary principles of atomic structure and valency theory as applied to the concepts of ionic, covalent and dative covalent (semi-polar, coordinate or co-ionic) bonds will be familiar.

The directed valency bonds which link the atoms of organic molecules are in electronic terms shared-pair or covalent bonds. Indeed, organic chemistry is above all else the study of the covalent bond and its behaviour in the various molecular environments provided by carbon compounds. What precisely is meant by saying that two atoms 'share' a pair of electrons has been examined in detail by mathematical methods beyond the scope of this book, but a qualitative picture is sufficient here.

Bohr's model of the atom pictures the electron as a particle of negative electricity revolving round the nucleus on a definite path or *orbit*. This picture proved inadequate to account for all the facts. Its inadequacy was shown to lie in the implicit assumption that an electron was a particle whose position and velocity could simultaneously be stated precisely. Heisenberg's famous 'Uncertainty Principle' contradicted this, stating that the product of the uncertainty in position and uncertainty in velocity of the particle could never be less than a certain finite minimum value. In accordance with this, the methods of wave-mechanics (associated with the name of Schrödinger) have led to the replacement of Bohr's particles-in-orbit by much less sharply limited regions in space (called *orbitals*) in which there is a high probability that the electron in question will be located. For pictorial purposes, therefore, it is often appropriate to think of the electron not as a particle, but as a 'cloud' of negative electricity. Its shape is that of the orbital, the cloud being of maximum density in those regions where the probability of finding the electron is greatest, and 'tailing off' indefinitely into those regions where the probability of finding the electron is very small. Any such orbital cannot be occupied by more than two electrons, which must differ from one another in having opposite *spins* (a concept whose precise meaning need not concern us here).

In an isolated atom, the electrons occupy *atomic orbitals* which have some degree of symmetry about the nucleus, since an isolated atom has no net polarity, its 'centroids' of negative and positive charge coinciding. When two atoms share a pair of electrons in a covalent bond, the electrons must occupy an orbital involving both nuclei, called a *molecular orbital*. We can picture this as a cloud (whose precise shape is not at this stage vital to the picture) in which are 'embedded' the nuclei of the two bonded atoms.

Now consider the atoms making up the methane molecule. The carbon atom has a completed K-shell of electrons, in a spherically symmetrical orbital surrounding the nucleus, and, in addition, four L-shell electrons. Each hydrogen atom has a single K-shell electron. If we suppose that each of the four hydrogen atoms is bonded to the carbon atom by pairing and sharing the hydrogen electron and one of the four L-electrons of the carbon atom, then we need a model in which four electron-pair clouds envelop in some way the carbon nucleus and the four hydrogen nuclei, one in each cloud. Whatever other principles may be involved, Coulomb's Law (the law of force between electrical charges) and energy considerations would lead us to expect that such a model must be symmetrical, and the four bonding clouds identical in shape. The mutual repulsion of these clouds of negative charge will lead them to take up an orientation with their axes as far apart as possible. This at once leads to a picture of the methane molecule in which each hydrogen atom is bonded to the carbon atom by an electron-pair cloud with axial symmetry. The four axes point to the corners of a regular tetrahedron with the carbon atom at the centre and the hydrogen nuclei equidistant from it on the four axes. This model agrees completely with the classical picture of the tetrahedral distribution of the four carbon valencies as postulated by van't Hoff.

Bond polarity

Consideration of Coulomb's Law and energy show that an electron-pair cloud linking two *identical* atoms must be symmetrical about the mid-point between the nuclei, so that, as with a single atom, a diatomic elementary molecule in isolation is non-polar. Where two *unlike* atoms are linked, this restriction no longer applies. Their difference in nuclear charge and the different number and distribution of their other electrons will lead to the cloud being non-symmetrical about the mid-point between the nuclei. One atom can thus be said to have a larger share of the electron pair than the other. The bond will have a certain net polarity, with a net negative charge at the end occupied by the atom with the greater share, and a net positive charge at the end occupied by the atom with the smaller share. Of any pair of atoms, the one which acquires the larger share of the electron pair linking them is the more electronegative, the other the more electropositive. In the extreme case, the electronegative atom may (hypothetically, at any rate) gain complete control of the electron pair, thus leading to the formation of a pair of ions, negative and positive. Hydrogen is more electropositive than carbon. Atoms in the short periods become more electronegative as the atomic number increases, from the alkali metal to the halogen. In a given group, the second short period element is less electronegative than the first (silicon less than carbon, for example). In the long periods, the situation is more complicated, but in the compounds described here we shall be little concerned with these, except for the halogens bromine and iodine, in which the trend to greater electropositivity continues with increasing atomic number.

Dipole moments

The polarity of a bond can in principle be expressed quantitatively by a *dipole moment*, that is, the restoring couple exerted on it by unit electrostatic field at right angles to the bond axis. (Compare the concept of a magnetic moment.) Although the CH bonds of methane will be polar, with the carbon atom at the negative end, the symmetry of the whole means that the vector sum of the dipole moments will be zero, and the molecule as a whole non-polar. This is not so with less symmetrical molecules. The molecule of methyl chloride, CH_3Cl, will have a net dipole moment, that is, the molecule as a whole is polar.

The dipole moments of *molecules* (as opposed to individual bonds) can be measured. When polar molecules in the vapour state or in dilute solution in a non-polar solvent, are placed between the plates of a condenser, they tend to orient themselves along the direction of the electrostatic field and so reduce the potential difference between the plates. Thermal agitation will oppose this 'ordering', and the molecular orientation will therefore become more random at higher temperatures. That is to say, the dielectric constant of the vapour or solution will vary with temperature and from measurements of the coefficient of temperature variation the dipole moment can be deduced. The dipole moment of any bond will be affected by all the other bonds and lone pairs in the molecule. Attempts have been made to allocate each type of bond (C—H; O—H; C—O; C—Cl, etc.) a fixed dipole moment. The molecular dipole moment is then the vector sum of the moments of the constituent bonds. However, the values arrived at are somewhat inconsistent and are at best rather rough approximations.

Thus although a molecule (as opposed to an ion) is as a whole uncharged, we may picture the individual atoms in it as bearing partial positive or negative charges. The charges are partial in the sense of being less than the atom in question would carry if all the bonds of the molecule were ionic. Furthermore, a non-polar or slightly polar molecule may become more polarized by the near approach of a polar molecule, on account of the distortion of the bonding clouds of the one by the dipole of the other. Such charges, permanent or induced, are of the greatest importance in affecting the behaviour of one molecule when approached by another—that is, in situations of possible chemical reaction. Partial charges of this kind are conveniently represented by a symbolism borrowed from the calculus, as $\delta+$ and $\delta-$; these symbols are used in this book.

Hydrogen bonding

One particular case of the interaction of polar molecules deserves special mention. It has been realized since the 1920s that molecules containing the bonds FH, —OH, and $>$NH tend to adhere exceptionally strongly to each other, and to other molecules containing oxygen, nitrogen and fluorine atoms attached to less electronegative elements. Evidence for this lies in

17

Organic Chemistry

such matters as the well-known associated liquid behaviour of ammonia, water and hydrogen fluoride, their great mutual solubility, the existence of the HF_2^- ion, and the abnormally small distances between certain pairs of oxygen or nitrogen atoms in crystalline substances (e.g. in solid bicarbonates) where one of the pair could be presumed on chemical grounds to be attached to hydrogen. (Presumed, since hydrogen atoms could not at that time be located by X-ray crystallography.) All the evidence points to the fact that in such cases, the molecules or ions are linked by the hydrogen atom, which appears to exert a sort of pseudo-bicovalency. (Indeed, in the early stages of electronic valency theory, it was assumed that hydrogen could form two shared-pair bonds, one covalent, the other by accepting a donated pair; this view is now untenable.) This phenomenon is known as *hydrogen bonding*, and we shall meet many examples of it in organic compounds containing the —OH and $>$NH groups. In explanation of these facts, it is assumed that the polarity of the O—H and N—H bonds, owing to the great difference in electronegativity of the two linked atoms, is large, and the hydrogen nucleus is almost 'denuded' of electron 'cover' on the side remote from oxygen or nitrogen. This means that along the OH or NH axis, on the far side of the H atom, there will be a considerable field of attraction for a negative charge. Now bicovalent oxygen carries two unshared ('lone') electron pairs, and tricovalent nitrogen one. Mutual repulsion of electron clouds means that the orbitals of the lone pairs will form electron clouds on the side of the atom most remote from the covalent bonding clouds. For example the 'back' of the oxygen and nitrogen atoms has a concentration of negative charge which can be attracted by the above-mentioned field of the OH or NH groups. Thus we can formally represent hydrogen bonding thus:

$$
\begin{array}{ll}
>\!\overset{\delta-}{O}\cdots\overset{\delta+}{H}\!-\!\overset{\delta-}{O}\!- & >\!\overset{\delta-}{O}\cdots\overset{\delta+}{H}\!-\!\overset{\delta-}{N}\!< \\[2mm]
>\!\overset{\delta-}{N}\cdots\overset{\delta+}{H}\!-\!\overset{\delta-}{O}\!- & >\!\overset{\delta-}{N}\cdots\overset{\delta+}{H}\!-\!\overset{-\delta}{N}\!<
\end{array}
$$

The same arguments apply to the HF bond but, owing to the univalency of fluorine, this only occurs in hydrogen fluoride itself.

Delocalized electrons; mesomerism or resonance

The formulation of organic molecular structures in terms of an integral number of covalent bonds linking each atom to its neighbours is satisfactory for many purposes. Not infrequently, however, this concept is insufficient; the graphical formula or 'bond-diagram' arrived at is inade-

18

quate to account for the known properties of the compound. The best example is that of benzene, where the obvious inadequacy of any conventional formula led to much speculation in the late nineteenth century.

In such cases it will invariably be found that, without contravening any valency rules and *without transposing any atoms* in the structure, it is possible to allocate the valency bonds in more than one way.

For example, carbonic acid can be formulated thus:

$$\begin{array}{c} HO \\ \diagdown \\ HO \diagup \end{array} C=O$$

and the carbonate ion thus:

$$\begin{array}{c} {}^{\ominus}O \\ \diagdown \\ {}_{\ominus}O \diagup \end{array} C=O$$

This latter can be re-written as

$$\begin{array}{ccc} {}^{\ominus}O & & O \\ \diagdown & & \diagdown \diagdown \\ & C-O^{\ominus} & \quad \text{or as} \quad & C-O^{\ominus} \\ \diagup \diagup & & \diagup \\ O & & {}_{\ominus}O \end{array}$$

The three formulae are of course identical in this case. Each one, however, implies that two of the oxygen atoms are singly linked to carbon and carry an ionic charge, whereas the third is doubly linked and does not. When we write the formula, we make an arbitrary choice among the three oxygen atoms as to which shall be the doubly linked one. X-ray crystallographic evidence, however, shows the carbonate ion as an equilateral triangle of oxygen atoms round a central carbon atom. There is no sign that one C—O distance is different from the other two, as we should expect if one oxygen atom was doubly linked (see p. 52). In such cases, it is accepted that the bond-diagrams are misleading. Such a diagram *must* show each shared electron-pair as 'localized' between two atoms only; whereas the fact that we can shift one electron-pair arbitrarily around the molecule and still obtain formulae which fit the rules is now held to imply that this electron pair is 'delocalized'; i.e. that the electron-pair cloud does not involve merely two nuclei, as the bond diagrams imply, but is a molecular orbital involving, in this example, all four atoms of the carbonate ion. The only way to represent this in a single formula would be to break away from the 'integral bond' concept, and write something like

$$\begin{array}{c} {}^{\frac{2}{3}-}O \diagdown_{\diagdown \diagdown} {}_{C} \diagup^{\diagup} O^{\frac{2}{3}-} \\ \| \\ O^{\frac{2}{3}-} \end{array}$$

in which carbon is linked to each oxygen by a 'one-and-a-third' bond. Molecules or ions of this kind are in a sense intermediate in structure between all the various bond-diagrams; such substances have been said to show *mesomerism* and to exist as a *mesomeric* form. An alternative description is to say that the carbonate ion is a *resonance hybrid* of the three *canonical structures* represented by the three bond-diagrams. This is symbolically written:

$$^{\ominus}O \diagdown \diagup C{=}O \quad \leftrightarrow \quad O^{\ominus} \diagdown \diagup C{-}O^{\ominus} \quad \leftrightarrow \quad O \diagdown \diagup C{-}O^{\ominus}$$

It is not essential that the various bond-diagrams shall be identical, as witness the case of acetic acid, discussed on p. 230, which can be written thus in resonance hybrid symbols:

$$CH_3{-}C\diagup_{O{-}H}^{O} \quad \leftrightarrow \quad CH_3{-}C\diagdown_{O^{\oplus}{-}H}^{\overset{\ominus}{O}}$$

It is essential to notice that the symbols $\leftrightarrow$ and $\rightleftharpoons$ have quite different meanings, and that the resonance hybrid description does *not* mean that molecules (or ions) corresponding to the various bond-diagrams exist in an equilibrium mixture. In view of this possible misunderstanding, the elementary student should think of such cases as often as possible in terms of 'delocalization' of electrons.

Detailed theoretical treatment shows that the resonance hybrid is more stable (i.e. is at a lower energy level) than any hypothetical molecule having one of the canonical structures. (In a sense, this is self-evident; if the electrons do not take up the arrangement implied in a bond-diagram, but some other arrangement, this must be because the latter is the more stable one. The point about resonance theory is that it successfully describes a structure which fulfils this requirement.) Where (as with acetic acid), the canonical structures are not equivalent, the actual molecule will be closest in structure and energy to the canonical structure of the greatest implied stability. Various cases of structures involving delocalized electron pairs are described in the succeeding chapters; the important case of benzene is discussed in chapter 7.

Reaction mechanisms

Chemists in the nineteenth century were principally concerned with practical methods of carrying out reactions and with elucidating the molecular structures of compounds. In the twentieth century, they began to ask what happened in the course of the reaction process to the molecules or other species involved in it, and why; what, in fact, was the *mechanism* of the reaction in question.

Chemical reactions of covalent substances must in general involve the breaking of existent covalent bonds and the forming of new ones. Clearly there are two ways in which a covalent bond can be broken. Either the electrons become unpaired, each atom retaining one,

$$AB \to A^{\bullet} + B^{\bullet}$$

or one of the initially bonded atoms retains both electrons of the bonding pair

$$AB \to A^{\oplus} + B^{\ominus}$$

or

$$AB \to A^{\ominus} + B^{\oplus}$$

The first way will lead to the formation of what are called free radicals; groups of covalently bonded atoms having an unpaired electron and hence, in older terms, a free valency. (The radical may in some cases be a single atom.) Bond fission of this type is said to be *homolytic*. The second way is known as *heterolytic* fission. (Taken in isolation, heterolytic fission of a molecule would yield a pair of oppositely charged ions, but the reacting species may itself be an ion, and in any case other steps may occur simultaneously, so a simple generalization is unprofitable.) Similarly, bond formation can clearly occur either datively, with one reactant providing both electrons of the bonding pair (the reverse of heterolysis) or by the combination of free radicals (the reverse of homolysis). Both types of process have been postulated in organic reactions, but by far the greater proportion of the reactions encountered by the elementary student are believed to occur by heterolysis and its reverse. Among the simplest of these are the displacement reactions of halides such as ethyl bromide, reviewed in chapter 10.

In general, a chemical reaction is accompanied by an energy change. The energy content of the initial reactants and final products will be different. Passage from one state to the other is not, however, simply a matter of sliding down an energy hill between the two (or being pushed up it for the reverse process) as represented by (*a*); rather is there supposed to be an energy barrier, as in (*b*), which the reaction process has to surmount. Such a picture is used to account in part for the fact that absolute reaction rates in molecules per unit time are normally only a small fraction of the collision rate between reacting species. It is assumed that reaction only occurs between or in the few molecules (or ions) which possess in some way sufficient energy to surmount this barrier. (It is also necessary to assume that in reactions between two molecules they must collide in the orientation favourable to reaction.) In the diagrams below, the horizontal co-ordinate has no quantitative meaning, merely representing the occurrence

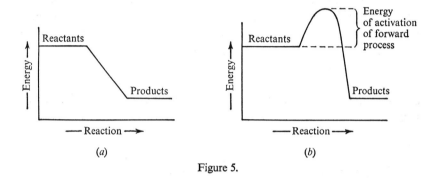

Figure 5.

of reaction. Such a reaction is a single-stage process in that no intermediate species which can be formulated as a molecule or ion appears between reactants and products. At the peak of the curve, the state of affairs is known as a *transition state*; the reacting species are here less stable relative to both reactants and products. On the other hand, the transition state will represent the system of *lowest* energy via which reaction can occur. For example in a halide displacement reaction such as

$$\overset{\ominus}{CN} + CH_3I \rightarrow CH_3CN + I^{\ominus}$$

it is pictured as a system in which the methyl–iodide bond is in the process of being ruptured while the methyl–cyanide bond is in process of formation:

$$NC^{\delta-} \text{---} CH_3 \text{---} I^{\delta-}$$

such a system being at a lower energy level than a hypothetical species with the reagents covalently bonded

$$(N{\equiv}C{-}CH_3{-}I)^{\ominus}$$

or a system in which the heterolysis of the CH_3I bond is complete while no methyl–cyanide bond has been initiated $(CN^{\ominus} + CH_3^{\oplus} + I^{\ominus})$. Any structural feature lowering the energy level of the transition complex will favour reaction.

Many reactions must however be pictured as occurring by successive steps, with the formation and subsequent removal of definite intermediate chemical species. The energy profile for such a reaction will be of the general form shown in Fig. 6.

In multi-stage reactions, one stage may be much slower than the others. This stage then acts as a 'bottleneck' in the reaction process and controls the overall rate; it is known as the *rate-determining* step. The existence of such a step is revealed by considering the kinetics of the reaction (that is by

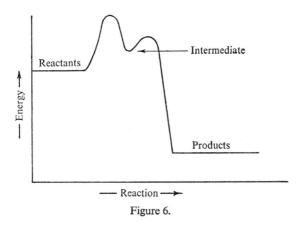

Figure 6.

studying the relation between the rate of the reaction and the reactant concentrations) because the overall kinetics will be those of the rate-determining step. The kinetics will be independent of those reactants which play no part in the rate-determining stage, though they are involved in the overall process. Examples of this are the so-called unimolecular substitution reactions of alkyl halides (see p. 112) and the bromination or iodination of acetone in certain conditions (see p. 189). If a reaction proceeds via an intermediate compound, then it is essential, for the overall process to have a determinate rate, that the rates of formation and removal of the intermediate shall be equal. That is, inasmuch as the overall reaction *rate* (measured by the slope of the concentration–time curve for the reaction) is instantaneously constant, so the *concentration* of the intermediate is instantaneously constant. This is known as the *steady state* requirement. (For a system in *equilibrium*, the overall rate is *zero*, and the concentration of the intermediate is *permanently* constant.) Reaction intermediates can rarely be isolated from the reaction mixture; their presence can often be inferred from the kinetics and sometimes confirmed by physical evidence (e.g. spectroscopic).

Types of reagent

In studying a reaction between two species, the chemist is often more immediately concerned with the changes produced in one of the reactants, and regards the other as an agent bringing about these changes. This distinction between the *substrate*, or substance attacked, and the *reagent*, or substance attacking, is arbitrary, but one we frequently make for convenience. In reactions proceeding by heterolysis and its reverse, two types of reagent can be distinguished. One type will have an unshared pair of electrons which it is able to share with a substrate capable of accommodating them. Such a reagent, we may suppose, will attack the substrate at a site where the density of the electron cloud is low, and is known as a *nucleophilic* reagent. The displacement reactions of alkyl halides already mentioned offer characteristic examples of nucleophilic attack (see chapter 10). Nucleophiles are often, but by no means always, negative ions. The other type of reagent is one which can accommodate a pair of electrons from the substrate (thus reversing the above behaviour of substrate and reagent). Such a reagent must either be electron-deficient (for example, the $Br^{\oplus}$ ion) or capable of bond-rearrangements to accommodate a further electron-pair (for examples, the nitronium ion $NO_2^{\oplus}$ or the sulphur trioxide molecule SO_3). Electrophiles will attack substrates at sites of high electron density, and are often, though by no means always, positive ions. The addition reactions of olefines (chapter 5) or the substitution reactions of benzene (chapter 8) offer characteristic examples of electrophilic attack.

Nucleophilicity and electrophilicity are obviously closely related to and to some extent identical with, base and acid behaviour respectively.

According to the Lowry–Brönsted concept, an acid is a species containing a hydrogen atom which can be detached from its bonding electron pair and transferred to an unshared pair of electrons of another species, which is the base. Thus in the simple inorganic example of hydrogen chloride reacting with ammonia, the process is as in the following equation. (Only the relevant electron pairs are shown.)

$$H_3N: + (H):Cl \longrightarrow (H_3N:H)^{\oplus} + (:Cl)^{\ominus}$$

Thus the hydrogen is transferred as a hydrogen nucleus, or proton, from acid to base. This proton transfer is often called '*protolysis*'. The relative strengths of acids *vis-à-vis* a given base depend very largely on the extent to which electronegative atoms in the rest of the molecule withdraw electrons from the neighbourhood of the hydrogen atom, thus rendering it a site of exceptionally low electron density and prone to attack by the base. (A well-known illustration is the case of the chloroacetic acids; see p. 277). Thus towards the acid as substrate, the base is characteristically nucleophilic; towards the base, the acid is an electrophile. If the scope of the word 'acid' is extended as in the Lewis concept, where it becomes any species capable of accepting a pair of electrons from a base, then the pairs of terms acid–base and electrophile–nucleophile become practically synonoymous. At most, the difference is one of habitual usage. An electron-pair acceptor is more likely to be called a Lewis acid when forming a simple addition compound with a base, or when acting catalytically, or in inorganic chemistry. It is more likely to be called an electrophile when acting as a reagent in organic chemistry, especially when attacking a carbon atom. In this book, the words acid and base, unqualified, will be used in the context of proton transfer. Quite apart from the acid and base behaviour of compounds regarded as such in everyday usage (such as acetic acid and aniline), proton transfers are believed to occur very widely in organic chemistry and are frequently postulated as rapid or even as slow steps in reaction mechanisms.

Since acid–base behaviour is a special case of electrophile–nucleophile interaction, we may expect that the reactivity of a species as a nucleophile (in current terminology, its 'nucleophilicity') will run more or less parallel with its basic strength. This is roughly so, though it must be borne in mind that the relative strengths of two bases are not absolutely fixed, but sometimes depend on the acid with which they react, so that an exact correspondence is still less to be expected when comparing nucleophilic attacks on combined hydrogen and combined carbon respectively.

Use of arrows in chemical formulae

Arrows of various types are much used in the formulation of organic compounds and their reactions. The straight 'reaction' arrow as used in equations or reaction schemes needs no further comment. The dative covalency or co-ionic bond is often represented by an arrow, thus:

$$\begin{array}{l} CH_3 \\ CH_3\!-\!\!\!\!>\!N \to O \\ CH_3 \end{array}$$

the tail of the arrow indicating the donor and the head the acceptor atom. The alternative formulation:

$$\begin{array}{l} CH_3 \quad \oplus \quad \ominus \\ CH_3\!-\!\!\!\!>\!N\!-\!O \\ CH_3 \end{array}$$

is preferable as indicating more specifically the ionic and covalent components of the bond.

Two other types of arrow symbol are useful for incorporating in formulae some of the concepts outlined in the present chapter. An arrow-head placed in the middle of a single bond:

$$\geq C \rightarrow Cl$$

indicates qualitatively the polarity of the bond, the arrow pointing to the atom with the larger share of the electron pair. (In other words the arrow indicates the direction of the distortion of the bonding electron cloud.) This polarity may be intrinsic to the bond between the pair of atoms involved, as in the above example; the arrow then points to the more electronegative atom. Alternatively it may indicate a polarity induced in the bond by the polarity of other parts of the molecule; thus in the formula:

$$\begin{array}{c} Cl \\ Cl \rightarrow C \leftarrow CHO \\ Cl \end{array}$$

the marked polarity of three carbon–chlorine bonds is shown as distorting the electron cloud of the adjacent carbon–carbon bond.

A particularly valuable convention is the use of curved arrows. The significance of such an arrow in words is 'the formula on the left may be transformed to the formula on the right by the movement of a pair of electrons from the site indicated by the tail of the arrow to that indicated by the head'. This convention is equally valuable in clarifying electron delocalization, as, for example, in the case of the acetate ion;

$$-C \overset{O}{\underset{O^{\ominus}}{<}} \longleftrightarrow -C \overset{O^{\ominus}}{\underset{O}{<}}$$

and in indicating the transference of electron pairs in a chemical reaction, and, for example, in the reaction between cyanide ions and methyl iodide:

$$N \equiv \overset{\ominus}{C} \colon \quad CH_3 \text{—} I \longrightarrow N \equiv C \text{—} CH_3 + I^{\ominus}$$

other example of the use of both these arrow symbols will be found in the remaining chapters of this book.

3

Analysis and determination of formulae

The classical method of determining the structural formula of an organic compound is:

(a) identification of the elements present in the substance;

(b) quantitative elementary analysis, giving the proportions by weight of the elements present;

(c) molecular weight determination.

From (b) and (c) and the atomic weights of the elements concerned, the molecular formula is found. From this, the structural formula is established by:

(d) reaction studies; particularly, with more complex molecules, controlled degradation to simpler molecules, and

(e) synthesis by unequivocal steps of the proposed structure and comparison of the product with the original.

Identification of the elements

(1)   Carbon and hydrogen

An intimate mixture of the dry compound is heated with a suitable dry oxidizing agent (usually cupric oxide). Evolution of carbon dioxide and steam, identified in the usual ways, establishes the presence of carbon and hydrogen.

(2)   Other elements: Lassaigne's test

The compound is heated with metallic sodium, and the product plunged into water to destroy excess sodium. Under these conditions, certain elements of the original form simple inorganic ions, which pass into the aqueous solution. (This is alkaline from the action of the excess sodium on the water). Thus:

$$\text{Nitrogen} \to C\equiv N^{\ominus}$$
$$\text{Chlorine} \to Cl^{\ominus}$$
$$\text{Bromine} \to Br^{\ominus}$$
$$\text{Iodine} \quad \to I^{\ominus}$$
$$\text{Sulphur} \to S^{2\ominus}$$

These are recognized as follows:

(*a*) $C\equiv N^{\ominus}$. A small quantity of ferrous salt is added to a portion of the filtered solution and the mixture is boiled for a minute or so. Under these conditions, ferrocyanide $[Fe(CN)_6]^{4\ominus}$ is formed, and some of the precipitate of ferrous hydroxide becomes oxidized by air to ferric. (A ferric salt can be added, but it is rarely necessary.) The mixture is cooled and just acidified, dissolving the hydroxide precipitate; $Fe^{3\oplus}$ and $[Fe(CN)_6]^{4\ominus}$ form Prussian blue. A blue precipitate or colour is therefore a positive indication of nitrogen in the original compound.

(*b*) $Cl^{\ominus}$, $Br^{\ominus}$, $I^{\ominus}$. (i) A portion of solution is acidified with nitric acid and silver nitrate solution added; a precipitate of silver halide indicates halogen in the original. If nitrogen is present, cyanide must first be driven off by boiling for a time with aqueous nitric acid, otherwise silver cyanide would be precipitated, masking any silver halides.

(ii) To identify the halogen, a portion of the solution is acidified and a few drops of chloroform or carbon tetrachloride, and a small amount of a suitable oxidizing agent (chlorine water; hypochlorite) are added. $Br^{\ominus}$ and $I^{\ominus}$ are oxidized to free halogen, which on shaking pass into the organic solvent, colouring it yellow to orange and pinkish purple respectively. No visible effect here and a positive test in (i) indicate chlorine.

(*c*) $S^{2\ominus}$. (A preliminary indication is given when carrying out (*a*) above, since in place of a green precipitate of ferrous hydroxide, a black precipitate of ferrous sulphide is formed.) A portion of the solution is tested with a little sodium nitroprusside solution. A purple solution (much the same colour as dilute potassium permanganate) is a positive indication of $S^{2\ominus}$, and hence of sulphur in the original.

(3) Beilstein's test

Halogens may also be detected by heating a roll of clean halide-free copper gauze in a flame, dipping it into the substance under test, and replacing it in the flame. A green-blue 'copper' flame is a positive indication of halogen. The test depends on the formation of copper halides by the destructive decomposition of the organic compound; these halides are volatile and vaporize in the flame, giving the characteristic colour.

The test is quicker but less reliable than Lassaigne's test. A marked positive or unequivocal negative result can reasonably be trusted; feeble positive results can arise from non-halogen-containing substances, especially if nitrogen is present (possibly because cuprous cyanide is formed and vaporized).

Quantitative estimation of elements

In principle, the substance under test is oxidized, and the products containing the various elements are collected and weighed or measured. Thus carbon is weighed as carbon dioxide, hydrogen as water, nitrogen is measured as gaseous elementary nitrogen. Sulphur is weighed as barium sulphate. The halogens are not oxidized under the conditions used for their estimation, and are weighed as silver halides. The older methods required a sample of about 0·2 g of the substance to be analysed. More refined methods have been developed using about 0·02 g (semi-micro scale) or about 0·005 g (micro scale). Such details as are given in the following descriptions apply to the semi-micro scale, as being the one the reader is most likely in due course to operate for himself.

(1) Carbon and hydrogen

The compound is completely burnt in a stream of oxygen in the presence of copper oxide, and the resulting water and carbon dioxide are weighed. Complications arise because nitrogen, halogens and sulphur, if present, form volatile products (NO_2, hydrogen halides or halogens, oxides of sulphur) which are also absorbed by the soda lime used to collect carbon dioxide. Such substances must therefore be converted to non-volatile or non-reactive compounds before the combustion products are passed through soda lime. The combustion tube and its packing are shown schematically below (not to scale).

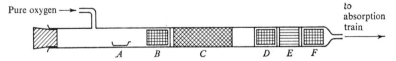

Figure 7. Combustion tube for the determination of hydrogen. *A*, Porcelain or platinum boat containing weighed sample; *B*, silver gauze roll to catalyse combustion; *C*, oxidative packing of (*a*) wire-form copper oxide (if sulphur absent) or (*b*) wire-form copper oxide and lead chromate (if sulphur present); *D*, silver gauze roll; *E*, lead dioxide; *F*, silver gauze roll.

The sample *A* is heated by an external flame or movable electric heater; the packings *B* to *F* are heated by tubular electric furnaces. The lead chromate in *C*(*b*) oxidizes sulphur to non-volatile lead sulphate. The rolls

29

of silver gauze *D* and *F* trap halogens as non-volatile silver halide. Lead oxide *E* absorbs oxides of nitrogen. The items of the packing are separated by asbestos. The water is absorbed first in a weighed absorption tube of anhydrous magnesium perchlorate; carbon dioxide passes on and is absorbed in a weighed tube of soda lime.

The numerous operational details necessary to get reliable results from this and the following methods will be found in text-books of practical organic analysis.

(2) Nitrogen

(*a*) *The Dumas method.* The compound is oxidized by heating with excess copper oxide in a stream of carbon dioxide. The gaseous products are collected over concentrated potassium hydroxide solution to absorb the carbon dioxide; the remaining volume of elementary nitrogen is measured. Oxides of nitrogen must be decomposed, since nitrogen dioxide would be absorbed by the alkali to give low results, and nitric oxide would be collected with the nitrogen to give high ones.

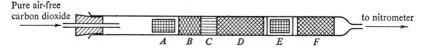

Pure air-free carbon dioxide →   *A* *B* *C* *D* *E* *F*   to nitrometer →

Figure 8. Combustion tube for the determination of nitrogen. *A*, Oxidized copper gauze roll; *B*, sample mixed with powder copper oxide; *C*, powder copper oxide; *D*, wire-form copper oxide; *E*, reduced copper spiral; *F*, wire-form copper oxide.

The reduced copper spiral *E* is present to decompose oxides of nitrogen. The other packings are to ensure complete oxidation. Packings *D*, *E* and *F* are heated by an electric furnace; *A*, *B* and *C* by an external flame or movable electric heater.

(*b*) *The Kjeldahl method.* A small sample is boiled in a long-necked flask with concentrated sulphuric acid for about an hour; the nitrogen is converted to ammonium sulphate. The product is diluted, made alkaline and steam-distilled. The ammonia thus evolved is absorbed in aqueous boric acid; this is so weak an acid that the resulting solution can be titrated with standard dilute hydrochloric acid as if it were aqueous ammonia.

Kjeldahl's method is less general than Dumas'. It is satisfactory for compounds having nitrogen attached to hydrogen; compounds with —N=N— or —N=O bonds may have to be reduced. Catalysts (mercuric compounds or selenium) may be added to the sulphuric acid to promote decomposition of the organic substances to ammonia.

(3) Halogens and sulphur

The Carius method. The sample is heated with fuming nitric acid and silver nitrate in a sealed tube. The tube is cautiously opened, and the silver halide removed, filtered off, dried and weighed.

Other methods are also available for halogen estimation. Sulphur can be estimated by the Carius technique; silver nitrate is omitted, and the sulphuric acid formed by the oxidation of the sample by the nitric acid is removed, and the sulphate precipitated as barium sulphate, which is filtered off, dried and weighed.

(4) Oxygen

There is no general qualitative test for oxygen, though evolution of recognizable oxygen compounds (e.g. CO_2, H_2O) when the substance is heated in the absence of air is often a clear indication. Before 1939, there was no general method for determining the oxygen content of organic compounds. The procedure was to sum the percentages of the other elements present, and to attribute the balance to oxygen; the obvious objection is that the figure arrived at contains the accumulated errors of all the other determinations. Nevertheless, the method sufficed for innumerable structural determinations.

Oxygen can now be estimated. The compound is vaporized in nitrogen and the products passed at a high temperature (over 1000 °C) over carbon. Oxygen is converted quantitatively to carbon monoxide. This is then passed over iodine pentoxide, which oxidises the carbon monoxide to dioxide, being itself reduced to iodine.

$$5CO + I_2O_5 \rightarrow 5CO_2 + I_2$$

The iodine vapour can be absorbed in potassium iodide and weighed; if desired, the carbon dioxide can be absorbed in soda lime and weighed also, giving a check.

Clearly
$$O \equiv \frac{I_2}{5} \equiv CO_2$$

Many analytical methods have been developed for determining specific groups in a compound of known molecular weight (e.g. —OH, —OCH$_3$, —NH$_2$). A number of these are outlined in the following chapters.

Molecular weights of organic compounds can be determined by vapour density measurement or any of the usual colligative property measurements as appropriate. Details can be found in text-books of physical chemistry.

A specimen calculation will illustrate the conversion of analytical results to a molecular formula.

31

Elements present: C, H, N, Br (O)
(i) C, H.

Mass of sample	$= 0.0273$ g
Mass of CO_2	$= 0.0447$ g
Mass of H_2O	$= 0.0094$ g

12.0 g C → 44.0 g CO_2

Sample contained $0.0447 \times \frac{12}{44}$ g C
$$= 0.0123 \text{ g C}$$

∴ percentage C $= \dfrac{100}{0.0273} \times 0.0123$
$$= 45.0\%$$

1.0 g H → 9.0 g water

Sample contained $0.0094 \times \frac{1}{9}$ g H
$$= 0.0010(4) \text{ g}$$

∴ percentage H $= \dfrac{100}{0.0273} \times 0.00104$
$$= 3.8(2)\%$$

(ii) N

Mass of sample	$= 0.0321$ g
Volume of N	$= 1.83$ cm³
Temperature	$= 20°$ C
Barometric height	$= 750$ mm.

Volume of N at s.t.p. $= 1.83 \times \frac{750}{760} \times \frac{273}{293}$ cm³
$$= 1.68 \text{ cm}^3$$

Mass of 22.4×10^3 cm³ or nitrogen at s.t.p.
$$= 28.0 \text{ g}$$

∴ mass of N in sample $= 1.68 \times \frac{28}{22400}$ g
$$= 0.00210 \text{ g}$$

∴ percentage N $= \dfrac{100}{0.0321} \times 0.00210$
$$= 6.5(2)\%$$

(iii) Br

Mass of sample	$= 0.0224$ g
Mass of Ag Br	$= 0.0196$ g

188 g Ag Br contains 80 g Br

∴ mass of Br in sample $= 0.0196 \times \frac{80}{188}$ g
$$= 0.00833 \text{ g}$$

∴ percentage Br $= \dfrac{100}{0.0224} \times 0.00833$
$$= 37.2\%$$

$$45 \cdot 0 + 3 \cdot 8(2) + 6 \cdot 5(2) + 37 \cdot 2 = 92 \cdot 5(4)\%$$

Balance (assumed O) $= 7 \cdot 4(6)\%$

Calculation of empirical formula

STEP 1. Divide percentage figures by atomic weights.

$$\frac{45 \cdot 0}{12} = 3 \cdot 75; \quad \frac{3 \cdot 8}{1} = 3 \cdot 8; \quad \frac{6 \cdot 52}{14} = 0 \cdot 466;$$
$$\text{(C)} \qquad\qquad \text{(H)} \qquad\qquad \text{(N)}$$

$$\frac{37 \cdot 2}{80} = 0 \cdot 465; \quad \frac{7 \cdot 46}{60} = 0 \cdot 466$$
$$\text{(Br)} \qquad\qquad \text{(O)}$$

STEP 2. Convert these to a near-whole number ratio by dividing by the smallest and multiplying the quotients (if necessary) by an appropriate integer.
$$\frac{3 \cdot 75}{0 \cdot 465} = 8 \cdot 06; \quad \frac{3 \cdot 8}{0 \cdot 465} = 8 \cdot 2; \quad \frac{0 \cdot 466}{0 \cdot 465} = 1 \cdot 00;$$

$$\frac{0 \cdot 465}{0 \cdot 465} = 1 \cdot 00; \quad \frac{0 \cdot 466}{0 \cdot 465} = 1 \cdot 00$$

(These figures are not exact integers; in particular, the hydrogen figure is some way out. The mass of water on which this figure depends is rather small, and deviation of this size in the hydrogen figure is not improbable.) Hence the empirical formula is probably C_8H_8ONBr (formula weight $= 214$).

Molecular weight (e.g. by an ebullioscopic determination in benzene)

Mass of sample	$= 1 \cdot 077$ g
Mass of benzene	$= 40 \cdot 7$ g
Elevation of b.p. of benzene	$= 0 \cdot 338°$ C
Molar elevation of b.p.	$= 2 \cdot 70°$ C per mol per kg benzene
Mole concentration of sample	$= \dfrac{0 \cdot 338}{2 \cdot 70}$ mol per kg
	$= 0 \cdot 125$ mol per kg
Mass concentration of sample	$= 1 \cdot 077 \times \dfrac{1000}{40 \cdot 7}$ g pe kg
	$= 26 \cdot 43$ g per kg
Molecular weight	$= \dfrac{26 \cdot 43}{0 \cdot 125}$
	$= 211 \cdot (4)$

Hence the above empirical formula is also the molecular formula.

Alternative calculation

Find the contribution of each element to the molecular weight, and divide the result by the appropriate atomic weight.

$$211 \times 45 \cdot 0\% \quad = 95; \qquad \div 12 = 7 \cdot 92 \quad (\div 8)$$
$$211 \times 3 \cdot 8(2)\% = 8 \cdot 05; \qquad \div \ 1 = 8 \cdot 05 \quad (\div 8)$$
$$211 \times 6 \cdot 52\% \quad = 13 \cdot 75; \quad \div 14 = 0 \cdot 984 \ (\div 1)$$
$$211 \times 37 \cdot 2\% \quad = 78 \cdot 6; \qquad \div 80 = 0 \cdot 984 \ (\div 1)$$
$$211 \times 7 \cdot 46\% \quad = 15 \cdot 75; \quad \div 16 = 0 \cdot 984 \ (\div 1)$$

Hence the *molecular* formula is C_8H_8ONBr.

The nitrogen figure can be derived even more directly; since 0·0321 g yields 1·68 cm³ nitrogen at s.t.p., 211 g (= 1 mole) would yield

$$\frac{211}{0 \cdot 0321} \times 1 \cdot 68 = 11\,050 \ \text{cm}^3,$$

i.e. nearly $\frac{1}{2}$ mole, or 1 g atom. Hence the molecule contains 1 atom of nitrogen.

The final figures in these alternative calculations all incorporate any error in the molecular weight determination.

(*p*-bromoacetanilide $Br.C_6H_4.NHCOCH_3 = C_8H_8ONBr$; molecular weight 214. Theoretical composition C, 44·9%; H, 3·7(4)%; O, 7·4(8)%; N, 6·5(5)%; Br 37·4%.)

When the molecular formula of a compound is known, its structure can be inferred from its reactions. The presence of the commoner functional groups in simple molecules (such as —OH in methanol, —NH_2 in methylamine, CH_3 and —COOH in acetic acid) can be logically deduced from the reactions of the compounds and the valencies of the elements as displayed in their binary compounds. (The arguments involved are given in the relevant chapters.) The presence of these functional groups in more complex molecules can then be inferred from their characteristic reactions. No rigid principles can be laid down for deciding which of the possible isomeric structures corresponds to a particular compound. Features such as molecular dissymmetry, revealed by resolution into optically active forms (p. 299), degradation reactions such as ozonolysis of olefins (p. 60), or oxidation of aromatic side chains (p. 82) which yield simpler and more easily recognizable fragments may help to decide in suitable cases. Alternatively, or in confirmation, a substance having the likely structure of the unknown may be synthesized from smaller molecules of known structure by unequivocal methods, and the product compared with the unknown for identity of physical and chemical behaviour. For this purpose, reactions such as acetoacetic ester syntheses (p. 199) or Grignard reactions (p. 120), by which carbon skeletons of known structure can be built from smaller molecules, have been much used.

Chapter 22 on carbohydrates, for example, will give some indication of the problems and methods involved in allocating structures to sugars of only moderate complexity.

To determine the structure of a substance of any degree of complexity by the above 'classical' methods may involve years of work. Organic chemists began from the late nineteenth century on to look for short cuts, and especially for ways of diagnosing specific structural features from the physical properties of a compound rather than its chemical reactions. The first properties investigated were macroscopic ones such as molecular volume $\left(\text{i.e. } \dfrac{\text{molecular weight}}{\text{density}}\right)$, or functions of molecular weight and surface tension, viscosity or refractive index. These proved of limited value. Really powerful methods arose from the study of the interaction between matter and oscillatory electric and magnetic fields with wavelengths of the same order as molecular dimensions (X-ray diffraction) or frequencies of the same order as the natural frequencies of molecules or atoms or their constituent particles (visible and infra-red spectroscopy, electron and nuclear magnetic resonance). Mass spectrometry has also been used (see p. 39). The principles involved and the kind of information they offer can be sketched briefly, but any detailed discussion is beyond the scope of this book.

X-ray diffraction

The distances separating atoms in molecules, or molecules or ions in a crystal, are of the order of 10^{-8} cm, or 1 Å. X-rays of this order of wavelength are therefore scattered by the atoms of crystals, just as visible light of wavelength about 10^{-5} is scattered by obstacles of the same order of size. A diffraction grating, ruled with a large number of equally spaced lines, scatters incident monochromatic visible light so that intensity maxima are observed at definite angles to the incident beam (the so-called diffraction spectra of first, second and higher orders). Monochromatic X-rays are similarly scattered by crystals to produce a definite diffraction pattern, indicating that the atoms and molecules are arranged in the crystal in a regular repeating pattern. Since the crystal is a three-dimensional structure, and may contain many different repeated atom spacings, the diffraction patterns are more complex than those obtained with a plane ruled grating and visible light. Diffracted X-rays can be recorded photographically and, from measurements of the direction and intensity of the various diffracted beams, the atomic spacings in the crystal can be deduced.

X-rays are diffracted by the electron clouds of the atoms, and the scattering effect depends on the electron density. X-ray crystallographic analysis leads ultimately to electron-density maps projected on to particular planes. The actual shapes of the molecules in the crystal are thus revealed. Atoms with low electron density produce only feeble scattering; hydrogen atoms in particular may be difficult to locate. Alternative methods of locating hydrogen atoms in molecules are therefore especially useful.

The application of X-ray diffraction methods is very largely responsible for the detailed and comparatively exact information now available about bond lengths and bond angles, and for the elucidation of the structures of such complex substances as proteins which present difficulties unsurmountable by 'classical' methods.

Electron diffraction

A beam of electrons of uniform velocity behaves as if it had a definite wavelength, and is diffracted by the molecules of a gas at low pressure. The gas molecules will be randomly oriented with respect to the direction of the beam, and this gives rise to a diffraction pattern, perpendicular to that direction, of a series of concentric circles, from which the interatomic spacings in the gas molecules may be deduced.

Methods involving the absorption of radiation use phenomena whose explanation depends on quantum theory. This was originally developed by Planck to account for the observed distribution of intensity with wavelength in black body radiation.

Briefly, any body which possesses energy in the form of periodic motion (rotational or vibrational) can only gain or lose energy by radiation in discrete 'packets' or quanta. The magnitude of the quantum is greater, the higher the frequency of the motion. Thus quantum theory is important in dealing with the behaviour of atoms and molecules, as opposed to macroscopic oscillating systems; it throws no light on the behaviour of a pendulum clock, but a good deal on, say, the methane molecule. A body gaining or losing energy in this way is said to undergo a transition from one energy level to another, and the magnitude E of the quantum of energy gained or lost as radiation is related to the frequency ν of this radiation by Planck's law: $\qquad E = h\nu,$

where h is Planck's constant, of magnitude $6 \cdot 55 \times 10^{-34}$ Js. This may also be expressed

$$E = \frac{hc}{\lambda},$$

where c is the velocity of propagation of the radiation (3×10^8 ms^{-1} *in vacuo*) and λ its wavelength. The body can therefore only absorb energy from radiation of such a wavelength that the corresponding energy quanta are equal to the difference in energy between the two energy levels involved.

The absorption of electromagnetic radiation in selected wavelengths only gives rise to absorption spectra of various kinds. The Fraunhofer lines of the solar spectrum are a well-known example, where the wavelengths absorbed correspond to energy transitions of the electrons in the atoms of various elements in the cooler outer layers of the sun.

Visible and ultraviolet absorption spectra

These arise from electron energy level transitions. They enable the presence of certain types of bonding (e.g. conjugated double bonds) to be detected in the molecule.

Infra-red spectra

Molecules may vibrate by elastic changes in bond length (stretching vibrations) or in bond angle ('scissoring' vibrations). The vibrational energy of molecules is 'quantized' in accordance with Planck's Law. The frequencies of the radiation absorbed or emitted in the transitions are of the order of 10^{13} Hz, corresponding to wavelengths in the infra-red region.

Infra-red absorption spectra of simple molecules give information about their shape and the force constants of the bonds. The spectra of complex molecules are usually used as 'finger prints'. That is, molecules in mixtures can be identified by their characteristic infra-red spectrum (a technique much used with hydrocarbon mixtures in the petroleum industry); specific atomic groupings in a compound of unknown constitution can be recognized by their characteristic infra-red absorption patterns.

Nuclear magnetic resonance (n.m.r.)

Certain atomic nuclei have a magnetic moment and may be considered as small spinning bar magnets. Among these are nuclei having odd-numbered masses (e.g. ^{1}H, ^{13}C, ^{15}N, ^{19}F, ^{31}P) and those of even mass but odd atomic number (e.g. ^{2}H, ^{10}B, ^{14}N). Other nuclei such as ^{12}C and ^{16}O do not have a magnetic moment.

37

When placed in an applied magnetic field the nucleus is constrained by quantum theory to lie in one of two orientations; a low-energy one aligned with the field or a high-energy one aligned anti-parallel to it. The difference between these two energy levels corresponds to an electromagnetic radiation frequency of the order of 10^8 Hz although the actual frequency depends on the magnetic flux density of the field surrounding the nucleus according to the relation $\nu = \gamma B$, where B is the flux density and γ a constant depending on the magnetic moment and the moment of inertia of the nucleus. Thus for a nucleus in an applied uniform magnetic field subjected to electro-magnetic radiation of the right frequency, energy is absorbed from the magnetic component of the radiation as the nucleus flips from one energy state to another.

The technique in principle is to place the sample in a highly uniform magnetic field (of flux density of the order of 1 tesla). The sample is ex-posed to a radio-frequency magnetic field (by, for example, placing it inside a coil supplied with radio-frequency current) and this is 'swept' through a range of frequency values where absorption is likely to occur. When a nucleus absorbs energy there is a small surge in the radio-frequency circuit which is detected and recorded on an oscilloscope or with a moving pen recorder. This is the phenomenon of 'nuclear magnetic resonance'; the name arises from the close analogy with resonances in the classical physical sense.

The hydrogen nucleus ^{1}H (i.e. the proton) exhibits this effect. In com-pounds containing hydrogen, the local magnetic field due to the nearby electron clouds slightly modifies the resonance conditions, and this local magnetic field will differ with the environment of the hydrogen nucleus within the molecule. Thus with ethanol, three absorption peaks are ob-served during a low resolution sweep of the radio field. These peaks correspond to the protons of the CH_3, CH_2 and OH groups respectively. The areas under the absorption peaks are in proportion to the number of protons in each location.

All organic compounds have characteristic proton n.m.r. spectra. A com-pound which n.m.r. spectroscopists find particularly useful is tetramethyl silane (TMS) which contains twelve equivalent protons giving rise to a sharp resonance peak at a radio-frequency just lower than that causing resonance in the vast majority of organic compounds. TMS is a volatile liquid which can be added in small amounts to the solvents generally used in n.m.r. spectroscopy and its signal is used as a reference point from which the displacements of the signals due to protons in other chemical environ-ments may be measured. These displacements, or chemical shifts as they are known, are entirely characteristic for the protons in each organic group. Thus study of an n.m.r. spectrum enables the chemist to identify the presence of hydrogen atom groupings in an unknown compound providing him with one of his most useful analytical tools.

Although n.m.r. can theoretically be applied to any nucleus having a net nuclear spin, most work has been done with ^{19}F, ^{31}P and more recently and importantly with ^{13}C in addition to ^1H.

Mass spectrometry

A mass spectrograph (or spectrometer) is a device for segregating ions in the vapour phase by magnetic 'focusing' so that all ions having the same value for the ratio of ion mass to electronic charge (m/e) are brought together on a suitable recording 'target'; the ion current can be measured either electronically (by varying the magnetic field, ions of different m/e can be focused and recorded in turn by the detector) or by the exposure of a photographic plate.

Organic compounds can be ionized in the vapour phase by bombardment with an electron beam. This not only removes outer electrons, but also breaks up the molecule, producing ionized fragments of the original molecule. These can be identified by their m/e and their relative abundance established by the magnitude of the ion current 'peak' for each value.

Not only can the technique distinguish between isotopic constituents such as ^{12}C, ^{13}C, but some fragments which seem, on a crude basis, to have the same mass e.g. $C_2H_5^+$, CHO^+, can, by careful tuning of a precision spectrometer, be resolved according to the small mass differences revealed in the fourth or fifth decimal place of the atomic masses (oxygen does not have an atomic mass exactly 16/12 times that of carbon). As a result of this ability mass spectrometry is now the principle tool of the chemist for establishing molecular weights. The particle with the largest m/e is often the molecule of the compound under study with just one electron removed, the molecular ion. Otherwise, using evidence from other sources such as n.m.r. spectroscopy as a guide to the structure, it is possible to reassemble several smaller m/e values to arrive at the value for the molecular ion.

Mass spectrometry is therefore a valuable and extremely accurate technique by which it is possible to work towards the establishment of a structure for an unknown compound by the identification of the fragments into which the molecule has been broken.

SECTION II

4

The paraffins or alkanes

The homologous series of *paraffins* or *alkanes*, of general formula C_nH_{2n+2}, has already been met in chapter 1, where the names and formulae of the members up to C_4H_{10} are listed. Alkanes with five or more carbon atoms in an unbranched carbon skeleton have names derived from the Greek numerals and the termination -*ane*.

n		n	
5	Pentane	11	Undecane
6	Hexane	12	Dodecane
7	Heptane	13	Tridecane
8	Octane	14	Tetradecane
9	Nonane	15	Pentadecane
10	Decane	16	Hexadecane

n = total number of carbon atoms.

To name a branched chain alkane, the longest chain of consecutively linked carbon atoms in the molecule is located. The compound is then named as a derivative of the unbranched alkane containing this length of chain. Alkyl group branches are named as substituents by prefixing their names, and their position is indicated by a numeral showing the atom in the main chain to which they are attached. Thus

$$\overset{1}{C}H_3.\overset{2}{C}H_2.\overset{3}{C}H_2.\overset{4}{C}H_2.\overset{5}{C}H_2.\overset{6}{C}H_2.\overset{7}{C}H_3$$

is heptane;

$$\begin{array}{cc} & CH_3 \qquad CH_3 \\ & \diagdown \quad \diagup \\ CH_3 & CH \\ | & | \\ CH_3.CH.CH_2.CH.CH_2.CH_2.CH_3 \end{array}$$

is 2-methyl-4-isopropylheptane; but

$$\begin{array}{cc} \overset{1}{C}H_3 \quad CH_3 \\ \diagdown \overset{2}{} \diagup \\ CH \qquad CH_3 \\ \overset{3}{|} \quad \overset{5}{|} \\ CH_3.\overset{3}{C}H.\overset{4}{C}H_2.\overset{5}{C}H.\overset{6}{C}H_2.\overset{7}{C}H_2.\overset{8}{C}H_3 \end{array}$$

is 2,3,5-trimethyloctane, since the longest continuous chain in the molecule is C_8, as numbered, and not the C_7 chain printed as straight. The atoms should be numbered from the end giving the lower numerals in the name; thus this last compound should not be called 4,6,7-trimethyloctane.

Although strictly speaking the name heptane implies therefore the unbranched or normal compound, the prefix n- is often added to avoid possible misunderstanding.

Physical characterization

The alkanes have the physical characteristics of non-associated substances. They are relatively low melting, volatile (compare e.g. the boiling point* of CH_4, $-161°$ C with those of NH_3, $-33°$ C; H_2O, $100°$ C; HF, $19·5°$ C) and very sparingly soluble in water. These properties reflect the practically complete absence of hydrogen bonding (see p. 17) in methane and its homologues.

The alkanes up to C_4 are all gases at ordinary temperatures and pressures, as is neopentane $C(CH_3)_4$. The higher members are liquids, then waxy solids. Of the isomers of a given molecular formula, the unbranched compound has the highest boiling point. Branching, leading to greater compactness of the molecule, lowers the boiling point but sometimes raises the melting point. The selection of melting and boiling points in the following table illustrate these points.

Alkane	m.p. °C	b.p. °C
CH_4	-184	-161
$CH_3(CH_2)_2CH_3$	-135	$- 0·6$
$(CH_3)_2CHCH_3$	-145	$- 10$
$CH_3(CH_2)_3CH_2$	-131	35
$(CH_3)_2CHCH_2CH_3$	-160	28
$(CH_3)_4C$	$- 20$	$9·5$
$CH_3(CH_2)_6CH_3$	$- 56$	125
$(CH_3)_3C.C(CH_3)_3$	104	$106·8$

As mentioned in chapter 1, alkanes are relatively unreactive substances; most of their reactions are inconvenient to carry out under ordinary laboratory conditions, and they are therefore rarely used as laboratory reagents. On the other hand, a plentiful supply of alkanes of all chain lengths from methane up to C_{30} or more is available from natural gas and petroleum (see p. 105) so that some of the technically feasible reactions of the alkanes are economically important.

* All boiling points quoted in this book are at 760 mm, unless otherwise indicated.

Reactions of alkanes

(1) Combustion

All alkanes burn in air or oxygen, yielding ultimately carbon dioxide and water or steam. The general equation is

$$C_nH_{2n+2} + \frac{3n+1}{2}\ O_2 \rightarrow nCO_2 + (n+1)\ H_2O.$$

It follows by using Avogadro's Law that 1 volume of gaseous alkane requires $\frac{3n+1}{2}$ volumes of oxygen for complete combustion, and yields n volumes of carbon dioxide and, if measurements are made at ordinary conditions, a small volume of liquid water, all volumes being measured at the same temperature and pressure. By taking measured volumes of gaseous alkane and oxygen (this in excess), exploding, and measuring the volume after cooling, before and after the addition of aqueous alkali to absorb carbon dioxide, the molecular formula of the alkane can be established from the reacting volumes thus found. This method (eudiometry) is applicable to all gaseous or readily vaporized hydrocarbons. (A considerable excess of oxygen may be needed to moderate the violence of the explosion.)

In the absence of excess oxygen and of properly designed burners, combustion of alkanes is incomplete, giving a luminous flame which deposits unburnt carbon (lamp-black) on a cool surface in contact with the flame. Lamp-black is a useful material. It is, for example, incorporated in black motor-tyre rubber.

Alkanes as a class form one of the most familiar and economically important groups of fuels. Methane is the main constituent of combustible natural gas (e.g. from under the Sahara or the North Sea). Propane and butane (the latter under the trade names of Calor gas, Bottogas, Butagaz, etc.) are marketed as liquids in moderate pressure cylinders for industrial and domestic use where portability of the gas supply is essential. Petrol (or gasoline) consists mainly of C_5 to C_8 alkanes; paraffin oil (in America, kerosene) contains C_9 to C_{18} alkanes, and diesel and fuel oils about C_{12} and upwards. Solid alkanes are the main constituents of the paraffin wax of candles. By far the most important source of these fuels is *petroleum*. Since petroleum refining involves the chemistry of not only alkanes but also alkenes and benzene derivatives, a brief sketch of the industry follows in chapter 9.

(2) Other oxidation reactions

Methane and other low molecular weight gaseous alkanes can be oxidized by steam in the presence of various catalysts (including metallic nickel) to carbon monoxide and hydrogen, e.g.

$$CH_4 + H_2O \rightarrow CO + 3H_2$$

This is the reverse of the methane synthesis (p. 46). Given abundant methane, the reaction in this direction is economically valuable as a source of hydrogen for ammonia manufacture or of 'synthesis gas' for producing higher hydrocarbons by the Fischer–Tropsch process (p. 46), and supplements or replaces water-gas from coke and steam. Various schemes have been proposed for the oxidation of the lower alkanes to formaldehyde, ethanol, acetaldehyde, acetic acid, etc.

High molecular weight alkanes can be oxidized in the liquid phase by air in the presence of heavy metal soaps (e.g. manganous stearate) as catalysts. The chains are broken down in the process; the main products are carboxylic acids, with various by-products.

(3) Halogenation

Methane acts with chlorine, with the progressive replacement of hydrogen by halogen:

$$CH_4 + Cl_2 \rightarrow \qquad CH_3Cl + HCl$$
methyl chloride (monochloromethane)

$$CH_3Cl + Cl_2 \rightarrow \qquad CH_2Cl_2 + HCl$$
methylene dichloride (dichloromethane)

and so on $\rightarrow$ $\quad CHCl_3 \quad \rightarrow \quad CCl_4$
chloroform   carbon tetrachloride
(trichloromethane)   (tetrachloromethane)

Reaction occurs when the gas mixture is exposed to light or heat (about 300° C); the initial step is probably the photochemical or thermal dissociation of a chlorine molecule, which initiates a chain reaction, involving the liberation of alkyl radicals, thus:

$$Cl_2 \rightarrow 2Cl\cdot$$
$$\left.\begin{array}{l} CH_4 + Cl\cdot \rightarrow CH_3\cdot + HCl \\ CH_3\cdot + Cl_2 \rightarrow CH_3Cl + Cl\cdot \end{array}\right\} \text{chain-propagating steps.}$$

The reaction is highly exothermic (ΔH for the overall reaction $CH_4 \rightarrow CH_3Cl$ is about -101 kJ mol^{-1} and may become explosive, with the formation of soot and hydrogen chloride. The corresponding reaction with bromine is much milder (ΔH for $CH_4 \rightarrow CH_3Br$ is about -25 kJ mol^{-1}). The iodination reaction is endothermic, reversible and impracticable.

Higher alkanes react similarly. Ethane gives rise to all products up to hexachloroethane C_2Cl_6. With higher alkanes still, all possible mono-chlorination products are obtained in the first stage reaction; thus propane gives a mixture of 1-chloro- and 2-chloro propanes (*n*- and iso-propyl chlorides) $CH_3CH_2CH_2Cl$ and $CH_3CHClCH_3$.

Halogenation, especially chlorination, of alkanes is technically important; it is scarcely convenient as a laboratory operation, and alkyl halides are usually made from alcohols (see p. 118).

(4) Nitration

Alkanes can be nitrated to yield *nitro alkanes*, containing the $\mathord{>}C\mathord{-}N\mathord{<}^O_O$ group. Thus methane reacts with nitric acid vapour at about 300° C:

$$CH_4 + HNO_3 \rightarrow CH_3NO_2 + H_2O$$

Higher alkanes react similarly; nitration occurs at all possible sites (e.g. butane yields $CH_3CH_2CH_2CH_2NO_2$ and $CH_2CH_2CHNO_2CH_3$) and some breaking down of the carbon skeleton usually occurs.

The conditions of nitration of alkanes should be contrasted with those used for the nitration of benzene (p. 89); alkane nitration, like halogenation in (3) above, is probably a homolytic process, whereas both substitution halogenation and nitration of benzene are heterolytic.

(5) Sulphonation

Concentrated sulphuric acid has no effect on alkanes, but oleum reacts with hexane and higher alkanes to yield sulphonic acids, containing the group $\mathord{>}C\mathord{-}SO_2OH$. The reaction is difficult, and oxidation and other side reactions occur. Again, this should be contrasted with the smooth sulphonation of benzene (p. 92) and its derivatives. Hydrogen is more readily replaced in this and similar reactions when attached to secondary or tertiary carbon atoms.

Sulphuryl chloride converts alkanes photochemically to sulphonyl chlorides, which can be hydrolysed to sulphonic acids, e.g.

$$CH_3CH_2CH_3 + SO_2Cl_2 \rightarrow \left. \begin{array}{l} CH_3CH_2CH_2SO_2Cl \\ CH_3CH(SO_2Cl)CH_3 \end{array} \right\} + HCl$$

$$-SO_2Cl + H_2O \rightarrow -SO_2OH + HCl$$

Again, the reaction is presumably homolytic.

This is more efficient than direct sulphonation with oleum, and has been applied to the manufacture of long-chain alkane sulphonic acids. Sulphonic acids being strong acids, such compounds have the strong electrolyte 'head' and long-chain hydrocarbon 'tail' typical of detergent molecules, and have applications as such.

Preparation of alkanes

(1) Hydrogenation of alkenes (olefins) and alkynes (acetylenes)

Compounds containing double or triple bonds (see the following chapters) can be hydrogenated with gaseous hydrogen over finely divided metals such as nickel or platinum. Thus ethylene and acetylene both yield ethane:

$$CH{\equiv}CH \xrightarrow{+H_2} CH_2{=}CH_2 \xrightarrow{+H_2} CH_3.CH_3$$

This reaction is used to prepare an alkane when, for example, iso-octene obtained by polymerizing iso-butene is converted to iso-octane (p. 108).

$$\underset{\underset{CH_3}{|}}{\overset{\overset{CH_3}{|}}{CH_3{-}C}}{-}CH{=}\overset{\overset{CH_3}{|}}{C}{-}CH_3 \xrightarrow[\text{catalyst}]{H_2} \underset{\underset{CH_3}{|}}{\overset{\overset{CH_3}{|}}{CH_3{-}C}}{-}CH_2{-}\overset{\overset{CH_3}{|}}{CH}{-}CH_3$$

(2) Reduction of halides

Alkyl halides can be reduced to alkanes by a variety of methods, including:

(*a*) the action of a zinc–copper couple in 95 % ethanol, e.g.

$$C_2H_5Br + H^{\oplus} + 2e \rightarrow C_2H_6 + Br^{\ominus}$$

(*b*) conversion to a Grignard reagent and subsequent addition of water or other hydroxylic reagent (see p. 121), e.g.

$$C_2H_5Br + Mg \rightarrow C_2H_5MgBr$$
$$C_2H_5MgBr + H_2O \rightarrow C_2H_6 + Mg^{2\oplus} + OH^{\ominus} + Br^{\ominus}$$

(3) Reduction of ketones by Clemmensen's reaction

Alkyl ketones on warming with amalgamated zinc and concentrated hydrochloric acid are reduced to alkanes; thus acetone yields propane:

$$CH_3COCH_3 + 4H^{\oplus} + 2Zn \rightarrow CH_3CH_2CH_3 + H_2O + 2Zn^{2\oplus}$$

Amalgamated zinc is a form of zinc which has been cleaned with aqueous alkali and then coated with zinc amalgam by immersion in mercuric chloride solution.

(4) Wurtz reaction and allied methods

Halides react with metallic sodium in dry ether; thus e.g.

$$2C_2H_5I + 2Na \rightarrow CH_3CH_2CH_2CH_3 + 2Na^{\oplus}I^{\ominus}$$

45

Alternatively, one mole of halide can be converted to a Grignard reagent and then reacted with a second mole of the same or another halide:

$$C_2M_5Br + Mg \rightarrow C_2H_5MgBr$$
$$C_2H_5MgBr + CH_3CH_2CH_2Br \rightarrow CH_3(CH_2)_3CH_3 + Mg^{2\oplus} + 2Br^{\ominus}$$

Side reactions reduce the yields in the Wurtz reaction, which only gives reasonable results with longer-chain halides (from C_{10} upwards). The Grignard method is usually preferable, especially in linking two different alkyl groups.

(5) Decarboxylation of fatty acids

Alkanes are obtained by heating the sodium salts of fatty acids with soda-lime:
$$CH_3COO^{\ominus} + OH^{\ominus} \rightarrow CH_4 + CO_3^{2\ominus}$$
Yields fall off with increasing chain length of the acid.

(6) Kolbe's electrolytic reaction

Electrolysis of the salts of fatty acids in aqueous solution yields alkanes and carbon dioxide at the anode; e.g.

$$2C_2H_5COO^{\ominus} - 2e \rightarrow CH_3(CH_2)_2CH_3 + 2CO_2$$

Thus the acid $R.CO_2H$ yields the alkane R—R by this method, but RH by simple decarboxylation as in (5).

(7) The Fischer–Tropsch reaction

Alkanes, together with variable amounts of alkenes and traces of oxygen-containing organic compounds, are obtained when carbon monoxide is hydrogenated over suitable metallic catalysts. Over reduced nickel (supported on kieselguhr and promoted by traces of thoria, etc.) the product is almost entirely methane:

$$CO + 3H_2 \rightarrow CH_4 + H_2O$$
and
$$2CO + 2H_2 \rightarrow CH_4 + CO_2$$

but by replacing nickel by cobalt and, later, by suitably prepared iron catalysts, Fischer and Tropsch in 1926 were able to prepare higher alkanes; the main reaction is:

$$nCO + (2n+1)H_2 \rightarrow C_nH_{2n+2} + nH_2O$$

but some of the oxygen appears as carbon dioxide:

$$2nCO + (n+1)H_2 \rightarrow C_nH_{2n+2} + nCO_2$$

the proportions of the two varying with catalyst composition.

The gas pressure can range from 1 to 10 atmospheres with cobalt catalysts. The products are almost entirely unbranched, of all chain lengths from methane up to high molecular weight waxes of C_{30} or more; the mean chain length in atmospheric pressure operation with cobalt is about C_7, but increased pressure increases the proportion of longer chains. There is no known way of favouring any particular chain length other than methane. Efficient temperature control is essential; the reaction is exo-thermic, and if the temperature is allowed to rise above the efficient operating figure (about 200° C), the product is almost entirely methane, and carbon deposits on the catalyst. In Germany, where the process was operated commercially during the Second World War, the catalyst was stationary ('fixed bed' operation) and reaction heat was carried off by water circulating at 10 atmospheres through pipes in the reaction vessel. 'Fluidized bed' techniques derived from catalytic cracking experience (see p. 107) have since been developed. The olefin content of the product can be increased by increasing the $CO:H_2$ ratio in the input gas, and by using iron catalysts at about 50 atmospheres.

Since the products are almost entirely straight chain and the olefins almost entirely α-olefins (i.e. with the double bond at the end of the chain, as in e.g. pent-1-ene $CH_3(CH_2)_2CH{=}CH_2$), 'straight' Fischer–Tropsch product is a poor motor fuel (see p. 106). The higher liquid fractions make a very high-grade diesel oil. The process is hardly competitive as a source of fuel, though it could be the basis of a straight-chain aliphatics chemical industry, should need arise.

Since carbon monoxide–hydrogen mixtures can be made either by the water-gas reaction or by the controlled oxidation of methane with steam or steam–oxygen mixtures, the Fischer–Tropsch process can be based either on coal or methane as raw material.

Alkyl groups

These, as stated in chapter 1, are the hydrocarbon residue remaining when a single hydrogen atom of an alkane has been replaced by a functional group of some kind. Superficially, at any rate, they retain some of the general inertness and the particular reactions of the alkanes themselves. They can often be halogenated and in many cases sulphonated. In detail, however, the reactions of alkyl groups are often modified by the attached functional group. This is particularly so of the α-C atom and its attached hydrogen atoms; that is, of the carbon atom to which the functional group is attached. These points are illustrated in later chapters of the book.

One feature of alkyl groups is that, though all alkanes are non-polar, so that replacement of hydrogen by alkyl has no effect on the polarity of the molecule, yet when other groups are present, alkyl groups act in comparison with hydrogen as electron-donating.

Cases where this effect can be adduced to give a plausible explanation of some feature of a particular reaction will be found in the following chapters. Caution is required; for one thing the methyl group, for example, is bulkier as well as more polarizable than a hydrogen atom. It could, for example, be argued that the following figures for K_A of the lower fatty acids exemplified the electron-repelling effect of CH_3— in place of hydrogen in rendering the ionizable hydrogen atom less easily detached by a base:

acid	K_A (25° C)
$H . CO_2H$	$17 \cdot 7 \times 10^{-5}$
CH_3CO_2H	$1 \cdot 76 \times 10^{-5}$
$CH_3CH_2CO_2H$	$1 \cdot 34 \times 10^{-5}$
$(CH_3)_3C . CO_2H$	$0 \cdot 95 \times 10^{-5}$

but the figure for isobutyric acid then requires some other explanation:

$$(CH_3)_2CH . CO_2H \qquad 1 \cdot 42 \times 10^{-5}$$

This example is perhaps a useful warning against over-facile theories and reading too much into limited data; it is not intended to throw doubt on the general picture of alkyl groups as in effect electron-repelling.

5

The ethylenic double bond function: $\diagup C{=}C\diagdown$

This functional group is present in the homologous series of *alkenes* or mono-olefins, of general formula C_nH_{2n}. The formulation of this group involves the concept that atoms may be linked by more than one valency bond. The development of this concept in the nineteenth century represents a remarkable advance in the ideas of valency. Before the chemistry of the olefins is considered in detail, we will review the evidence which justifies this concept of 'multiple bonding' in experimental terms. This is closely connected with the phenomenon of *unsaturation*.

Unsaturation

Many compounds undergo *addition reactions*. That is to say, they combine with another reagent so that one or more atoms or groups of atoms from the latter combine with the molecules of the reacting substance without any part of these being split off; hence the molecular weight of the product is the sum of the molecular weight of the original substance and the atomic or formula weights of the added groups.

In this broad sense, a number of simple inorganic substances undergo addition reactions; a few are listed below:

$$PCl_3(g) + Cl_2(g) \rightleftharpoons PCl_5(g)$$
$$2NO + O_2 \rightarrow 2NO_2$$
$$SO_2 + Cl_2 \rightarrow SO_2Cl_2$$
$$NH_3 + BF_3 \rightarrow BF_3NH_3$$
$$SO_3 + H_2O \rightarrow H_2SO_4$$
$$SO_3 + HCl \rightarrow HSO_3Cl \text{ (chlorosulphonic acid)}$$

The capacity to perform addition reactions implies that some part of the chemical combining power of one or more atoms of the original molecule is latent, and capable of being brought into use to form valency bonds with the added atoms or groups. Another way of making the same point about

49

the original molecule is to say that the combining power or valency is not *saturated*. Hence substances capable of undergoing addition reactions are termed *unsaturated*, or are said to show *unsaturation*. This unsaturation may be referred to certain atoms or 'centres' in the unsaturated molecule, thus, in the first example above, it is clear that it resides in the capacity of the phosphorus atom to form two additional bonds to univalent chlorine; in the last two examples, on the other hand, any plausible formula for sulphuric acid and chlorsulphonic acids implies that the water or hydrogen chloride molecules become split into two groups, one of which adds to oxygen and one to sulphur.

(Note that it is strictly not correct to define an addition reaction as one in which two substances combine to form a single product, since such a definition would include for example the reaction:

$$H_2 + Cl_2 \rightarrow 2HCl$$

which is not an addition reaction, nor is it ideal to define it as a reaction in which two or more molecules combine to form a single molecule, since this would exclude addition reactions in which the reagent is for example an oxidizing agent, of which only part becomes attached to the reacting molecules.)

Such reactions may be contrasted with *substitution reactions* in which part of the reacting molecule becomes detached, and another atom or group of atoms is *substituted* for it. Simple inorganic examples related to and contrasted with the above addition reactions would include:

$$SO_2 + PCl_5 \rightarrow SOCl_2 + POCl_3$$
$$H_2SO_4 + PCl_5 \rightarrow SO_2Cl_2 + POCl_3 + 2HCl$$
$$NH_3 + HOCl \rightarrow NH_2Cl + H_2O$$
$$\text{monochloramine}$$

It is by no means impossible for the same substance to undergo an addition reaction in one context and a substitution reaction in another; this is true, as we shall see, even of the hydrocarbons of the olefin series. We might conclude, however, that a substance which *never* underwent addition reactions had its combining power saturated; such a substance could be described as a *saturated* compound.

The hydrocarbon ethylene C_2H_4 and its homologues the mono-olefins or alkenes (general formula C_nH_{2n}) characteristically show unsaturation, and undergo addition reactions. We shall discuss these in detail later. For the present a few of the most characteristic are listed below:

$$C_2H_4 + Br_2 \rightarrow C_2H_4Br_2 \quad \text{ethylene dibromide}$$
$$C_2H_4 + HBr \rightarrow C_2H_5Br \quad \text{ethyl bromide}$$
$$C_2H_4 + HOCl \rightarrow C_2H_4ClOH \quad \text{ethylene chlorohydrin}$$

Ethylene and its homologues may thus be contrasted with methane and the alkanes, which undergo only substitution reactions and are therefore saturated substances.

Further consideration of the alkenes and their unsaturation reveals several important points. First, no hydrocarbon CH_2 has ever been isolated; *two carbon atoms at least* are necessary for the existence of the unsaturated function of an alkene. Secondly, the reactions described above lead to the addition of two univalent atoms or groups to the ethylene molecule. Thirdly, where it is possible to produce independent evidence, this points to the fact that these two univalent groups are added to *adjacent* carbon atoms in the molecule. For example the addition of bromine to ethylene yields ethylene dibromide $C_2H_4Br_2$; an *isomeric* substance is obtained by the addition of hydrogen bromide to acetylene or by the action of phosphorus pentabromide on acetaldehyde. This isomer formed in these latter circumstances is called ethylidene dibromide. Ethylidene dibromide yields acetaldehyde on hydrolysis with water in sealed vessels (*alkaline* hydrolysis will not, of course, yield acetaldehyde, see p. 194); acetaldehyde may be shown by arguments independent of the structure of ethylene (e.g. from its chlorination and subsequent hydrolysis to chloroform), to contain a methyl group in its molecule. Hence if we are to formulate the isomeric dibromides as dibromoethanes, ethylidene dibromide must from its relation to acetaldehyde be CH_3CHBr_2, and hence ethylene dibromide is $CH_2Br.CH_2Br$; that is, the two Br atoms have been added to adjacent C atoms of ethylene, which therefore must be formulated CH_2CH_2.

Such a molecule could be formulated graphically:

$$\begin{array}{ccc} H & & H \\ & \diagdown C - C \diagup & \\ H & & H \end{array}$$

This was obviously unsatisfactory to the nineteenth-century chemists who laid the basis of structural organic chemistry, since no compounds containing isolated tervalent carbon atoms (CH_3, for example) could be obtained. It was therefore supposed that *two* valency bonds linked the two carbon atoms, forming a *double bond*, thus:

$$\begin{array}{ccc} H & & H \\ & \diagdown C = C \diagup & \\ H & & H \end{array}$$

making the carbon atom quadrivalent, as in the saturated alkanes. It was assumed that when addition reactions occurred, the second link of the double bond became broken, leaving two 'free valencies' on adjacent carbon atoms, to which the two added univalent groups or atoms became attached.

Once put forward, the double bond concept proved remarkably adaptable to the experimental facts. If we assume that in methane, the four valency bonds of the carbon atom are symmetrically disposed, then it follows that in the ethylene molecule they must be distorted from their 'natural' directions (i.e. those of lowest potential energy) in order that *two* bonds shall link two carbon atoms. This implies that some 'strain' energy must be incorporated in the molecule; that is, *less* energy will be *evolved* in forming a *double* bond between carbon atoms than would be evolved in forming two *separate single* bonds between carbon atoms, the missing energy being 'stored' in the 'bent' bonds. (This is easily appreciated with a ball-and-spring model, in which the springs simulate the properties we are postulating in a valency bond, namely, that it has a minimum potential energy when of a certain length and direction, and cannot be distorted from these without the input of energy.) *Direct* verification of this involves data which were not available to nineteenth-century chemists (see p. 54 later), but Baeyer, who in 1885 introduced the idea of strain in double bonds, pointed out that in the addition reactions of ethylene and its homologues, this strain would be eliminated in the formation of the saturated and single-bonded product, and the energy stored in the double bond would be released. He used this idea to explain why unsaturated compounds containing double bonds underwent addition reactions so readily.

If, following van't Hoff (p. 300), we make the undistorted directions of the carbon valencies point to the corners of a tetrahedron, then a model of an ethylene molecule turns out to be flat; the two carbon atoms and the four hydrogen atoms lie in one plane. This is in accordance with all later evidence; one piece of negative evidence is that no compound has ever been found resolvable into mirror-image isomers (see p. 299) as a consequence of any unsymmetrical substitution of the four hydrogen atoms of ethylene by different groups.

When models of ethylene and ethane are compared, we find that in ethane one methyl group may rotate relative to the other about the single C—C bond, but in ethylene the C=C bond inhibits the relative rotation of the CH_2 groups. This lack of free rotation leads to *geometrical* or *cis–trans isomerism* in ethylene derivatives of the type CHX:CHX; see p. 310.

In a ball-and-spring model of the ethylene molecule (see Fig. 9), the two carbon atoms are closer together than in a model of ethane molecule on the same scale. Classical methods were, of course, quite unable to confirm this implication of the model, but physical methods show that the C—C distance in ethylene is 0·133 nm (1·33 Å), whereas in ethane it is 0·154 nm.

The idea of unsaturation and the concept of the double bond have been developed here without reference to any particular theory of valency or atomic structure, since chemists found them necessary long before such theories were established. In terms of an electronic theory of valency,

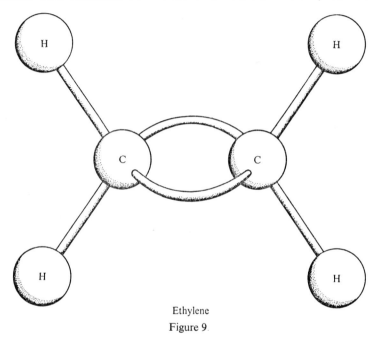

Ethylene

Figure 9

unsaturation clearly arises from the presence in the molecule of electrons which can be brought into play to link fresh atoms to the molecule. These will either be unshared (lone) pairs, as in the case of phosphorus trichloride combining with chlorine, or pairs of electrons shared between atoms which are linked by more than one such pair, so that a pair can be disengaged from the bond without totally disrupting the linkage between the atoms. (In the comparatively rare cases of 'odd molecules' such as NO, unsaturation arises from the presence of one or more *unpaired* electrons in the molecule.) This second type is present in ethylene (and in sulphur trioxide in the last two examples of inorganic unsaturation), and is much the more important type in organic chemistry. It is so widespread that unsaturation is often considered as synonymous with the presence in a molecule of one or more multiple bonds, although this is somewhat illogical on any experimental definition of unsaturation.

Thermochemistry of ethylene

From the heats of combustion of a hydrocarbon, hydrogen and graphite, the heat of formation of the hydrocarbon from hydrogen and graphite can be calculated. The change

$$2C_{graphite} + 3H_2 \rightarrow C_2H_6$$

is exothermic, ΔH being -101 kJ mol^{-1}, whereas the change

$$2C_{graphite} + 2H_2 \rightarrow C_2H_4$$

is endothermic, ΔH being 29 kJ mol^{-1}.

On casual inspection, these figures appear to confirm Baeyer's Strain Theory, but the figures represent the net change in heat content per mole for a succession of changes. Thus the first reaction can be broken down to the atomization of two moles of graphite and the dissociation of 3 moles of hydrogen into atoms, followed by the formation of 6 moles of CH bonds and one mole of C—C bonds; the second involves the dissociation of the same quantity of graphite, but of only 2 moles of hydrogen, and the formation of 4 moles of C—H bonds and 1 mole of C=C bonds. In order to compare the values of ΔH for the formation of a mole of single C—C bonds and a mole of double bonds we also need to know the heat of dissociation of hydrogen and the heat of formation of the C—H bond (assuming for the moment that this is the same in ethane as in ethylene), which also involves knowledge of the heat of atomization of graphite. This last value in particular is difficult to determine accurately. Given the following values, however, the required values can be obtained.

$$CH_4 + 2O_2 \rightarrow CO_2 + 2H_2O(l)$$
$$\Delta H = -895 \text{ kJ mol}^{-1}$$
$$C_2H_6 + 3\tfrac{1}{2}O_2 \rightarrow 2CO_2 + 3H_2O(l)$$
$$\Delta H = -1542 \text{ kJ mol}^{-1}$$
$$C_2H_4 + 3O_2 \rightarrow 2CO_2 + 2H_2O$$
$$\Delta H = -1387 \text{ kJ mol}^{-1}$$
$$\tfrac{1}{2}H_2 \rightarrow H; \Delta H = 218 \text{ kJ mol}^{-1}$$
$$C_{graphite} \rightarrow C_{atomic}; \Delta H = 716 \text{ kJ mol}^{-1}$$
$$H_2 + \tfrac{1}{2}O_2 \rightarrow H_2O_l; \Delta H = -286 \text{ kJ mol}^{-1}$$
$$C_{graphite} + O_2 \rightarrow CO_2; \Delta H = -393 \text{ kJ mol}^{-1}$$

The student should calculate first the mean heat of formation *from atoms* of the C—H bonds in methane; this, of course, is not the same as the heat of formation per mole of the CH bond from equal numbers of isolated carbon and hydrogen atoms, but the *mean* heat of formation is more informative in this case. If we assume this value applies to the CH bonds of ethane and ethylene, the heat of formation of C—C in ethane and C=C in ethylene can be found. It will be found that the latter is less than twice the former, as stated above, p. 52; the balance of energy is therefore in some sense or other 'stored' in the molecule. The extent to which this is regarded as confirming Baeyer's Strain Theory depends on how literally strain is interpreted in terms of bending bonds, and what picture of the double bond is provided by more detailed application of current valency theory concepts. These are beyond the scope of the present book.*

Nomenclature

Systematically, the alkenes or mono-olefins are named after the corresponding alkanes or paraffins by replacing the termination -*ane* by -*ene* to indicate the presence of the double bond. If necessary, the position of this in the molecule is indicated by inserting before the termination the *lower* of the two integers indicating the positions in the chain of the carbon atoms joined by the double bond.

These points are illustrated below for the first few members of the alkene series.

CH_2=CH_2 ethene (ethylene)
CH_2=CH—CH_3 propene (propylene)
CH_2=CH—CH_2CH_3 but-1-ene (α-butylene)
CH_3—CH=CH—CH_3 but-2-ene (β-butylene)
CH_2=C—CH_3 2-methylpropene (isobutylene)
        |
        CH_3

Properties

In simple physical properties the alkenes are similar to the corresponding alkanes. In general the alkene has a slightly lower boiling point and a slightly higher solubility in water than the corresponding alkane.

Chemical reactions

The chemical properties of the alkenes are dominated by their tendency to undergo almost exclusively addition rather than substitution reactions. In these reactions, as already mentioned above, the product is a saturated substance. For example ethylene gives rise in such reactions to derivatives of ethane.

The following are among the best-known addition reactions of ethylene and other compounds containing the $\rangle C{=}C\langle$ functional group.

* The description of double bonding in terms of 'sp² hybridization of carbon orbitals', with the second link regarded as a pure 'π bond', which may well be encountered is only an approximation, and in no way invalidates an alternative description in terms of 'bent' bonds.

(1) Hydrogenation

Compounds with olefinic double bonds can be hydrogenated by the action of hydrogen at suitable temperature and pressure in the presence of a metallic catalyst, usually nickel or platinum. Thus ethylene yields ethane; the conditions required vary greatly with the effectiveness of the catalyst employed.

$$CH_2{=}CH_2 + H_2 \rightarrow CH_3.CH_3$$

Pioneer work in catalytic hydrogenation was carried out by Sabatier and his co-workers in the early twentieth century. The process is used in the 'hardening' of fish, whale and vegetable oils. These are esters of unsaturated carboxylic acids (see p. 209 for an explanation of these terms), and are liquids at ordinary temperatures, often with disagreeable smells; the corresponding saturated compounds have higher melting points (hence the term 'hardening') and inoffensive smells, and are used in the manufacture of margarine.

(2) Addition of halogens

Chlorine and bromine add readily to olefinic double bonds; thus if ethylene is passed through water-cooled bromine (with a layer of water on top to minimize volatilization of the bromine), ethylene dibromide or 1,2-dibromoethane is obtained.

$$CH_2{=}CH_2 + Br_2 \rightarrow CH_2Br.CH_2Br$$

(Note that, in spite of the name ethylene dibromide, this product is saturated and contains no double bond; it must be clearly distinguished from a dibromoethylene, which would be $CHBr{:}CHBr$ or $CH_2{:}CBr_2$.) Chlorine may be added to ethylene by passing both gases into a solvent, such as ethylene dichloride itself.

A naïve view of this reaction would perhaps picture the halogen molecule as colliding sideways on to and reacting with an ethylene molecule, thus:

$$\begin{array}{ccc} Br & CH_2 & Br{-}CH_2 \\ | \; + \; || & \rightarrow & | \\ Br & CH_2 & Br{-}CH_2 \end{array}$$

rather as hydrogen and iodine molecules are supposed to collide and change partners in the formation of hydrogen iodide. Experimental evidence, however, shows that this picture is far from correct. For example, when ethylene reacts with bromine in the presence of sodium chloride solution 1-bromo-2-chloroethane (ethylene chlorobromide) is found in the product. Since any possible equilibrium concentration of BrCl is minute and far too small to account for the proportion of $CH_2Cl.CH_2Br$ formed, this result implies that one of the Br atoms of ethylene dibromide is added as a $Br^\ominus$ ion, and its place in the reaction can be taken by $Cl^\ominus$ if this is present. Thus either prior to or in the course of the reaction process the bromine molecule must become polarized as $Br^{\delta\oplus}{-}Br^{\delta\ominus}$. Presumably since the ethylene molecule is unsaturated by virtue of the availability for reaction of the second electron pair of the double bond, it is the electron-deficient positive bromine atom which attacks the ethylene molecule, leading to the liberation of $Br^\ominus$ which then adds to the electron-deficient intermediate:

$$CH_2{=}CH_2+Br^{\delta\oplus}{-}Br^{\delta\ominus} \rightarrow \left(\begin{matrix}CH_2{-}CH_2\\ |\\ Br\end{matrix}\right)^{\oplus}+Br^\ominus \rightarrow CH_2Br.CH_2Br$$

Furthermore, it has been established in a number of cases that the two bromine atoms become attached on *opposite* sides of the olefinic bond (so-called *trans-addition*), and this is presumably the normal course of the reaction. A particularly clear case of this is shown by the addition of bromine to maleic and fumaric acids, which is discussed on p. 313.

Iodine has little tendency to add to double bonds.

(3) Addition of hydrogen halides

Hydrogen bromide adds to olefinic double bonds; thus ethylene is absorbed by concentrated hydrobromic acid, forming ethyl bromide (bromo-ethane).

$$CH_2{=}CH_2+HBr \rightarrow CH_3CH_2Br$$

Hydriodic acid behaves similarly, but hydrochloric acid reacts very slowly if at all with ethylene itself, though it adds to higher olefins. Ethylene is however absorbed by liquid hydrogen chloride in the presence of aluminium chloride.

Clearly, when, for example, hydrogen bromide adds to an olefin in which the double bond is not symmetrically situated, there are two possible products. Thus propylene might give rise to 1-bromopropane $CH_3CH_2CH_2Br$ or 2-bromopropane $CH_3CHBrCH_3$. In such cases, addition normally takes place in accordance with *Markovnikov's Rule*: the halogen atom becomes attached to the carbon atom carrying the smaller number of hydrogen atoms, and the hydrogen atom to that carrying the larger number. (A useful mnemonic is the scriptural text: 'unto every one that hath shall be given', the carbon atom which already has more hydrogen gets the added hydrogen atom.)

On the analogy of the addition of bromine, we may suppose that the olefin bond is first attacked by the positive hydrogen atom of the hydrogen halide, perhaps even as a hydrogen ion, and that the negative halide ion adds subsequently. Markovnikov's rule therefore requires us to account for the fact that the olefin carbon atom carrying the larger number of hydrogen atoms is the more nucleophilic. It is suggested that, as alkyl groups act as rather weak sources of electrons, an unsymmetrical olefin molecule such as propylene has its electron distribution distorted thus:

$$H_3C \diagdown_{\diagdown} \quad \diagup H$$
$$C = C$$
$$H \diagup \qquad \diagdown H$$

leading to attack by the $\overset{\oplus}{H}$ of the hydrogen halide on the carbon atom remote from the alkyl group.

It has been shown that in the presence of peroxides (which are very liable to form with olefins in the presence of air) 'anti-Markovnikov' addition of hydrogen bromide may occur. A different reaction mechanism, involving bromine atoms, is involved in this. Markovnikov's rule only applies to addition to simple olefins; where other functional groups are present, their polarity and constitution may affect the course of the addition. Thus hydrogen bromide adds to acrylic acid $CH_2{=}CH.CO_2H$ to yield β-bromopropionic acid $CH_2Br.CH_2.CO_2H$ and not the α-bromo-acid which would be expected if Markovnikov's Rule applied.

(4) Addition of sulphuric acid

Olefins are absorbed by 98% sulphuric acid forming the corresponding alkyl bisulphates; thus, ethylene yields ethyl hydrogen sulphate:

$$CH_2{=}CH_2 + HOSO_2OH \rightarrow CH_3.CH_2OSO_2OH$$

These bisulphates yield alcohols and sulphuric acid on hydrolysis by heating with water. Since Markovnikov's rule applies to the addition of sulphuric acid, the higher olefins will always yield secondary or tertiary alcohols in this way, and never primary, since this would require the addition of the bisulphate group to the terminal $={=}CH_2$, whereas this *must* carry more hydrogen atoms than the other carbon atom of the $C{=}C$ bond, and therefore must acquire the added H atom.

(5) Addition of water

Olefins do not add water under ordinary laboratory conditions, but ethanol is manufactured by the direct catalysed hydration of ethylene by steam.
$$CH_2{=}CH_2 + HOH \rightarrow CH_3.CH_2OH$$

The catalyst is basically phosphoric acid on a siliceous support.

(6) Addition of hypohalous acids

Hypochlorous and hypobromous acids add to olefinic double bonds, forming compounds known as chloro- and bromo-hydrins. If a mixture of ethylene and carbon dioxide is passed into sodium hypochlorite solution, the hypochlorous acid liberated by the action of the (stronger) carbonic acid on the hypochlorite adds to the ethylene forming ethylene chlorohydrin (β-chloroethyl alcohol; 2-chloroethanol)

$$CH_2{=}CH_2 + HOCl \rightarrow CH_2OH \cdot CH_2Cl$$

(Technically, ethylene is absorbed in milk of lime at 200 atmospheres and ordinary temperatures. Chlorine is passed in. Under these conditions, the hypochlorite reacts as hypochlorous acid, leaving calcium chloride.) Here again, with unsymmetrical higher olefins two products could be formed; the rule here is that the main product has *halogen* attached to the carbon atom richer in hydrogen. The obvious conclusion in the light of the above interpretation of Markovnikov's rule is that the hypohalous acid behaves as $\overset{\delta\ominus}{H}O{-}\overset{\delta\oplus}{C}l$, providing the electrophilic positive halogen atom or ion to attack the electrons of the double bond.

On hydrolysis with caustic alkali, chloro- and bromo-hydrins yield *alkylene oxides* rather than vicinal diols (alcohols with —OH groups on adjoining carbon atoms). For example, ethylene chlorohydrin yields ethylene oxide:

$$CH_2Cl \cdot CH_2OH + OH^\ominus \rightarrow \underset{O}{CH_2{-}CH_2} + Cl^\ominus + H_2O$$

(7) Oxidation of olefins

Cold aqueous alkaline permanganate solution is reduced by olefinic double bonds, first to a green manganate, then to a suspension of manganese dioxide. The rapid discharge of the purple colour of an ice-cold dilute solution of potassium permanganate in aqueous sodium carbonate may be used as a test for the olefinic double bond if other strongly reducing groups (e.g. —CHO) are known to be absent. The olefin is oxidized to a dihydric alcohol with —OH groups on adjacent C atoms. Thus ethylene is converted to ethylene glycol (ethan-1,2-diol).

$$CH_2{=}CH_2 + H_2O + (O) \rightarrow CH_2OH \cdot CH_2OH$$

Unlike halogen addition, this reaction proceeds with both —OH groups adding to the *same* side of the olefin molecule (*cis*-addition) though with other oxidizing agents such as selenium dioxide *trans*-addition occurs. This point is discussed further in connection with the behaviour of maleic and fumaric acids (p. 313). More drastic oxidation may lead to the fission of the molecule at the $>C=C<$ bond; the products will in general be the same as those obtained by ozonolysis (see the next section).

(8) Addition of ozone; ozonolysis

If ozonized oxygen is passed into an ice-cooled solution of an olefinic compound, in e.g. chloroform, ozone is absorbed, and on evaporation of the solvent at room temperature and reduced pressure, the *ozonide* of the olefin remains. A molecule of ozone adds across the double bond, ultimately to form:

$$>C{-}O{-}C< \atop \;\;\;O{-}O$$

Ozonides are usually highly unstable and explode if heated. On cautious warming with water, they are hydrolysed, and the products have $>C=O$ at the carbon atoms which were linked by the double bond in the original compound. Thus, for example, the olefin

$$\begin{array}{cc} CH_3CH_2 & CH_3 \\ & C=C \\ CH_3 & CH_3 \end{array}$$

will yield on treating with ozone and subsequent hydrolysis the ketones $CH_3CH_2.CO.CH_3$ and $CH_3.CO.CH_3$. The remaining oxygen appears as free oxygen, hydrogen peroxide, etc., and under these conditions aldehydes will be extensively oxidized to carboxylic acids (see p. 188); thus the olefin

$$\begin{array}{cc} CH_3 & H \\ & C=C \\ CH_3 & CH_3 \end{array}$$

will yield $CH_3.CO.CH_3$, $CH_3.CHO$ and $CH_3.CO_2H$.

The fission of olefins by treatment with ozone followed by water is called *ozonolysis*. If the resulting ketones, aldehydes or carboxylic acids are isolated and identified, the position of the double bond in the parent compound is established. This procedure offers a valuable method for elucidating this feature in the structure of an unknown molecule, and has been extensively used. Ozonides may alternatively be decomposed by catalytic hydrogenation with hydrogen over a platinum catalyst. The same types of product are obtained, but excessive oxidation is avoided.

(9) Polymerization

Since the $\diagup$C$=$C$\diagdown$ bond is potentially capable of behaving as $\diagup$C—C$\diagdown$ and adding other groups or atoms, it is possible that olefin molecules should add to one another. This could lead to ring formation, or to the formation of long chains, in which, for example, ethylene molecules would combine together thus:

$$\text{--- } + CH_2{=}CH_2 + CH_2{=}CH_2 + CH_2{=}CH_2 + \text{ ---}$$
$$\rightarrow -CH_2.CH_2.CH_2.CH_2.CH_2.CH_2-$$

forming a chain of indefinite length.

Such a reaction is a *polymerization*; that is, the combination together of a number of molecules of a simple substance to form a product whose molecular weight is an integral multiple of that of the parent substance. The simple substance is called the monomer (from the Greek meaning 'one part') and the product is the polymer (many parts).

Such reactions can in fact be brought about with compounds containing $\diagup$C$=$C$\diagdown$ bonds. Thus ethylene can be polymerized to *polythene* and propylene to *polypropylene*. These and a number of other polymers of substances containing olefin bonds are among the most familiar plastics and are of great technical importance. Their production is further discussed in chapter 23.

(The above is a strictly formal definition of polymerization but in practice the term is applied, at any rate in technical processes, to any reaction which approximates to this description, even though the molecular weight of the product is not an integral multiple of that of the monomer. For instance, it is clear that ethylene can only polymerize in a pedantically strict sense to a ring compound; the open chain polymer must have its terminal carbon valencies occupied by some extraneous groups or atoms. In any case, the molecules of an industrial polymer are not all of the same size, so the *mean* molecular weight need not be an integral multiple of that of the monomer. Apart from the introduction of extraneous end groups, a so-called polymerization may in fact involve the elimination of groups from the molecule; thus an aldehyde resin (p. 182) is often called a polymer of the aldehyde, though in fact extensive elimination of water occurs in its formation.)

Substitution reaction in olefins

Although addition reactions are by far the most familiar and easily elicited reactions of olefines, it is by no means impossible to find conditions

61

which favour substitution in the non-olefin part of the molecule. For example, if propylene is treated with chlorine at about 450° C (the so-called 'hot chlorination' of propylene) allyl chloride is obtained:

$$CH_3—CH=CH_2+Cl_2 \rightarrow CH_2Cl—CH=CH_2+HCl$$

This is a step in a possible route to glycerol ($CH_2OH.CHOH.CH_2OH$) from propylene as raw material.

Preparation of olefins: introduction of the $>C=C<$ link into molecules

(1) Elimination methods

(*a*) Olefins are obtained from alcohols by elimination of water; thus ethylene is prepared from ethanol by heating to about 160° C with excess of concentrated sulphuric acid, though much charring and reduction of the sulphuric acid also occurs. Alternative methods include passing ethanol vapour over heated pumice soaked in phosphoric acid or over heated alumina.

$$CH_3CH_2OH \rightarrow CH_2=CH_2+H_2O$$

The ease of elimination of the water molecule varies greatly from one —OH compound to another. The reaction is discussed on p. 134.

(*b*) Olefins are obtained from halides by the elimination of hydrogen halide. Thus ethylene is obtained when ethyl bromide vapour is passed over heated soda-lime.

$$CH_3CH_2Br \rightarrow CH_2=CH_2+HBr$$

In general, this reaction involves the use of a base as catalyst; it is discussed further on p. 115.

(*c*) Olefins are obtained from vicinal dihalides (i.e. carrying the two halogen atoms on adjacent carbon atoms) by heating with metals; thus ethylene dibromide (1,2-dibromoethane) yields ethylene on distillation with zinc dust.

$$CH_2Br.CH_2Br+Zn \rightarrow CH_2=CH_2+ZnBr_2$$

(2) Condensation methods

Olefinic double bonds are present in the products of the many variants of the aldol condensation in which aldehydic or ketonic $>C=O$ reacts with —CH_2— in a suitably 'activated' situation. These reactions are really addition reactions, followed by spontaneous eliminations of water as in 1(*a*) above (see p. 182).

Technical production of olefins

Olefins of various chain lengths are obtained by the *thermal cracking* of fairly long chain paraffins. Thus, if a paraffin fraction of range say C_{14} to C_{18} is passed into a tube packed with silica chippings at about 600° C, the product contains a substantial proportion of olefins from ethylene upwards, the higher homologues being largely α-olefins (i.e. having the double bond at one end of the chain). Ethylene is manufactured by the cracking of suitable petroleum fractions in the presence of steam.

Technical uses of olefins

Ethylene is used for the manufacture of ethanol and of polythene; propylene is used for the manufacture of polypropylene, isopropyl alcohol and acetone (including that obtained via the cumene process for making phenol; see p. 142). Higher olefins are converted to secondary alcohols for use as industrial solvents, etc. Long-chain olefins can be 'sulphated' by the addition of sulphuric acid to the double bond; the products have detergent properties.

6

The acetylenic triple bond function: $-C\equiv C-$

This functional group is present in the homologous series of *alkynes* or mono-acetylenes, of general formula C_nH_{2n-2}. The concept of a triple bond linking two carbon atoms in these compounds is a natural extension of the concept of the double bond as developed in the preceding chapters.

Nomenclature

Alkynes are named systematically on principles exactly analogous to those outlined for alkenes on p. 55. The first member of the series is commonly called acetylene, and higher members of the series may be named as substituted acetylenes; some of them have rather rarely used trivial names. The following examples illustrate these points:

$CH\equiv CH$	ethyne (acetylene)
$CH_3-C\equiv CH$	propyne (methyl acetylene; allylene)
$CH_3CH_2-C\equiv CH$	but-1-yne (ethyl acetylene; crotonylene)
$CH_3-C\equiv C-CH_3$	but-2-yne (dimethyl acetylene)

Physical properties

In simple physical characteristics, the alkynes differ rather more markedly from alkanes and alkenes than these do from one another. Thus alkynes have in general *higher* boiling points than either the alkanes or alkenes with the same carbon skeleton. (Compare butane, 0·5° C; but-1-ene, −6·5° C; *cis*-but-2-ene, −3·7° C; but-1-yne, 8·6° C; but-2-yne, 27·2° C.) They are also somewhat denser in the liquid state, and slightly more soluble in water.

Chemical behaviour

The presence of the acetylenic bond is associated with considerable thermal instability. Thus, acetylene itself under pressure or in the liquid state will detonate under shock. It is therefore marketed in cylinders packed with porous material soaked in acetone, in which it has a high solubility; in this way for a given (safe) gas-phase acetylene pressure (in practice about 12 atmospheres) a considerably greater weight of acetylene is present in the cylinder than if it were simply present as compressed gas in the absence of a solvent.

Alkynes, like alkenes, show unsaturation. It will at once be seen that addition reactions may be expected in general to go in two stages, with the successive addition of two pairs of univalent groups to the triply bonded pair of carbon atoms, yielding first an ethylenic compound and then by further addition an alkane or substituted alkane. Indeed, it is the fact that addition reactions of alkynes proceed in this way that forms the principal classical experimental evidence for the presence of the triple bond.

The elementary student is unlikely to meet any alkynes other than acetylene itself. The main reactions of the acetylenic bond are summarized below for the case of acetylene, except where the presence of carbon instead of hydrogen attached to the triply bound carbon atoms causes important modifications.

(1) Hydrogenation

Alkynes can be hydrogenated by hydrogen at suitable temperatures and pressures in the presence of metallic catalysts.

$$CH{\equiv}CH \xrightarrow[\substack{+\text{catalyst} \\ (\text{e.g. Raney nickel})}]{H_2} CH_2{=}CH_2 \xrightarrow[+\text{catalyst}]{H_2} CH_3{-}CH_3$$

The reaction can be stopped after the first stage by using a catalyst whose activity is reduced by being supported on a sulphur-containing compound.

The reaction has little or no practical value in the case of simple acetylenes, but has been used in laboratory synthesis of more complex substances.

(2) Addition of halogens

Acetylene and chorine inflame or explode when mixed, forming much soot and hydrogen chloride. The addition of chlorine to acetylene is best achieved by using substances such as antimony pentachloride or ferric chloride as halogen carriers. Acetylene and chlorine can be passed separately into a stirred solution of antimony pentachloride in tetrachloroethane; tetrachloroethane is the final product.

$$CH\equiv CH + Cl_2 \xrightarrow{SbCl_5} \underset{\text{1,2-dichloroethylene}}{CHCl\!=\!CHCl} \xrightarrow{SbCl_5} \underset{\text{1,1,2,2-tetrachloroethane}}{CHCl_2.CHCl_2}$$

It is possible to stop at the intermediate stage. Both products are useful solvents.

Acetylene adds bromine rather slowly.

(3) Addition of hydrogen halides

In the absence of catalysts, hydrogen chloride adds very slowly to acetylene. Reaction occurs at about $200°$ C in the presence of adsorbent charcoal (or similar materials) impregnated with aqueous solutions of mercury and other salts. The main product is mono-chloroethylene, which is also known as vinyl chloride, $CH_2\!=\!CH-$ being the vinyl group. This is a possible technical route to this compound, which can then be polymerized (see p. 339).

Vinyl acetylene $CH\equiv C-CH\!=\!CH_2$ (made by polymerizing acetylene, see below p. 68) adds hydrogen chloride in accordance with Markovnikov's Rule, in the presence of aqueous cuprous and ammonium salts to give 2-chlorobutadiene $CH_2\!=\!CCl-CH\!=\!CH_2$. This is chloroprene, the monomer of neoprene rubber (see p. 342).

Further addition of hydrogen chloride is difficult and technically, of course, undesirable, since the vinyl compounds are the required products. Presumably ethylidene dichloride would be formed, since hydrogen bromide and hydrogen iodide, which add more readily to acetylene than hydrogen chloride, yield ethylidene halides as the final product.

$$CH\equiv CH \xrightarrow{HBr} \underset{\text{vinyl bromide}}{CH_2\!=\!CH-Br} \xrightarrow{HBr} \underset{\text{ethylidene dibromide}}{CH_3CHBr_2}$$

Thus, although Markovnikov's Rule is not strictly applicable, since vinyl bromide is not a simple alkene (see p. 57), it is in fact obeyed.

(4) Addition of acetic acid

Acetylene adds acetic acid in the presence of mercuric sulphate (from oleum and mercuric oxide) to yield vinyl acetate and, by further addition, ethylidene diacetate, Markovnikov's Rule again operating.

$$CH\equiv CH + CH_3COOH \xrightarrow{Hg^{II} \text{ salts}} CH_2\!=\!CHO.COCH_3$$
$$CH_2\!=\!CHO.COCH_3 + CH_3COOH \rightarrow CH_3.CH(OCOCH_3)_2$$

Vinyl acetate is polymerized industrially to polyvinyl acetate (see p. 340); it cannot be made by direct esterification of vinyl alcohol, since this does not exist, except in undetectable amounts in equilibrium with acetaldehyde, of which it is the enol form (see p. 202).

(5) Addition of water (hydration)

Acetylene adds water on being passed into hot aqueous sulphuric acid containing mercuric sulphate.

Direct addition of water would be expected to yield vinyl alcohol:

$$CH{\equiv}CH + HOH \rightarrow CH_2{=}CH.OH$$

but this is a highly unstable 'enol' and cannot be isolated, the product in fact being the 'keto' form, acetaldehyde.

$$CH_2{=}CH.OH \rightarrow CH_3.CH{=}O$$

The relation between keto and enol forms and their interconversion is discussed on pp. 202 et seq.

This reaction forms a valuable route to acetaldehyde from acetylene and hence from calcium carbide (see below).

Higher alkynes can be similarly hydrated; in these cases ketones will be formed, in accordance with Markovnikov's Rule. Thus methyl acetylene will yield acetone:

$$CH_3.C{\equiv}CH + HOH \rightarrow \underset{\text{unstable}}{CH_3C(OH){=}CH_2} \rightarrow CH_3.\underset{\|\atop O}{C}.CH_3$$

In reactions (4) and (5) above, acetylene differs from ethylene, which does not add either acetic acid or water under these conditions. The use in both of these reactions of mercuric salts as catalysts is significant; mercuric salts are known to react readily with alkynes, and organic mercury compounds of some kind are almost certainly intermediates in addition reactions using mercuric catalysts.

(6) Oxidation

(*a*) Combustion. Acetylene burns in air with a luminous very smoky flame, forming much free carbon (soot). In the days of acetylene car and cycle lamps, burners were devised to bring about more or less complete combustion. The reaction is highly exothermic (see below) and practical use is made of the high temperature flame obtained by the rapid combustion of acetylene with oxygen in the oxy-acetylene torch for 'cutting' steel.

(*b*) Alkynes reduce cold aqueous permanganate solutions in the same general way as alkenes. The main product from acetylene is oxalic acid; on the analogy of ethylene, glyoxal might be expected:

$$\begin{matrix} CH \\ \||\| \\ CH \end{matrix} + 2H_2O + 2(O) \rightarrow \left(\begin{matrix} CH(OH)_2 \\ | \\ CH(OH)_2 \end{matrix}\right) \rightarrow \begin{matrix} CHO \\ | \\ CHO \end{matrix} + 2H_2O$$

but the oxidation proceeds further.

$$\begin{matrix} CHO \\ | \\ CHO \end{matrix} + 2[O] \rightarrow \begin{matrix} COOH \\ | \\ COOH \end{matrix}$$

oxalic acid

Acetylene is said to form an ozonide.

(7) Polymerization

Acetylene polymerizes in a number of ways according to the conditions used. Two of these may be mentioned.

(*a*) If acetylene is heated at ordinary pressures (for example, by passing through a heated tube) some benzene, mixed with other aromatic hydrocarbons, is formed. $3C_2H_2 \rightarrow C_6H_6$

(*b*) Acetylene can be polymerized to its dimer, vinylacetylene, by passing into aqueous solutions of copper (I) chloride complexes.

$$2CH{\equiv}CH \rightarrow CH_2{=}CH{-}CH{\equiv}CH$$

This compound can then be converted to 'chloroprene' (see above p. 66).

In all the above reactions except combustion acetylene shows characteristically unsaturated behaviour.

(8) Formation of metal derivatives

Alkynes containing the C≡C—H group differ from alkanes and alkenes in the ease in which the hydrogen atom attached to the acetylenic carbon atom is removed, leaving the carbon either with an ionic charge or possibly covalently attached to a metal atom.

If acetylene is passed into a solution of sodium in liquid ammonia, monosodium acetylide $CH{\equiv}C^{\ominus}Na^{\oplus}$ is formed; more drastic conditions, such as passing acetylene over molten sodium, yield the disodium derivative ('sodium carbide'). Another possible procedure, at any rate for higher alkynes, is the reaction with sodamide:

$$CH_3.C{\equiv}CH + Na^{\oplus}NH_2^{\ominus} \rightarrow CH_3.C{\equiv}C^{\ominus}Na^{\oplus} + NH_3$$

In such reactions acetylene and its homologues are clearly showing a markedly acidic function. This acidic function is much weaker than that of water, which hydrolyses these ionic acetylides back to the hydrocarbon and alkali; thus, for example,

$$H.C{\equiv}C^{\ominus} + H_2O \rightarrow H.C{\equiv}CH + OH^{\ominus}$$

Silver and cuprous acetylides, on the other hand, can be obtained in aqueous conditions by passing acetylene into solutions of silver and cuprous ammines (i.e. 'ammoniacal' silver nitrate and cuprous chloride) respectively.

$$CH{\equiv}CH + 2[Ag(NH_3)_2]^{\oplus} \rightarrow AgC{\equiv}CAg + 2NH_4^{\oplus} + 2NH_3$$

Cuprous acetylide appears as a red, silver acetylide as a cream precipitate. Both substances when dry detonate on slight shock; we thus have the unusual case of an explosion yielding solid products only—the metal and free carbon. These compounds are supposed to be largely covalent in character. Alkynes of the general type $R.C{\equiv}CH$ behave like acetylene itself, yielding $R.C.{\equiv}C.Cu$ as a red precipitate; ammoniacal cuprous solutions can therefore be used as a test reagent for the functional group $-C{\equiv}C-H$.

Although unaffected by water, silver and cuprous acetylides and their homologues yield the free alkyne on treatment with aqueous cyanide; presumably because of the great stability of the cuprous and argentous cyanide complexes.

The term 'carbide' has sometimes been held to denote the ion $\overset{\ominus}{C}{\equiv}\overset{\ominus}{C}$ and compounds (like sodium carbide Na_2C_2 and calcium carbide CaC_2) containing it; these have ionic lattices. 'Acetylides' are then the 'covalent' substances like cuprous acetylide. Current practice seems to be to use the term acetylide for all derivatives of acetylene, whether predominantly ionic or covalent, and to confine 'carbide' to substances like aluminium carbide or silicon carbide in which the carbon atoms, whatever their bonding, are not present as triply linked pairs.

Thermochemistry of acetylene

Acetylene, like ethylene and unlike ethane, is an endothermic substance; from the following data:

$$H_2 + \tfrac{1}{2}O_2 \rightarrow H_2O \qquad \Delta H = -286 \text{ kJ mol}^{-1}$$
$$C_{graphite} + O_2 \rightarrow CO_2 \qquad \Delta H = -393 \text{ kJ mol}^{-1}$$
$$C_2H_2 + 2\tfrac{1}{2}O_2 \rightarrow 2CO_2 + H_2O \qquad \Delta H = -1309 \text{ kJ mol}^{-1}$$

it can be deduced that ΔH for the reaction:

$$2C_{graphite} + H_2 \rightarrow C_2H_2$$

is $+237$ kJ mol^{-1}. By a calculation similar to that suggested for C=C on p. 54, it will be found that the differences in the values of ΔH for forming a mole of C—C, C=C and C≡C bonds respectively from free atoms become successively smaller. (The validity of assuming the same value of ΔH for the formation of the C—H bond as in methane is, however, more obviously questionable for the C≡C calculation, in view of the special behaviour of —C≡C—H as reviewed above.) The conclusion can be tentatively drawn therefore that, as the mean energy released in the formation of each link of an olefinic bond is less than that for a single bond, so similarly that for each link of a triple bond is smaller still, and that herein in some way lies the instability of the acetylene molecule.

C≡C bond length and shape of the acetylene molecule

The acetylenic bond follows the trend shown by the C—C and C=C bonds in length as well as in heat of formation; the C≡C length in acetylene is 0·120 nm (compare C=C in ethylene 0·133 nm and C—C in ethane 0·154 nm). Simple considerations from the tetrahedral model lead to the assumption that the acetylene molecule is linear, with the two hydrogen and two carbon atoms all on the same axis; more elaborate valency theory leads to the same conclusion, which is confirmed by physical evidence. There is therefore no question of geometrical isomerism as with olefins, and in fact no such isomers of acetylene derivatives are known.

Technical uses of acetylene

Acetylene is used in oxyacetylene torches, as a source of vinyl compounds (vinyl chloride, vinyl acetate) for the manufacture of polyvinyl plastics, as a source of acetaldehyde and hence of ethanol, acetic acid, acetone, butanol, butadiene and many other industrially important materials. It was at one time used for lighting, but this use has largely disappeared.

Manufacture of acetylene

For industrial purposes, acetylene is obtained by the action of water on calcium carbide; essentially the reaction is:

$$C_2^{2\ominus} + 2H_2O \rightarrow C_2H_2 + 2OH^\ominus$$

'Carbide' is made by heating lime and anthracite in an electric furnace. It contains impurities, notably phosphide and sulphide from the limestone;

the acetylene obtained therefore contains phosphine and hydrogen sulphide as important impurities, and these are responsible for its rather unpleasant smell. They may largely be removed by washing the gas with copper sulphate solution.

Clearly the economic use of acetylene as an industrial raw material depends on the availability of cheap electric power for manufacturing calcium carbide.

General method for introducing $C \equiv C$ into organic molecules

(1)   The action of alkalis on dihalides

If a suitable dihalogeno-alkane is refluxed with alcoholic potassium hydroxide, two molecules of hydrogen halide are eliminated and an alkyne is formed. The two halogen atoms may be attached to the *same* C atom (in a so-called *gem*-dihalide such as $CH_3 . CHBr_2$) or to adjacent carbon atoms (in a *vicinal* dihalide, such as $CH_2Br . CH_2Br$). Thus acetylene itself is obtained when either 1,2-dibromo- or 1,1-dibromo-ethane is dropped into boiling alcoholic potash.

$$\left\{ \begin{matrix} CH_2Br . CH_2Br \\ or \\ CH_3 . CHBr_2 \end{matrix} \right\} + 2OH^{\ominus} \rightarrow CH{\equiv}CH + 2H_2O + 2Br^{\ominus}$$

With higher dihalides of either type, the alkyne and not the theoretically possible alternative allene is formed. Thus $CH_3CHBr . CH_2Br$ or $CH_3CBr_2CH_3$ yield $CH_3C{\equiv}CH$ and not $CH_2{=}C{=}CH_2$.

(2)   The action of alkyl halides on sodium alkynides

Higher alkynes containing a methyl group can be obtained by the action of methyl halides (e.g. methyl iodide) on sodium alkynides. Thus for example, monosodium acetylide and methyl iodide yield methyl acetylene.

$$H . C{\equiv}C^{\ominus} + CH_3I \rightarrow H . C{\equiv}C{-}CH_3 + I^{\ominus}$$

This does not of course create the $C{\equiv}C$, but merely attaches the residue containing it to the methyl group. Yields are poor with higher alkyl halides.

7

Benzene: aromatic systems

In 1825, Faraday isolated the hydrocarbon now known as benzene from gas obtained by the thermal decomposition of fish-oils. Later (in 1845), Hofmann obtained it from coal-tar, a complex mixture of organic substances obtained as a distillate when coal is heated in retorts in the absence of air, as in a gasworks or in coke-ovens. This is still the main source of benzene and many related compounds.

Benzene is in many respects notably different from the hydrocarbon types reviewed in the preceding three chapters. Quantitative combustion and vapour density show it to have the molecular formula C_6H_6. This is a very low hydrogen to carbon ratio—compare the fully saturated hexanes C_6H_{14}—and would suggest a highly unsaturated substance. In fact, however, although benzene does undergo addition reactions, these are more difficult to elicit than the corresponding reactions of olefins or acetylenes, and do not in any case lead to substituted hexanes; the characteristic familiar reactions of benzene are *substitution* reactions, leading in the first place therefore to derivatives of the general type C_6H_5X.

Addition reactions of benzene

These may be summarized in the equations:

$$C_6H_6 + 3H_2 \xrightarrow{\text{catalytic}} C_6H_{12}$$

$$C_6H_6 + 3Cl_2 \xrightarrow[\text{sunlight}]{\text{vapour-phase}} C_6H_6Cl_6$$
$$\text{(or } 3Br_2) \qquad\qquad (C_6H_6Br_6)$$

$$C_6H_6 + 3O_3 \longrightarrow C_6H_6(O_3)_3$$
$$\text{benzene triozonide}$$

A few practical details of these reactions are discussed in the next chapter. We see at once that benzene adds six univalent atoms (or three effectively bivalent 'ozonide' groups); that is, two univalent groups less then required to yield a substituted hexane.

Furthermore, whereas the hydrogenation of ethylene and other mono-olefins is exothermic:

$$C_2H_4 + H_2 \rightarrow C_2H_6 \quad \Delta H = -117 \text{ kJ mol}^{-1}$$

the *first* step of hydrogenation of benzene is endothermic:

$$C_6H_6 + H_2 \rightarrow C_6H_8 \quad \Delta H = +23 \cdot 5 \text{ kJ mol}^{-1}$$

and although the overall hydrogenation reaction is exothermic, the mean heat change per mole of hydrogen added

$$\tfrac{1}{3}C_6H_6 + H_2 \rightarrow \tfrac{1}{3}C_6H_{12} \quad \Delta H = -68 \cdot 2 \text{ kJ mol}^{-1}$$

is considerably less than the above value for the hydrogenation of ethylene. The implication of these figures is that there is in benzene some additional 'barrier' to hydrogenation not present with ethylene; in a sense then, in this reaction at any rate, benzene is less unsaturated than its H:C ratio would imply.

Unlike ethylene, benzene does not undergo addition reactions with hypohalous acids, undergoes substitution and not addition with concentrated sulphuric acid, is extremely resistant to the attack of the common oxidizing agents in aqueous solution and shows no tendency to polymerize.

Substitution reactions of benzene

The most familiar of these may be summarized as follows:

$$C_6H_6 \xrightarrow{H_2SO_4} C_6H_5SO_3H$$

$$C_6H_6 \xrightarrow{HNO_3, \ H_2SO_4} C_6H_5NO_2$$

$$C_6H_6 \xrightarrow[+\text{catalysts}]{Cl_2 \ (\text{or } Br_2)} C_6H_5Cl \quad (\text{or } C_6H_5Br)$$

$$C_6H_6 \xrightarrow[+\text{catalysts}]{RCl} C_6H_5R \quad (\text{R can be alkyl or acyl})$$

These reactions are discussed in detail in the next chapter. In each case a hydrogen atom is replaced by a univalent group. Only one compound C_6H_5X, where X is of any particular type, is obtainable in this way; no isomeric mono-substituted benzenes are formed. This strongly suggests that all the hydrogen atoms occupy identical sites in the molecule, so that the same mono-substituted derivative is obtained, whichever hydrogen atom is replaced. (This can be proved formally by experiment, but the details are of largely academic interest.) Disubstitution, either to yield

$C_6H_4X_2$ or C_6H_4XY (substituents the same or different), leads to *three* isomers of any type.

These features taken together posed a considerable problem to the nineteenth-century chemists seeking a structural formula for the benzene molecule. Clearly no open-chain structure with olefinic or acetylenic unsaturation will fit the requirements. Indeed, isomers of benzene are known whose reactions and properties conform with such structure as

$$CH \equiv C-CH_2-CH_2-C \equiv CH \quad \text{(dipropargyl)}$$
$$CH_2 = CH-C \equiv C-CH = CH_2 \quad \text{(divinyl acetylene)}$$

and they are highly unsaturated substances remarkably unlike benzene. The basic feature of the solution to the problem was proposed by Kekulé, in 1865, as a result according to his own account of sudden inspiration rather than logical deduction. He proposed a closed 'ring' of six carbon atoms, each carrying a single hydrogen atom:

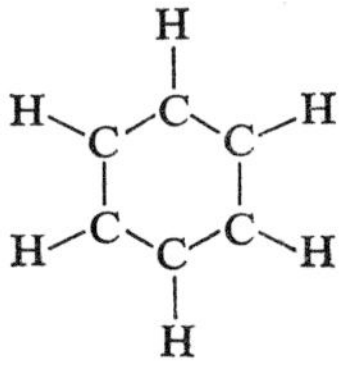

This formula gives the benzene molecule the symmetry of a regular hexagon, and thus accounts for the non-existence of isomeric mono-substitution products, and predicts the correct number of disubstitution products, which may for the moment be conventionally represented thus:

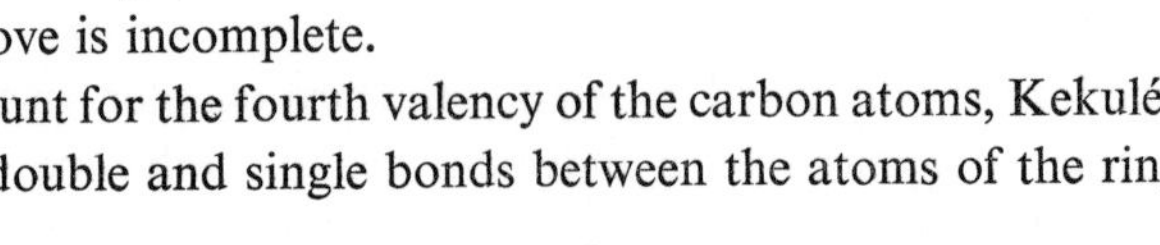

Each carbon atom, however, is attached to only *three* other atoms, and hence if we accept, as Kekulé did, that carbon is quadrivalent, the formula shown above is incomplete.

To account for the fourth valency of the carbon atoms, Kekulé suggested alternate double and single bonds between the atoms of the ring:

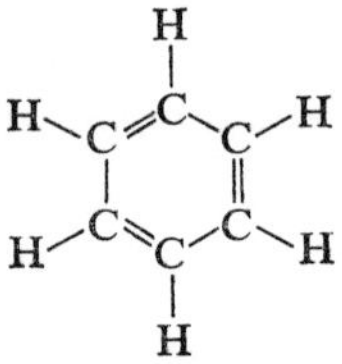

conveniently conventionalized as:

and this arrangement is now universally known as the 'Kekulé Structure'.

There are clearly two main objections to this formula. First, it incorporates double bonds, so that, although it satisfactorily accounts for the addition, for example, of only six hydrogen atoms and not eight, some form of special pleading is needed to explain why the unsaturation of benzene is so 'suppressed'. Secondly, the formula implies that with two univalent substituents on adjacent carbon atoms, two isomers should exist, with the relevant carbon atoms joined respectively by a double and a single bond;

making *four* isomers of $C_6H_4X_2$ and not the three required by the experimental facts.

To counter the second objection, Kekulé suggested that the double and single bonds in the benzene ring were continually oscillating between the two arrangements.

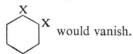

In this way the distinction between the two hypothetical isomers of

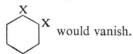 would vanish.

In spite of its defects, Kekulé's formula gained fairly general acceptance, and none of the various alternatives which were propounded in the late nineteenth century is of more than passing interest. Any rejecting the hexagonal arrangement of carbon atoms were experimentally disproved, and those which retained this but attempted to eliminate Kekulé's system of oscillating double and single bonds did so by inventing bonds with special characteristics not implicit in the general idea of a valency bond.

In fact, no useful progress beyond Kekulé's idea is possible so long as valency is conceived in terms of integral numbers of bonds linking pairs of atoms.

In terms of an electronic theory of valency, the problem of the benzene molecule can be seen as the problem of the location in the molecule of the six electrons (one per carbon atom) which are 'redundant' to the linking of the six carbon atoms to each other and to the six hydrogen atoms by single bonds (that is, by shared electron pairs):

$$
\begin{array}{c}
\text{H} \\
\overset{\times\bullet}{\text{C}}
\end{array}
$$

The current view of the benzene molecule rejects the idea (which is implicit in the nineteenth-century concept of a valency bond) that these six electrons are located in pairs engaged in bonding specific pairs of atoms. Rather they are considered to be 'delocalized' in 'molecular orbitals' involving all six atoms of the ring. An alternative statement of the same idea is to describe benzene as a 'resonance hybrid' of the two Kekulé structures.

(Strictly speaking, an adequate description of benzene in terms of 'resonance' concepts should include some contribution from the three 'Dewar' structures* of the type:

This can be neglected for qualitative purposes.)

Either description implies that the 'electron density' of the six electrons in question is uniform over the whole ring, and that the bonding of the carbon atoms of the ring is neither by single covalent bonds as in a paraffin, nor by ethylenic double bonds, nor by a periodic alternation of one and the other, but by a bond with its own individual character, consisting of a single covalent bond together with the contribution of the six delocalized electrons to the bonding of each pair of atoms.

Physical measurements such as X-ray diffraction studies give a picture of the benzene ring which is completely consistent with the above description. Thus, for example, Robertson showed that in hexamethyl benzene $C_6(CH_3)_6$ the twelve carbon atoms lie, within the limits of accuracy of the data, in a single plane, forming the apices of two regular hexagons. The atoms of the inner hexagon form the benzene ring. The interatomic distance

---

* This was one of the late-nineteenth-century formulae mentioned on p. 75.

is 0·139 nm, being thus between the value of 0·154 nm for the carbon–carbon distance in paraffins and 0·133 nm, the interatomic distance for carbon atoms joined by an olefinic bond. The atoms of the outer hexagon (the six methyl groups) lie symmetrically outside those of the benzene ring, so that the sides of the two hexagons are parallel, and the interatomic distance from the methyl carbon to the corresponding ring carbon atom is 0·150 nm, almost but not quite equal to the single C—C bond length in paraffins.

It is a characteristic of structures with delocalized electrons (resonance hybrids), as mentioned in chapter 2, that they are more stable—that is, at a lower energy level—than any hypothetical alternative structure linking the atoms in the same spatial arrangement but by localized 'shared pair' bonds. It is this feature that accounts for the great stability of the benzene ring, and its reluctance to perform addition reactions, since these can only occur with a disruption of the full symmetry of the ring and at any rate a partial localization of the delocalized electron 'sextet'.

This picture of the benzene molecule presents the chemist with the tiresome difficulty of finding an acceptable representation for the benzene ring on paper. It is one of the most frequently encountered structures in chemistry, and yet no single formulation is adequate, since the conventions of writing structural formulae require bonds to be shown as 'integral' in character—that is, single, double or triple—which is precisely what the benzene ring bonds are not. For many years a simple hexagon was used; all the atoms of benzene itself were omitted and substituents were shown alongside the corner representing the carbon atom to which they are joined. Thus:

benzene   chlorobenzene   a dichlorobenzene

Provided it is recognized that this is a convention, it is unexceptionable. It did, however, preclude the use of the same symbol for cyclohexane

and its derivatives, for which it would otherwise be suitable. Alternatively, a Kekulé type symbol

77

has been used, but this has the undesirable implication of alternate double and single bonds, and it is unfortunate to adopt a convention directly opposed to the accepted model. A fairly recent tendency has favoured symbols such as

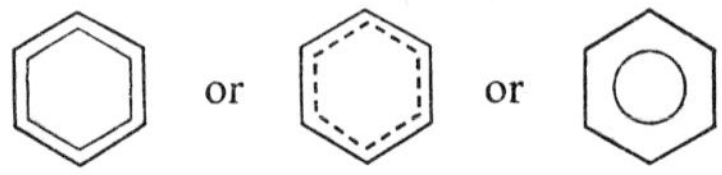

or   or

which use the old hexagon convention with an added conventional symbol to indicate the special nature of the bonding. This is hardly ideal for certain 'condensed' benzene ring systems of the types mentioned below (p. 87), where the bonds are no longer all identical in character. In this book the symbol

has been adopted in spite of the objection raised above, as being simple and widely used. Kekulé-type symbols have been retained in contexts where it is important to emphasize the presence of three electron pairs in the aromatic sextet. An obvious case is in the discussion of aromatic substitution in the following chapter.

By a historical accident, many of the earlier known benzene derivatives were isolated from 'spicy' natural sources, and were therefore known as 'aromatic' compounds. The name has stuck, first to benzene and its derivatives, and then to all ring systems and their derivatives in which there is appreciable delocalization of electrons (as described above) in the bonding of the ring atoms. Some of these other aromatic systems are reviewed very briefly at the end of this chapter.

Isomerism in benzene derivatives

As shown above, the regular hexagonal shape of the benzene ring leads to the existence of three isomers of any derivative of the type $C_6H_4X_2$ or C_6H_4XY. The problem therefore arises of deciding which formula to allocate to each of the three isomeric substances of a given set. This problem faced chemists several decades before X-ray diffraction studies offered the possibility of a direct physical investigation of the shapes of the molecules. Two main solutions were found.

The three xylenes (dimethyl benzenes) occur in coal tar and can be oxidized to the three benzene dicarboxylic acids $C_6H_4(COOH)_2$. Of these, only one (known as phthalic acid, from its preparation by the oxidation of the hydrocarbon na*phthal*ene) loses water on heating to its melting point to form an anhydride, which in turn reverts to the acid on hydrolysis; the other two isomers melt unchanged. Presumably phthalic acid has the carboxyl groups so situated that they readily interact to form the anhydride ring, while in the other two acids the groups are too far apart. Phthalic acid is therefore assumed to be

This arrangement, with the substituents attached to adjacent atoms of the ring, is known as the *ortho*-isomer.

Acetone on heating with sulphuric acid yields a trimethyl benzene known as mesitylene. From the likely mode of formation from acetone (see p. 186, chap. 14) and from the fact that on controlled oxidation, only one dimethyl benzene monocarboxylic acid $C_6H_3(CH_3)_2CO_2H$ is formed, mesitylene is assumed to be the symmetrical 1,3,5-trimethylbenzene.

| three molecules of acetone | mesitylene (1,3,5-trimethylbenzene) | 3,5-dimethylbenzoic acid |

(The significance of the numbers should be clear from the above formulae. The naming of benzene derivatives is discussed later, p. 81.) Decarboxylation of 3,5-dimethylbenzoic acid (see chap. 15, p. 227, for the decarboxylation reaction) must therefore yield the xylene

and this on oxidation yields the acid known as isophthalic acid, which must therefore be

This arrangement is known as the *meta*-isomer.

79

By elimination, the third isomer, known as terephthalic acid, must be:

CO₂H

CO₂H

This is the *para*-isomer.

This method obviously depends on the chemical arguments used to decide the relative positions of the substituents in phthalic acid and mesitylene, and offers no independent positive evidence for their positions in terephthalic acid.

Körner in 1874 pointed out that an alternative method independent of chemical arguments was available; this depends on determining the number of tri-derivatives formed when a third substituent group is introduced into each of the di-derivatives. This is easily seen diagrammatically.

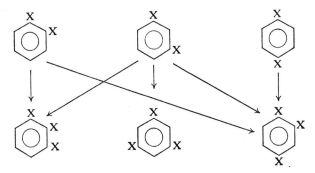

Clearly the di-derivative which yields *three* tri-derivatives has the *meta* orientation of the substituents, that which yields *two* must be the *ortho*-isomer, while that which yields only *one* is the *para*-isomer.

(The word 'orientation' is used to describe either the relative positions of the substituents in a benzene derivative—for example, in a di-derivative, whether they are *ortho*, *meta* or *para*—or the experimental determination of these positions. It has also been used to describe the 'directing' effect of benzene substituents (see p. 94) but this use is better avoided.)

The principal practical difficulty of this method is that owing to the *directing* effect of substituents in the benzene ring (see p. 94, chapter 8) isomers which should be obtained according to the above scheme may form an extremely small proportion of the total product. Thus, for example, the further nitration of meta-dinitrobenzene will yield almost exclusively 1,3,5-trinitrobenzene. Körner, however, succeeded in establishing the orientation of the groups in the dibromo- and tribromo-benzenes. The method can clearly be operated in reverse; that is, the ortho compound is the one which arises from the elimination of X from only two of the three tri-derivatives, and so on. It can also be adapted to cases where different substituents are present, although the number of possible tri-derivatives is then greater.

It is not, of course, necessary to determine in this way from first principles the orientation of the groups in all sets of isomeric di-substituted benzenes. Once a few 'reference' compounds have had their orientation established, the orientation in other compounds can be decided by transforming their functional groups to those of a selected 'reference' set by suitable reactions, and discovering which isomer is formed.

The two methods of orientation outlined above (the chemical argument for the dicarboxylic acids and the 'absolute' method of Körner) have been shown in this way to agree with one another.

The prefixes *ortho-*, *meta-* and *para-* are usually abbreviated to *o-*, *m-*, and *p-*. In the naming of trisubstituted benzenes and other more complex derivatives it is customary to number the atoms of the ring as indicated above; in a name like 2,4,6-trinitrobenzoic acid, carbon atom number 1 is that to which the un-numbered functional group implied in the name of the compound (in this case, carboxyl) is attached.

benzoic acid   *o*-nitrobenzoic acid   2,4,6-trinitrobenzoic acid

Homologues of benzene

The successive replacement of H— by CH_3—, starting with benzene, clearly gives rise to a homologous series of hydrocarbons of general formula C_nH_{2n-6}. The formulae and names of the second member and the four isomeric third members are shown below:

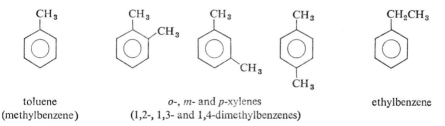

toluene   *o*-, *m*- and *p*-xylenes   ethylbenzene
(methylbenzene)   (1,2-, 1,3- and 1,4-dimethylbenzenes)

81

Unlike benzene itself, its homologues contain hydrogen bonded to carbon which is not part of the aromatic ring, and they may therefore be said to be partly aliphatic and partly aromatic in constitution. These two parts of the molecule tend to show their own characteristic reactions, somewhat modified by the presence of the other part. The presence of the alkyl group modifies the reactivity of the CH groups of the benzene ring; this is discussed in the next chapter, in which the reactions of the benzene ring are discussed in detail.

Two reaction of the alkyl groups may be noted:

(1) Oxidation

By persistent vigorous oxidation (for example by prolonged refluxing with alkaline permanganate, chromium trioxide or concentrated nitric acid) alkyl groups (and substituted alkyl groups) attached to the benzene ring become converted to carboxyl groups, whether the alkyl groups (the so-called 'side chains') contain one or more than one carbon atom. Thus the number of side chains and their points of attachment to the ring in a benzene derivative can be decided if the number and location of the carboxyl groups in the final product of oxidation can be found. For example, the compound

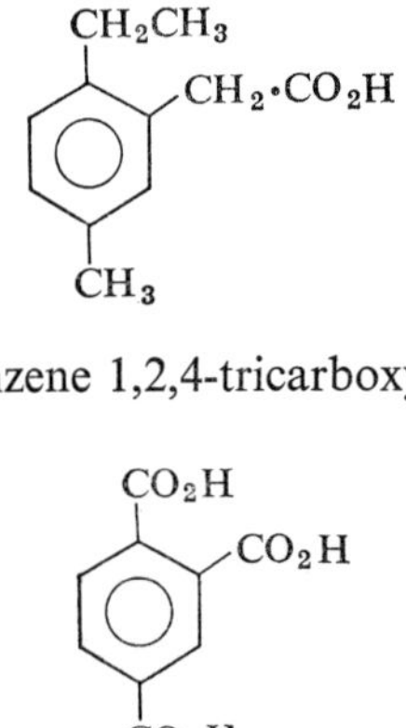

$$\underset{\text{CH}_3}{\overset{\text{CH}_2\text{CH}_3}{\bigcirc}}\text{CH}_2 \cdot \text{CO}_2\text{H}$$

would yield ultimately benzene 1,2,4-tricarboxylic acid:

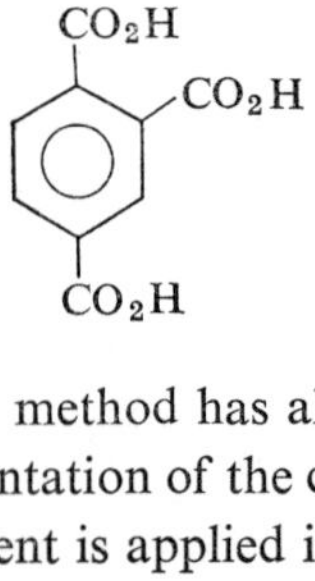

$$\underset{\text{CO}_2\text{H}}{\overset{\text{CO}_2\text{H}}{\bigcirc}}\text{CO}_2\text{H}$$

on prolonged oxidation. This method has already been referred to above (p. 79) in determining the orientation of the carboxyl groups in isophthalic acid, though there the argument is applied in reverse.

(2) Halogenation

This discussion will be limited to the case of toluene.

If chlorine is passed through boiling toluene in sunlight or ultraviolet irradiation, progressive replacement of the hydrogen atoms of the methyl group occurs (*side-chain* halogenation).

CH₃   CH₂Cl   CHCl₂   CCl₃

| toluene | (+HCl) benzyl chloride | benzal dichloride (benzylidene dichloride) | benzotrichloride (often called trichlorotoluene) |

These conditions are strongly suggestive of vapour-phase photochemical chlorination, such as occurs with methane (p. 43).

Halogenation of toluene in the absence of sunlight or ultraviolet light and in the presence of suitable catalysts gives rise to *nuclear* halogenation— that is, replacement of hydrogen atoms attached to the benzene ring. This is dealt with in the following chapter. (No conditions seem to be known in which benzene homologues undergo halogen addition.)

Sources of benzene and its homologues

(1) Coal tar

The composition of the tar obtained by the destructive distillation of coal depends considerably on the temperature at which this is carried out. Thus low-temperature distillation (at about 450° C), such as is used in the manufacture of smokeless 'semi-cokes' used for burning in open grates, yields a tar rich in paraffins and non-aromatic ring compounds such as cyclohexane, and poor in aromatics.

As the temperature of distillation of the coal is raised, the aromatic content increases at the expense of the non-aromatic, so that tars from gas-works for making town gas (operating temperatures *ca.* 1000° C) and coke-ovens (for making metallurgical coke, *ca.* 1300° C) are largely aromatic.

In addition to hydrocarbons, the tar contains (*a*) weakly acidic substances, which are mostly phenols, that is, compounds with OH attached to an aromatic ring (see p. 124) and (*b*) weakly basic substances; nitrogenous compounds such as pyridine:

and analogous compounds. (For the pyridine and other aromatic rings, see p. 86.)

83

After a preliminary fractionation into 'cuts' of fairly wide boiling range, the neutral components of each fraction (largely hydrocarbons) are separated from the 'tar acids' and 'tar bases'.

The fraction is first washed with aqueous sodium hydroxide solution, which converts the sparingly soluble phenols to their water-soluble conjugate bases (in other words, removes them in solution as sodium salts). Acidification of the aqueous extract with dilute sulphuric acid (or even carbon dioxide) regenerates the phenols.

phenol   phenate ion

The non-aqueous layer is then washed with dilute sulphuric acid, which converts the bases to their water-soluble conjugate acids. (For example, pyridine is converted to pyridinium ions). Pyridine itself is miscible with water (a remarkable contrast with benzene) and would therefore in any case be partitioned between the aqueous and non-aqueous layers. The pyridinium salts, however, like nearly all strong electrolytes, have very low solubilities in hydrocarbons, and hence are practically totally removed in the aqueous layer, from which the bases may be regenerated by addition of alkali:

pyridine   pyridinium ion

Thus the non-aqueous layer which remains after alkali and acid washing contains neutral compounds only.

The three sub-fractions thus obtained—acids, bases, and neutral compounds—can then be subjected to further fractionation by distillation, centrifuging or chemical methods.

In addition to the original distillates, the tar yields a residue of *pitch* which is run out of the stills while hot and allowed to set to a moderately hard glassy material. It can be powdered and used as a boiler fuel, or used for road surfacing. It is known to contain cancer-producing substances, including 3,4-benzpyrene:

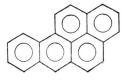

and derivatives.

Benzene has a considerable vapour pressure at the temperature of the condensers of a gas works or coke oven installation, and important amounts of benzene therefore escape condensation and pass on in the crude gas. These can be recovered by 'scrubbing' the gas with a spray of oil ('benzene wash-oil') in which the benzene dissolves and from which it can be recovered by distillation.

(2)   Petroleum and other sources

As mentioned in chapter 9 (p. 105) the chemical character of crude oil varies from field to field. Some crude oils ('asphaltic crudes'), notably those from the Rumanian and Borneo fields, contain appreciable quantities of aromatic substances. These aromatics are not extensively recovered from the oil. However, aromatic compounds can be obtained catalytically from non-aromatics. For example, when *n*-heptane vapour is passed over suitable heated catalysts (such as a specially prepared mixture of chromic and aluminium oxides), toluene is produced. The process involves several stages, including loss of hydrogen in ring closure (*cyclization*), and further loss of hydrogen. Overall, it is referred to as *aromatization*.

n-heptane   methylcyclohexane   toluene

Cyclohexane derivatives, which occur in 'naphthenic' crude oils, can be aromatized by passing over the same catalysts. In this case no cyclization step is involved.

These processes involve preliminary fractionation of the crude oil to isolate or at any rate concentrate the hydrocarbons to be aromatized.

The formation of benzene and its homologues in the polymerization of acetylene and the condensation of acetone has been mentioned on pp. 68 and 79 respectively.

Aromatic systems in general

A precise experimental definition of what constitutes an aromatic system need hardly be attempted; apart from the points discussed earlier in this chapter in relation to the structure of the benzene molecule, there are a number of striking ways in which the behaviour of the commoner functional groups is modified when they are attached to the benzene ring rather than to an aliphatic system. If, when the behaviour of the functional groups has been studied, these points are collected together, a picture of what constitutes aromatic character in benzene and its derivatives will emerge.

The theoretical discussion of the precise structural features which give rise to aromatic character is beyond the scope of this book. In practice however, the single ring systems which show to any extent the aromatic character we associate with benzene all possess associated with the atoms of the ring a group of six electrons 'in excess' of those essential to the bonding of the ring atoms. These electrons (sometimes known as the 'aromatic sextet') are more or less delocalized in the way outlined above for benzene, but since no other aromatic system has the complete symmetry of benzene, their distribution over the ring will be less uniform.

Since the nitrogen atom and the CH group are isoelectronic, it is not surprising that the former can replace the latter in benzene to some extent without the aromatic character disappearing. Thus pyridine (formulated above) and its homologues are characteristically aromatic. Other such systems are known with up to three nitrogen atoms in place of CH groups.

In pyridine, the lone pair of electrons of the nitrogen atom are not essential to the aromatic character of the ring, and pyridine can act as a base without losing its aromatic character. In certain 5-membered aromatic ring systems, however, a lone pair of electrons from a ring atom has to be taken into account as part of the aromatic sextet; an example of this type is *thiophen*,

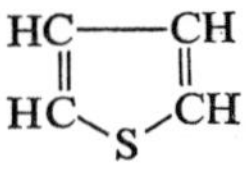

$$
\begin{array}{c}
\text{HC}\!\!-\!\!\text{CH} \\
\| \quad \| \\
\text{HC} \diagdown_{\text{S}} \diagup \text{CH}
\end{array}
$$

Physically, thiophen is very like benzene, and is normally present in coal-tar benzene unless special steps are taken to remove it by chemical means. Other similar aromatic systems are shown below:

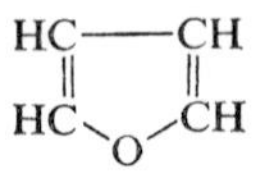

$$
\begin{array}{c}
\text{HC}\!\!-\!\!\text{CH} \\
\| \quad \| \\
\text{HC} \diagdown_{\text{O}} \diagup \text{CH}
\end{array}
\qquad
\begin{array}{c}
\text{HC}\!\!-\!\!\text{CH} \\
\| \quad \| \\
\text{HC} \diagdown_{\text{N}} \diagup \text{CH} \\
\text{H}
\end{array}
$$

furan 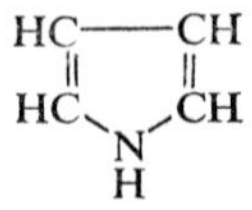   pyrrole

(It is striking confirmation of the incorporation of the lone pair in the bonding of the aromatic ring that pyrrole is practically non-basic, unlike secondary amines—see chapter 13—with the —NH— group not in an aromatic ring. To form the pyrrolium ion, the lone pair would have to be withdrawn from the bonding of the ring.)

One other striking case can be mentioned. The immediate neighbours of carbon (element no. 6) in the Periodic Table are boron (no. 5) and nitrogen (no. 7). The molecule $B_3N_3H_6$ is therefore isoelectronic with the benzene molecule; that is, they each have the same total number of electrons distributed over the same number of atoms. This compound (borazole) is known, and is remarkably like benzene; it has, in fact, been called 'inorganic benzene'. It can be allotted a Kekulé-type formula:

$$
\begin{array}{c}
\text{H} \\
|\\
\text{H}-\text{N}\diagup\overset{\text{B}}{\diagdown}\text{N}-\text{H} \\
|\quad\downarrow| \\
\text{H}\diagup\overset{\text{B}}{\diagdown}\text{N}\diagdown\overset{\text{B}}{\diagup}\text{H} \\
|\\
\text{H}
\end{array}
$$

but there must be extensive delocalization of the aromatic sextet of electrons. (It is of course possible to redraw the above formula with the dative bonds from the nitrogen atoms to the boron atoms on the other side of them.) The reader curious to know more about this remarkable substance should consult an advanced text-book of inorganic chemistry.

In addition to single-ring aromatic systems such as the above, many *fused ring* systems are known in which two or more aromatic rings share pairs of common atoms. Some of the best known are shown below:

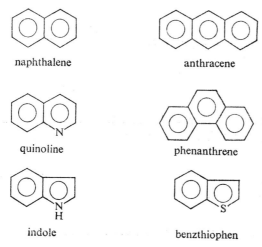

naphthalene   anthracene

quinoline   phenanthrene

indole   benzthiophen

8

The benzene ring as a functional group

Addition reactions of benzene

(1) Hydrogenation

Benzene may be catalytically hydrogenated to *cyclo*hexane by passing benzene vapour and hydrogen over, e.g. a nickel catalyst

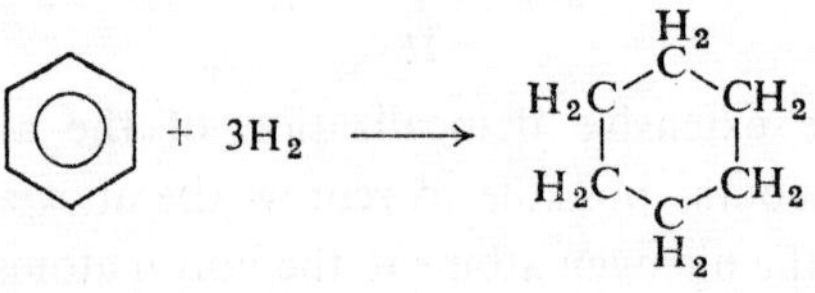

$$\bigcirc + 3H_2 \longrightarrow$$

cyclohexane

(2) Addition of halogens

Chlorine and bromine vapour add to benzene vapour in sunlight.

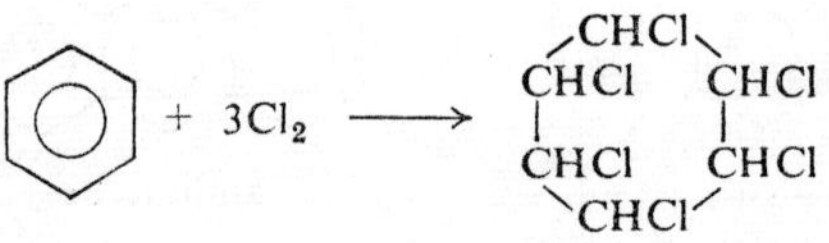

$$\bigcirc + 3Cl_2 \longrightarrow$$

'benzene hexachloride'

The closed ring of carbon atoms fixes the relative configurations of any pair of hydrogen and chlorine atoms, thus

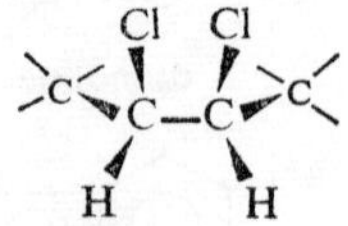

and

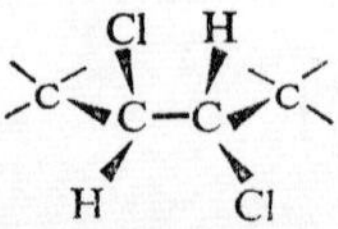

represent isomeric

configurations of that part of the molecule (see chapter 2).

Benzene hexachloride therefore exists in a number of isomeric forms (one of which is the insecticide 'Gammexane').

Substitution often accompanies or succeeds the addition reaction.

(3) Ozone addition

Benzene adds ozone to form an unstable triozonide, $C_6H_6(O_3)_3$, which on hydrolysis yields glyoxal $\begin{matrix} H-C=O \\ | \\ H-C=O \end{matrix}$ and its oxidation products such as oxalic acid.

These three addition reactions indicate the unsaturated nature of benzene. The point has been discussed in detail in chapter 7.

Substitution reactions of benzene

(1) Nitration

Benzene reacts with a mixture of concentrated nitric and sulphuric acids ('nitrating mixture') at temperatures below 50° C to yield mononitrobenzene; the overall stoichiometric equation is:

$$C_6H_6 + HNO_3 \rightarrow C_6H_5NO_2 + H_2O$$

The reaction is not appreciably reversible; nitrobenzene is not hydrolysed to benzene and nitric acid by boiling with water or aqueous acid; the function of the sulphuric acid is *not* therefore to displace the equilibrium of a reversible change by removing water. Furthermore, 100% nitric acid in the absence of sulphuric acid is a poor nitrating agent, so that the main function of the sulphuric acid is not to concentrate the nitric acid by combining with water, though it undoubtedly does this. (Ordinary 'concentrated' nitric acid is about $\frac{2}{3}HNO_3$, $\frac{1}{3}H_2O$ by weight.) It is well-established that nitric acid behaves as a base towards sulphuric acid in solution in the latter; first as a simple Lowry–Bronsted proton acceptor:

$$HONO_2 + H_2SO_4 \rightarrow [(HO)_2NO]^{\oplus} + HSO_4^{\ominus}$$

but then losing water:

$$[(HO)_2NO]^{\oplus} \rightarrow NO_2^{\oplus} + H_2O$$

which itself acts as a base:

$$H_2O + H_2SO_4 \quad \rightarrow \quad H_3O^{\oplus} + HSO_4^{\ominus}$$

i.e. $\qquad HNO_3 + 2H_2SO_4 \quad \rightarrow \quad NO_2^{\oplus} + H_3O^{\oplus} + 2HSO_4^{\ominus}$

This view is confirmed by the fact that the depression of the freezing point of sulphuric acid by dissolved nitric acid is nearly four times that produced by the same molar concentration of a solute such as sulphuryl chloride, which dissolves unchanged.

Salts of this *nitronium ion* such as the perchlorate $NO_2^{\oplus}ClO_4^{\ominus}$ have been isolated, and studies of reaction rates leave no doubt that this is the active species in 'nitrating mixture'. The reaction may be regarded as proceeding thus

followed by the loss of a proton to a basic species, presumably $HSO_4^{\ominus}$:

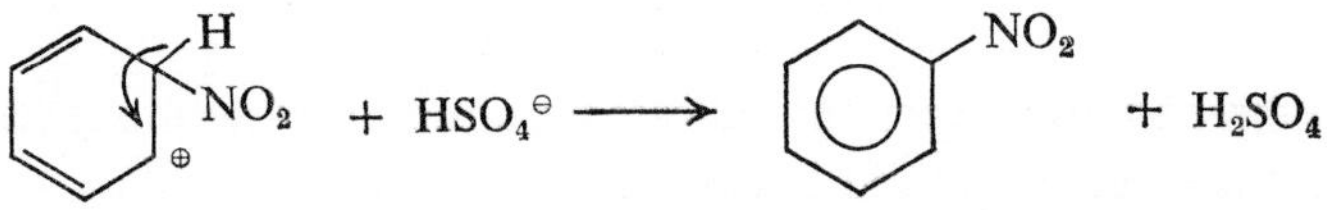

with a restoration of the aromatic ring. In this and the following discussions of aromatic substitution, the formation of intermediates of this type is probably a more complex process than this, but further discussion is beyond the scope of this book. It should also be borne in mind that the positive charge would be distributed over the ring:

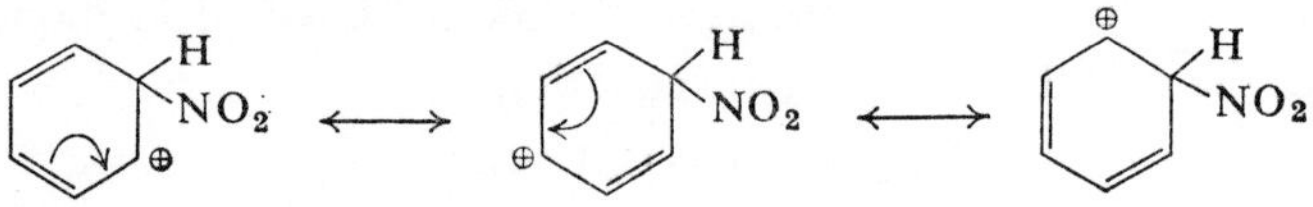

This applies to all such intermediates.

(2) Halogenation

Benzene reacts with chlorine and bromine in the presence of various catalysts, collectively known as halogen carriers, yielding first the mono-halogenobenzene, e.g.

$$C_6H_6 + Cl_2 \rightarrow C_6H_5Cl + HCl$$

Further substitution will occur, though much more slowly, yielding ultimately hexachlorobenzene. With bromine, the introduction of three bromine atoms per molecule is about the practical limit of the reaction.

Possible catalysts include iron filings, aluminium powder, anhydrous ferric chloride or aluminium chloride, and pyridine; a seemingly heterogeneous collection.

A plausible mechanism suggests that the catalysts function by polarizing the halogen molecule, either partially or completely, and that the electron-deficient $Cl^{\oplus}$ (or the equivalent positive atom of a partially polarized molecule) attacks the benzene ring analogously to the nitronium ion:

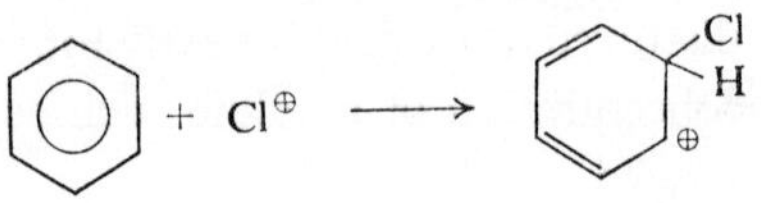

Thus, for example, with aluminium chloride, which in its monomeric form is a powerful electron acceptor:

$$Cl—Cl+AlCl_3 \rightarrow Cl^{\oplus}[AlCl_4]^{\ominus} \quad (\text{or } \overset{\delta+}{Cl} \rightarrow —Cl \rightarrow \overset{\delta-}{AlCl_3})$$

The elimination of $H^{\oplus}$ by combination with a base, e.g.

$$H^{\oplus}+AlCl_4^{\ominus} \rightarrow HCl+AlCl_3$$

completes the reaction.

The metal catalysts presumably function by preliminary reaction with the halogen to form the metal halide.

(3) The Friedel–Crafts reactions

In its simplest form, this involves the reaction of the benzene ring with an alkyl or an acyl halide in the presence of a catalyst, typically aluminium chloride. With an alkyl halide, a higher homologue of benzene is formed; with an acyl halide the product is a ketone. For example:

(a) $\quad C_6H_6+C_2H_5Br \rightarrow C_6H_5.C_2H_5+HBr$
ethylbenzene

(b) $\quad C_6H_6+CH_3COCl \rightarrow C_6H_5COCH_3+HCl$
acetophenone

A plausible mechanism is, for example, as follows:

$$CH_3COCl + AlCl_3 \longrightarrow CH_3\overset{\oplus}{CO} + AlCl_4^{\ominus}$$

On this basis, the reactive species is an electron-deficient acyl or alkyl ion, or the positive acyl or alkyl group of a partially polarized molecule.

There are practical differences between reactions of type (a) and (b) above. With alkyl halides, only a small quantity of aluminium chloride is needed to bring about reaction; moreover, since the reaction product, the alkyl benzene, is more reactive than benzene itself (see p. 93), further substitution is bound to occur. (Ultimately with a methyl halide, hexamethyl benzene can be obtained.) With acyl halides, the ketone forms an addition compound with the aluminium chloride, rendering it inactive as a catalyst; a little over a mole of catalyst must therefore be used per mole of acyl halide, and the addition product must be decomposed with cold aqueous acid to liberate the ketone. Acyl groups deactivate the benzene ring (p. 94), so little or no further substitution occurs.

A further limitation on the reaction is the fact that with C_3 and larger alkyl groups, isomerization is liable to occur with some catalysts, including aluminium chloride itself; thus *n*-butyl halides in such cases yield mainly secondary butyl benzene.

Many variants of the Friedel–Crafts reactions are known, and it is beyond the scope of this book to list them. Two that are likely to be met with frequently are the use of tertiary alcohols in place of halides (thus, tertiary butyl alcohol can effectively be used to make tertiary butyl benzene) and the use of anhydrides in the place of acyl halides for the preparation of ketones (thus, acetic anhydride can replace acetyl chloride in the preparation of acetophenone).

It will be seen that in each of the above three reactions, it is supposed that reaction occurs between the 'aromatic' electrons of the benzene ring and an electrophilic reactive intermediate ($NO_2^{\oplus}$, $Cl^{\oplus}$, $CH_3\overset{\oplus}{C}O$ or the corresponding positive part of a polarized molecule) and that the function of the catalyst or added reagents is to convert the initially ineffective molecule (HNO_3, Cl_2, CH_3COCl) into the reactive species.

(4) Sulphonation

The benzene ring reacts with concentrated sulphuric acid yielding sulphonic acids; for example:

$$C_6H_6 + HOSO_2OH \rightleftharpoons C_6H_5SO_2OH + H_2O$$
benzenesulphonic acid

With benzene and 98% H_2SO_4, refluxing for about twenty hours is required, but benzene reacts quite rapidly in the cold with oleum.

The reaction is certainly of the same type as the other three, and the reactive species is probably the SO_3 molecule (hence the much greater effectiveness of oleum rather than the 98% acid).

Unlike the nitronium ion, or acylium cations mentioned above, the sulphur trioxide molecule carries no cationic charge. Nevertheless the sulphur atom has a considerable partial positive charge owing to the polarity of the sulphur–oxygen bonds. The sulphur atom is hence the site of the electrophilic reactivity of sulphur trioxide, and this accounts for the formation of a carbon–sulphur bond when it attacks the aromatic ring.

Sulphonation is appreciably reversible. Some practical aspects of sulphonation are dealt with in chapter 17.

These four reactions are characteristic not only of benzene, but of many of its homologues and their derivatives. Unless they contain some group which is sensitive to the attack of nitric acid or sulphuric acid, practically all aromatic compounds can be nitrated and sulphonated, and many can be halogenated.

Friedel–Crafts reactions cannot be carried out, on, for example, nitrobenzene, which is inert to them (and indeed can be used as a solvent in which to perform the reactions). Some compounds (such as phenol and aniline) act as Lewis bases and form inert addition compounds with the aluminium chloride acting as a Lewis acid and cannot therefore undergo the ordinary Friedel–Crafts reaction; phenol ethers, however, often react normally.

These reactions represent some of the most typical features of the behaviour of the aromatic nucleus. It would be untrue to suppose that reactions to some extent analogous do not occur in aliphatic chemistry. The paraffins can be nitrated (methane, for example, by heating to 300° with nitric acid vapour) and the higher ones can be sulphonated by heating with oleum. What is characteristic of the aromatic series is the comparatively mild conditions of the reactions, the way they respond to the presence of substituents in the ring (see the next section), and the characteristic conditions, catalyst types and probable mechanisms. A striking illustration of this is afforded by the two types of halogenation undergone by toluene; photochemical halogenation in the vapour phase attacks the alkyl side-chain; halogen-carrier catalysis brings about attack on the nucleus;

$$C_6H_5CH_3 + Cl_2 \xrightarrow[\text{Sunlight or u.v.}]{\text{boiling}} C_6H_5CH_2Cl + HCl$$
$$\text{benzyl chloride}$$

$$C_6H_5CH_3 + Cl_2 \xrightarrow[\text{carrier}]{\text{halogen}} CH_3C_6H_4Cl + HCl$$
$$\text{(}o\text{- and }p\text{-chlorotoluenes)}$$

(See chapter 7.)

Aromatic substitution in benzene derivatives

The presence of a substituent attached to the benzene ring in place of hydrogen affects the course of further substitution in two important ways.

First, the rate of reaction may be greater or less than the rate for benzene itself under the same conditions.

Monosubstituted benzene derivatives containing any one of the following functional groups undergo substitution (e.g. nitration) more rapidly than benzene itself:

(*a*) —CH₃ and other alkyl groups, —OH, —OCH₃, —NH₂

On the other hand, mono-substituted benzene derivatives containing

93

any one of the following functional groups undergo substitution more slowly than benzene:

(*b*) —NO_2, —SO_3H, —CO_2H, —CN, —CHO, —CO.R, —$\overset{\oplus}{N}Me_3$, —Cl, —Br, —I

These facts can be established by detailed studies of reaction rates, or, more crudely, by allowing an equimolecular mixture of two compounds to compete for a small quantity of reagent and comparing the quantities which are obtained of the substitution products of each.

The second effect relates to the proportions of the three possible disubstituted derivatives (*o*-, *m*- and *p*-) obtained from a given mono-substituted benzene. If the rates of reaction at each of the five available sites were identical, then the product would contain 40% of the *o*-, 40% of the *m*- and 20% of the *p*-isomer (since there are two ortho- and two meta-sites, but only one para-).

In fact, the actual distribution of isomers in the product rarely even approximates to this. Thus, for example, the nitration of nitrobenzene yields a product containing over 90% of *m*-dinitrobenzene, and only small amounts of the *o*- and *p*-isomers:

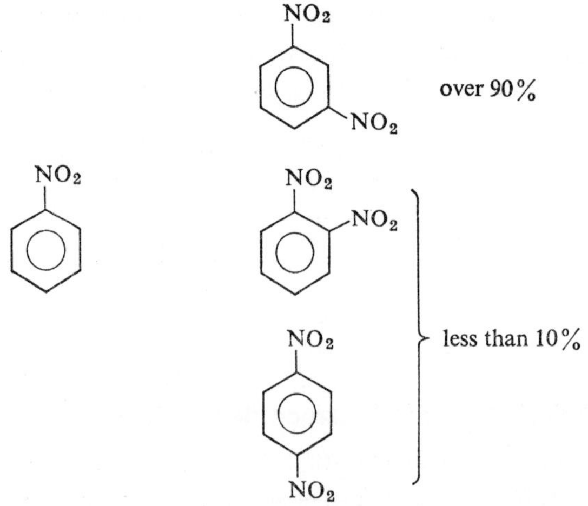

On the other hand, nitration of toluene yields a product with over 90% *o*- and *p*-nitrotoluene, and only 4% *m*-nitrotoluene (see formulae on p. 95).

In the case of nitrobenzene, therefore, the rate of nitration in the meta-positions must be much greater than the rate in the ortho- and para-positions, while in the nitration of toluene the reverse is true.

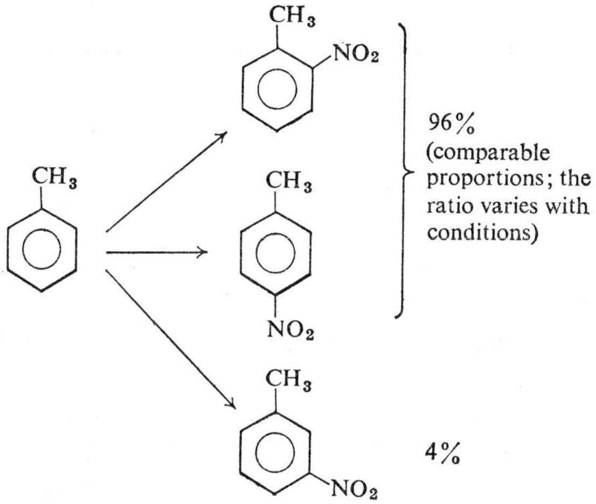

The following groups in a mono-substituted benzene cause the attacking reagent to react more rapidly at the ortho- and para-sites than at the meta-:

(c) —CH$_3$ (etc.), —OH, —OCH$_3$, —NH$_2$, —Cl, —Br, —I

The following groups in a mono-substituted benzene cause the attacking reagent to react more rapidly at the meta- sites than at the ortho- and para-sites:

(d) —NO$_2$, —SO$_3$H, —CO$_2$H, —CN, —CHO, —CO.R —$\overset{\oplus}{\text{N}}Me_3$

It will at once be noticed that the lists corresponds closely to those which speed up and slow down reaction respectively, with the important exception of the halide groups, which alone among the common groups favouring ortho- and para- substitution also slow down the substitution reactions.

The effect of a substituent group in causing further substitution in the benzene ring to proceed more rapidly at some sites than at others has been called its 'directing effect'. Of the lists of groups above, therefore, (c) is a list of so-called *ortho–para-directing* groups, and (d) a list of *meta-directing* groups.

Theory of aromatic substitution in benzene derivatives

(a) The speeding up or slowing down of further substitution by a functional group already attached to the benzene ring depends on the effect of this group on the electron density of the ring.

If the dipole moments (see p. 16) of the mono-substituted benzenes are measured, it is found that in those compounds which undergo substitution more slowly than benzene, the substituent group already present is at the negative end of the dipole and the ring at the positive end, while in those which react more rapidly, the polarity is the reverse of this. For example:

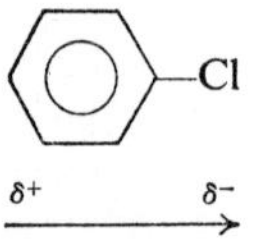

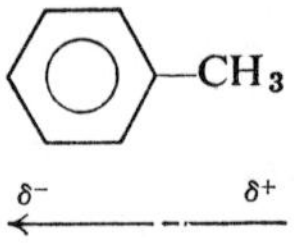

$$\delta+ \longrightarrow \delta-$$

$$\delta- \longleftarrow ---- \delta+$$

0·033   24

relative rate of nitration (benzene = 1)

These results mean that the substituent causes a displacement of electrons in the direction of the arrow of the dipole symbol. Thus in chlorobenzene, the electron density of the ring is less than in benzene, while in toluene it is greater. Since the reagents which characteristically attack the benzene ring are electrophilic, we should expect more rapid reaction where the electron density in the ring is greater, slower reaction where it is less. This accords with the facts as set out above.

Two major effects are responsible for the drift of electrons to or from the benzene ring. The well-established electron-repelling effect of alkyl groups (see p. 48) will increase the electron density of the ring:

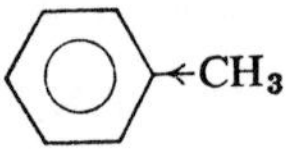

An electronegative halogen atom attached to the ring will induce a drift of electrons away from it:

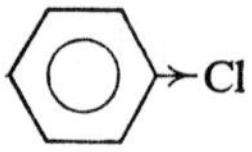

A strongly dipolar group with its positive end attached to the ring, such as —NO_2, will have the same effect:

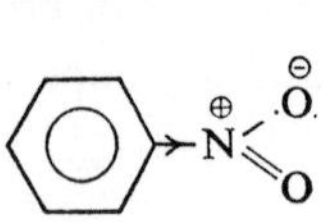

However, inspection of list (*a*) above shows that several important groups which speed up reaction have in fact an electronegative atom (nitrogen or oxygen) attached to the ring, which would be expected to withdraw electrons from the ring. A second effect must therefore operate to account for the observed dipole moments, which are *opposite* to those of chloro- and nitro-benzene. These groups have lone pairs of electrons on the oxygen and nitrogen atoms, and these electrons are delocalized in benzene derivatives according to the following scheme:

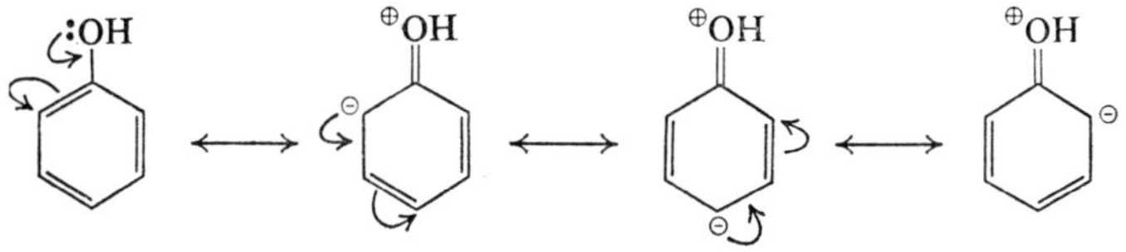

This *increases* the electron density of the ring. The evidence of the dipole moments shows that this effect predominates over the first-mentioned for —OH, —OCH$_3$ and —NH$_2$; the overall effect of these groups is therefore to increase the electron density in the ring and to speed up electrophilic substitution.

In the halogenobenzenes, however, the first ('induced drift') effect predominates over the delocalization effect, as shown by the direction of the dipole moment of the molecule. The overall effect of a halide group is therefore to *reduce* electron density in the ring and to slow down electrophilic substitution.

Substituents with an electronegative atom attached by a multiple bond to the atom joined to the ring, such as —C$\begin{smallmatrix} H \\ \\ O \end{smallmatrix}$, can show a converse delocalization effect, thus:

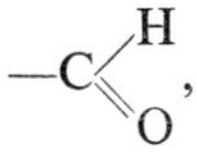

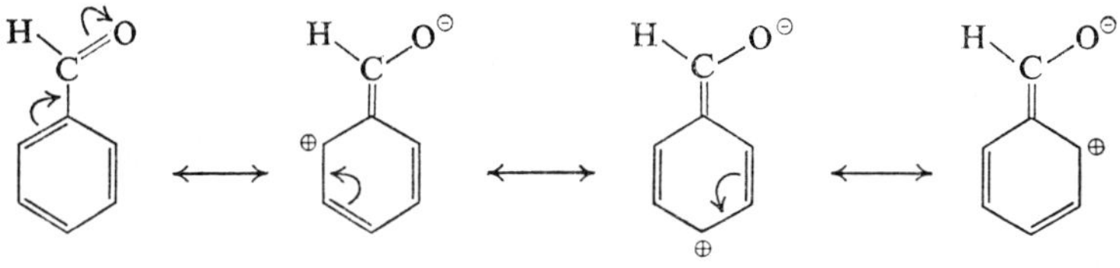

This reduces the electron density of the ring, reinforcing the 'induced drift' effect. The overall effect is a lower electron density in the ring, and slowing up of substitution.

(*b*) To account for the different rates of attack at different sites in nitrobenzene we must consider the factors which favour or disfavour the formation of reaction intermediates of the type shown above for the nitration of benzene. In the nitration of benzene itself, it is a matter of indifference which carbon atom is attacked by the nitronium ion, but in the nitration of nitrobenzene this is not so. The nitro-group has the structure:

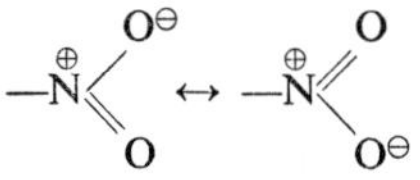

and the nitrogen atom carries a positive charge. When a bond is formed between a ring carbon atom of nitrobenzene and an attacking nitronium ion, the intermediate carries another positive charge which is delocalized over the sites ortho and para to the *entering* NO_2 group. This is shown in the following diagrams, which represent the intermediates formed when the nitronium ion attacks the nitrobenzene molecule at the positions ortho-, meta- and para- respectively to the original nitro-group.

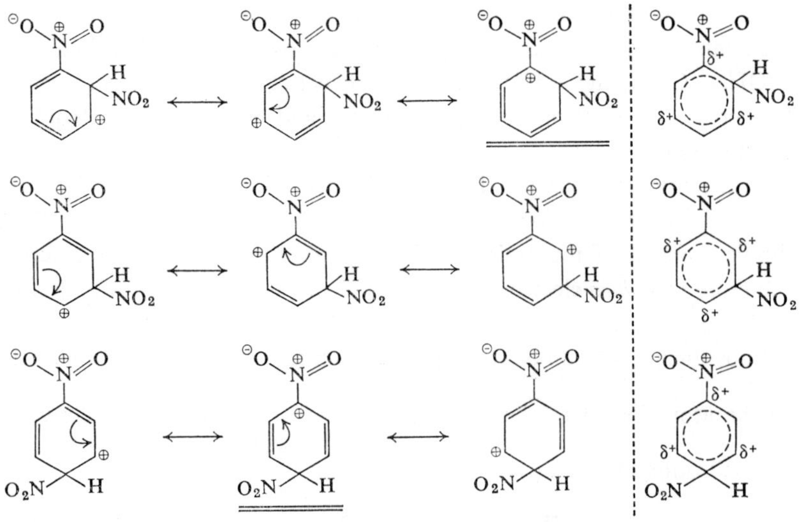

It can be seen by inspecting the bond-diagrams underlined that substitution ortho or para- to the nitro-group produces an intermediate with a partial positive charge *on the ring carbon atom attached to the positive nitrogen*. In the intermediate which results from meta attack by the nitronium ion, however, this carbon atom carries no positive charge; the nearest carbon atoms so charged are those *next* to the one bearing the positive nitrogen. On purely electrostatic grounds, therefore, the ortho and para intermediates are at a higher energy than the meta-, since their formation requires the establishment of two adjacent positively charged atoms, while in the meta intermediate the positively charged ring atoms are as far remote as possible from the positive nitrogen. On account of the greater difficulty of forming the ortho- and para-intermediates, nitrobenzene would therefore be expected to undergo further nitration more slowly at the ortho- and para-sites than at the meta-site. This agrees with the observed result.

In toluene, on the other hand, the carbon atom of the methyl group carries a partial *negative* charge:

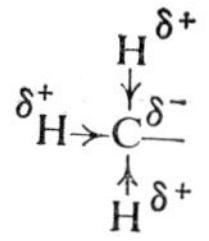

$$\overset{\delta+}{H}\!\!\!\uparrow$$
$$\overset{\delta+}{H}\!\!\rightarrow\!\overset{|}{\underset{|}{C}}\!\overset{\delta-}{\underline{\quad}}$$
$$\underset{H}{\uparrow}\,\delta+$$

hydrogen being slightly electropositive relative to carbon. The intermediates formed in nitration can be shown in the same way as above to be:

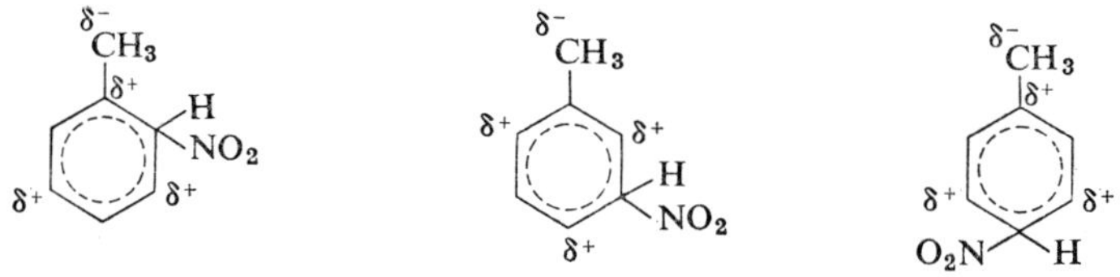

and, of these, the ortho- and para-forms, with *opposite* charges in closer proximity, are at a lower energy and will be more readily formed than the higher-energy meta-form. Toluene therefore would be expected to undergo nitration more rapidly at the ortho- and para-sites; again, this agrees with experiment.

A further effect lowers the energy level of the ortho- and para-intermediates in some cases. The oxygen atom of the methoxyl group $-OCH_3$, for example, carries lone pairs of electrons, which can participate in the delocalization of the positive charge in the ortho- and para-reaction intermediates, but not in the meta-intermediate, as the following bond-diagrams show.

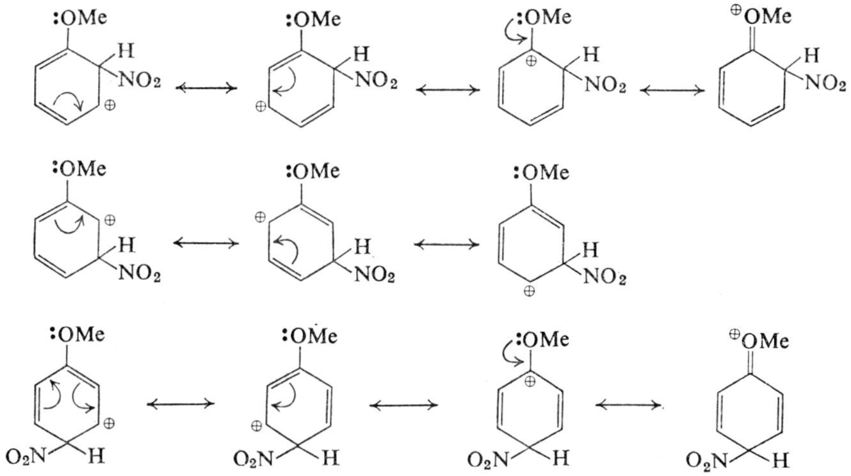

The greater delocalization of the positive charge (over four sites as against three) makes the energy level of the ortho- and para-intermediates lower than that of the meta-. Anisole (methoxybenzene) would therefore be expect to undergo nitration more rapidly at the ortho- and para-sites than at the meta.

Although the above discussion has been in terms of nitration, it is applicable to the attack of any of the usual electrophilic reagents which carry out aromatic substitution.

In all the meta-directing groups listed above (p. 95), the atom attached to the ring is positively charged; either by being the site of an ionic charge, as with $-\overset{\oplus}{N}Me_3$, or by being linked by a co-ionic bond (dative covalency), as with $-\overset{\oplus}{N}\overset{\diagup O}{\diagdown O^{\ominus}}$ or by being attached to other more electronegative atoms, usually by highly polarized multiple bonds, as with $-C\overset{\diagup H}{\diagdown O}$ and $-C\equiv N$.

The above theory therefore accounts for their meta-directing effect.

All the ortho–para-directing groups listed above (p. 95), with the exception of the alkyl groups which have been dealt with separately, have lone pairs on the atoms attached to the ring. The above theory therefore accounts for their ortho–para-directing effect.

An interesting set of cases is set out below. The progressive replacement of electropositive hydrogen by electronegative chlorine changes the sign of the partial charge on the carbon atom of the substituent, and brings about a corresponding change in the directing effect.

CH_3 | CH_2Cl | $CHCl_2$ | CCl_3

% meta isomer on nitration

| 4 | 12 | 34 | 64 |

It is often stressed that directing effects are due entirely to the group already present and are independent of the entering group; that, for example, nitrobenzene yields predominantly the meta-isomer whether on nitration or halogenation, while chlorobenzene whether on nitration or halogenation yields predominantly ortho- and para-isomers. This is because the reagents which commonly attack the benzene ring are all electrophiles. Certain exceptional reactions are known (though not among the familiar reactions of benzene and its simple derivatives) in which nucleophiles attack the aromatic ring; in such cases, directing effects are reversed, and, for example, groups which are normally meta-directing become ortho–para-directing.

Two words of warning: first, in ortho–para-direction, the proportions of the two isomers formed vary widely according both to the directing group and the reaction conditions, some reactions yielding very little ortho-isomer; and second, in some reactions (notably sulphonation and Friedel–Crafts acylation) it is sometimes possible to manipulate conditions to get substantial yields of the 'wrong' isomer. These points need not concern the elementary student, but he should keep an open mind for meeting them later.

Aromatic substitution reactions in phenols and amines

—OH in phenols (and the conjugate base —$O^\ominus$) and —NH_2 in amines are both markedly ortho–para-directing and activating. Phenol and aniline and their homologues therefore undergo certain substitution reactions under much milder conditions than used with benzene and its homologues, and certain others which cannot be carried out at all with the parent hydrocarbon. Some of these are listed below.

(1) Nitration

Phenol is quite rapidly nitrated at room temperature by 20% aqueous nitric acid, yielding a mixture of o- and p-nitrophenols. Clearly the concentration of nitronium ion in this reagent must be quite negligible, and another mechanism (believed to involve nitrous acid) must operate.

Addition of concentrated nitric acid to a solution of phenol in concentrated sulphuric acid yields 2,4,6-trinitrophenol by substitution in all available ortho- and para-positions.

There are no convenient conditions for the direct nitration of aniline. Nitric acid (or nitrating mixture) will convert aniline to the conjugate acid; in the presence of a considerable excess of concentrated sulphuric acid, aniline is slowly nitrated in the meta-position (see above, p. 100) if considerable care is used. Concentrated nitric acid in the absence of sulphuric acid oxidizes aniline and the mixture ultimately inflames.

The most convenient route to o- and p-nitroaniline is first to 'protect' the —NH_2 group by acetylation (see p. 158); acetanilide is nitrated normally by nitrating agents, and the acetyl group can then be removed from the product by hydrolysis with aqueous strong acid.

(and o-isomer)

(2) Halogenation

Both phenol and aniline react very rapidly with bromine water, yielding 2,4,6-tribromophenol and 2,4,6-tribromoaniline respectively.

The reactions are practically quantitative and can be used as the basis of methods of estimating phenol and aniline in solution.

(3) Sulphonation

Both phenol and aniline are sulphonated by heating with concentrated sulphuric acid for a short time, yielding respectively a mixture of o- and p-phenolsulphonic acids and p-aminobenzenesulphonic acid (sulphanilic acid).

In comparison with the extremely mild conditions for nitration of phenol and the very rapid bromination of phenol and aniline, the increase in the rate of sulphonation over that of benzene seems comparatively insignificant, but in concentrated sulphuric acid, both aniline and phenol will be very largely converted to the unreactive positively charged conjugate acids

$C_6H_5\overset{\oplus}{O}H_2$ and $C_6H_5\overset{\oplus}{N}H_3$. The concentration of the reactive free phenol and aniline will therefore be extremely small.

(4) Special reactions of phenol or the phenate ion:

(i) *The Kolbé reaction.* If dry sodium phenate is heated with carbon dioxide under pressure, sodium salicylate and some sodium *p*-hydroxy-benzoate are formed.

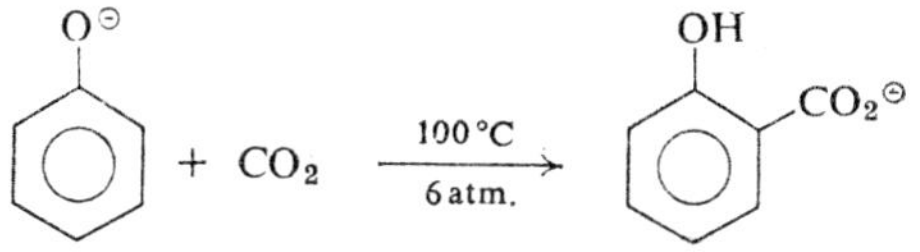

(and *p*-isomer)

Salicylic acid is made commercially by this reaction.

(ii) *The Reimer–Tiemann reaction.* If phenol is refluxed in sodium hydroxide solution with chloroform, the conjugate base of salicylaldehyde (together with some *p*-hydroxybenzaldehyde) is formed. Addition of acid liberates the free aldehydes.

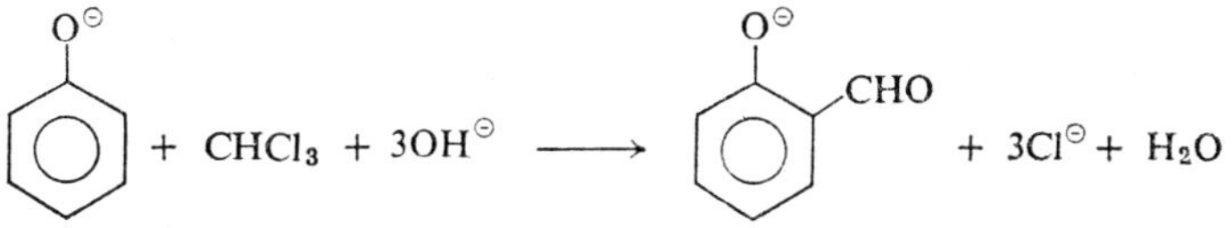

(and *p*-isomer)

Presumably the substitution reaction leads to

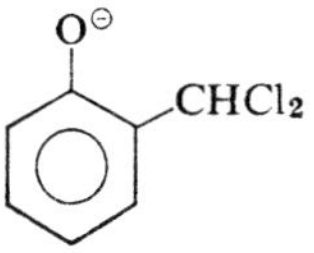

which yields the aldehyde in the usual way (compare p. 194).

If carbon tetrachloride is used in place of chloroform, the product is sodium salicylate.

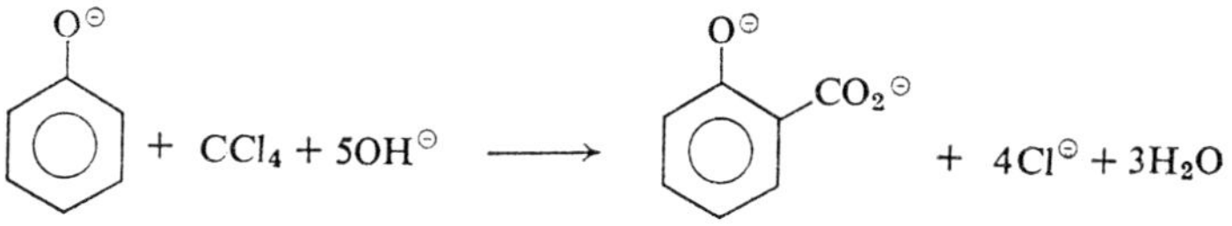

Again, 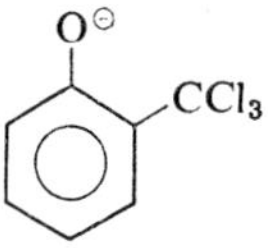 is presumably the intermediate.

(iii) *Phthalein formation.* A number of phenols, including phenol itself, react with phthalic anhydride on warming in the presence of a little concentrated sulphuric acid to yield products called phthaleins. For example:

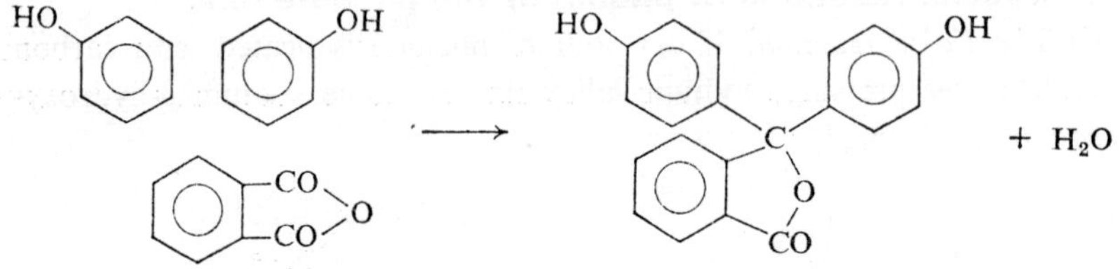

phenolphthalein.

(Succinic anhydride $\begin{array}{c} CH_2CO \\ | \quad \quad \rangle O \\ CH_2CO \end{array}$ yields similar products).

Resorcinol (*m*-dihydroxybenzene) yields fluorescein:

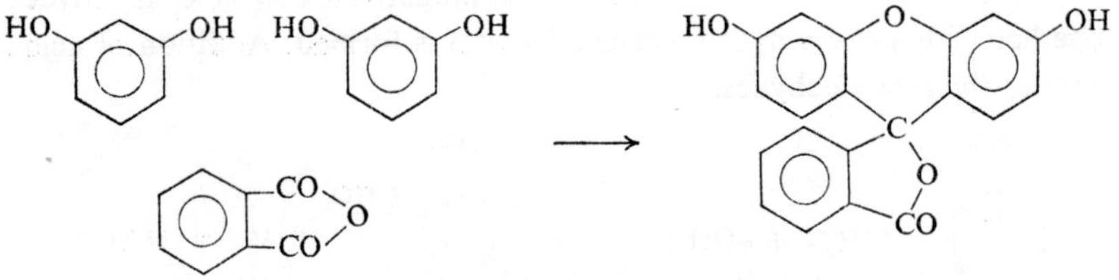

These substances (like phenols themselves) are weak acids. They undergo characteristic colour changes with alkali on forming their conjugate bases; hence the use of phenolphthalein as an acid-base indicator.

9

The petroleum industry

Petroleum, or crude oil, a dark viscous fluid, is a complex mixture of substances (over 90% and sometimes over 99% hydrocarbons by weight) found trapped in certain porous geological strata. It is believed probably to originate from the organic parts of deposits of dead marine organisms, subjected geologically to heat and pressure, though other theories of its origin have been advanced. Natural gas is normally associated with petroleum in oil-bearing strata, and may be confined above it under pressure by the overlying impervious rock. In such cases, when a drilling strikes the oil, it may 'gush' out; normally it has to be pumped to the surface. The main oil fields of the world are in the U.S.A., Venezuela and the neighbouring islands, the Middle East, the Caspian region of the U.S.S.R., and Indonesia.

Crude oils differ considerably in composition from field to field. They are broadly divided, in the language of petroleum technology, into *paraffinic crudes*, consisting mainly of paraffins, *naphthenic* crudes, containing important quantities of naphthenes; i.e. *cyclo*paraffins (saturated closed-ring hydrocarbons), and *aromatic (or asphaltic) crudes*, containing a significant (though not predominant) proportion of aromatic compounds (up to about 40% in Borneo crudes). Crude oil is distilled in conventional industrial fractionating stills, yielding fractions or cuts on the following broad pattern:

Product	C number	B.p. range (° C)
Gas	C_1—C_4(C_5)	<20
Petroleum ether	C_5—C_6(C_7)	20–80
Petrol	(C_5)C_6—C_8(C_9, C_{10})	40–180
Paraffin oils	C_9—C_{18}	170–300
Diesel oils	C_{12}—C_{20}	200–340
Heavy fuel oils	>C_{13}	>300
Lubricating oils and waxes	>C_{19}	>300

(The figures are only approximate).

The still residue may be usable as heavy fuel oil, or may be asphalt, according to the character of the crude oil. Lubricating oils are more highly branched and cyclized than waxes of the same molecular weight; they can be separated by solvent extraction with low-boiling petroleum ether, in which the waxes are much the less soluble.

The major economic importance of petroleum is as a source of motor fuel, i.e. of petrol. Straight distillation of petroleum is inadequate to supply present needs for two reasons. First, the proportion of petroleum in the C_6 to C_8 range is too small, and that in the higher molecular weight ranges too high. Secondly, much so-called 'straight-run distillate' petrol performs poorly in modern spark-ignition engines, easily causing 'knocking' or 'pinking'. Many of the processes of petroleum refining are directed to correcting these two drawbacks.

'Knocking' results from the premature explosion of part of the air–fuel mixture in the cylinder of a spark-ignition engine. The flame initiated by the spark should advance rapidly but smoothly through the mixture, producing a steady thrust on the piston; instead, when knocking occurs, the unburnt mixture in front of the flame front, by the double effect of compression and radiated heat, suddenly detonates. This is wasteful of power. It is found that unbranched hydrocarbons such as *n*-heptane are particularly likely to cause knocking, especially in high compression engines, while highly branched alkanes, such as 2,2,4-trimethylpentane. ('iso-octane')

$$
\underset{\underset{\displaystyle CH_3}{|}}{\overset{\overset{\displaystyle CH_3}{|}}{CH_3\!-\!C}}\!-\!CH_2\!-\!\overset{\overset{\displaystyle CH_3}{|}}{CH}\!-\!CH_3
$$

have a much lower tendency to knock. (The prefix 'iso'- is used loosely here, and not according to the meaning given on p. 9.)

The anti-knock rating of a fuel is expressed by an octane number, which gives the percentage of iso-octane (octane number 100), in a mixture with heptane (octane number 0) which gives the same performance as the fuel in a test engine under standard conditions. (An octane number above 100 implies that heptane must be added to the fuel to reduce its performance to that of iso-octane; a negative octane number implies that iso-octane must be added to bring its performance up to that of heptane.)

The manufacture of anti-knock fuels involves therefore the production of branched in preference to unbranched-chain alkanes. Alkenes have better anti-knock properties than unbranched alkanes, especially if the double bond is *not* in the terminal or α-position; so have benzene and its derivatives.

Lower molecular weight hydrocarbons can be made from higher ones by '*cracking*'. Petroleum fractions of higher chain length are heated, with or without catalysts; the carbon chains are disrupted, and a range of lower molecular weight hydrocarbons is obtained. *Thermal* cracking—that is, by heat alone—occurs at about 500 to 600° C. The products show little change in the type of carbon skeleton—straight-chain 'feed stocks' produce straight-chain cracked products. The products contain a high proportion of olefins, especially in the lower C numbers, and much ethylene is formed. The olefins are mainly α-type; that is, the double bond is at the end of the chain. Thermal cracking increases the yield of hydrocarbons in the petrol range, but the products, mainly paraffins and α-olefins with little branching have only moderate 'anti-knock' characteristics. Catalytic cracking ('cat-cracking', in oil refinery jargon) is a later development. This operates at a rather lower temperature (450–500° C) in the presence of catalysts, such as natural or artifical alumino-silicates. The products are more highly branched, and the olefins have the double bonds in non-terminal positions; both features give better anti-knock properties. The yield of C_4 and higher products is also greater at the expense of the ethylene. The catalyst is often 'fluidized' by being suspended in a rapid vapour stream; this encourages mixing and efficient heat-transfer. ('Fluidization' implies the suspension of a solid of uniform granular size in a rapid gas stream, the mixture behaving in many ways like a liquid.)

Thermal cracking probably proceeds by homolytic fission of the alkane chain to yield two radicals; these may interact with other alkane molecules with transfer of hydrogen to yield smaller alkanes and other radicals, and suitable radicals may disproportionate into smaller radicals and α-olefins. Catalytic cracking may involve heterolytic reactions, as it is known that alkyl cations (so-called carbonium ions, with an electron-deficient carbon atom—e.g. $CH_3\overset{\oplus}{C}HCH_2CH_3$) readily isomerize to branched chains.

Although cracking increases the proportion of petrol to high molecular weight products, it leads in turn to over-production of gaseous hydro-carbons. These must therefore be recombined to give products in the petrol range. The following processes are operated:

(*a*) *Polymerization.* C_3 and C_4 olefins combine over a supported phos-phoric acid catalyst. Thus, for example, two molecules of isobutylene (2-methylpropene) combine to form (among other isomers) the so-called 'iso-octene':

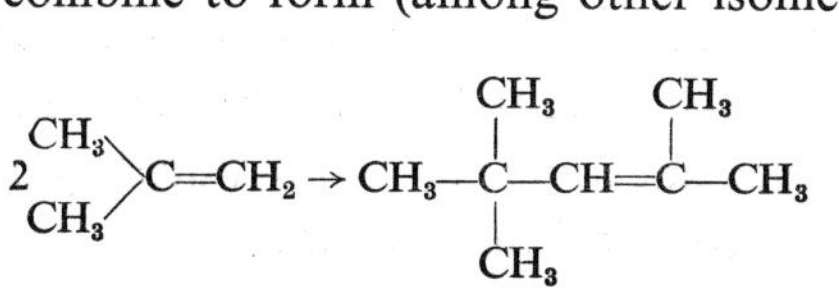

$$2\ \overset{CH_3}{\underset{CH_3}{>}}C=CH_2 \rightarrow CH_3-\underset{\underset{CH_3}{|}}{\overset{\overset{CH_3}{|}}{C}}-CH=\overset{\overset{CH_3}{|}}{C}-CH_3$$

which on hydrogenation yields the compound iso-octane mentioned above.

(*b*) *Alkylation.* A *branched-chain* alkane reacts with an olefin in the presence of fairly concentrated sulphuric acid or anhydrous hydrogen fluoride as catalyst. Thus for example isobutane (2-methylpropane) and isobutene yield isomeric branched octanes, especially iso-octane:

$$CH_3 \diagdown CH-CH_3 + CH_2=C \diagup CH_3 \diagdown CH_3 \rightarrow CH_3-\overset{\overset{\displaystyle CH_3}{|}}{\underset{\underset{\displaystyle CH_3}{|}}{C}}-CH_2-\overset{\overset{\displaystyle CH_3}{|}}{CH}-CH_3$$

(In effect, the tertiary CH of the alkane adds across the double bond of the olefin.)

(Isobutane can be made available in larger quantities by *isomerizing* *n*-butane over anhydrous aluminium chloride or other catalysts.

$$CH_3(CH_2)_2CH_3 \overset{AlCl_3}{\rightleftharpoons} (CH_3)_2CH.CH_3$$

The equilibrium favours the branched-chain isomer.)

Cracking, polymerization and alkylation between them still fail to meet the modern need for high-octane motor and aviation fuels. Much straight-run petrol is therefore *re-formed*. By passing over catalysts such as a mixture of aluminium and molybdenum oxides, straight-chain alkanes isomerize to branched compounds, undergo ring closure and dehydrogenation, both to olefins and (with ring closure) to aromatics, all processes tending to increase the anti-knock rating of the re-formed product.

As well as being a major source of fuel, petroleum is the basis of the 'petrochemicals' industry. References will be found in various chapters of the present book to economically important organic compounds for which the ultimate raw material is, or can be, a hydrocarbon obtained from petroleum.

Hydrocarbon fuels can also be obtained by the catalytic hydrogenation of coal or tar, by the low temperature distillation of coal and by the Fischer–Tropsch hydrocarbon synthesis (p. 46). None of these is genuinely competitive with petroleum in a free world market, though all three were operated intensively in Germany as part of the national self-sufficiency programme in preparation for and during World War II. Where there is abundant methane, the Fischer–Tropsch process can be used to convert this via carbon monoxide and hydrogen to liquid hydrocarbons, either for fuels or for organic chemical manufacture.

10

The halide groups: −Cl, −Br, −I

Structurally, the simplest derivatives of hydrocarbons are obtained when one hydrogen atom is replaced by another univalent atom, namely a halogen atom. Fluorine derivatives differ in many important ways from those of the other halogens, and their chemistry is largely a modern development. The following discussion is confined to chlorine, bromine and iodine compounds. Where a halogen is attached to the carbon atom of a carbonyl group $\diagup$C=O, the reactions are so drastically modified that the groups $-C\diagup\overset{O}{\diagdown}_{Cl}$ etc. are regarded as of a separate functional type (see p. 209).

Nomenclature

Monohalogeno-hydrocarbons are systematically named by adding the prefixes chloro-, bromo-, iodo- to the name of the parent hydrocarbon, together if necessary with a number or Greek letter to indicate the position of the halogen atom.

The older names, treating the compounds as a union of two radicals also persist. For example:

CH_3CH_2Br bromoethane or ethyl bromide

$CH_2CHClCH_3$ 2-chloropropane or isopropyl chloride

o-bromotoluene (rarely o-cresyl bromide)

α-iodotoluene or benzyl iodide

Physical and general properties

Chloromethane, bromomethane and chloroethane are gases at room temperature and atmospheric pressure; their critical temperatures are above ordinary room temperature, and they can be liquified by compression. Methyl chloride is sold in steel cylinders, methyl bromide in sealed glass tubes. Ethyl chloride is sold in ethanolic solution as an anaesthetic, and methyl chloride has been used as a refrigerator-operating fluid; both compounds have been largely replaced for these purposes by fluorinated compounds. The higher homologues are liquids, then solids. The halogeno-benzenes are liquids; higher homologues are liquids or solids. They have low solubilities in water.

All halogeno-compounds are more or less toxic though chloroform, $CHCl_3$, is a safe anaesthetic. Important exceptions include certain highly fluorinated compounds, like fluoroform CHF_3, which seem physiologically quite inert.

Reactions

(1) With nucleophilic reagents

An important group of reactions of the mono-halogen compound comprises those in which the halogen atom is replaced by another group or atom by reaction with a nucleophilic reagent. The effective reagents are mainly negative ions with strongly electron-donor properties, but molecular bases such as ammonia and amines also react. A list of the more familiar reactions of this type follows, with bromoethane as example:

(*a*) With aqueous alkali, halides are hydrolysed to the corresponding hydroxy-compound.

$$C_2H_5Br + OH^\ominus \rightarrow C_2H_5OH + Br^\ominus$$

(*b*) With alcoholic solutions of alkoxides, for example, sodium *n*-propoxide, ethers are formed; for example:

$$C_2H_5Br + CH_3CH_2CH_2O^\ominus \rightarrow C_2H_5OCH_2CH_2CH_3 + Br^\ominus$$
ethyl *n*-propyl ether

This is Williamson's ether synthesis and can be used to obtain symmetrical ethers or (as in the example) 'mixed' ethers, i.e. those with two different groups attached to oxygen.

(*c*) With aqueous-alcoholic solutions of alkali-metal cyanides, organic cyanides (or nitriles) are produced:

$$C_2H_5Br + CN^\ominus \rightarrow C_2H_5CN + Br^\ominus$$
ethyl cyanide
(propionitrile)

(*d*) With alkali-metal nitrites, mixtures of alkyl nitrites and nitro-hydrocarbons are produced. With simple halogeno-paraffins, the main product is the nitrite.

$$C_2H_5Br + NO_2^{\ominus} \rightarrow \begin{cases} C_2H_5ONO + Br^{\ominus} \\ C_2H_5NO_2 \end{cases}$$

(*e*) With alkali-metal iodide solutions, alkyl iodides are produced from chlorides and bromides (Finkelstein reaction).

$$C_2H_5Br + I^{\ominus} \xrightarrow[\text{in acetone}]{} C_2H_5I + Br^{\ominus}$$

(*f*) With ammonia and amines, substituted ammonium salts are produced; for example:

$$C_2H_5Br + NH_3 \rightarrow \underbrace{C_2H_5\overset{\oplus}{N}H_3}_{\text{ethylammonium bromide}} + Br^{\ominus}$$

$$C_2H_5Br + C_2H_5NH_2 \rightarrow (C_2H_5)_2\overset{\oplus}{N}H_2 + Br^{\ominus}$$

In spite of the difference in charge-type of reagent and product, this last reaction is clearly of the same type as the preceding ones. This reaction is discussed in further detail in chapter 13. Other reactions of the same type include the Gabriel amine synthesis (p. 162) and the syntheses involving ethyl acetoacetate and ethyl malonate (p. 199).

The general method for these reactions is to reflux the halide with the other reagent. It is often preferable to use ethanol or aqueous ethanol as solvent rather than water, so that halide and reagent are in the same phase. Where one reagent is highly volatile (e.g. when using methyl chloride or bromide, or with ammonia or a gaseous amine), the reaction may have to be carried out in a sealed tube.

There are considerable differences in reactivity between various halides in these reactions:

(*a*) In general, iodides react faster than bromides, and bromides than chlorides. Simple alkyl chlorides often react sluggishly.

(*b*) *Halides with halogen atom attached to a carbon atom involved in a carbon–carbon multiple bond* (*including the carbon atom of a benzene ring*) *are extremely inert.* Thus chlorobenzene is unaffected by boiling aqueous sodium hydroxide solution at atmospheric pressure. At about 350° C, however, it is hydrolysed by 10% aqueous sodium hydroxide to sodium phenate:

$$C_6H_5Cl + OH^{\ominus} \rightarrow C_6H_5OH + Cl^{\ominus}$$
$$\downarrow OH^{\ominus}$$
$$C_6H_5O^{\ominus} + H_2O$$
$$\text{phenate ion}$$

To keep the reagents liquid at this temperature, a pressure of about 350 atmospheres is required.

Again aqueous ammonia will only react with the chlorobenzene at temperatures around 200° C (pressures of 50 atmospheres) in the presence of cuprous salts:

$$C_6H_5Cl + NH_3 \rightarrow C_6H_5NH_3^{\oplus} + Cl^{\ominus}$$
$$\downarrow NH_3$$
$$C_6H_5NH_2 + NH_4^{\oplus}$$
$$\text{aniline}$$

(Since ammonia is a much stronger base than aniline, free aniline will be formed.)

Bromobenzene forms benzonitrile (phenyl cyanide) with aqueous alkali cyanide at 200° C under pressure, again in the presence of cuprous salts:

$$C_6H_5Br + CN^{\ominus} \rightarrow C_6H_5CN + Br^{\ominus}$$

Bromobenzene and iodobenzene are little if at all more reactive than chlorobenzene. There are no practicable conditions for carrying out the other reactions listed above with aromatic halides of this type.

Similar inertness is shown where the halogen atom is attached directly to an unsaturated carbon atom of an olefin. Thus the monohalogeno-ethylenes (vinyl halides) such as bromoethylene $CH_2{=}CH.Br$ (vinyl bromide), undergo these reactions slowly if at all.

(c) In contrast to (b), halides in which the halogen atom is attached to carbon atom which is then attached to an aromatic ring (e.g. benzyl chloride $C_6H_5CH_2Cl$) or to an unsaturated olefinic carbon atom (e.g. allyl bromide $CH_2{=}CH.CH_2Br$) show enhanced reactivity. For example, benzyl chloride may often be used where, say, n-hexyl chloride would react very sluggishly.

Examples of this type of reaction have been investigated kinetically in much detail, and since the overall reactions are very simple ones they form a convenient illustration of the relation between kinetics and suggested mechanisms. We will therefore consider them in some detail. Two characteristic reaction types appear; in one type, the reaction rate depends on the first power of the activities of the halide and the other reagent:

$$\text{Rate} = k[\text{Halide}] [\text{reagent}]$$

and, in the other, the rate depends on the first power of the activity of the halide and is independent of the concentration of the other reagent:

$$\text{Rate} = k[\text{Halide}].$$

(This must not be taken to imply that intermediate cases do not occur, nor that a given pair of reagents cannot show both types of reaction according to conditions.)

In the first type, it is believed that the reaction step involves the simultaneous extrusion of a halide ion and combination with the reagent:

$$HO^\ominus + CH_3I \rightarrow \overset{\delta-}{HO} \text{ - - - } CH_3 \text{ - - - } \overset{\delta-}{I} \rightarrow HOCH_3 + I^\ominus$$
$$\text{transition complex}$$

That is, the reaction is bimolecular.

In the second type, it is believed that the reaction consists of a slow and rate-determining *ionization* of the halide, followed by a rapid combination of the 'carbonium' ion intermediate with the reagent:

$$(CH_3)_3CI \rightarrow (CH_3)_3C^\oplus + I^\ominus \quad \text{slow}$$
$$(CH_3)_3C^\oplus + OH^\ominus \rightarrow (CH_3)_3COH \quad \text{fast}$$

Since the overall rate is determined by the rate of the first step, the rate equation

$$\text{Rate} = k[\text{Halide}]$$

is accounted for.

The suggested mechanisms are further confirmed by the fact that reactions of the second type are favoured by solvents which encourage ionization. Thus tertiary butyl bromide is hydrolysed by water about 10^8 times as fast as methyl bromide. However with iodide ions in acetone as solvent it reacts about $10^{-4.4}$ times as fast as methyl bromide. Formic acid is a highly polar solvent of high dielectric constant, and favours the ionization mechanism, even for primary alkyl halides; acetone, on the other hand, is a poor solvent for ionization, and favours the bimolecular mechanism, even for tertiary alkyl halides.

Although ionization has been shown above as a process involving the simple separation of a molecule into ions, it is in fact a reaction with the solvent, the ions being solvated; the equation given above should therefore be thought of as a shorthand version of:

$$(CH_3)_3CI + \text{solvent} \rightarrow (CH_3)_3C^\oplus(\text{solvent}) + I^\ominus(\text{solvent})$$

The picture then becomes broadly this. The organic halide itself is a polar molecule $\overset{\delta+}{R}\text{—}\overset{\delta-}{Hal}$; this polarization can proceed to completion with the separation of the halogen atom as a halide ion if suitable reagents are present. In the displacement reactions we have outlined (of whichever type) these reagents perform two essential processes; the attack of a nucleophilic agent on the more-or-less positively charged (i.e. electron-deficient) carbon atom, and the stabilization, normally by solvation, of the halide ion. (Nucleophile and solvent can, of course, be the same reagent—water, for example, might in favourable cases perform both functions.) Whether the reaction follows the first or the second of the two mechanisms, with their associated kinetics, depends on which of these two processes—nucleophilic attack or solvation—provides the 'driving force' of the reaction. This in turn depends on three factors; the nucleophilic affinity of the reagent, the solvating power of the solvent, and the structure of the halide itself. This last point will affect the relative importance of its two essential features in these reactions, namely the affinity of the α-carbon atom for an electron pair, and the ease of ionization of the carbon–halogen bond. Broadly we can say that primary alkyl halides, except in powerfully ionizing solvents, tend to react by the first, bimolecular mechanism, while tertiary alkyl halides, except in poorly ionizing solvents, tend to react by the second, unimolecular mechanism. Secondary halides can react by either mechanism, or by both simultaneously, depending mainly on the balance of the three factors mentioned above.

(2) With silver salts

In a second group of reactions, alkyl halides react with silver salts. In some cases, they give a product different from that obtained with an alkali metal salt; in others, the silver salt is effective where the alkali metal salt is not, or is at any rate much less so. Some of these reactions are listed below.

(*a*) With silver cyanide, the main product is the isocyanide and not the cyanide or nitrile:

$$C_2H_5Br + AgCN \rightarrow C_2H_5NC + AgBr$$
ethyl isocyanide

(*b*) With silver nitrite, the main product is the nitro-compound, even with simple alkyl halides:

$$C_2H_5Br + AgNO_2 \rightarrow C_2H_5NO_2 + AgBr$$
nitroethane

(*c*) With dry silver oxide, an ether is obtained. (Alkali metal oxides are not normally available as reagents, so that comparison here has little significance.)

$$2C_2H_5I + Ag_2O \rightarrow (C_2H_5)_2O + AgI$$
diethyl ether

(*d*) With silver salts of carboxylic acids, esters are formed; e.g.

$$CH_3CO_2Ag + C_2H_5I \rightarrow CH_3CO_2C_2H_5 + AgI$$
ethyl acetate

This is a possible method of obtaining an ester where reaction between the acid and the alcohol is slow and ineffective.

Two factors may be operating here. In the first place, some silver salts are known not to have simple ionic lattices of the same type as the alkali metal salts. This is so for the cyanide and nitrite, and although it cannot be said that the structures of the salts show conclusively why the different products are formed, at least it is clear that the reagent is no longer the simple cyanide or nitrite ion.

Secondly, although silver chloride and bromide (and one form of silver iodide) have cubic lattices of the sodium chloride type, the silver ion is much smaller than even the sodium ion, and exerts a much greater deforming field on the halide ion, especially if this is iodide. The reaction is therefore 'driven' not only by the affinity of the nucleophilic reagent for the alkyl carbon and of the solvent (if any) for the halide ion, but by that of the silver ion for the halide ion. This may at any rate partly account for the greater effectiveness of silver salts in (*d*), and of the particular desirability of using iodides in this reaction. The formation of argentohalide complex ions may also help.

(3)   Elimination reactions

Halides capable of so doing often form olefins by overall elimination of a hydrogen halide molecule; thus, formally:

$$CH_3CH_2Br \rightarrow CH_2{=}CH_2 + HBr$$

Various reagents and conditions can bring this about. Thus some elimination very frequently accompanies the reactions listed under (1). For example, in the alkaline hydrolysis of halides to alcohols, olefins are also formed and with tertiary alkyl halides they may be the main product; for example,

$$(CH_3)_3CBr + OH^{\ominus} \rightarrow (CH_3)_2C{=}CH_2 + H_2O + Br^{\ominus}$$
2-methyl propene

It is believed that elimination reactions occur by the removal of a hydrogen atom as a *proton* from the β-carbon atom (i.e. that adjacent to the carbon atom carrying the halogen). The nucleophilic reagent is in this case acting specifically as a base in the Lowry–Brönsted sense. The picture is therefore somewhat as follows, the curved arrows indicating the transference of electron pairs:

115

(If the base is a neutral molecule, then of course the conjugate acid will have a cationic charge.)

As with the displacement reactions discussed above, kinetic studies indicate that the ionization of the halogen atom as halide ion may either precede or accompany the loss of the proton, and the circumstances favouring the one version of the reaction rather than the other are essentially the same for eliminations as for displacements.

Elimination as opposed to substitution is especially favoured when the nucleophilic reagent is a strong proton base. This is to be expected from the suggested mechanism, and lies behind the use of the traditional reagent 'alcoholic potash' for the preparation of olefins from alkyl halides, since owing to the equilibrium

$$C_2H_5OH + OH^\ominus \rightleftharpoons C_2H_5O^\ominus + H_2O$$

the very strong proton base $C_2H_5O^\ominus$ is present. In fact, this reagent is not necessarily very effective and, with bromoethane, substitution is still the predominant reaction (yielding therefore ethanol and some diethyl ether), less than 1% of ethylene being formed. With other halides, however, good olefin yields can be obtained and, with some tertiary halides, Williamson's synthesis is impossible, the olefin alone being formed. Tertiary amines and $OH^\ominus$ itself also cause considerable elimination.

High temperatures favour elimination rather than substitution. Heating with the tertiary base quinoline  b.p. 235° C is thus often an effective method for converting an alkyl halide to an olefin.

(4) Halides react with certain metals

(*a*) In dry ethereal solution, alkyl halides and aryl bromides and iodides react with magnesium yielding compounds called Grignard reagents, e.g.

$$C_2H_5Br + Mg \rightarrow C_2H_5MgBr$$
ethyl magnesium
bromide

Bromobenzene similarly yields phenyl magnesium bromide C_6H_5MgBr.

In general, iodides react most rapidly, chlorides least; chlorobenzene reacts too slowly to be of practical use. Side reactions (such as the Wurtz reaction, (*d*) below) occur most readily with iodides.

(*b*) Provided a non-oxidizing and dry atmosphere is maintained, lithium reacts with alkyl halides under the same conditions as magnesium, yielding lithium alkyls:

$$C_2H_5Br + 2Li \rightarrow C_2H_5Li + LiBr$$

116

Both Grignard reagents and lithium alkyls are valuable synthetic reagents (see this chapter, p. 120).

(*c*) Zinc forms compounds similar to the Grignard reagents, and these on distillation yield the zinc dialkyls:

$$2C_2H_5ZnI \rightarrow (C_2H_5)_2Zn + ZnI_2$$

Zinc alkyls were formerly used for the same synthetic purposes as the Grignard reagents, but being spontaneously inflammable in air and also toxic, they became largely obsolete with the discovery of the latter. Alkyl zinc halides are occasionally useful where Grignard reagents are too reactive.

(*d*) *The Wurtz reaction.* Alkyl halides react in dry ethereal solution with sodium or potassium to yield paraffin hydrocarbons e.g.

$$2C_2H_5I + 2Na \rightarrow CH_3CH_2CH_2CH_3 + 2NaI$$
$$n\text{-butane}$$

The reaction is not easy to carry out effectively, and halides other than iodides often react very sluggishly.

The 'mixed' reaction, using two different halides R^1I and R^2I, yields three possible products R^1R^1, R^2R^2 and R^1R^2.

As a method of preparing R^1R^2 it is effective when one halide is an aryl halide. Thus bromobenzene and bromoethane react with sodium to give a reasonable yield of ethylbenzene (Fittig reaction).

$$C_6H_5Br + BrC_2H_5 + 2Na \rightarrow C_6H_5.C_2H_5 + 2NaBr$$

The action of a halide on a Grignard reagent (p. 121) is usually more effective than the Wurtz reaction as a method of linking two alkyl or similar groups.

(*e*) Alkyl halides are reduced by a zinc–copper couple (that is, zinc powder coated with copper by immersing it for a short time in copper sulphate solution) in the presence of ethanol.

The corresponding hydrocarbon is produced; stated formally for the case of ethyl bromide:

$$C_2H_5Br + H^\oplus + 2e \rightarrow C_2H_6 + Br^\ominus$$

In fact, zinc is the reducing agent, the proton presumably arising from the ionizable —OH of the alcohol (see p. 127):

$$C_2H_5Br + Zn \rightarrow C_2H_5{}^\ominus + Zn^{2\oplus} + Br^\ominus$$
$$C_2H_5{}^\ominus + C_2H_5OH \rightarrow C_2H_6 + C_2H_5O^\ominus$$

(The three ions shown in the first equation need not in fact become separated before the attack of the ethanol; if not, then the reaction becomes very close to the formation of ethyl zinc bromide, followed by its alcoholysis.)

Aryl halides do not react with the zinc–copper couple.

Preparation of monohalogenohydrocarbons and allied compounds: introduction of halogens into organic molecules

(1) Direct replacement of hydrogen by halogen

Hydrogen attached to carbon can be replaced by the direct action of chlorine or bromine. The halogenation of paraffins has been discussed in chapter 4, and of aromatic compounds in chapter 8. With propane and higher alkanes, all possible monochloroisomers are present in the product, as well as products of further chlorination.

Chlorination and bromination of alkyl groups in other types of compound is often possible. For example, the α-H atoms of fatty acids can be replaced by bromine in the presence of red phosphorus, e.g.

$$CH_3CH_2CO_2H + Br_2 \rightarrow CH_3CHBr.CO_2H + HBr$$

and the methyl group of acetic acid can be progressively chlorinated, yielding ultimately, trichloroacetic acid CCl_3CO_2H, by the action of chlorine on boiling acetic acid in the presence of sulphur, phosphorus or iodine.

Direct iodination is not normally a practicable method of preparing iodohydrocarbons, being slow and reversible. Benzene, however, can be iodinated to iodobenzene if iodic acid or other oxidizing agents are present to oxidize the hydrogen iodide formed and thus to prevent the reverse reaction.

Alkyl iodides are often best made from alkyl chlorides or bromides by the action of sodium iodide (see p. 111).

The reagents are refluxed in solution in acetone.

(2) Replacement of —OH by halogen

(*a*) By the action of hydrohalic acids. Alcohols react in suitable conditions with aqueous hydrogen halides, yielding the corresponding halide. This reaction is discussed in detail on p. 129, for example,

$$C_2H_5OH + HBr \rightarrow C_2H_5Br + H_2O$$

This is the most widely applicable method for preparing alkyl halides in the laboratory.

—OH *attached to the benzene ring cannot be replaced in this way.* Thus phenol does not yield bromobenzene on refluxing with concentrated hydro-bromic acid.

For practical purposes, bromides are usually made by using a mixture of sodium bromide and fairly concentrated aqueous sulphuric acid, giving an overall bromide concentration about equal to that in constant boiling hydrobromic acid.

For iodides, this cannot be used owing to the oxidizing action of concentrated aqueous sulphuric acid on iodides. Syrupy phosphoric acid can often be used in place of sulphuric acid.

Primary and secondary alcohols react on refluxing with excess of the reagents, tertiary ones often react in the cold.

Concentrated hydrochloric acid reacts rapidly in the cold with tertiary alcohols, but is ineffective with others. A saturated solution of zinc chloride in concentrated hydrochloric acid is an effective reagent for preparing primary and secondary alkyl chlorides.

(*b*) By the action of phosphorus halides and similar compounds. Reactions of the following types are among those possible when an alcohol or a phenol reacts with a phosphorus halide:

$$3C_2H_5OH + PBr_3 \rightarrow 3C_2H_5Br + H_3PO_3$$
$$C_2H_5OH + PCl_5 \rightarrow C_2H_5Cl + POCl_3 + HCl$$

Other reactions also occur, leading to the formation of esters of phosphorus and phosphoric acids. The method is therefore of limited value. It has probably been used most often to prepare *iodides* using an intimate mixture of *red phosphorus and iodine* to provide phosphorus iodide in situ but bromine and red phosphorus also give good yields of bromides in suitable cases. Phosphorus oxychloride can sometimes be used.

Chlorides can be made by the action of thionyl chloride on hydroxy compounds, e.g.

$$CH_3(CH_2)_3OH + SOCl_2 \rightarrow CH_3(CH_2)_3Cl + SO_2 + HCl$$

Yields are usually good and since the inorganic by-products are gaseous the chloride is easily purified. Bromides can be made using thionyl bromide; thionyl iodide does not exist.

(3) Addition of hydrogen halides to olefins

Hydrogen bromide and hydrogen iodide add to ethylenic double bonds. The olefine is refluxed with the concentrated aqueous acid (or, if gaseous, passed into the boiling acid). Markovnikov's Rule normally determines the position taken up by the halogen atom (see p. 57); for example,

$$CH_3\!-\!CH\!=\!CH_2 + HBr \rightarrow CH_3CHBrCH_3$$

The method is not of great laboratory value, since the alcohols are normally more readily available than the olefins.

(4) Replacement of —$N_2^{\oplus}$ in diazonium salts by halogen

Aromatic diazonium salts react with chloride or bromide ions in the presence of finely divided copper as a catalyst (Gattermann's method) to yield nuclear-substituted halides; for example, phenyl diazonium ions and chloride yield chlorobenzene:

$$C_6H_5N_2^{\oplus}+Cl^{\ominus} \xrightarrow{Cu} C_6H_5Cl+N_2\uparrow$$

Iodide ions need no catalyst.

Alternatively, the diazonium ion may be made to react with complex cuprous halide solutions (i.e. cuprous chloride in hydrochloric acid, or the corresponding bromide reagent). This is the Sandmeyer reaction; for example, phenyl diazonium salts and a cuprochloride solution yield chlorobenzene. $\quad C_6H_5N_2^{\oplus}+CuCl_2^{\ominus} \rightarrow C_6H_5Cl+N_2\uparrow+CuCl$

The reactions are further discussed in chapter 19.

Since the simpler primary aromatic amines are readily available, this is a useful alternative to direct halogenation of hydrocarbons, especially for the iodo-compounds. It is clearly only applicable to nuclear aromatic halides, since diazonium salts can only be formed with —$N_2^{\oplus}$ attached to an aromatic nucleus (see chapter 13).

Grignard reagents and their use in organic synthesis

A Grignard reagent is a compound of general formula R.Mg.Hal where R can be alkyl, aryl or other types of hydrocarbon radical. They are named after François Antoine Victor Grignard, who discovered them and introduced them into organic synthesis at the beginning of this century.

Grignard reagents are prepared by the action of the corresponding halide in dry ethereal solution on magnesium turnings; the reaction normally proceeds briskly and spontaneously at the boiling point of the ethereal solution. Thus, for example, iodomethane yields methylmagnesium iodide CH_3MgI, and bromobenzene phenylmagnesium bromide C_6H_5MgBr. The Grignard reagent is not normally isolated, the ethereal solution being used directly. Unlike the zinc alkyls, whose use for synthetic purposes they rendered obsolete, and the more recently developed lithium alkyls, Grignard reagents are relatively slowly oxidized. Provided water is carefully excluded and the normal precautions in handling ethereal solutions are observed, they can be handled in the laboratory without further special measures.

Reactions of Grignard reagents

(1) With —OH compounds

Water, alcohols, phenols and carboxylic acids decompose Grignard reagents, yielding the hydrocarbon RH from R.Mg.Hal. Thus methyl-magnesium iodide yields methane; for example,

$$CH_3MgI + H_2O \rightarrow CH_4 + MgIOH$$
$$CH_3MgI + EtOH \rightarrow CH_4 + MgIOEt$$

The reaction is therefore of no synthetic value, and leads simply to the reduction of the halide from which the reagent was prepared. It has however been used to determine the number of OH groups in a compound of known molecular weight (Zerewitinoff's method). If a known weight of the hydroxyl compound is added to an excess of methyl magnesium iodide, the number of moles of hydroxyl added can be found by measuring the volume of methane evolved, since 1 mole of —OH liberates 1 mole of methane (22·4 dm^3 at s.t.p.). Diethyl ether has a very high vapour pressure at ordinary temperatures, the correction for which would be large and uncertain; the Grignard reagent for Zerewitinoff's method is therefore prepared in dipentyl ether, which is much less volatile.

(2) Reaction with halides

Grignard reagents react with alkyl and similar halides, yielding a hydro-carbon by the union of the radicals of the Grignard reagent and the halide. Thus, for example, allyl magnesium bromide and *n*-butyl bromide yield hept-1-ene.

$$CH_2=CH-CH_2MgBr + CH_3(CH_2)_3Br$$
$$\rightarrow CH_2=CH(CH_2)_4CH_3 + MgBr_2$$

(One of the valuable features of Grignard reagents is that, since their reactions are in general carried out at about the boiling point of diethyl ether, the risk of undesirable rearrangements of the product is small; thus in the example quoted, there is little or no 'migration' of the double bond from the 1–2 to the 2–3 position, such as might occur in, for example, the dehydration of heptan-1-ol.)

(3) Reactions with carbonyl compounds

Grignard reagents add to carbonyl compounds according to the general formal scheme:

These products (which often crystallize from the ethereal solution) are hydrolysed by water or dilute mineral acid to yield a product of the general type:

$$\begin{array}{c} \diagdown \\ \diagup \end{array} C \begin{array}{c} \diagup R \\ \diagdown OH \end{array}$$

and inorganic magnesium salts.

(a) Aldehydes therefore yield secondary alcohols, except for formaldehyde, which yields primary alcohols. Thus benzaldehyde and methylmagnesium iodide yield phenylmethyl carbinol:

$$C_6H_5.CHO \xrightarrow{CH_3MgI} C_6H_5\underset{\underset{OMgI}{|}}{\overset{\overset{CH_3}{|}}{CH}} \xrightarrow{H^\oplus} C_6H_5\overset{\overset{CH_3}{|}}{CHOH}$$

and formaldehyde and phenylmagnesium bromide yield benzyl alcohol

$$H.CHO \xrightarrow{C_6H_5MgBr} C_6H_5CH_2OMgBr \xrightarrow{H^\oplus} C_6H_5CH_2OH$$

(b) Ketones yield tertiary alcohols; thus acetophenone and ethylmagnesium bromide yield ethyl methyl phenyl carbinol

$$C_6H_5COCH_3 \xrightarrow{C_2H_5MgBr} C_6H_5\underset{\underset{C_2H_5}{|}}{\overset{\overset{CH_3}{|}}{COMgBr}} \xrightarrow{H^\oplus} C_6H_5\underset{\underset{C_2H_5}{|}}{\overset{\overset{CH_3}{|}}{COH}}$$

(c) Carbon dioxide yields carboxylic acids; only one $\diagup C{=}O$ group reacts. Thus n-butyl magnesium chloride yields pentanoic acid (valeric acid).

$$CH_3(CH_2)_3MgCl+CO_2 \rightarrow CH_3(CH_2)_3CO_2MgCl \xrightarrow{H^\oplus} CH_3(CH_2)_3CO_2H$$

(Dry carbon dioxide can be passed into the ethereal solution of the Grignard reagent; alternatively, powdered 'dry ice' can be added to the stirred solution.)

(d) The esters of carboxylic acids react with Grignard reagents in the mole ratio 1 ester:2 reagent; the final product is a tertiary alcohol. Presumably addition to the carbonyl group occurs according to the above general scheme, and elimination of a magnesium compound of the alkoxyl group of the ester may be assumed to follow: this regenerates a carbonyl group with which with second molecule of reagent reacts as in (b). Thus the action of phenylmagnesium bromide on ethyl acetate, for example, yields methyldiphenyl carbinol:

122

$$CH_3.COOEt \xrightarrow{C_6H_5MgBr} CH_3.C\underset{OMgBr}{\overset{C_6H_5}{\underset{\Big\backslash}{\overset{\diagup}{-}OEt}}} \rightarrow CH_3COC_6H_5$$

$$\xrightarrow{C_6H_5MgBr} CH_3.\overset{\overset{\displaystyle C_6H_5}{|}}{\underset{\underset{\displaystyle C_6H_5}{|}}{C}}OMgBr \xrightarrow{H^\oplus} CH_3.\overset{\overset{\displaystyle C_6H_5}{|}}{\underset{\underset{\displaystyle C_6H_5}{|}}{C}}OH$$

Two of the groups attached to the tertiary carbon atom must of course be the same. It is not as a rule possible to stop at the ketone stage.

Grignard reagents also react with amides, acyl halides and nitriles; with the last especially it is often possible to stop after one molar proportion of Grignard reagent has reacted and thus obtain a ketone. For further details and for other reactions of Grignard reagents, more advanced text-books should be consulted.

In the reactions listed under (2) and (3) above, a C–C link is formed between the alkyl or similar group of the Grignard reagent and a carbon atom of the other reagent, thus building a larger carbon skeleton from two smaller ones.

Grignard reagents may in certain cases act as reducing agents rather than normally as outlined above. Sometimes they fail to react at all; possibly for steric reasons, if the carbon atom that would be attacked is made inaccessible by large neighbouring groups, or possibly for reasons of abnormal electron distribution (for example, rendering a carbonyl carbon atom much less electrophilic than usual). In some cases where Grignard reagents fail, a lithium alkyl may react successfully. These can usually be made from lithium and an alkyl halide in the same way as Grignard reagents, but oxygen as well as moisture must be excluded. In general they yield the same types of product with the same types of reagent.

11

The hydroxyl group : —OH

Compounds containing the —OH group attached to a saturated carbon atom of an aliphatic radical or in the side chain of an aromatic compound are called *alcohols*. (Compounds with —OH attached to an *ethylenic* carbon atom are called 'enols', and exist in equilibrium with a greater or lesser proportion of an isomeric carbonyl compound, see p. 202.) When —OH is attached directly to a carbon atom of an aromatic ring, the resulting compounds are sufficiently different from alcohols in their behaviour to have a different name and are known as *phenols*. The two series may, however, be considered together. As with other functional groups, attachment of —OH to the carbon of a carbonyl group to form the group —CO₂H drastically modifies its properties. The resulting compounds, *carboxylic acids*, are therefore considered as a separate functional type.

Alcohols are further classified according to the number of hydrogen atoms attached to the carbon atom bearing the —OH group. Those containing the group —CH₂OH are *primary* alcohols, those containing $\geqslant$CHOH *secondary* alcohols, and those containing $\geqslant$COH *tertiary* alcohols, the remaining bonds being linked to carbon atoms in each case.

The following formulae illustrate these points:

CH₃CH₂OH ethyl alcohol (ethanol)	CH₃CH₂CH₂OH (primary) *n*-propyl alcohol (propan-1-ol)
CH₃CHOHCH₃ isopropyl alcohol (propan-2-ol)	CH₃CH₂CHOHCH₃ (secondary) secondary butyl alcohol (butan-2-ol)
CH₃.COH.CH₃ ⎮ CH₃ tertiary butyl alcohol (2-methylpropan-2-ol)	(tertiary)

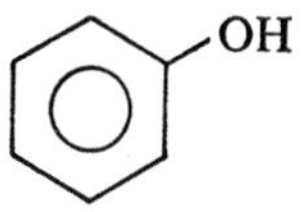

CH$_3$

OH

OH

phenols

phenol

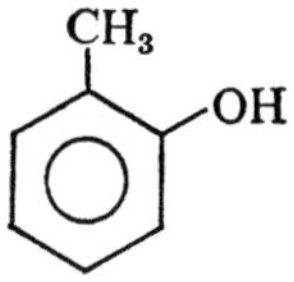

o-cresol

CH$_2$OH

(contrast

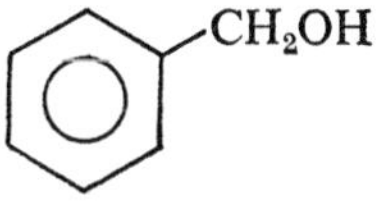

a primary alcohol).

Nomenclature   benzyl alcohol

The names under the formulae illustrated here follow the old-established nomenclature of the simpler alcohols, which are named from the alkyl radical attached to the —OH group. The names in brackets illustrate the systematic method, in which the —OH group is indicated by the termination —ol added to the name of the parent alkane, together (if necessary) with a number indicating to which carbon atom of the longest chain it is attached.

Yet another alternative, convenient for alcohols of moderate complexity, is to regard the alcohol as derived by the replacement of the hydrogen atoms of the simplest alcohol, methanol (CH_3OH), by other radicals. The names of these radicals are prefixed to the word 'carbinol' which in this context signifies methanol. Thus $(C_6H_5)_3COH$ is triphenyl carbinol.

General and physiological properties

Methanol and ethanol are liquids with boiling points 65 and 78° C respectively. Phenol is a solid of melting point about 40° C. The physiological effects of aqueous ethanol are well known; in fact, the term 'intoxication', strictly applicable to any poisoning of the higher nervous centres, is almost universally supposed to apply specifically to the effects of ethanol. Methanol is said to be more toxic. 'Industrial methylated spirit' is technical ethanol to which methanol has been added to make it (supposedly) undrinkable, while for retail sale in Great Britain it is further contaminated with pyridine and coloured with methyl violet. Phenol ('carbolic acid') has a limited use as disinfectant and antiseptic, and has been extensively replaced by substances less toxic to human beings. Neat phenol in contact with the skin produces painful blisters or 'phenol burns'. The simple physical characteristics of alcohols and phenols are directly related to the presence of the hydroxyl group, and are discussed in the next section.

Alcohols and phenols have extensive technical uses. Thus methanol,

125

ethanol, isopropyl alcohol and several higher alcohols are used as solvents. In addition, they are important sources of other materials; thus methanol is a source of methyl derivatives generally, and of formaldehyde; ethanol of ethyl derivatives, acetic acid, acetaldehyde and hence of many other materials. Isopropyl alcohol is an intermediate in the manufacture of acetone. Phenol has extensive uses in the manufacture of drugs, dyestuffs and fine chemicals. It is a major raw material for phenol-formaldehyde resins (bakelite). Both of the reactants for making '66 Nylon' (adipic acid and hexamethylenediamine) can be obtained from phenol.

Properties and reactions dependent on the —OH group

(1) Physical characteristics

The OH group is, of course, present in the water molecule itself, and alcohols and phenols can be regarded as mono-alkyl and mono-aryl waters; an approach adopted over a century ago by Gerhardt. In ice and liquid water, there is strong hydrogen bonding (p. 17) between the molecules, giving water its well-known properties as an associated liquid (notably its exceptionally high boiling point in comparison with H_2S). This hydrogen bonding between —OH groups is also present in alcohols, which show association in the same way as water. Thus alcohols have higher boiling points than the isomeric ethers, in which the —OH group is absent (compare ethanol CH_3CH_2OH, b.p. 78° C with dimethyl ether CH_3OCH_3, b.p. $-24°$ C). The lower alcohols are miscible with water, presumably because hydrogen bonding can occur between water and alcohol molecules. The effect of the —OH group in conferring solubility in water is very noticeable in polyhydroxy compounds such as glycerol ($CH_2OH.CHOH.CH_2OH$), the sugars, and the di- and tri-hydric phenols such as catechol (*o*-dihydroxy benzene. (An alcohol or phenol is said to be *monohydric* if its molecule contains one hydroxyl group, *dihydric* if two, and so on.) These effects become less conspicuous as the number of carbon atoms in the molecule increases; thus *n*-butyl alcohol $CH_3CH_2CH_2CH_2OH$ has a finite solubility in water, and the higher homologues are less soluble still.

Within a group of isomeric alcohols, such as the butyl alcohols, the straight-chain isomer with —OH on the terminal carbon atom (the 'normal' alcohol) has the highest boiling point. Change of position of the —OH to a non-terminal carbon atom and branching of the chain both lower the b.p. Compare:

butan-1-ol (*n*-butyl alcohol) $CH_3CH_2CH_2CH_2OH$ b.p. 118° C.
butan-2-ol (secondary butyl alcohol) $CH_3CH_2CHOHCH_3$ b.p. 100° C.

2-methylpropan-1-ol (isobutyl alcohol) $(CH_3)_2CHCH_2OH$ b.p. 107° C.
2 methylpropan-2-ol (tertiary butyl alcohol) $(CH_3)_3COH$ b.p. 83° C.

On the other hand, of these alcohols, the tertiary has the highest melting point and the highest solubility in water (being miscible with it). Probably a number of effects are operating here; the actual compactness of the molecule, the effect of the alkyl group on the polarity of the molecule (tertiary butyl is more 'polarizable' than normal butyl, and thus the effect of the polarity of —OH will be to some extent neutralized in tertiary butyl alcohol) and the 'steric' effect of the crowding of groups round the —OH.

Phenol is moderately soluble in water at room temperatures, its solubility increasing with rise of temperature and becoming infinite at 68° C; again, the effect of the —OH group is conspicuous if this is compared with the very low solubility in water of benzene or of an ether such as $C_6H_5OCH_3$.

Although the lower alcohols are in some respects similar to water, they are much less effective solvents for simple salts. This is presumably partly due to their much lower dielectric constants; the replacement of one hydrogen atom in H_2O by an organic radical will also somewhat decrease the polarity and increase the bulk of the molecule, and both effects would be expected to reduce the solvating power of the molecule (that is, its tendency to cling to the ions of the solute and thus reduce the energy required to separate the ions from the crystal lattice).

(2)   Acid–base behaviour

The —OH group in the alcohols, as in water, is capable of losing a proton to a base;
$$ROH + B \rightleftharpoons RO^\ominus + BH^\oplus$$

and, on account of the lone pairs of the oxygen atom, of gaining a proton from an acid;
$$ROH + HA \rightleftharpoons ROH_2^\oplus + A^\ominus$$

Thus alcohols and phenols, like water, are potentially both acids and bases.

With alcohols, as with water, these functions are both comparatively feeble; for example, alcohols have no effect on the hydrogen ion concentration of water, although they exchange deuterium with heavy water in the presence of bases, confirming that ionization of the alcohol occurs. Nevertheless, both functions are highly important in the chemical behaviour of alcohols.

In accordance with the above properties, alcoholic solutions of strong alkalis contain alkoxide ions in equilibrium with hydroxide (see p. 116); for example,
$$C_2H_5OH + OH^\ominus \rightleftharpoons C_2H_5O^\ominus + H_2O$$
the ethoxide
ion

and alcoholic solutions of acids are ionized and therefore conducting; for example:

$$C_2H_5OH + HCl \rightleftharpoons C_2H_5OH_2^{\oplus} + Cl^{\ominus}$$

the 'ethoxonium' ion being the 'hydrogen ion' present in solutions of acids in ethanol. (This is, of course, apart from any subsequent reaction between the acid and the alcohol.)

Alcohols, like water, are believed to undergo 'autoprotolysis'; that is, alcohol molecules act as acid and base towards each other:

$$2C_2H_5OH \rightleftharpoons C_2H_5O^{\ominus} + C_2H_5OH_2^{\oplus}$$

but the extent of this is even less than in water itself.

Unlike alcohols, phenols are detectably though feebly acidic in aqueous solution, and this is one of the most striking differences between the two types. The conventional dissociation constant for phenol itself, ionizing in aqueous solution

$$C_6H_5OH + H_2O \rightleftharpoons C_6H_5O^{\ominus} + H_3O^{\oplus}$$

is $1 \cdot 2 \times 10^{-10}$ at 25° C. (The old name 'carbolic acid' emphasizes this point.) This is considerably less than the first dissociation constant of carbonic acid:

$$2H_2O + CO_2 \rightleftharpoons H_2CO_3 + H_2O \rightleftharpoons H_3O^{\oplus} + HCO_3^{\ominus}$$

($K_A = 4 \cdot 3 \times 10^{-7}$ at 25° C). Thus phenol is liberated when carbon dioxide is passed into a solution of sodium phenate in water.

$$C_6H_5O^{\ominus} + H_2CO_3 \rightleftharpoons C_6H_5OH + HCO_3^{\ominus}$$

(It is often stated that phenol is no more soluble in sodium carbonate solution than in water; but this is clearly a matter of the relative magnitudes of K_A for phenol and for the bicarbonate ion, the value for this last being $5 \cdot 6 \times 10^{-11}$ at 25° C. These figures suggest that the equilibrium

$$C_6H_5OH + CO_3^{2\ominus} \rightleftharpoons C_6H_5O^{\ominus} + HCO_3^{\ominus}$$

should be appreciably displaced to the right.)

This enhanced acidity of phenols can be accounted for by the stabilization of the phenate ion by the distribution of the ionic charge over the ortho- and para-atoms of the ring. The ion is in fact a 'resonance hybrid'.

(Alternatively, one can say that the lone pairs of the $-O^{\ominus}$ atom are to some extent delocalized.)

128

The complementary aspect of this is that the phenate ion is a much weaker base than the ethoxide ion. Phenates can exist in aqueous solution (though such solutions are quite strongly alkaline);

$$C_6H_5O^\ominus + H_2O \rightleftharpoons C_6H_5OH + OH^\ominus$$

while sodium ethoxide when added to water is practically totally hydrolysed to alcohol and sodium hydroxide.

$$C_2H_5O^\ominus + H_2O \rightleftharpoons C_2H_5OH + OH^\ominus$$

(This is of course a radically different situation from that in *alcoholic* alkalis, where the alcohol is in large excess.)

This is of practical importance in the working-up of coal tar. The phenolic constituents can be removed as phenates by agitating the tar with aqueous sodium hydroxide solution; the aqueous layer is separated and the phenols can then be liberated by addition of sulphuric acid, or even by passing in gases with a large CO_2 content (such as cleaned flue gases).

(3) The action of alkali metals on alcohols

Sodium displaces hydrogen from alcohols, forming sodium alkoxides; for example,

$$2C_2H_5OH + 2Na \rightarrow 2C_2H_5O^\ominus Na^\oplus + H_2\uparrow$$
$$\text{sodium ethoxide}$$

This is obviously analogous with its action on water. Sodium ethoxide is a white crystalline solid, not unlike sodium hydroxide. It is soluble in alcohol, but practically completely hydrolysed by water (see above).

Sodium will behave similarly with molten phenol, but of course sodium phenate (or phenoxide) can be prepared by adding an equivalent of aqueous sodium hydroxide to phenol and evaporating to dryness. It is used in the Kolbé reaction for making salicylic acid (see p. 103).

(4) Replacement of —OH by halogen; reaction with hydrohalic acids

If alcohols are refluxed with an excess of constant boiling point hydrobromic acid, they are converted to alkyl bromides; for example,

$$C_2H_5OH + HBr \rightarrow C_2H_5Br + HOH$$

Refluxing with bromide solution in the absence of acid has no effect.

The most likely explanation of this reaction is that, while bromide ions are ineffective in displacing the hydroxyl group as an ion (the reaction, in fact, proceeding practically to completion in the reverse direction; see p. 110), in the strongly acid conditions used here some of the alcohol will be converted to the conjugate acid.

$$C_2H_5OH + H^\oplus \rightleftharpoons C_2H_5OH_2^\oplus$$

Reaction of this with bromide ions involves the displacement of a *water* molecule, which is a much weaker nucleophile than $OH^{\ominus}$ and correspondingly more readily liberated by heterolysis of the C—O bond.

$$Br^{\ominus} + C_2H_5OH_2^{\oplus} \rightleftharpoons BrC_2H_5 + H_2O$$

An excess of hydrobromic acid in high concentration ensures a good yield of halide.

Hydriodic acid reacts similarly, but in some cases the reaction may be complicated by the reducing action of hydriodic acid on the product:

$$RI + HI \rightarrow RH + I_2$$

Concentrated hydrochloric acid reacts rapidly with tertiary alcohols; a mixture of hydrochloric acid and tertiary butyl alcohol becomes turbid in a few seconds as the water-insoluble chloride forms. For making primary and secondary alkyl chlorides, however, a concentrated solution of zinc chloride in hydrochloric acid is used. This reagent presumably contains the complex $ZnCl_4^{2\ominus}$, but its function has not been established.

This difference between primary, secondary and tertiary alcohols is the basis of Lucas's Test. The unknown alcohol is added to a concentrated solution of anhydrous zinc chloride in concentrated hydrochloric acid. If the alcohol is tertiary the insoluble alkyl chloride separates immediately. Secondary alcohols dissolve also, and yield the insoluble chloride within about five minutes. Primary alcohols dissolve, but no separation of the chloride occurs except on prolonged refluxing.

Certain other strong mineral acids react with alcohols in the same way as the halogen hydracids. Thus when, for example, ethanol is mixed with concentrated sulphuric acid, an equilibrium mixture is formed containing *ethyl hydrogen sulphate*.

$$C_2H_5OH + HOSO_2OH \rightleftharpoons C_2H_5OSO_2OH + H_2O$$
$$\text{ethyl hydrogen}$$
$$\text{sulphate}$$

(5) Replacement of —OH by halogen; reaction with phosphorus halides

In general, —OH in organic compounds can be replaced by halogen by reaction with one of the appropriate phosphorus halides. The typical reactions are

$$3ROH + PX_3 \rightarrow 3RX + H_3PO_3$$
$$(X = Cl, Br, I)$$

and

$$ROH + PX_5 \rightarrow RX + HX + POX_3$$
$$(X = Cl, Br)$$

130

In place of phosphorus chlorides, phosphorus oxychloride or thionyl chloride may be used to obtain alkyl chlorides:

$$3ROH + POCl_3 \rightarrow 3RCl + H_3PO_4$$
$$ROH + SOCl_2 \rightarrow RCl + SO_2 + HCl$$

The preparative aspects of the replacement of —OH by halogen are dealt with on p. 118.

(6) Ether formation

When ethanol is heated with sulphuric acid in appropriate conditions, diethyl ether is formed:

$$2C_2H_5OH \rightarrow C_2H_5OC_2H_5 + H_2O$$

The reaction is thus formally a dehydration of the alcohol. The preparative aspects of this are discussed on p. 147.

Other acids will bring about this reaction, including benzene sulphonic acid, hydrofluoric acid and, even with some alcohols, dilute hydrochloric acid. It seems likely, therefore, that the acid protonates some alcohol molecules, which are then attacked by other alcohol molecules. Loss of a proton completes the process.

$$ROH + ROH_2^{\oplus} \rightleftharpoons ROR + H_2O^{\oplus} + I^{\oplus}$$

Lewis acids such as boron trifluoride also bring about the reaction.

(As always in suggested general mechanisms of this type, it is possible that the polarization resulting from proton addition may in some cases proceed as far as ionization: $ROH_2^{\oplus} \rightarrow R^{\oplus} + OH_2$. The reactive intermediate is then the ion $R^{\oplus}$. The function of the catalyst remains the same.)

There is no justification for the view sometimes found that etherification with H_2SO_4 occurs via the formation of the alkyl hydrogen sulphate. Etherification with other acid catalysts, such as HCl, often occurs under conditions where the alcohol has little or no action on the alkyl chloride, which would be the corresponding intermediate.

(7) Ester formation—acylation

Alcohols react with carboxylic acids to form compounds known as *esters*; for example:

$$C_2H_5OH + CH_3CO_2H \rightleftharpoons CH_3CO_2C_2H_5 + H_2O$$
$$\text{acetic acid} \qquad \text{ethyl acetate}$$

(An *ester* can be *formally* defined as a compound derived from an acid by the replacement of its ionizable hydrogen atoms by alkyl or similar groups. See, however, chapter 15.)

The reaction is catalysed by small concentrations of strong acids; the commonest procedures are to reflux the acid and alcohol together with a small amount of concentrated sulphuric acid or, where this would cause undesirable side-reactions, to pass dry hydrogen chloride into the refluxing mixture (Fischer–Speier method). There is little or no justification for using *large* amounts of sulphuric acid with the aim of removing water and displacing the equilibrium in favour of the ester. This is likely to lead to loss of alcohol by etherification or elimination of water to yield an olefin. The reaction is reversible; esters are hydrolysed by refluxing with aqueous acids (an example of the principle that a catalyst operates to speed up a reversible reaction in both directions). Alcohols also form esters on reaction with acyl chlorides; for example,

$$C_2H_5OH + CH_3COCl \rightarrow CH_3CO_2C_2H_5 + HCl$$
acetyl chloride

This reaction is more vigorous than that of the acid itself, and is not reversible.

In place of acyl chlorides, acid anhydrides can be used; for example,

$$C_2H_5OH + (CH_3CO)_2O \rightarrow CH_3CO_2C_2H_5 + CH_3CO_2H$$
acetic anhydride

(if reaction is prolonged, especially if an acid catalyst is added, then a second molecule of alcohol will react with the carboxylic acid liberated in the first reaction, but the reaction is not usually performed so as to do this). The anhydride reacts more rapidly than the acid but less rapidly than the chloride. A mixture of acetic acid and acetic anhydride is often used for acetylation.

Acetylation by acetic anhydride is of great technical importance in the conversion of *cellulose* (a long-chain molecule with alcoholic—OH groups) into *cellulose acetate* in the manufacture of acetate rayon. Alcohols also react with the esters of other alcohols. Thus, if ethanol and methyl acetate are refluxed in the presence of a little sulphuric acid, equilibrium is established.

$$CH_3CO_2CH_3 + C_2H_5OH \rightleftharpoons CH_3CO_2C_2H_5 + CH_3OH$$

The analogy with the esterification of the acid itself is obvious; indeed, the latter may be thought of as a special case (R or R^1=H) of the more general reaction:

$$CH_3CO_2R + R'OH \rightleftharpoons CH_3CO_2R' + ROH$$

Phenols as a rule react very slowly with carboxylic acids, even in the presence of strong acid catalysts, and the equilibrium favours the free phenol. Clearly the successful preparation of esters by this reaction therefore requires (*a*) long reaction time, (*b*) a fairly high temperature (to increase the reaction rate), and (*c*) removal of one product. Satisfactory yields have been obtained by lengthy refluxing when both phenol and acid have fairly high boiling points, and the water is allowed to distil off as formed.

Phenols react readily with acyl chlorides and anhydrides, and these are the usual reagents for preparing phenol esters. The aromatic acyl chlorides, such as benzoyl chloride, are only slowly hydrolysed by aqueous alkali. The conversion of phenols to their esters with benzoic and similar aromatic acids can therefore be carried out by dissolving the phenol in about 2M sodium hydroxide solution (thus converting it almost completely to the phenate ion) and shaking this with benzoyl chloride (the so-called Schotten-Baumann reaction):

$$C_6H_5O^{\ominus} + C_6H_5COCl \rightarrow C_6H_5CO.OC_6H_5 + Cl^{\ominus}$$
$$\text{phenyl benzoate}$$

Some aspects of the mechanism of acylation (which can also be performed on —NH_2 and —NH— groups) are discussed in chapter 15. It should be mentioned here, however, that it has been shown that in the esterification of carboxylic acids, the —OH group of the *acid* is replaced by the —OR group of the alcohol or phenol. The reaction is therefore *not* analogous with the conversion of alcohols to halides (see (4), p. 129, above). Strikingly, primary alcohols are in general more rapidly esterified than secondary by carboxylic acids, and secondary more rapidly than tertiary, while the rates of reaction with halogen hydracids are in the reverse order.

Many alcohols and phenols are liquids or low melting solids. They can be characterized by conversion to *crystalline* esters by the use of suitable acyl chlorides, such as *p*-nitrobenzoyl chloride:

$O_2N\langle\bigcirc\rangle COCl$ or 3, 5-dinitrobenzoyl chloride: $\overset{\displaystyle O_2N}{\underset{\displaystyle O_2N}{\langle\bigcirc\rangle}} COCl$

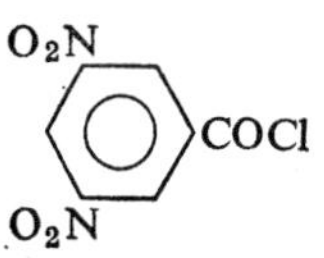

The above reactions are potentially carried out by any alcohol or phenol, since they involve the —OH group only (although they may proceed with difficulty with individual compounds). There are a number of other reactions which involve the —OH group and other parts of the molecule, but whether or not these can occur depends on the structure of the group attached to the —OH.

(8) Elimination of water to form olefins

If ethanol is heated with excess of concentrated sulphuric acid to about 160° C, the main product is not diethyl ether, as in (6) above, but ethylene.

$$CH_3CH_2OH \rightarrow CH_2{=}CH_2 + H_2O$$

(Considerable charring and reduction of the sulphuric acid also occur.) The —OH group has been eliminated together with an hydrogen atom from the β-carbon atom, forming an ethylenic bond. The reaction is formally therefore a dehydration of the alcohol. Ortho-phosphoric acid at about 200° C may be used in place of sulphuric acid; the oxidizing effects of the latter are then avoided.

The reaction may possibly proceed via the conversion of the alcohol to its hydrogen sulphate.

$$C_2H_5OH + HOSO_2OH \rightarrow C_2H_5OSO_2OH + H_2O$$

(a reaction analogous to alkyl halide formation; see (4), p. 129, above).

The bisulphate ion is a much weaker nucleophile than OH$^\ominus$, and the bisulphate group will therefore correspondingly be more easily lost as an ion; simultaneous or subsequent loss of a proton, with transfer of an electron pair to form a double bond completes the process.

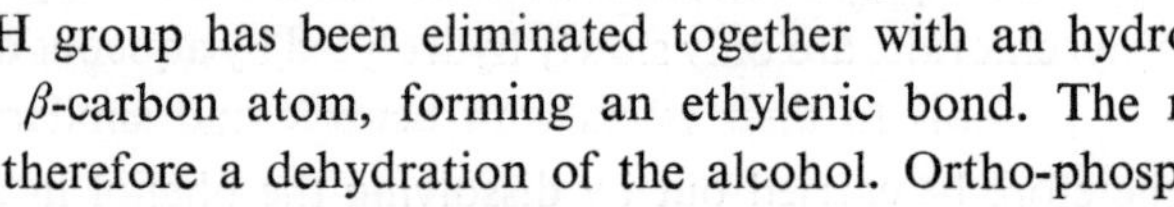

Alternatively, the acid may simply convert the alcohol to the oxonium ion, and H$^\oplus$ and H$_2$O are then eliminated by processes analogous to the above.

Secondary alcohols are dehydrated by boiling with 50% aqueous sulphuric acid, and tertiary alcohols with even more dilute acid.

Alcohols may also be dehydrated to olefins by passing the vapour over suitable catalysts, such as alumina.

Hydrogen atoms cannot be eliminated (i.e. as opposed to undergoing replacement) from the benzene ring; phenol will therefore not undergo the above reaction. It is clearly impossible with methanol CH$_3$OH and with any alcohol in which no β-carbon atom carries an hydrogen atom (such as tritertiarybutyl carbinol [(CH$_3$)$_3$C]$_3$COH or triphenyl carbinol (C$_6$H$_5$)$_3$COH).

(9) Oxidation of alcohols

The main products of oxidation of an alcohol differ according to whether the alcohol is primary, secondary or tertiary.

Thus primary alcohols are first oxidized to aldehydes:

$$\begin{array}{c} H \\ | \\ -C-OH+(O) \\ | \\ H \end{array} \rightarrow \begin{array}{c} H \\ | \\ -C=O+H_2O \end{array}$$

For example, $CH_3CH_2OH+(O) \rightarrow CH_3CHO+H_2O$
                                        acetaldehyde

These are readily oxidized further to carboxylic acids (see p. 188).

$$\begin{array}{c} H \\ | \\ -C=O+(O) \end{array} \rightarrow -C\begin{array}{c} OH \\ \diagdown\diagup \\ O \end{array}$$

The preparative aspects of this reaction are dealt with on p. 191.

Secondary alcohols are oxidized to ketones, the reaction being exactly analogous with the first stage of oxidation of primary alcohols:

$$\rangle CHOH+(O) \rightarrow \rangle C=O+H_2O$$

For example, $(CH_3)_2CHOH+(O) \rightarrow (CH_3)_2C=O+H_2O$
               isopropyl alcohol   acetone

Further oxidation can only occur with C—C bond fission, by prolonged treatment with vigorous oxidizing agents.

Clearly these reactions required the presence of an α-hydrogen atom. Tertiary alcohols, which do not possess this, can therefore only be oxidized by vigorous agents which produce C—C bond fission.

These differences in behaviour can be used to distinguish the three classes of alcohols; if, for example, the four butyl alcohols are warmed with a solution of dichromate in M sulphuric acid, three of them (the two primary alcohols, $CH_3(CH_2)_3OH$ and $(CH_3)_2CHCH_2OH$ and the secondary alcohol $CH_3CH_2CHOHCH_3$) will rapidly reduce the dichromate, while the tertiary alcohol $(CH_3)COH$ will have little or no effect. The distillates from the reaction in the first two cases contain aldehydes, and will reduce ammoniacal silver oxide solution; that from the third contains a ketone, and does not give a silver mirror. (The oxidizing power of dichromate depends markedly on the acidity of the solution; a mixture of dichromate and 50% aqueous sulphuric acid oxidizes tertiary butyl alcohol rapidly.)

Primary and secondary alcohols may be *dehydrogenated* by passing the alcohol vapour over heated metal catalysts (e.g. finely divided copper or nickel, see also p. 193).

$$\rangle CHOH \rightleftharpoons \rangle C=O+H_2$$
(primary or
secondary)

This reaction with nickel as a catalyst is used in the industrial production of acetone from propan-2-ol. Under these conditions tertiary alcohols will normally be dehydrated to an olefin.

Phenols, like tertiary alcohols, possess no α-H atom, and can only be oxidized by reactions affecting the aromatic ring itself. In fact, the aromatic ring in phenols is comparatively easily oxidized—much more so than in benzene itself—and phenol rapidly reduces acid permanganate solutions on warming.

(10) The Haloform reaction

All alcohols containing the CH_3CHOH— group (that is to say, ethanol and all methyl secondary alcohols) yield iodoform CHI_3 when treated in the cold or on gentle warming with a hypoiodite solution. The hypoiodite ion is unstable, disproportionating rapidly to iodide and iodate. The reagent is prepared as required, either by adding a hypochlorite solution to a mixture of the alcohol with an iodide solution, or by adding aqueous alkali to a mixture of the alcohol with a solution of iodine in potassium iodide solution.

Presumably the alcohol is oxidized to a carbonyl compound (acetaldehyde or a methyl ketone) by the hypoiodite. The oxidation product then undergoes halogenation and hydrolysis. These last two reactions are discussed in detail on p. 189.

The overall reactions for ethanol, for example, are therefore:

$$CH_3CH_2OH + OI^\ominus \rightarrow CH_3CHO + I^\ominus + H_2O$$
$$CH_3CHO + 3OI^\ominus \rightarrow CI_3CHO + 3OH^\ominus$$
$$\text{tri-iodoacetaldehyde}$$
$$CI_3CHO + OH^\ominus \rightarrow CHI_3 + HCOO^\ominus$$
$$\text{formate ion}$$

and for secondary butyl alcohol:

$$CH_3CHOHC_2H_5 + OI^\ominus \rightarrow CH_3COC_2H_5 + I^\ominus + H_2O$$
$$\text{methyl ethyl ketone}$$
$$CH_3COC_2H_5 + 3OI^\ominus \rightarrow CI_3COC_2H_5 + 3OH^\ominus$$
$$\text{tri-iodomethyl}$$
$$\text{ethyl ketone}$$
$$CI_3COC_2H_5 + OH^\ominus \rightarrow CHI_3 + C_2H_5CO_2^\ominus$$
$$\text{propionate ion}$$

The appearance of a pale yellow precipitate of iodoform in the conditions mentioned above is a very general and reliable test for the CH_3CHOH— group. (Thus, for example, of the four butyl alcohols, the secondary alcohol is the only one which responds to the test, and can rapidly be distinguished from the other isomers.)

Special reactions of certain —OH compounds

(1) Methanol

In general, methanol behaves as a primary alcohol in the same way as ethanol. It cannot, of course, yield an olefin on dehydration, but only dimethyl ether $CH_3.O.CH_3$. Dehydrogenation to formaldehyde:

$$CH_3OH \rightarrow HCHO + H_2$$
formaldehyde

is best carried out by passing the vapour *plus air* over a metallic catalyst at about 400° C. The hydrogen is then oxidized to water; the overall process is thus made exothermic (the simple dehydrogenation is endothermic) and the catalyst temperature is maintained.

Methanol is converted to the important ester *dimethyl sulphate* by first preparing methyl hydrogen sulphate, either by mixing methanol and excess of concentrated sulphuric acid, or by absorbing sulphur trioxide in ice-cooled methanol:

$$CH_3OH + HOSO_2OH \rightleftharpoons CH_3OSO_2OH + H_2O$$
$$CH_3OH + SO_3 \rightleftharpoons CH_3OSO_2OH$$

and then distilling this product

$$2CH_3OSO_2OH \rightarrow \begin{matrix} CH_3O \\ CH_3O \end{matrix}{>}SO_2 + H_2SO_4$$

Dimethyl sulphate is a liquid, dangerously poisonous both by skin absorption and by breathing the vapour. It is a valuable methylating agent, and can be used for many purposes in place of the more expensive methyl iodide. For example, phenol in aqueous alkali reacts with dimethyl sulphate on shaking to yield methyl phenyl ether by a Williamson synthesis (compare (2), p. 148).

$$C_6H_5O^\ominus + (CH_3)_2SO_4 \rightarrow C_6H_5OCH_3 \quad + \quad CH_3SO_4^\ominus$$
phenyl methyl ether (anisole) — (the methosulphate ion—the conjugate base of methyl hydrogen sulphate).

(2) Chlorination of ethanol

If chlorine is passed into ethanol, the ultimate product is the 'alcoholate' of trichloroacetaldehyde (chloral). In effect, the alcohol is oxidized, the acetaldehyde chlorinated and the trichloroacetaldehyde combines with a molecule of unchanged alcohol though the reactions do not necessarily occur in this order (see p. 136).

$$CH_3CH_2OH \rightarrow CH_3CHO \rightarrow CCl_3CHO \rightarrow CCl_3CH{<}\begin{matrix} OH \\ OC_2H_5 \end{matrix}$$

Chloral itself is obtained by distilling the alcoholate with sulphuric acid.

(3) Combustion of ethanol

Like almost all organic compounds, ethanol burns in air or oxygen with complete combustion yielding carbon dioxide and steam. As a readily available material, ethanol is therefore a possible fuel. Ethanol in small quantities has been used as an anti-knock additive to petrol.

The special aromatic substitution reactions of phenol and the phenate ion are dealt with in chapter 8.

Preparation of alcohols and phenols—introduction of the hydroxyl group into organic molecules

(1) By hydrolysis of halides

Alkyl halides and similar aliphatic halogen compounds yield alcohols on hydrolysis by refluxing with aqueous alkali, or even in some cases with water only, for example,

$$C_2H_5Br + OH^\ominus \rightarrow C_2H_5OH + Br^\ominus$$

Since the halogen atom can often be introduced by direct replacement of a hydrogen atom by the action of elementary chlorine or bromine, this is a useful route for replacing hydrogen by hydroxyl.

Simple nuclear aromatic halides are hydrolysed with great difficulty. Phenol can be made by heating chlorobenzene with aqueous sodium hydroxide at about 300° C.

$$C_6H_5Cl + OH^\ominus \rightarrow C_6H_5OH + Cl^\ominus$$

These reactions are discussed on p. 111.

(2) By the hydration of olefins

If olefins are absorbed in cold 98% sulphuric acid, and the product is diluted, alcohols are obtained. The effect is the addition of water to the olefin. The reaction is discussed on p. 58, and is the reverse of the dehydration of alcohols to olefins (see p. 134).

Ethylene yields ethanol. With other olefins, the addition follows Markovnikov's Rule, and thus, for example, propylene yields iso-propyl alcohol.

$$CH_3-CH=CH_2 + H_2O \rightarrow CH_3CHOHCH_3$$

This reaction is valuable for converting olefins from the cracking of petroleum fractions to technical secondary alcohols (which are in general therefore much more readily available than the isomeric primary alcohols).

Ethanol is now largely manufactured by the catalysed addition of steam to ethylene at 300° C and 70 atmospheres, over a supported phosphoric acid catalyst.

(3) By the reduction of carbonyl compounds

Aldehydes on reduction yield primary alcohols. Ketones yield secondary alcohols.

$$>C=O+2(H) \rightarrow >CHOH$$

Reduction can be carried out by a variety of methods including catalytic hydrogenation (the reverse of the catalytic dehydrogenation of alcohols) or, where reduction of another group in the molecule must be avoided, the Ponndorf–Meerwein reagent aluminium isopropoxide (see p. 187).

For example, catalytic hydrogenation of crotonaldehyde

$$CH_3CH=CH.CHO$$

(obtainable from aldol, see p. 181) will yield *n*-butyl alcohol

$$CH_3CH_2CH_2CH_2OH$$

but Ponndorf–Meerwein reduction yields the unsaturated alcohol

$$CH_3CH=CH.CH_2OH$$

More conventional chemical reducing agents for carbonyl compounds include sodium and ethanol, sodium amalgam and water, and other 'nascent hydrogen' type agents. A more recent and more effective reagent is sodium borohydride $NaBH_4$.

(4) By the action of nitrous acid on primary amines

If sodium nitrite is added to an acidified solution of a primary aliphatic amine and the mixture is warmed, the nitrous acid attacks the amine. Nitrogen is liberated, and among the products is the corresponding alcohol. For example, ethylamine will yield some ethanol.

$$CH_3CH_2NH_2+HNO_2 \rightarrow CH_3CH_2OH+N_2+H_2O$$

Several other reactions occur simultaneously, and yields are often poor. Moreover, with longer chain alkyl groups, isomerization occurs. Thus *n*-propylamine yields more iso-propyl than *n*-propyl alcohol.

The practical applicability of the method is therefore severely limited.

(5) By the use of Grignard reagents

These are dealt with in chapter 10.

(6) Preparation of phenols by the hydrolysis of diazonium salts

Primary *aromatic* amines when treated with acid and sodium nitrite in the cold yield diazonium salts (see p. 160). These on warming in aqueous solution yield phenols; the overall effect is therefore exactly analogous with method (4). Thus, for example, phenyl diazonium salts yield phenol:

$$(C_6H_5NH_2 \xrightarrow{HNO_2}) C_6H_5N_2^{\oplus} + H_2O \longrightarrow C_6H_5OH + N_2\uparrow + H^{\oplus}$$
$$\text{(aniline)} \qquad \text{(phenyl diazonium ion)}$$

Yields are sometimes only moderate, tarry by-products being formed.

Since a hydrogen atom of the benzene ring can be replaced by a nitro-group (see p. 89) and this reduced to a primary amino-group, the following sequence of reactions effects the introduction of —OH into the benzene ring.

$$C_6H_6 \xrightarrow[H_2SO_4]{HNO_3} C_6H_5NO_2 \xrightarrow[HClaq]{Sn} C_6H_5NH_2 \xrightarrow{HNO_2} C_6H_5N_2^{\oplus} \xrightarrow[warm]{H_2O} C_6H_5OH$$

The steps are too many and some of the reagents too costly for this to be a technical method of making phenol, but as a general laboratory method it has obvious advantages of convenience over (1) above or (7) below.

(7) Preparation of phenols from aromatic sulphuric acids by alkali fusion of sodium salts

If sodium benzene sulphonate is fused with sodium hydroxide, sodium phenate is formed.

$$C_6H_5SO_3^{\ominus} + OH^{\ominus} \rightarrow C_6H_5OH + SO_3^{2\ominus}$$
$$+ \Big| OH^{\ominus}$$
$$C_6H_5O^{\ominus} + H_2O$$

This was used in the traditional technical process for manufacturing phenol, now obsolete. The sequence of reactions is

$$C_6H_6 \xrightarrow{H_2SO_4} C_6H_5SO_3H \xrightarrow[\ (a)\ ]{base} C_6H_5SO_3^{\ominus} \xrightarrow[fuse]{NaOH} C_6H_5O^{\ominus} \xrightarrow[\ (b)\ ]{acid} C_6H_5OH$$

Some economy in materials is achieved by using sodium sulphite formed as an end-product for the base of stage (a) and the sulphur dioxide thus liberated for the acid of stage (b).

Processes have been patented for the direct oxidation of benzene to phenol by atmospheric oxygen, but they do not seem to be operated commercially.

The manufacture of methanol

Methanol was at one time a product of the destructive distillation of wood. It is now made by the catalytic hydrogenation of carbon monoxide over metallic oxide catalysts at about 300° C and 300 atmospheres.

$$CO + 2H_2 \longrightarrow CH_3OH$$

The manufacture of ethanol by fermentation of carbohydrates

The two main primary sources of carbohydrates for fermentation to industrial ethanol are starch (from grain or potatoes) and sucrose (from molasses). Glucose in fruit juices, especially grape juice, is the main source of ethanol in wines, and in the event of over-production, lower grade wines are sometimes distilled to yield industrial ethanol.

Sucrose and glucose solutions are fermented by the action of *yeast*, a unicellular plant which provides the essential enzymes. An *enzyme* is a complex protein or protein-like substance occurring in a natural organism and acting as a catalyst for the biochemical reactions involved in the life processes of the organism. The enzymes of yeast were the first to be recognized—hence the name, which is from the Greek, meaning simply 'in yeast'. The older name 'ferment' for an enzyme also refers to the example of yeast and its action on sugars, and the word 'fermentation' in a chemical context simply means a technical process carried out by the use of enzymes. Its everyday implications of turmoil or agitation arise from the agitation of the fermenting carbohydrate solution by the evolved bubbles of carbon dioxide. Sucrose is hydrolysed in the presence of the yeast enzyme invertase:

$$C_{12}H_{22}O_{11} + H_2O \rightarrow C_6H_{12}O_6 + C_6H_{12}O_6$$
$$\text{glucose} \quad \text{fructose}$$

to the isomeric sugars glucose and fructose; the so-called 'inversion of sucrose' (see p. 326). The glucose and fructose are converted to ethanol by a complex series of reactions catalysed by various enzymes in the yeast, known collectively as 'zymase'. The overall reaction is approximately

$$C_6H_{12}O_6 \rightarrow 2C_2H_5OH + 2CO_2$$

although some glycerol ($CH_2OH.CHOH.CH_2OH$) is always formed, and some ethanol is further oxidized to CO_2 and water.

If starch is the primary material for ethanol production, it must first be hydrolysed to the disaccharide maltose (an isomer of sucrose, $C_{12}H_{22}O_{11}$) which is then further hydrolysed to glucose. Yeast contains an enzyme (maltase) which catalyses this latter reaction:

$$C_{12}H_{22}O_{11} + H_2O \rightarrow 2C_6H_{12}O_6$$
$$\text{maltose} \quad\quad \text{glucose}$$

but not the enzyme diastase (or amylase) required for the hydrolysis of starch. The starch is therefore first treated in a warm aqueous suspension with either 'malt' or a suitable mould, both of which contain a diastase. ('Malt' is barley which has been allowed to germinate; its temperature is then raised sufficiently to kill the plant without destroying the enzyme.) The overall reaction is approximately

$$(C_6H_{10}O_5)_n + \frac{n}{2} H_2O \rightarrow \frac{n}{2} C_{12}H_{22}O_{11}$$
$$\text{starch} \qquad\qquad \text{maltose}$$

Yeast is then added to complete the conversion to ethanol as already described.

The dilute aqueous solution of ethanol so obtained is fractionally distilled; the distillate from the head of the column is approximately 95% ethanol, 5% water, which is nearly the composition of the constant boiling mixture or azeotrope of the two substances. The water can be removed on a large scale by adding benzene and redistilling. A ternary mixture of benzene, ethanol and water distils off first, followed by a mixture of alcohol and benzene, and finally almost pure alcohol, substantially water-free but containing traces of benzene. A description of the drying of 95% ethanol in the laboratory is given below.

The process of beer-making or brewing is substantially the formation of alcohol from barley-starch (and added sucrose) by the use of malt and yeast. Wine-making begins from the glucose in the grape-juice. In these cases there is no distillation stage. Whisky and gin are distilled from fermented grain, rum from fermented cane sugar (sucrose) and brandy from wine.

Dry ethanol

'Rectified spirit' contains about 5% water, and is adequate for many laboratory purposes where ethanol is required, either as reagent or solvent. In many reactions, however, water must be completely absent. It can be removed by first refluxing the moist ethanol with freshly burnt calcium oxide, then distilling off the alcohol and refluxing over metallic magnesium from which it is finally distilled. Dry ethanol is exceedingly hygroscopic and must be protected from atmospheric moisture.

The manufacture of phenol

Phenol can be manufactured from benzene via sulphonation or via chlorination, as already outlined. Substantial amounts of phenol and its homologues are recovered from suitable fractions of coal tar by extraction with alkali and reliberation by addition of acid (see p. 29).

Much phenol is now made by the oxidation of isopropyl benzene, or cumene:

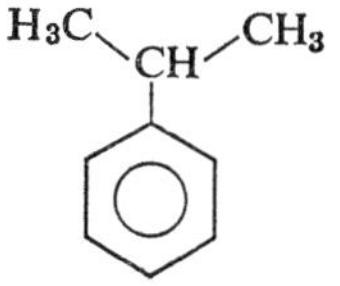

Benzene and propylene (from the cracking of petroleum) combine at high pressure and temperature over a catalyst such as phosphoric acid on kieselguhr.

$$C_6H_6 + CH_2=CH-CH_3 \rightarrow C_6H_5.CH(CH_3)_2$$

The cumene is then oxidized by air at high pressure to a peroxide which with sulphuric acid breaks down to phenol and acetone.

$$C_6H_5CH(CH_3)_2 + O_2 \rightarrow C_6H_5C(CH_3)_2.O.OH$$
$$\rightarrow C_6H_5OH + CH_3COCH_3$$

The presence of —OH in alcohols, etc.

Methanol (molecular formula CH_4O) must be formulated

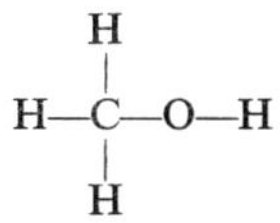

with a hydroxyl group if the elements present are taken to exert their normal valencies. This formulation is supported by the fact that:

(*a*) Only one hydrogen atom is 'replaced' when sodium reacts with methanol, indicating that one hydrogen atom is attached differently from the other three.

(*b*) The action of, for example, phosphorus and iodine yields CH_3I. That is, one oxygen and one hydrogen atom are together replaced by a single univalent atom, and hence they must be present as a single univalent group —O—H. Ethanol (C_2H_6O) shows precisely analogous behaviour, and must therefore be

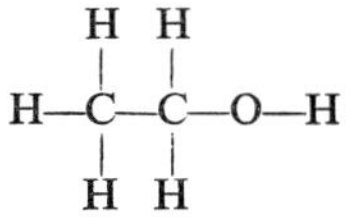

and not the alternative

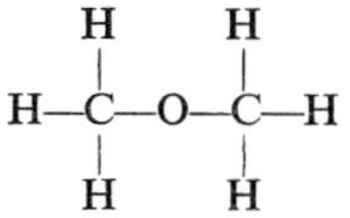

The characteristic reactions of —OH in methanol and ethanol can therefore be used to diagnose its presence in other molecules.

143

The ether group: $>C{-}O{-}C<$

Compounds containing the functional group $>C{-}O{-}C<$, whose molecules therefore consist of two alkyl or aryl groups linked via a single oxygen atom, are known as *ethers*. If the groups so linked are different, the compound is known as a *mixed ether*.

Nomenclature

Ethers are usually named from the two groups joined by the ether link; systematically, the names of these are placed in alphabetical order, but habit and euphony often lead to disregard of this rule. A few aromatic ethers have trivial names in fairly common use.

$$C_2H_5{-}O{-}C_2H_5$$ diethyl ether

$$CH_3{-}O{-}CH_2.CH_2.CH_3$$ methyl *n*-propyl ether

$O \cdot CH_3$ methyl phenyl ether (anisole)

$O \cdot C_2H_5$ ethyl phenyl ether (phenetole)

diphenyl ether

In everyday laboratory language, 'ether' unqualified means diethyl ether.

Physical properties

Dimethyl ether and methyl ethyl ether are gases at ordinary temperatures and pressures; diethyl ether is a very volatile liquid b.p. 35° C, with a vapour pressure of over half an atmosphere at ordinary temperatures. Anisole and phenetole are liquids, diphenyl ether a solid at ordinary temperatures; all three have pleasantly aromatic smells.

Diethyl ether has a limited but appreciable solubility in water (8%), and water in it (1%); hydrogen bonding must occur between the water molecules and the oxygen atoms of the ether molecules.

Ethers are isomeric with alcohols and phenols; thus the simple aliphatic ethers have the general formula $C_nH_{2n+2}O$. Ethers, as mentioned in the preceding chapter, are much more volatile than the isomeric alcohols, since hydrogen bonding is practically absent between ether molecules; compare the above value for diethyl ether with the boiling points of the butyl alcohols, which range from 83° C (tertiary) to 118° C (normal). The effective absence of hydrogen bonding is shown by the closeness of the b.p. of the ethers to those of the analogous paraffins with $-CH_2-$ in place of the isoelectronic $-O-$; compare diethyl ether and pentane, b.p. 36° C.

Chemical properties

Ethers are chemically unreactive substances. They are unattacked by metals at ordinary temperatures. Diethyl ether is used as a solvent for the preparation of Grignard reagents from magnesium and organic halides, and for this purpose is dried by standing over sodium. Ethers are extremely resistant to hydrolysis by aqueous alkali, or by dilute aqueous acid at ordinary pressures. Hydrolysis by dilute acids occurs at about 280° C under the appropriate pressure (about 120 atmospheres).

Reactions

(1) Base behaviour

Ether molecules are potentially basic on account of the unshared electron pairs of the oxygen atom. Diethyl ether is much more soluble in concentrated hydrochloric acid than in water, presumably because it forms diethyl oxonium ions:

$$(C_2H_5)_2O + H_3O^\oplus \rightleftharpoons (C_2H_5)\overset{\oplus}{O}H + H_2O$$

or

$$(C_2H_5)_2O + HCl \rightleftharpoons (C_2H_5)\overset{\oplus}{O}H + Cl^\ominus$$

No crystalline oxonium salts of the simple ethers can however be isolated at ordinary temperatures.

(2)   Fission by hydriodic acid

Ethers, as mentioned, resist hydrolysis by normal methods. Refluxing with constant-boiling hydriodic acid brings about fission of the ether molecule. Dialkyl ethers yield two molecules of alkyl iodide; alkyl aryl ethers yield a molecule of alkyl iodide and a molecule of phenol.

$$CH_3OCH_2CH_2CH_3 + 2HI \longrightarrow CH_3I + CH_3CH_2CH_2I + H_2O$$

Ethers may thus be identified by identifying the halides produced.

Many natural products, for example, the flavouring material vanillin:

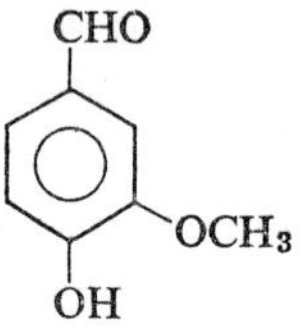

contain the methoxyl group attached to an aromatic nucleus. The fission of such aromatic methyl ethers by hydriodic acid is the basis of the *Zeisel method* for determining their methoxyl content. A known fraction of a mole of the substance is refluxed with constant-boiling hydriodic acid, and the methyl iodide formed is carried off in a stream of carbon dioxide and absorbed in aqueous-ethanolic silver nitrate solution. An alcoholate of silver iodide is precipitated; on adding excess of water, this is converted to silver iodide, which is filtered off and weighed. 1 mole of silver iodide (235 g) is obtained from 1 mole of methoxyl group; hence the number of methoxyl groups in one molecule of the ether is found. Hydrobromic acid brings about a similar fission.

(3)   Reaction with sulphuric acid

Ethers dissolve as bases in concentrated sulphuric acid, as in (1). On heating the solution the ether is slowly broken down to two molecules of alkyl hydrogen sulphate. For example,

$$C_2H_5 . O . CH_2CH_2CH_3 + 2H_2SO_4$$
$$\rightarrow C_2H_5OSO_2OH + CH_3CH_2CH_2OSO_2OH + H_2O$$

(4)   Oxidation

Ethers are combustible. Diethyl ether vapour and air form explosive mixtures; the flash point of ether is very low ($-4°$ C), and precautions to avoid igniting ether or ether vapour are stressed in every manual of practical chemistry.

Ethers exposed to air and light are liable to form small amounts of *peroxides*, probably of the type R—O—O—R. These are less volatile than the ether, and on distilling, are liable to become concentrated in the residue in the distillation flask, and may explode if heated too strongly. They may be removed by shaking with a ferrous salt solution, which reduces them.

Uses of ethers

Diethyl ether is a familiar and valuable laboratory solvent. Most organic substances are readily soluble in it (exceptions include those with a high proportion of —OH groups, such as glycerol) but do not react with it. As it has a low solubility in water, it can be used to extract organic substances from aqueous solution or suspension, leaving inorganic substances and strong electrolytes in the aqueous layer. Ether being so volatile, the solute can be recovered by distilling off the ether over a hot water bath.

Ether was one of the earliest anaesthetics used in surgery, and is still so used.

Diphenyl ether is a constituent of 'Dowtherm', a proprietary product of the Dow Chemical Co. with a melting point in the region of 180° C, which is used as a heating jacket fluid. It has a pleasant smell, and has been used in small quantities in scenting soap.

Preparation of ethers

(1) Dehydration of alcohols

Dialkyl ethers are made by heating alcohols with strong mineral acids; the mechanism of this reaction has been discussed on p. 13. Thus diethyl ether is obtained from ethanol by mixing it with concentrated sulphuric acid (in a mole ratio of about $2EtOH : 1H_2SO_4$), heating to about 120–140° C, and dropping in further ethanol. Since the function of the acid is essentially catalytic, the process can be operated continuously if conditions are adjusted so that the water produced distils off with the ether (and some unchanged ethanol).

Industrially, ethanol vapour is passed into a heated mixture of ethanol and sulphuric acid. Under these conditions, the heat of reaction is sufficient to vaporize the water formed.

Diaryl ethers cannot in general be made by this method. On the

147

mechanism postulated on p. 131, this is not unexpected, being comparable with the difficulty of displacing halogen from aryl halides by the attack of nucleophilic reagents.

(2) Williamson's synthesis

Ethers can be made by the action of the conjugate base of an alcohol or phenol on an alkyl halide, or similar alkylating agent (such as an alkyl sulphate or benzenesulphonate). For example, *n*-butyl ethyl ether is obtained by refluxing *n*-butyl bromide with a solution of sodium ethoxide in excess of ethanol:

$$C_4H_9Br + C_2H_5O^{\ominus} \rightarrow C_4H_9OC_2H_5 + Br^{\ominus}$$

Methyl phenyl ether is obtained by shaking aqueous sodium phenate solution with dimethyl sulphate:

This method is clearly well-adapted to the preparation of mixed ethers, which cannot be effectively made by method (1) above.

Diphenyl ether is obtained as a by-product of the preparation of phenol by the action of aqueous alkali on chlorobenzene under high pressure (see p. 111); presumably it is formed by the Williamson reaction of phenate ions with chlorobenzene under the drastic conditions used.

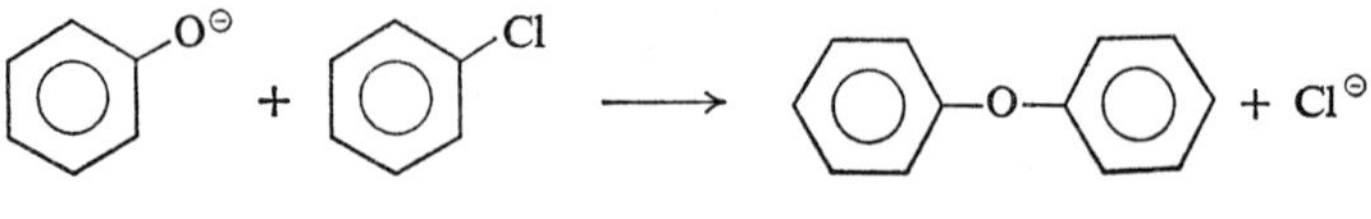

Cyclic ethers

These are compounds whose molecules contain an oxygen atom as part of a ring, the rest of which is made up of CH_2 groups. A few of the best known are shown below:

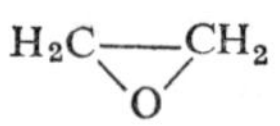

ethylene oxide 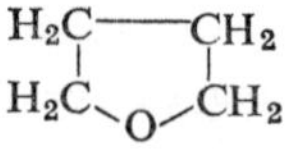   tetrahydrofuran 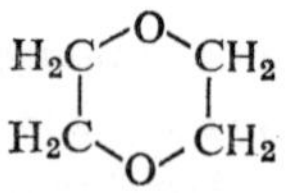   dioxan
                                                   (a cyclic diether)

Ethylene oxide is a gas (b.p. 11° C at 760 mm). At its boiling point it is miscible with water. Chemically it is considerably more reactive than the dialkyl ethers, as the following points will illustrate.

148

(1) Hydrolysis

Ethylene oxide is rapidly hydrolysed by warming with very dilute aqueous acid (e.g. $\frac{1}{2}\%$ aqueous sulphuric) under pressures only slightly greater than atmospheric. This is a step in one of the practicable methods for manufacturing ethylene glycol.

$$\begin{array}{c} CH_2-CH_2 \\ \diagdown \diagup \\ O \end{array} + H_2O \rightarrow CH_2OH.CH_2OH$$

(2) Ammonolysis

Ethylene oxide is ammonolysed to ethanolamine by fairly concentrated aqueous ammonia at about 60° C.

$$\begin{array}{c} CH_2-CH_2 \\ \diagdown \diagup \\ O \end{array} + NH_3 \rightarrow \underset{\text{monoethanolamine}}{CH_2OH.CH_2NH_2}$$

The ethanolamine formed itself reacts with ethylene oxide to form diethanolamine $(CH_2OH.CH_2)_2NH$ and this by a further step forms triethanolamine $(CH_2OH.CH_2)_3N$. Excess of ammonia will clearly disfavour these steps.

The ethanolamines are technically valuable as emulsifying agents and for synthetic purposes.

(3) Alcoholysis

Ethylene oxide reacts with ethanol at about 150–200° C under the appropriate pressure (about 10–20 atmospheres).

The main product is glycol monoethyl ether, a valuable solvent for cellulose esters.

$$\begin{array}{c} CH_2-CH_2 \\ \diagdown \diagup \\ O \end{array} + C_2H_5OH \rightarrow CH_2OH.CH_2OC_2H_5$$

Methanol and other alcohols behave similarly.

Ethylene oxide will also react with carboxylic acids in the presence of sulphuric acid to yield esters, and with Grignard reagents to yield alcohols of the general type $R.CH_2CH_2OH$. It is thus a useful substance in a variety of organic syntheses.

The comparative reactivity of ethylene oxide may well in part be a 'strain' effect in the three-membered ring, since tetrahydrofuran shows the same general inertness as the dialkyl ethers.

Ethylene oxide is obtained by:

   (a) the catalytic oxidation of ethylene by air in the presence of metallic silver.

(b) the hydrolysis of ethylene chlorohydrin with aqueous caustic alkali:

$$CH_2OH.CH_2Cl + OH^\ominus \rightarrow CH_2\!\!-\!\!CH_2 + H_2O + Cl^\ominus$$
$$\underset{O}{\diagdown\!\!\diagup}$$

As a technical method this is practically obsolete.

Analogous compounds (e.g. propylene oxide $CH_3.CH.CH_2$) can be

obtained from higher olefins by either method, and have analogous properties.

The presence of —O— in ethers

Alkyl ethers are isomeric with alcohols ($C_nH_{2n+2}O$), but show none of the reactions of the —OH group. They are therefore formulated as R—O—R^1. This is confirmed by:

(a) The Williamson synthesis from RO$^\ominus$ and R^{1}I or RI and R^{1}O$^\ominus$, and the fact that both yield the same ether (e.g. methyl iodide and sodium ethoxide and ethyl iodide and sodium methoxide yield the same product.)

(b) Fission by hydriodic acid to yield the alkyl iodides RI and R^{1}I.

The amino group: $-NH_2$

Compounds containing the $-NH_2$ group attached to an alkyl, aryl, or similar group are called *primary amines*. (As with other functional groups, when the NH_2 group is attached to the carbon atom of a carbonyl group to form the group $CONH_2$, its properties are so drastically modified that the resulting compounds are regarded as a different functional type, and are called *amides*.) Primary amines may be regarded as derivatives of ammonia in which one H atom has been replaced by an organic radical, and the older nomenclature is based on this, the name 'amine' (standing for ammonia) being prefixed by the name of the substituting group.

Systematic nomenclature indicates the NH_2 group and its point of attachment to the skeleton by the prefix 'amino' with the appropriate numeral or letter. Thus:

CH_3NH_2	methylamine	aminomethane
$CH_3.CH_2NH_2$	ethylamine	aminoethane
$CH_3.CH_2.CH_2NH_2$	n-propylamine	1-aminopropane
$CH_3.CH(NH_2)CH_3$	iso-propylamine	2-aminopropane
(ring)$-NH_2$	phenylamine	aminobenzene aniline
(ring with CH_3)$-NH_2$	o-tolylamine o-aminotoluene	1-methyl-2-aminobenzene o-toluidine
(ring)$-CH_2NH_2$	benzylamine	α-aminomethylbenzene

The underlined names are those in common use.

Secondary and tertiary amines have respectively two and three of the hydrogen atoms of the parent NH_3 molecule replaced by organic radicals, thus:

$CH_3NHCH_2CH_3$
ethylmethylamine

—$NHCH_3$
N-methylaniline

secondary amines

CH_3
CH_3CH_2—N
$CH_3CH_2CH_2$
ethylmethyl
n-propylamine

—$N(CH_3)_2$
NN-dimethylaniline

tertiary amines

The prefix *N*-, not to be confused with *n*-, indicates that the substituent group is attached to the nitrogen atom and not to a carbon atom of the parent compound. It is often omitted where no ambiguity arises; thus the name methylaniline is adequate, since a derivative of aniline in which CH_3— replaces H— attached to carbon is called a toluidine.

Notice that secondary and tertiary amines do *not* contain the amino group, and also that the use of the terms 'primary', 'secondary' and 'tertiary' is different from their use in the alcohol series.

Physical and physiological properties of the primary amines

Of the alkylamines, methylamine and ethylamine are gases at ordinary temperatures and pressures and are highly soluble in water (methylamine at $0°$ C has the highest solubility of any gas). Higher members are liquids, then solids, their solubilities falling off with increasing molecular weight. This high solubility of the lower alkylamines can be compared with the high solubility of ammonia in water, and with the high solubility of the lower aliphatic alcohols, and in all cases is associated with the hydrogen-bonding between the —NH_2 or —OH groups and the water molecules.

Of the more familiar amines containing benzene rings, benzylamine, aniline and *o*-toluidine are liquids at ordinary temperatures; *p*-toluidine is a solid. They are much less soluble in water than the lowest aliphatic amines though they are still somewhat soluble. This is partly a matter of higher molecular weight, making for lower solubility. Another factor is that amines with —NH_2 attached to the benzene ring are much less soluble than their isomers with —NH_2 in the side chain.

The lower alkylamines have notorious 'fishy-ammonia' smells. Benzylamine has a similar smell. When the amino group is attached directly to a benzene ring, the smell is quite different, though characteristic.

Aniline is markedly toxic by absorption through the skin.

Reactions of primary amines

The reactions of primary amines reveal that the dominant feature of their chemistry is the nucleophilic character of the NH_2 group, with the unshared electron pair of the nitrogen atom.

$$R : \overset{\overset{\text{H}}{\cdot\cdot}}{\underset{\overset{\cdot\cdot}{\text{H}}}{\text{N}}} :$$

This is shown in the markedly basic character of the amines and in their acylation and alkylation reactions.

By contrast, acid behaviour (loss of a proton from the $-NH_2$ group) is only exceptionally shown. Replacement of the NH_2 by other groups is confined in elementary chemistry to the reactions with nitrous acid.

(1) The basic character of amino-compounds

All primary amines are bases, undergoing reactions of the general type:

$$RNH_2 + HA \rightleftharpoons R\overset{\oplus}{N}H_3 + A^{\ominus}$$
$$\text{conjugate}$$
$$\text{acid of the amine}$$

The simpler alkylamines are only a little stronger as bases than ammonia (K_B of the order of 10^{-4}). The lower members of the series are highly soluble in water, presumably, like ammonia on account of hydrogen bonding, and their solutions are markedly alkaline, e.g.

$$C_2H_5NH_2 + H_2O \rightleftharpoons C_2H_5NH_3^{\oplus} + OH^{\ominus}$$

The actual degree of ionization of the base is small, the above value of K_B signifying that the equilibrium is well to the left. With acids, they form well-defined crystalline salts; e.g. ethylamine yields ethylammonium salts:

$$C_2H_5NH_2 + HCl \rightarrow C_2H_5NH_3^{\oplus}Cl^{\ominus}$$
$$\text{ethylammonium chloride}$$

Ethylamine and other volatile amines therefore show the characteristic 'white cloud' with hydrogen chloride (or any other acid in the vapour state at moderate temperatures) in the same way and for the same reason as ammonia itself. These salts are often known by obsolete or loose names (e.g. ethylammonium chloride as ethylamine hydrochloride; ethylammonium sulphate as ethylamine sulphate).

Like simple ammonium salts, these salts dissociate in the vapour phase on heating

$$C_2H_5NH_3^{\oplus}Cl^{\ominus} \rightleftharpoons \underbrace{C_2H_5NH_2 + HCl}_{\text{vapour phase}}$$

and are only feebly acidic in aqueous solution. (Since K_B for ethylamine is $5 \cdot 6 \times 10^{-4}$ and K_W is 10^{-14} at $25°$ C, K_A for the ethylammonium ion is $1 \cdot 8 \times 10^{-11}$.)

The salts of the lower aliphatic amines are as a rule highly soluble in water, but more soluble in ethanol than the corresponding ammonium salts. The solids have ionic lattices, and they behave as strong electrolytes in aqueous solution.

Benzylamine, with the amino group in the *side chain* of an aromatic radical, is similar to the simple alkylamines in basic character and salt formation.

Direct attachment to a carbon atom of an aromatic ring greatly reduces the basic strength of the NH_2 *group.* Thus K_B for aniline $C_6H_5NH_2$ is 4×10^{-10} and hence K_A for the conjugate acid, the phenylammonium or anilinium ion, is $2 \cdot 5 \times 10^{-5}$—very close to that for acetic acid.

This marked fall in basic strength can be accounted for by assuming that the unshared electron pair of the nitrogen atom is partly involved in bonding the nitrogen to the aromatic ring.

On the general principle that the 'relocalization' of delocalized electron pairs requires the input of energy, it is clear that such energy will have to be supplied in this case to render the lone pair of the nitrogen atom available for base behaviour. This should be compared with the explanation of the weakness of the phenate ion as a base in comparison with alkoxide ions (see p. 128).

Although aniline forms well-defined salts with the strong mineral acids:

$$C_6H_5NH_2 + HCl \rightleftharpoons C_6H_5\overset{\oplus}{N}H_3Cl^{\ominus}$$
phenylammonium chloride
('aniline hydrochloride')

these salts are quite strongly acidic in aqueous solution, with pH approximately equal to that of an acetic acid solution of the same molarity. They can therefore be titrated with aqueous alkali, using phenolphthalein as indicator.

The acid behaviour of ammonium and organic substituted ammonium salts is often referred to as 'hydrolysis' of the salt, and K_A for the cation is identical with the so-called 'hydrolysis constant' of a salt of the amine with a strong acid.

154

A salt such as phenylammonium acetate, derived from a weak acid and a very weak base (aniline), will be roughly 50% hydrolysed in aqueous solution; contrast ethylammonium acetate, about 1% hydrolysed in molar aqueous solution.

The amines, both aliphatic and aromatic, are liberated from their salts by the addition of aqueous alkali, e.g.

$$C_6H_5\overset{\oplus}{N}H_3+OH^\ominus \to C_6H_5NH_2+H_2O$$

Aniline and its homologues, being sparingly water-soluble, form a separate non-aqueous layer; the lower alkylamines are water-soluble but volatile, and can therefore be driven off by heating, just as ammonia can in the same circumstances.

(2) Alkylation of amines

This is the conversion of RNH_2 to $RR'NH$ (and to $RR'R''N$, and ultimately to $RR'R''R'''N^\oplus$) where R', etc. are alkyl groups. This will be illustrated by a discussion of *methylation* (R', R'', R''' all $= CH_3$). The points made will apply to alkylation generally, bearing in mind the greater sluggishness of the higher alkyl halides and allied reagents, and of bromides (and, *a fortiori*, chlorides) compared with iodides.

As already stated in chapter 10, primary amines, like ammonia itself, react with methyl iodide to form substituted ammonium iodides. Thus, with ethylamine:

$$C_2H_5NH_2+CH_3I \to \begin{array}{c} C_2H_5 \\ CH_3 \end{array}\!\!\!\!\!>\overset{\oplus}{N}H_2+I^\ominus$$

ethylmethylammonium iodide (ethylmethylamine hydriodide) is formed, and with aniline

$$C_6H_5NH_2+CH_3I \to \begin{array}{c} C_6H_5 \\ CH_3 \end{array}\!\!\!\!\!>\overset{\oplus}{N}H_2+I^\ominus$$

phenylmethylammonium iodide (methylaniline hydriodide).

(Under practical conditions ammonia and volatile amines such as ethylamine react easily in ethanolic solution in a sealed vessel. Aniline and methyl iodide react readily on mixing and warming.)

As with all substituted ammonium salts having at least one hydrogen atom attached to the nitrogen atom, the cations of these salts are weak acids. On dissolving the reaction product in water and adding alkali, therefore, the conjugate base is regenerated:

$$\underset{CH_3}{\overset{C_2H_5}{>}}\overset{\oplus}{N}H_2 + OH^\ominus \rightarrow \underset{CH_3}{\overset{C_2H_5}{>}}NH + H_2O$$

ethylmethylamine

$$\underset{CH_3}{\overset{C_6H_5}{>}}\overset{\oplus}{N}H_2 + OH^\ominus \rightarrow \underset{CH_3}{\overset{C_6H_5}{>}}NH + H_2O$$

N-methylaniline

(Compare the action of alkali on ammonium salts.) The water-soluble but volatile ethylmethylamine could be distilled off; the sparingly soluble methylaniline will form a separate layer. Sodium iodide will remain in the aqueous solution.

The *net result* of the action of methyl iodide followed by the addition of alkali is therefore the replacement of one hydrogen atom in the original primary amine by a methyl radical, thus producing a secondary amine; hence the term 'alkylation' applied to the reaction.

The reaction is accompanied by an inconvenient complication. As the secondary ammonium salt is formed, an acid–base equilibrium with unchanged primary amine is bound to be established by simple proton transfer:

$$\underset{CH_3}{\overset{C_2H_5}{>}}\overset{\oplus}{N}H_3 + C_2H_5NH_2 \rightleftharpoons \underset{CH_3}{\overset{C_2H_5}{>}}NH_2 + C_2H_5\overset{\oplus}{N}H_3$$

The reaction mixture will therefore contain the free secondary amine as well as the primary amine, and the side reaction,

$$C_2H_5NHCH_3 + CH_3I \rightarrow \underset{CH_3}{\overset{C_2H_5}{>}}\overset{\oplus}{N}\underset{CH_3}{\overset{H}{<}} + I^\ominus$$

will occur. This in turn will yield some free tertiary amine leading to the further side reaction:

$$C_2H_5N(CH_3)_2 + CH_3I \rightarrow \underset{CH_3}{\overset{C_2H_5}{>}}\overset{\oplus}{N}\underset{CH_3}{\overset{CH_3}{<}} + I^\ominus$$

This *quaternary* ammonium ion has no hydrogen attached to nitrogen, and is therefore *not* an acid, so the process stops here. Even therefore if molar proportions of amine and alkyl halide are mixed, the product will contain primary, secondary, tertiary and quaternary ammonium compounds, and some separation will have to be devised (see p. 250).

Methyl iodide is a relatively costly reagent, but there are alternatives. The disadvantages of methyl bromide and chloride have been discussed in chapter 10. Methyl sulphate is rapid, cheap and convenient, but highly toxic. It reacts thus:

$$C_6H_5NH_2 + (CH_3O)_2SO_2 \rightarrow \underset{CH_3}{\overset{C_6H_5}{>}} \overset{\oplus}{N}H_3 + CH_3OSO_3^{\ominus}$$

The methyl esters of aromatic sulphonic acids (e.g. methyl *p*-toluene-sulphonate $CH_3 - \langle\bigcirc\rangle - SO_2OCH_3$) are also effective.

N-methylaniline and *NN*-dimethylaniline are technically important. The *technical* methylation of aniline to yield these compounds is carried out by heating aniline hydrochloride and methanol in sealed vessels.

(3) Acylation of amines: conversion of the amine RNH² to RNH.COR′

This reaction achieves the replacement of an hydrogen atom of the NH_2 group by an *acyl* group $R'CO$.

In general acylation can be carried out by four characteristic reagent types. These are, in order of decreasing vigour of reaction:

acyl chlorides	$R'COCl$
acid anhydrides	$(R'CO)_2O$
carboxylic acids	$R'CO_2H$
carboxylate esters, e.g.	$R'CO_2C_2H_5$

Thus for the acetylation of ethylamine, the four possible reactions would be:

$$C_2H_5NH_2 + CH_3COCl \rightarrow C_2H_5NH.COCH_3 + HCl$$
$$C_2H_5NH_2 + (CH_3CO)_2O \rightarrow C_2H_5NH.COCH_3 + CH_3CO_2H$$
$$C_2H_5NH_2 + CH_3CO_2H \rightarrow C_2H_5NH.COCH_3 + H_2O$$
$$C_2H_5NH_2 + CH_3CO_2C_2H_5 \rightarrow C_2H_5NH.COCH_3 + C_2H_5OH$$

Acetic acid or hydrochloric acid will of course form salts with some unchanged amine.

The reaction is in each case exactly comparable with the conversion of the reagent in question to the amide by the action of ammonia (see chapter 15), and the products with amines can be regarded not only as acylamines, but also as alkyl (or aryl) amides. Thus $CH_3CONH.C_2H_5$ is *N*-acetylethylamine or *N*-ethylacetamide; $CH_3CONH.C_6H_5$ is *N*-acetyl-aniline or *N*-phenylacetamide (its usual laboratory name is acetanilide).

By selecting a suitable acyl group, a liquid or gaseous amine can be converted to a crystalline *N*-acyl derivative, whose melting point after purification may be used to characterize the original amine.

Practical considerations. For elementary students, practical experience of the acylation of amines is normally confined to the acetylation and benzoylation of aniline and its immediate homologues.

Acetylation of aniline. (*a*) By acetyl chloride.

Aniline and acetyl chloride react violently on mixing in the cold.

$$C_6H_5NH_2 + CH_3COCl \rightarrow C_6H_5NH.COCH_3 + HCl$$

Some diacetyl derivative ($C_6H_5N(COCH_3)_2$), may be formed. Acetyl chloride is an unnecessarily vigorous reagent here.

(*b*) By acetic anhydride.

If aniline is mixed with acetic anhydride, the mixture becomes hot as acetylation (exothermic) occurs; the reaction mixture may be further heated to complete the process. Acetanilide crystallizes on cooling (and, if necessary, scratching).

$$C_6H_5NH_2 + (CH_3CO)_2O \rightarrow C_6H_5NH.COCH_3 + CH_3CO_2H$$

Refluxing with a mixture of equal volumes of acetic anhydride and glacial acetic acid is sometimes recommended.

Aniline may be acetylated cleanly and smoothly in a few seconds by adding acetic anhydride to an aqueous suspension of aniline, with shaking. The use of concentrated sodium acetate solution instead of water, possibly as a basic catalyst, is sometimes recommended.

Acetic anhydride is the obvious reagent to choose when an aromatic amine is to be characterized by the melting point of its acetyl derivatives.

(*c*) By acetic acid.

If aniline is refluxed with glacial acetic acid, acetylation occurs smoothly but slowly.

$$C_6H_5NH_2 + CH_3CO_2H \rightarrow C_6H_5NH.COCH_3 + H_2O$$

This method has two applications:

(i) if an unknown carboxylic acid is used in place of the acetic acid, it can be characterized by the melting point of the resulting anilide.

(ii) Acetic acid being a much cheaper reagent than acetic anhydride, this method is the first choice for technical acetylation; e.g. protection of the NH_2 group (see below).

(*d*) Ethyl acetate has no appreciable action on aniline, though it converts ethylamine slowly to *N*-ethylacetamide.

Apart from its use for characterization, acetylation is used for the so-called 'protection' of the amino group. Acetanilide is in many cases a much less uncontrollably reactive substance than aniline. For example, it can be smoothly chlorosulphonated with chlorosulphonic acid, whereas aniline, owing to the reactivity of the NH_2 group to acid chlorides in general, cannot.

$$NH \cdot COCH_3 \qquad\qquad NH \cdot COCH_3$$

$$\underset{\text{(ring)}}{\bigcirc} + 2HOSO_2Cl \longrightarrow \underset{\substack{\text{(ring)}\\ SO_2Cl}}{\bigcirc} + HCl + H_2SO_4$$

After subsequent synthesis stages, the acetyl group may be removed by hydrolysis with hot aqueous mineral acid.

$$-NH.COCH_3 + H_2O \rightarrow -NH_2 + CH_3CO_2H$$
$$\left(\overset{H^{\oplus}\downarrow}{-N^{\oplus}H_3} \right)$$

Similarly, acetanilide can be smoothly nitrated, and the nitro-acetanilides hydrolysed to *o*- and *p*-nitroaniline and acetic acid.

Benzoylation of aniline. Aniline is usually benzoylated by shaking with an equimolar quantity of benzoyl chloride in suspension in roughly 2M aqueous sodium hydroxide solution. (Schotten-Baumann method; compare benzoylation of phenol p. 133.)

The alkali, in addition to neutralizing the acid liberated in the reaction:

$$C_6H_5NH_2 + C_6H_5COCl \rightarrow C_6H_5NH.COC_6H_5 + HCl$$
benzanilide
(N-phenylbenzamide)

may act as a catalyst, but in fact, aniline and benzoyl chloride, like aniline and acetic anhydride, react rapidly in suspension in water alone.

Benzoyl derivatives often have higher melting points than the corresponding acetyl derivatives, and thus may be more suitable for characterizing an amine whose acetyl derivative is low-melting.

Mechanism of alkylation and acylation. Although it is less obviously the case than with salt formation, both alkylation and acylation are, from the point of view of the amine, the consequence of its nucleophilic behaviour. This behaviour results from the tendency of the unshared electron pair on the nitrogen atom to become shared. In methylation, for example, this pair becomes a shared-pair covalent bond with the carbon atom of the methyl group, while the pair which originally bonded this atom to the iodine atom has been totally transferred to the latter to form an iodide ion:

$$\geq N: \quad CH_3 - I \longrightarrow \geq \overset{\oplus}{N} - CH_3 + I^{\ominus}$$

This type of reaction has been discussed in detail in chapter 10.

Acylation involves the attack of the unshared pair of the nitrogen atom on the carbon atom of the $>C=O$ group of the acylating agent. Acylation in general, including the acylation of amines, is discussed in chapter 15.

(4)   Reactions of amines with nitrous acid

Amines react with nitrous acid in various ways. With simple aliphatic primary amines, replacement of —NH_2 by—OH with evolution of nitrogen, is among the reactions occurring. With ethylamine, ethanol is among the products:

$$C_2H_5NH_2 + HONO \rightarrow C_2H_5OH + N_2\uparrow + H_2O$$

Since nitrous acid is unstable it must be generated where the reaction is actually taking place by the action of another acid (a mineral acid or acetic acid) on a nitrite. In the acidic solution, the amine will be present very largely, but not entirely, as the conjugate acid. Nitrogen is evolved freely on warming.

As a diagnostic test for primary amines the reaction has two drawbacks:

(*a*) Effervescence will occur whether an amino compound is present or not, since the nitrous acid decomposes:

$$3HNO_2 \rightarrow H_2O + 2NO\uparrow + HNO_3$$

This will occur to some extent in any case. For test purposes, comparison with a 'blank' is essential, and may well be indecisive.

(*b*) A number of side-reactions occur and, in particular, the reaction with higher amines is notoriously accompanied by isomerization. Thus the action of nitrous acid on *n*-propylamine $CH_3CH_2CH_2NH_2$ produces not only *n*-propyl alcohol $CH_3CH_2CH_2OH$ but also isopropyl alcohol $CH_3CHOHCH_3$ and propylene $CH_3.CH{=}CH_2$.

Side chain aromatic amines such as benzylamine behave in the same way as alkylamines with nitrous acid.

When the amino group is attached directly to the carbon atom of an aromatic ring (as e.g. in aniline) the action of nitrous acid in the cold yields a diazonium salt. Diazonium salts *cannot* be obtained from aliphatic or side-chain aromatic amines. This reaction is one of the most striking features of aromatic behaviour.

Thus with aniline, a phenyldiazonium salt is formed. The reaction is called 'diazotization' of the amine, and is represented by the overall equation:

phenyldiazonium ion

Aniline itself reacts fairly rapidly with phenyldiazonium ions to give a product called diazoaminobenzene (see p. 269).

$$C_6H_5N_2{}^{\oplus} + C_6H_5NH_2 \rightleftharpoons C_6H_5{-}N{=}N{-}NHC_6H_5 + H^{\oplus}$$

The reaction is reversible and is disfavoured by acid. Diazotization itself is fairly slow, but not reversible. To avoid forming diazoaminobenzene therefore, diazotization is carried out in acidic solution (in which the aniline will be present very largely but not entirely as its conjugate acid, the anilinium ion). Since diazonium salts decompose in aqueous solution, the reaction must be carried out below temperatures at which this decomposition is too rapid. For aniline and its immediate homologues, it is advisable not to exceed 10° C. Since diazotization is fairly slow, and like all reactions is slower at lower temperatures, the temperature must not be too low; for aniline, not much below 5° C.

These requirements determine the usual conditions for diazotizing aniline. In mole ratios, a solution of 1 part of aniline in at least 2·5 parts of aqueous hydrochloric or sulphuric acid is cooled to 5° C, and a solution of about 1·1 parts of sodium nitrite is slowly added with stirring, keeping the temperature below 10° C. (The excess of nitrite allows for some decomposition of the nitrous acid.) Too great an excess of nitrous acid oxidizes the aniline and must be avoided. The resulting solution contains the phenyldiazonium salt.

On warming diazonium salt solutions, nitrogen is evolved and the corresponding phenol (together with tarry by-products) is formed. For example,

$$C_6H_5\overset{\oplus}{N}_2 + H_2O \rightarrow C_6H_5OH + N_2{\uparrow} + H^{\oplus}$$

The *overall* effect of diazotizing aniline and warming the resulting solution is therefore:

$$C_6H_5NH_2 + HONO \rightarrow C_6H_5OH + N_2{\uparrow} + H_2O$$

which is analogous with the above action of nitrous acid on primary aliphatic amines.

Although the aniline is almost all present as anilinium ion during diazotization, kinetic studies leave little doubt that it is the free base which takes part in the reaction.

The structure of the diazonium ion and the applications of diazotization are discussed in chapter 19.

Preparation of primary amines—introduction of the amino group into organic molecules

(1) Ammonolysis of halogen compounds

A general method of wide application for preparing primary amines may be summarized by the equations:

$$RX + NH_3 \rightarrow R\overset{\oplus}{N}H_3 + X^{\ominus} \quad (X = Cl, Br, I)$$
$$R\overset{\oplus}{N}H_3 + OH^{\ominus} \rightarrow RNH_2 + H_2O$$

That is, the action of ammonia on a halogen compound yields an organic primary ammonium halide, which is converted to the free base by alkali (or by excess of ammonia, if RNH_2 is markedly weaker than ammonia as a base). With alkyl halides and side-chain aromatic halides this proceeds readily. Thus ethylamine is obtained when alcoholic ammonia and ethyl bromide are heated in a sealed tube and the product is made alkaline with sodium hydroxide solution.

$$C_2H_5Br + NH_3 \rightarrow C_2H_5\overset{\oplus}{N}H_3 + Br^{\ominus}$$
$$C_2H_5\overset{\oplus}{N}H_3 + OH^{\ominus} \rightarrow C_2H_5NH_2 + H_2O$$

The reaction has been discussed in chapter 10, and the complications leading to secondary, tertiary and quaternary ammonium salts have been dealt with above. These complications seriously limit the preparative value of the method for simple amines, but it is effective for some amino acids (see chapter 20).

Ammonolysis of aryl halides, like their hydrolysis, proceeds with great difficulty. Aniline can be obtained technically from chlorobenzene by heating with aqueous ammonia at 200° C and 50 atmospheres in the presence of cuprous salts as catalysts.

$$C_6H_5Cl + 2NH_3 \rightarrow C_6H_5NH_2 + NH_4Cl$$

Since aniline is a much weaker base than ammonia, the phenylammonium ion will not persist in the solution. Conversion of chlorobenzene to aniline is about 90% of the theoretical, phenol and diphenylamine $(C_6H_5)_2NH$ being by-products.

(2) Use of potassium phthalimide

A synthesis of primary aliphatic and side-chain aromatic amines which avoids the further reaction steps of direct ammonolysis is that due to Gabriel.

Phthalimide NH is a very weak acid (see p. 251) and yields

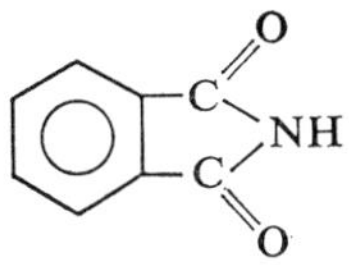

a potassium salt:

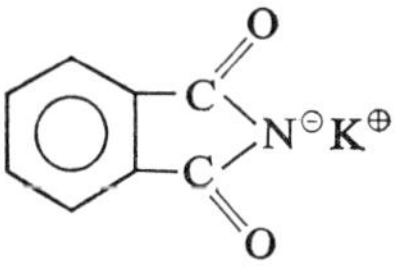

This on heating with an alkyl halide performs a typical displacement reaction:

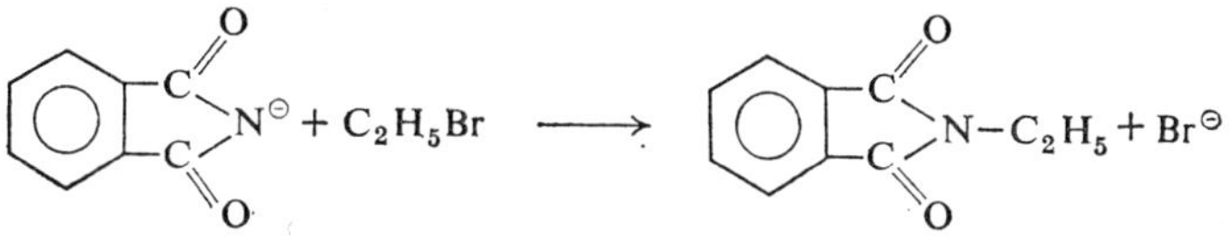

N-ethylphthalimide

The N-alkylphthalimide can be hydrolysed liberating the amine.

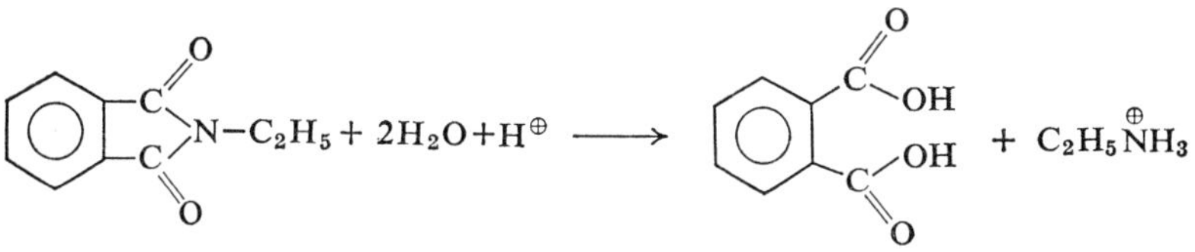

(Boiling with strong aqueous mineral acid is usually needed; free phthalic acid and the alkyl ammonium ion are formed. Excess alkali will then liberate the amine.) Since the other two bonds of the tercovalent nitrogen

atom are occupied by the 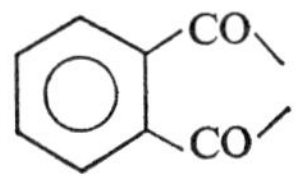 which is only removed in the

final hydrolysis, it is clear that only one alkyl radical can become attached to the nitrogen atom by this method.

Both simple ammonolysis and the Gabriel method are applicable to the synthesis of amino-acids from halogeno acids (see p. 283).

Since halogen atoms can be introduced into organic molecules by a variety of methods (see chapter 10), the above reactions can be adapted to obtain primary amines from a corresponding variety of source materials.

(3) Reduction methods

Since the amino group represents the most highly reduced state of nitrogen attached to carbon, the reduction of other functional types containing nitrogen atoms linked to one carbon atom will yield primary amines.

The most useful subjects for reduction to primary amines are:

Nitro compounds $R—NO_2$

oximes $\underset{R'}{\overset{R}{>}}C{=}NOH$ (R′ = H in aldoximes)

cyanides $R—C{\equiv}N$

amides $R—CONH_2$

The applicability of these to amine synthesis depends on the availability of methods of introducing these functional groups into organic compounds.

(*a*) *Reduction of nitro-compounds.* Simple aliphatic nitro-compounds are usually made by the action of inorganic nitrites on halogen compounds (see chapter 10). Their reduction to amines offers no great advantage over ammonolysis or the Gabriel method. However, paraffins *can* be nitrated directly (see chapter 4) and the reduction of these nitro-compounds could be a technical source of alkylamines should their development warrant it. Useful reducing agents are metal and acid, or hydrogen with a Raney nickel catalyst. Since aromatic compounds are usually readily nitrated (see chapter 8) this method is readily applicable to the production of amines with NH_2 attached to an aromatic ring, and is the most useful of all methods for doing this.

Aniline is readily obtained from nitrobenzene in the laboratory by reducing it with tin and hydrochloric acid. Formally:

$$Sn \rightarrow Sn^{2\oplus} + 2e$$
$$Sn^{2\oplus} \rightarrow Sn^{4\oplus} + 2e$$
$$C_6H_5NO_2 + 6H^{\oplus} + 6e \rightarrow C_6H_5NH_2 + 2H_2O$$
$$C_6H_5NH_2 + H^{\oplus} \rightleftharpoons C_6H_5\overset{\oplus}{N}H_3$$

Under acid conditions, the phenylammonium ion is formed, from which aniline is liberated by excess alkali and isolated by steam distillation.

(The operations, though not the organic chemistry, are complicated by the transformations of the tin atom which occur concurrently. In the excess of chloride ion present, hexachlorostannate ions are formed:

$$Sn^{4\oplus} + 6Cl^{\ominus} \rightarrow SnCl_6{}^{2\ominus}$$

If the mixture after reduction is left to stand, phenylammonium hexa-chlorostannate, $(C_6H_5\overset{\oplus}{N}H_3)_2SnCl_6{}^{2\ominus}$, crystallizes out. On adding alkali, the tin is first precipitated as hydrated stannic oxide, $Sn(OH)_4$ or $SnO_2.xH_2O$, and then partly redissolves in further alkali as the stannate ion:

$$Sn(OH)_4 + 2OH^{\ominus} \rightarrow Sn(OH)_6{}^{2\ominus})$$

Tin is far too costly a reagent for the large-scale technical reduction of nitrobenzene. This is carried out with scrap-iron turnings in the presence of a small quantity of dilute hydrochloric acid. The iron appears to be oxidized to hydrated Fe_3O_4, in which case the formal material balance would be:

$$4C_6H_5NO_2 + 9Fe + 4H_2O \xrightarrow{\text{H}^{\oplus}} 4C_6H_5NH_2 + 3Fe_3O_4$$

(*b*) *Reduction of oximes*. Aldoximes and ketoximes (see chapter 14) are readily reduced by such reagents as sodium amalgam in weakly acid conditions. For example, formally:

$$Na \rightarrow Na^{\oplus} + e$$

$$\underset{\text{benzaldoxime}}{C_6H_5CH{=}NOH} + 4H^{\oplus} + 4e \rightarrow \underset{\text{benzylamine}}{C_6H_5CH_2NH_2} + H_2O$$

$$\underset{\text{acetoxime}}{(CH_3)_2C{=}NOH} + 4H^{\oplus} + 4e \rightarrow \underset{\text{isopropylamine}}{(CH_3)_2CHNH_2} + H_2O$$

The reduction of aldoximes will yield primary amines of the type $R.CH_2NH_2$, which can also be obtained by the reduction of cyanides. Ketoximes yield amines of the type $\dfrac{R}{R'}{>}CHNH_2$, where R and R' may be the same or different. Ketones can be made by a variety of methods (see chapter 14); this is often the neatest route to amines of this type.

(*c*) *Reduction of cyanides (nitriles)*. Organic cyanides (nitriles) are readily reduced by a variety of agents, such as sodium and alcohol or by catalytic hydrogenation, to amines of the general type $R.CH_2NH_2$. For example,

$$C_6H_5CN + 4H^{\oplus} + 4e \rightarrow C_6H_5CH_2NH_2$$

$$CH_3CH_2CN + 4H^{\oplus} + 4e \rightarrow CH_3CH_2CH_2NH_2$$

Since nitriles can be made by a variety of methods, this is a versatile route to amines of this type. However yields may be reduced by the formation of secondary amines and other by-products. Notice that if the nitrile is made by introducing the —CN group (e.g. by the action of potassium cyanide on an alkyl halide) then the final amine contains one more carbon atom per NH_2 group than the starting material.

(*d*) *Reduction of amides*. Amides, of course, contain the NH_2 group and can be obtained from carboxylic acids and their derivatives (see chapter 15). Their reduction to primary amines,

$$R.CONH_2 + 4H \rightarrow RCH_2NH_2 + H_2O$$

is not practicable with any classical reagents, but can be effected smoothly in some cases by lithium aluminium hydride.

165

(4)   The Hofmann degradation $R.CONH_2 \rightarrow RNH_2$

Amides are converted to amines containing one less carbon atom per molecule by the action of bromine and caustic alkali. The usual procedure is to add bromine to the amide followed by sufficient aqueous alkali to discharge the bromine colour. The resulting solution, which contains the conjugate base of the *N*-bromoamide, is slowly added to hot aqueous alkali, when the amine distils off.

$$R.CONH_2 \xrightarrow[OH^\ominus]{Br_2} R.CONHBr \xrightarrow{-HBr} RNCO \xrightarrow{OH^\ominus aq} RNH_2$$

The reaction proceeds via the formation and hydrolysis of an isocyanate and is discussed on p. 229. The method is equally applicable to aromatic amides; thus benzamide, $C_6H_5CONH_2$, yields aniline.

(5)   Hydrolysis methods

Amines are formed when their acyl derivatives are hydrolysed. However, this represents a regeneration of the amine from a derivative and not a method of introducing the NH_2 group.

Alkyl and aryl isocyanides are rapidly hydrolysed by aqueous acid (though not by aqueous alkali) yielding primary amines and formic acid. For example:

$$CH_3NC + 2H_2O + H^\oplus \rightarrow CH_3\overset{\oplus}{N}H_3 + H.COOH$$

The reaction is of little preparative value.

(6)   Ammonolysis of the simple alcohols

Methyl- and ethylamines can be made technically by the ammonolysis of methanol and ethanol at high temperatures and pressures in the presence of alumina; for example:

$$CH_3OH + NH_3 \rightarrow CH_3NH_2 + H_2O$$

Secondary and tertiary amines

(1)   Reactions with nitrous acid

Both aliphatic and aromatic secondary amines react with nitrous acid to produce *N*-nitrosamines, i.e. compounds having the nitroso group $-N{=}O$ attached to the amine nitrogen atom in place of hydrogen. For example,

$$(C_2H_5)_2NH + HONO \rightarrow (C_2H_5)_2N{-}N{=}O + H_2O$$
diethylamine   diethyl *N*-nitrosamine

$$C_6H_5.NHCH_3 + HONO \rightarrow \underset{CH_3}{\overset{C_6H_5}{{>}}}N{-}N{=}O + H_2O$$
N-methylaniline   phenyl methyl *N*-nitrosamine

The nitrosamines are practically non-basic and, except for dimethyl nitrosamine, sparingly soluble in water. They therefore separate as yellow oils when sodium nitrite solution is added to an acidified solution of the secondary amine. The aliphatic nitrosamines are readily hydrolysed by refluxing with aqueous acid:

$$(C_2H_5)_2N\text{—}N\text{=}O + H_2O \xrightarrow{H^\oplus} (C_2H_5)_2NH + HNO_2$$

yielding the parent amine and decomposition products of nitrous acid. Excess acid should therefore be avoided in preparing dialkyl nitrosamines.

Aromatic N-nitrosamines are reduced to the parent amine and ammonia by tin and hydrochloric acid:

$$C_6H_5N(NO)CH_3 + 8H^\oplus + 6e \rightarrow C_6H_5\overset{\oplus}{N}H_2CH_3 + \overset{\oplus}{N}H_4 + H_2O$$

Secondary amines can therefore be purified from primary and tertiary amines by conversion to the nitrosamine and purification of this, followed by regeneration of the secondary amine by one of the above methods.

Tertiary aliphatic amines do not react with nitrous acid. NN-Dialkyl aromatic amines, however, undergo nitrosation of the ring. This occurs in the p position if this is vacant. Thus for example:

NN-dimethylaniline   p-nitroso (NN)-dimethylaniline

Unlike N-nitrosamines, the p-nitrosamines are still basic; the above compound therefore forms as its conjugate acid, which is red, when sodium nitrite is added to a solution of aniline in aqueous mineral acid. The free nitrosamine is liberated as a green precipitate on adding alkali.

red in aqueous solution   green

(2) Acylation

Secondary amines can be acylated; tertiary amines cannot, having no hydrogen atom attached to the nitrogen atom (see above p. 157). Tertiary amines can therefore be purified from traces of primary and secondary amines by refluxing with acetic anhydride and steam-distilling off the unchanged tertiary amine.

(3) Alkylation

The alkylation of amines has been discussed above (p. 155). Tertiary amines in general react smoothly on warming with methyl iodide to form crystalline quaternary ammonium iodides, many of which melt sharply without decomposition and can be used to characterize the amine. For example,

$$C_6H_5N(CH_3)_2 + CH_3I \rightarrow C_6H_5\overset{\oplus}{N}(CH_3)_3I^{\ominus}$$
phenyl trimethyl
ammonium iodide

The three types of amine can be distinguished by their behaviour with nitrous acid and with acylating agents, as shown in the table.

Reagent	Primary	Secondary	Tertiary
HNO_2	$-NH_2 \rightarrow -OH$ (etc.) N_2 off.	$\rangle NH \rightarrow \rangle N-N=O$ (yellow oil if pure)	aliphatic—no action. aromatic —*NN*-dimethyl-aniline and similar amines → *p*-nitrosamine (red in acid aq. $\overset{OH^{\ominus}}{\longrightarrow}$ green ppt.)
acylating agents	$-NH_2 \rightarrow -NH.COR$	$\rangle NH \rightarrow \rangle N.COR$	No action

For the reaction of primary and secondary amines with sulphonyl chlorides, see page 250.

Quaternary ammonium salts

These can be regarded as derivatives of the ammonium ion in which all four hydrogen atoms have been replaced by alkyl or similar groups; the ultimate product of the alkylation of any amine is a quaternary ammonium ion.

Quaternary ammonium salts have no acidic properties, and are unaffected by aqueous alkali.

If halide ion is removed from a solution of a quaternary ammonium halide by shaking with an excess of silver oxide and filtering off the silver compounds, a strongly alkaline solution is left, which on evaporation leaves the solid *quaternary ammonium hydroxide*. For example,

$$2(CH_3)_4N^{\oplus} + 2I^{\ominus} + Ag_2O + H_2O \rightarrow \underbrace{2(CH_3)_4N^{\oplus} + 2OH^{\ominus}} + 2AgI$$

tetramethylammonium hydroxide

These ionic solids are caustic alkalis, highly water-soluble and deliquescent, absorbing carbon dioxide rapidly from the air and in general behaving very like alkali metal hydroxides.

They decompose on heating. Tetramethylammonium hydroxide yields trimethylamine and methanol; those with one higher alkyl group (e.g. ethyltrimethylammonium hydroxide) yield as a rule an olefin, trimethylamine and water. These reactions are closely comparable with the displacement and elimination reactions of alkyl halides (see pp. 110–16):

$$HO^{\ominus} \quad CH_3 \overset{\curvearrowright}{-} \overset{\oplus}{N}(CH_3)_3 \longrightarrow HOCH_3 + N(CH_3)_3$$

$$HO^{\ominus} \quad H \overset{\curvearrowright}{-} CH_2 - CH_2 \overset{\curvearrowright}{-} \overset{\oplus}{N}(CH_3)_3 \longrightarrow HOH + CH_2{=}CH_2 + N(CH_3)_3$$

Quaternary phosphonium and arsonium compounds are also known, and with suitable substituents, sulphur, iodine and many other elements, can form the central atom of such fully substituted -onium cations.

Tertiary amine oxides

Tertiary amines are oxidized by aqueous hydrogen peroxide to 'amine oxide hydrates' which on heating yield the amine oxides; thus trimethylamine yields trimethylamine oxide, $(CH_3)_3\overset{\oplus}{N}{-}\overset{\ominus}{O}$.

These compounds presumably contain the dative $\overset{\oplus}{N}{-}\overset{\ominus}{O}$ bond, uncomplicated by electron delocalization.

Trimethylamine oxide is the somewhat surprising end-product in which teleost fishes (those with bony skeletons, such as herring or cod) excrete surplus nitrogen from protein metabolism. (Sharks and other elasmobranch fish, like man, excrete mainly urea.)

The presence of the —NH₂ group in primary amines

Methylamine (CH_5N) can only be formulated:

$$H-\overset{\overset{\textstyle H}{|}}{\underset{\underset{\textstyle H}{|}}{C}}-N\overset{\textstyle H}{\underset{\textstyle H}{\diagdown}}$$

This formula is confirmed by the formation of methylamine from methyl iodide and ammonia, followed by alkali.

The four isomeric amines C_3H_9N can be formulated:

(1) $CH_3CH_2CH_2NH_2$

(2) $\begin{matrix} CH_3 \\ \\ CH_3 \end{matrix} \!\!\! \searrow\!\!\!\nearrow CH-NH_2$

(3) $\begin{matrix} CH_3CH_2 \\ \\ CH_3 \end{matrix} \!\!\! \searrow\!\!\!\nearrow NH$

(4) $\begin{matrix} CH_3 \\ CH_3 \\ CH_3 \end{matrix} \!\!\! \rightarrow\!\! N$

Synthesis from *n*-propyl halides and ammonia yields *n*-propylamine, which must be (1); isopropylamine similarly is (2). Both of these show the behaviour of the —NH$_2$ group as in methylamine. Isopropylamine is also obtained by the reduction of acetoxime, $CH_3\!-\!\underset{\underset{NOH}{\|}}{C}\!-\!CH_3$. A third isomer is obtained from methylamine and ethyl halides, and must be ethylmethylamine, (3).

A fourth isomer obtained from methyl halides and ammonia must be trimethylamine, (4). It differs from the other three in not undergoing acylation with, for example, acetic anhydride; it therefore lacks the —NH— group, thus confirming (4).

The characteristic behaviour of these isomers towards nitrous acid (see p. 168) and acylating agents can be thus used to diagnose —NH$_2$, —NH— and $\geqslant$N in other molecules.

14

The carbonyl group : $\rangle C{=}O$

The carbonyl group is present in *aldehydes,* where it is attached to a single hydrogen atom and to an organic radical (except in the special case of formaldehyde, where it is attached to two hydrogen atoms). Aldehydes therefore have the general formula

$$\begin{array}{c} R \\ \diagdown \\ H \diagup \end{array} C{=}O \quad \text{or} \quad R.CHO$$

The carbonyl group is also present in *ketones,* where it is attached to two organic radicals. Ketones therefore have the general formula

$$\begin{array}{c} R \\ \diagdown \\ R^1 \diagup \end{array} C{=}O \quad \text{or} \quad R.CO.R^1$$

If R and R^1 are different (as, e.g. in $CH_3.CO.C_2H_5$) the compound is called a 'mixed' ketone.

The carbonyl group is formally present in carboxylic acids

$$\begin{array}{c} R \\ \diagdown \\ HO \diagup \end{array} C{=}O \quad \text{or} \quad R.COOH$$

and their related compounds amides ($R.CONH_2$) acid chlorides ($R.COCl$) anhydrides (($R.CO)_2O$) and esters ($R.COOR^1$), but these compounds differ so greatly from aldehydes and ketones, and show so few reactions of the carbonyl group alone, that they must be considered separately.

Nomenclature

In the older nomenclature, aldehydes are named from the acids they yield on oxidation (see p. 188). Thus $CH_3CHO[+(O) \rightarrow CH_3CO_2H$, acetic acid] is acetaldehyde; $C_2H_5.CHO$ is propionaldehyde. Symmetrical aliphatic ketones are named after the acid from whose salts they are obtained on pyrolysis (see p. 195). Thus $CH_3.CO.CH_3$ (by heat on calcium acetate) is *acetone*; $C_2H_5.CO.C_2H_5$ is *propionone*. Unsymmetrical ketones are usually named from the two radicals present: thus $CH_3COC_2H_5$ is *methyl ethyl ketone*. Phenyl ketones are called '*phenones*', with a prefix indicating the acyl radical attached to the ring, thus:

$C_6H_5COCH_3$ $C_6H_5COC_6H_5$ $C_6H_5COC_2H_5$

acetophenone   benzophenone   propionophenone

Systematically, the doubly-bonded oxygen in an *aldehyde* is indicated by the ending *-al*; since it must occur on a terminal carbon atom of a chain, it need not be numbered. Thus:

$CH_3CH_2CH_2CHO$ is butanal;

$(CH_3)_2CH.CHO$ is 2-methylpropanal.

The doubly-bonded oxygen of a ketone is indicated by the ending *-one*, if necessary with a numeral indicating to which carbon atom of the chain it is attached. Thus CH_3COCH_3 is propanone; $CH_3CH_2COCH_2CH_3$ is pentan-3-one.

Physical and general properties of aldehydes and ketones

Formaldehyde is a gas at ordinary temperatures and pressures; all other aldehydes and ketones are liquids or solids. (Acetaldehyde boils at 21° C.) Acetone and acetaldehyde are miscible with water; the higher members of both series have limited solubilities. Aromatic aldehydes and ketones are sparingly soluble. Acetone is extensively used as a laboratory and industrial solvent, notably for acetylated cellulose in the manufacture of acetate rayon. Formaldehyde is marketed as a 40% aqueous solution 'formalin', used in the preservation of biological specimens. The major industrial use of formaldehyde is in the production of resins with phenol (bakelite) and urea (see p. 343). Benzaldehyde occurs (combined with hydrogen cyanide and a sugar) in almonds and similar kernels; it has a limited use in flavouring, and in dyestuff manufacture.

Aldehydes and ketones in solution

Although the anhydrous compounds contain the $C{=}O$ group, there is no doubt that in aqueous solution the equilibrium

$$\text{>}C{=}O + H_2O \rightleftharpoons \text{>}C\overset{OH}{\underset{OH}{<}}$$

between water and certain carbonyl compounds, especially aldehydes, is established at a measurable rate. The product on the right-hand side is the *diol* of the carbonyl compound. In certain special cases the diol can be isolated as a more or less stable hydrate, e.g. the following are all known:

$$CH(OH)_2 \qquad\qquad CHO$$
$$|\qquad\qquad\qquad |$$
$$CH(OH)_2 \quad \text{the (bis) diol of} \quad CHO$$
$$\text{glyoxal}$$

$$CCl_3.CH(OH)_2 \quad \text{the diol of} \quad CCl_3.CHO$$
$$\text{(chloral hydrate)} \qquad\qquad \text{chloral}$$
$$\text{(trichloroacetaldehyde)}$$

$$COOH \qquad\qquad COOH$$
$$|\qquad\qquad\qquad |$$
$$C(OH)_2 \quad \text{the diol of} \quad CO$$
$$|\qquad\qquad\qquad |$$
$$COOH \qquad\qquad COOH$$
$$\text{mesoxalic acid}$$

Simple ketones like acetone appear to undergo this reaction extremely slowly in the absence of acids and bases, and little or no diol is present in a solution of acetone in water.

Other hydroxylic solvents can behave in the same way; for example, ethanol:

$$\rangle C{=}O + C_2H_5OH \rightleftharpoons \rangle C\!\!\!<^{OC_2H_5}_{\ OH}$$

Again, in favourable cases the 'alcoholate' can be isolated; chloral alcoholate $CCl_3.CH\!\!\!<^{OC_2H_5}_{\ OH}$ is known as a stable substance.

Acid–base behaviour

Aldehydes and ketones are neutral in aqueous solution. Nevertheless, those containing the group

$$\rangle CH{-}C{-}$$
$$\qquad\; \| $$
$$\qquad\; O$$

(i.e. having an α-hydrogen atom) behave as feebly acidic, and will react with bases:

$$B + \rangle CH{-}C{-} \rightleftharpoons BH^{\oplus} + \rangle\overset{\ominus}{C}{-}C{-}$$
$$\qquad\qquad \|\qquad\qquad\qquad\qquad \|$$
$$\qquad\qquad O\qquad\qquad\qquad\qquad O$$

This can be attributed to the electron-attracting effect of the electronegative oxygen atom, 'relayed' through the molecule, thus:

$$\rangle\underset{\underset{H}{\uparrow}}{C} \rightarrow \underset{\underset{O}{\|}}{C}{-}$$

which has the effect of withdrawing electrons from the α-hydrogen atom and rendering it more easily lost to a base. Moreover, the ion produced will be stabilized by electron delocalization:

$$\underset{\underset{O}{\parallel}}{\overset{\ominus}{>}C}-C- \leftrightarrow >C=C-\underset{O\ominus}{\overset{|}{}}$$

This reaction is important as an initial step in aldol-type reactions (see p. 180) and in the halogenation of aldehydes and ketones in the presence of bases (as, for example, in the haloform reaction, p. 189).

The lone pairs of the oxygen atom make it potentially a source of basic properties, thus:

$$>C=O+HA \rightleftharpoons >C=\overset{\oplus}{O}-H+A^{\ominus}$$

The acid and base properties of carbonyl compounds are important in giving rise to keto–enol tautomerism (p. 202). It must be emphasized again that these properties are too feeble to have any effect on the $H^{\oplus}$ ion concentration of water; aqueous solutions of simple aldehydes and ketones are neutral.

Reactions of aldehydes and ketones

The representation of the carbonyl group as containing a double bond, $>C=O$, on the analogy of the ethylenic bond $>C=C<$, is justified by the fact of unsaturated behaviour in both aldehydes and ketones. Thus the following addition reactions can occur in suitable conditions:

$$>C=O+H_2 \xrightarrow{\text{catalytic}} >CHOH$$

$$>C=O+HCN \longrightarrow >C\underset{CN}{\overset{OH}{<}}$$

$$>C=O+NH_3 \longrightarrow >C\underset{NH_3}{\overset{OH}{<}}$$

$$>C=O+NaHSO_3 \longrightarrow >C\underset{SO_3Na}{\overset{OH}{<}}$$

The addition of hydroxylic solvents has already been mentioned. Apart from these addition reactions, the $>C=O$ group undergoes a number of reactions in which the initial steps are believed to be additions, but the subse-

174

quent steps lead to the elimination of simple molecules such as water, so that the final product is not a simple addition product. Such *condensation* reactions include the reactions with hydroxylamine and phenylhydrazine:

$$\text{>C=O + NH}_2\text{OH} \rightarrow \text{>C=NOH + H}_2\text{O}$$

$$\text{>C=O + C}_6\text{H}_5\text{NHNH}_2 \rightarrow \text{>C=N.NHC}_6\text{H}_5 + \text{H}_2\text{O}$$

A condensation reaction can be defined as one in which two or more molecules combine together, with or without the elimination of a simpler molecule. The term is therefore loosely used as a matter of convenience rather than systematically. Thus, the aldol condensation (p. 180) is in its simplest form just an addition reaction; on the other hand, the esterification of acids by alcohols, though a condensation reaction within this definition, is rarely so called.

It is conspicuous that, apart from the catalytic addition of hydrogen, the addition and allied reactions of the carbonyl group involve quite different reagents from those which attack ethylene. Thus neither halogens, hydrogen halides nor hypohalous acids form stable addition compounds with the carbonyl group, while, for example, hydrogen cyanide and ammonia do not add to ethylene. This is plausibly explained by supposing that the electronegative oxygen atom tends to withdraw electrons from the carbon atom attached to it, so that this carbon becomes susceptible to attack by *nucleophilic* (electron-donor) reagents. This is in contrast to the behaviour of olefins, where the 'motive force' of the addition reactions is the attack of *electrophilic* (electron acceptor) reagents on the electrons of the ethylenic bond.

From this point of view, the classication of carbonyl reactions into additions and condensations is therefore superficial, based on differences in type in the final products and obscuring the essential similarity of the reaction between >C=O and the attacking reagent in all cases.

These reactions (including those listed above) are therefore discussed together in the following parts of this chapter.

Aldehydes differ from ketones in the chemical behaviour associated with the hydrogen atom attached to the >C=O group. There are also certain differences in the behaviour of the >C=O group itself resulting from its attachment to hydrogen rather than to carbon. On the other hand, as might be expected, many reactions are common to both classes of compound, and they are conveniently considered together.

Addition and condensation reactions of aldehydes and ketones involving attack by nucleophilic reagents

(1) Cyanohydrin formation—reaction with hydrogen cyanide

Aldehydes and ketones add hydrogen cyanide to form compounds called cyanohydrins; thus, for example, with acetaldehyde:

$$\begin{array}{c} CH_3 \\ \diagdown \\ H \diagup \end{array} C{=}O + HCN \rightarrow \begin{array}{c} CH_3 \diagdown \quad \diagup OH \\ C \\ H \diagup \quad \diagdown CN \end{array}$$

acetaldehyde cyanohydrin

The usual method of carrying this out, especially with the lower, water-soluble carbonyl compounds, is to add the compound to aqueous potassium cyanide solution, and then to add acid. Anhydrous hydrogen cyanide is relatively slow and ineffective. This suggests that the effective reagent is the cyanide ion, a typical nucleophilic reagent, and that the reaction proceeds thus:

$$\begin{array}{c} \diagup \\ {>}C{=}\overset{\frown}{O} \\ \uparrow \\ \big(\\ \diagdown :\underset{\ominus}{C}N \end{array} \longrightarrow \begin{array}{c} \diagup \overset{\ominus}{O} \\ {>}C \\ \diagdown CN \end{array}$$

followed by the rapid addition of a proton:

$$\begin{array}{c} O^{\ominus} \\ {>}C{<} \\ \diagdown CN \end{array} + H^{\oplus} \rightarrow \begin{array}{c} OH \\ {>}C{<} \\ CN \end{array}$$

Cyanohydrins can also be made by the action of potassium cyanide solution on bisulphite addition compounds (see below, p. 177): this is especially convenient with aromatic aldehydes, which undergo the benzoin condensation (p. 184) with cyanide ion as catalyst. Thus for example, benzaldehyde:

$$C_6H_5CH{\diagdown}^{OH}_{SO_3{}^{\ominus}Na^{\oplus}} + CN^{\ominus} \rightarrow C_6H_5CH{\diagdown}^{OH}_{CN} + SO_3{}^{2\ominus} + Na^{\oplus}$$

This would seem to be a displacement reaction of the same type as the action of cyanide ion on halides (p. 110).

Cyanohydrin formation is reversible. Thus boiling with aqueous alkali regenerates the original carbonyl compound (unless this is itself further attacked by alkali). Refluxing with aqueous *acid*, however, hydrolyses the cyanide radical to the carboxylic acid radical, thus yielding the α-hydroxy acid of which the cyanohydrin is the nitrile; compare p. 233 and p. 239. Thus:

$$CH_3CH(OH)CN + 2H_2O + H^{\oplus} \rightarrow CH_3CHOHCO_2H + NH_4^{\oplus}$$

acetaldehyde cyanohydrin   lactic acid

This is a valuable method of synthesizing α-hydroxy acids. Cyanohydrin formation becomes difficult with some higher ketones.

(2) The Strecker synthesis

If a carbonyl compound is added to potassium cyanide solution, and an ammonium salt is added, then instead of the cyanohydrin an amino-cyanide is obtained:

$$CH_3CHO + CN^\ominus + NH_4^\oplus \rightarrow CH_3CH(NH_2)CN + H_2O$$
$$CH_3CH(NH_2)CN + 2H_2O \rightarrow CH_3CH(NH_2)CO_2H + NH_3$$

This on acid hydrolysis yields the corresponding α-amino acid, to which it therefore forms a useful route (see p. 283).

(3) Addition of sodium bisulphite

Many aldehydes and ketones react exothermically with saturated sodium bisulphite solution yielding crystalline addition compounds; for example with acetone:

$$(CH_3)_2CO + Na^\oplus HSO_3{}^\ominus \rightarrow (CH_3)_2C\begin{smallmatrix}OH\\SO_3{}^\ominus Na^\oplus\end{smallmatrix}$$

'acetone sodium bisulphite compound'

The reaction is probably of the same type as cyanohydrin formation, the nucleophilic reagent being the sulphite ion:

$$HSO_3{}^\ominus \rightleftharpoons H^\oplus + SO_3{}^{2\ominus}$$

$$\begin{smallmatrix}O^\ominus\\\end{smallmatrix}$$
$$>C=O + SO_3{}^{2\ominus} \rightarrow >C\begin{smallmatrix}O^\ominus\\SO_3{}^\ominus\end{smallmatrix} \xrightarrow{H^\oplus} >C\begin{smallmatrix}OH\\SO_3{}^\ominus\end{smallmatrix}$$

These compounds may sometimes be useful in separating carbonyl compounds from others, since the solid addition compound may be filtered off and the aldehyde or ketone regenerated by the action of dilute alkali or alkali carbonate solution, for example:

$$C_6H_5CH(OH)SO_3{}^\ominus + OH^\ominus \rightarrow C_6H_5CHO + SO_3{}^{2\ominus} + H_2O$$

This is essentially a reversal of the reaction forming the bisulphite compound. Bisulphite addition occurs in aqueous sulphite as well as bisulphite solutions; in this case $OH^\ominus$ ions are liberated. Thus if acetaldehyde or formaldehyde is added to excess of neutralized sodium sulphite solution, the mixture can be titrated with standard acid with phenolphthalein as indicator. A mole of aldehyde liberates a mole of hydroxyl ion; the aldehyde can therefore be estimated. The bisulphite compounds of acetaldehyde and formaldehyde are readily soluble in water.

Ketones with the carbonyl group attached directly to an aromatic ring (e.g. acetophenone $C_6H_5COCH_3$) do not form bisulphite compounds, and even the higher aliphatic ketones form them slowly and partially.

(4) Reaction of aldehydes and ketones with NH_2 compounds

(*a*) *Formation of oximes and phenyl hydrazones.* Aldehydes and ketones in general, aliphatic and aromatic alike, condense readily with hydroxylamine and phenylhydrazine to yield compounds called *oximes* and *phenylhydrazones* respectively. For examples:

$$CH_3CHO + NH_2OH \quad \rightarrow CH_3CH{=}NOH + H_2O$$
acetaldehyde hydroxylamine   acetaldoxime
(an 'aldoxime')

$$(CH_3)_2CO + NH_2OH \rightarrow (CH_3)_2C{=}NOH + H_2O$$
acetone   acetoxime
(a 'ketoxime')

$$C_6H_5CHO + C_6H_5NHNH_2 \rightarrow C_6H_5CH{=}N.NHC_6H_5 + H_2O$$
benzaldehyde phenylhydrazine   benzaldehyde phenylhydrazone

To prepare the oxime, the carbonyl compound is warmed in aqueous or aqueous-ethanolic solution with hydroxylammonium chloride and an equivalent of alkali (to liberate free hydroxylamine).

Carbonyl compounds often react with phenylhydrazine on simple mixing of the reagents. Alternatively, the carbonyl compound can be added to a solution of phenylhydrazine in aqueous acetic acid. Since phenylhydrazine is a very weak base, sufficient free phenylhydrazine is present in such a solution. The —NH_2 group is characteristically nucleophilic, and we may suppose that the initial step in both these reactions is the attack of the nitrogen atom with an unshared pair of electrons on the carbon atom of the $\diagdown C{=}O$ group, in the same way as with $CN^\ominus$ or $SO_3{}^{2\ominus}$; for example:

$$\diagdown C{=}\overset{\frown}{O} \quad \longrightarrow \quad \diagdown \underset{\overset{|}{\overset{\oplus}{N}H_2OH}}{C} - O^\ominus$$
$$\underset{:NH_2OH}{}$$

Subsequent reaction steps include the addition and removal of protons and the spontaneous elimination of water. A pH of 4 to 6 is most favourable for oxime and phenylhydrazone preparation; the reactions may be carried out in acetate buffer solutions.

Acetaldoxime is low-melting and water-soluble; other oximes are in general crystalline solids at ordinary temperatures, and less soluble in water. Acetaldehyde and acetone phenylhydrazones separate as oils, though they crystallize on chilling and scratching. Other phenylhydrazones are usually well-defined crystalline solids. Both oximes and phenylhydrazones can therefore be used for characterizing aldehydes and ketones. (Substituted phenylhydrazones, such as *p*-nitrophenylhydrazone and 2,4-dinitrophenylhydrazone often give more readily crystalline and higher melting products than phenylhydrazine itself.)

Semicarbazide $NH_2.CONH.NH_2$ and hydrazine itself $NH_2.NH_2$ react similarly forming respectively semicarbazones; for example:

$$\begin{array}{c} C_6H_5 \\ \diagdown \\ C{=}N.NH.CONH_2 \\ \diagup \\ CH_3 \end{array}$$

acetophenone semicarbazone

and azines:

$$C_6H_5CH{=}N{-}N{=}CH.C_6H_5$$
dibenzalazine

Oximes may be reduced to primary amines; a useful preparative method (see p. 165).

(*b*) *Reaction of aldehydes and ketones with ammonia.* In contrast to the uniformity of behaviour of carbonyl compounds with hydroxylamine and phenyl hydrazine, their behaviour with ammonia is varied. Some form simple addition compounds; for example chloral:

$$CCl_3CHO + NH_3 \rightarrow CCl_3.CH{\Big\langle}\begin{array}{l} OH \\ NH_2 \end{array}$$

(Compare the behaviour of chloral with water and ethanol, p. 173.)

Acetaldehyde reacts with dry ammonia (for example, in ethereal solution) to form a crystalline addition compound. Possibly the simple product is first formed:

$$CH_3CH{\Big\langle}\begin{array}{l} OH \\ NH_2 \end{array}$$

but this rapidly polymerizes and condenses to more complex products. The freshly made product is readily soluble in water. It regenerates acetaldehyde on distillation with aqueous strong acid.

Ketones do not form simple addition compounds with ammonia at ordinary temperatures.

Formaldehyde and benzaldehyde do not yield simple addition products, but condense with ammonia to more complex materials. Thus formaldehyde yields hexamethylene tetramine:

$$6HCHO + 4NH_3 \rightarrow (CH_2)_6N_4 + 6H_2O$$

179

which has the structure:

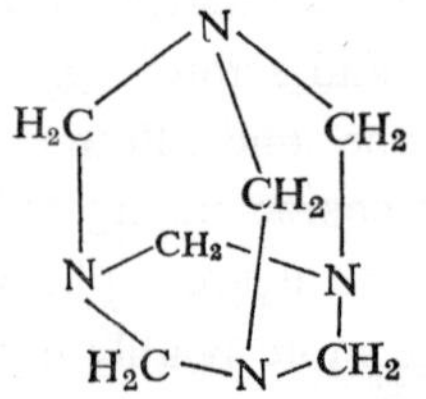

Hexamethylene tetramine is used in medicine, as a condensing catalyst in one stage of manufacture of bakelite, and in the manufacture of the explosive cyclonite.

Benzaldehyde forms the so-called 'hydrobenzamide' on standing with concentrated aqueous ammonia:

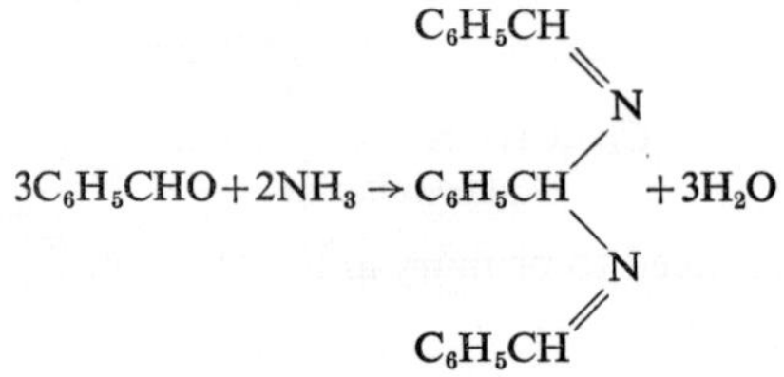

$$3C_6H_5CHO + 2NH_3 \rightarrow \begin{matrix} C_6H_5CH \\ \diagdown \\ N \\ \diagup \\ C_6H_5CH \\ \diagdown \\ N \\ \diagup \\ C_6H_5CH \end{matrix} + 3H_2O$$

Even in these cases, however, there is no reason to doubt that the initial reaction step is the attack of the nitrogen atom of the ammonia molecule on the carbon atom of the $>C{=}O$ group.

(c) *Reaction of aldehydes and ketones with primary amines.* Again, various types of product are obtained. The only reaction of this type that the elementary student will meet is, however, that between aromatic aldehydes and aromatic primary amines, which condense together to form compounds known as 'Schiff's bases'. For example, benzaldehyde and aniline condense rapidly on mixing and warming to give benzal-aniline (or benzylidene aniline):

$$C_6H_5CHO + H_2NC_6H_5 \rightarrow C_6H_5CH{=}NHC_6H_5 + H_2O$$
benzal-aniline

This reaction is exactly comparable with the formation of a phenylhydrazone [see (a) above].

(5) The aldol condensation and related reactions

(a) *The simple aldol condensation.* In the presence of dilute alkali carbonate solution at 0° C, acetaldehyde forms a *dimer* β-hydroxy-butyraldehyde (3-hydroxybutanal) known as aldol:

$$2CH_3CHO \rightarrow CH_3.CHOH.CH_2.CHO$$

Other weak bases are known to catalyse this reaction.

180

Notice in the alternative names for aldol that a possible confusion arises from the two systems of labelling carbon atoms in a chain. Every carbon atom in the chain is numbered, that in the aldehyde group being 1; when Greek letters are used, however, the α-carbon atom is that *attached to* the functional group

$$O\!-\!\overset{|}{\underset{\underset{1}{|}}{C}}\!-\!\overset{|}{\underset{\underset{2}{\underset{\alpha}{|}}}{C}}\!-\!\overset{|}{\underset{\underset{3}{\underset{\beta}{|}}}{C}}\!-\!\overset{|}{\underset{\underset{4}{\underset{\gamma}{|}}}{C}}$$

When, as in aldehydes, the functional group contains a carbon atom, $\alpha \neq 1$.

A likely mechanism for the base-catalysed aldol condensation is that some molecules of acetaldehyde react with the base as indicated on p. 173, thus:

$$CH_3CHO + B \rightleftharpoons \overset{\ominus}{C}H_2.CHO + BH^{\oplus}$$

The anion thus produced will behave as a nucleophilic reagent and attack the carbonyl carbon atom of a second aldehyde molecule in the way postulated above for nucleophilic reagents in general.

$$CH_3\!-\!C\!\overset{H}{\underset{O}{\diagdown}} \longrightarrow CH_3\!-\!\overset{\overset{H}{|}}{\underset{\underset{CH_2CHO}{|}}{C}}\!-\!O^{\ominus}$$

$$:CH_2CHO \\ \ominus$$

Proton addition from water or any other acid species present ($H_3O^{\oplus}$, $BH^{\oplus}$) completes the reaction:

$$CH_3CHO^{\ominus} + H^{\oplus} \rightarrow CH_3CHOHCH_2CHO \\ \underset{CH_2CHO}{|}$$

Aldol and similar compounds eliminate water easily, often on simple distillation, or in the presence of acids or bases, yielding an unsaturated aldehyde. Thus aldol itself yields crotonaldehyde $CH_3.CH\!=\!CH.CHO$. Acid-catalysed elimination of water is the rule for —OH compounds (see p. 134); the base-catalysed reaction here presumably arises because the aldol itself can lose a hydrogen atom as a proton just as the original aldehyde did:

$$CH_3CHOHCH_2CHO + B \rightleftharpoons CH_3CHOH\overset{\ominus}{C}HCHO + BH^{\oplus}$$

and the resulting anion contains, as it were, a 'built-in' nucleophilic reagent capable of displacing hydroxyl from the carbon atom:

$$CH_3\!-\!\overset{\overset{OH}{\diagup}}{\underset{\underset{\cdot\cdot}{\frown}}{C}H}\!-\!\overset{\ominus}{C}HCHO \longrightarrow CH_3CH\!=\!CHCHO + OH^{\ominus}$$

Aldol, being itself an aldehyde, cannot only form an anion in this way but can also be attacked by an anion from an acetaldehyde molecule. Thus on warming in the presence of strong bases such as the $OH^\ominus$ ion, the reaction does not stop at the aldol stage, but proceeds further with elimination of water and addition of further aldehyde units to form a yellowish orange 'aldehyde resin'.

Homologues of acetaldehyde, provided they have the essential α-hydrogen atom, undergo the aldol reaction, though the tendency to resin formation with caustic alkali is less marked.

Ketones with α-hydrogen atoms can also condense in this way, but usually much less readily. Thus with acetone, the reaction is markedly reversible, the equilibrium greatly favouring the monomeric ketone:

$$2CH_3COCH_3 \rightleftharpoons (CH_3)_2COH.CH_2COCH_3$$
'diacetone alcohol'
(4-hydroxy-4-methyl pentan-2-one)

A good yield can therefore only be obtained by using a catalyst which is insoluble in acetone (such as barium hydroxide), separating the equilibrium mixture from the catalyst, and distilling off and recycling the acetone (a procedure conveniently operated in a Soxhlet apparatus). No polymerization to form a resin occurs.

From the above account of the aldol condensation, it is clear that two aldehyde molecules perform different functions. One provides the electrophilic carbon atom of the $>C=O$ group, while the other ionizes as a weak acid to provide the nucleophilic anionic reagent. Carbonyl compounds with no α-hydrogen atom cannot perform this latter function; such compounds (for example, formaldehyde $H.CHO$; trimethyl acetaldehyde $(CH_3)_3C.CHO$; benzaldehyde $C_6H_5.CHO$) cannot therefore undergo the simple aldol condensation. With strong alkalis, these compounds undergo Cannizzaro's reaction (see p. 183). On the other hand, there is no general reason why they should not perform the former function and react with anions from aldehydes and similar species which *have* the α-hydrogen atom. A number of such reactions of benzaldehyde are considered in the next section.

(*b*) *Reactions of benzaldehyde related to the aldol condensation.* Benzaldehyde undergoes the following condensations, which are essentially base-catalysed and analogous with aldol condensations with subsequent elimination of water.

(i) With acetaldehyde in the presence of aqueous or aqueous-ethanolic alkali (the Claisen reaction):

$$C_6H_5CHO + CH_3CHO \rightarrow C_6H_5CH=CH.CHO + H_2O$$
cinnamic aldehyde

(ii) Similarly with acetone and one or two molecules of benzaldehyde, according to conditions:

$$C_6H_5CHO + CH_3COCH_3 \rightarrow C_6H_5CH{=}CHCOCH_3 + H_2O$$
benzalacetone

$$(\xrightarrow{C_6H_5CHO} C_6H_5CH{=}CHCOCH{=}CHC_6H_5)$$
dibenzalacetone

(iii) A similar reaction, though not with an aldehyde or ketone, is the Perkin reaction. Benzaldehyde is refluxed with acetic anhydride and anhydrous sodium acetate (the base catalyst) for some hours and the product is poured into water, yielding cinnamic acid.

$$C_6H_5CHO + CH_3CO.O.COCH_3$$

$$\rightarrow C_6H_5CH{=}CH.CO.O.COCH_3 + H_2O$$
(the 'mixed anhydride' of
acetic and cinnamic acids)

$$\rightarrow C_6H_5CH{=}CH.CO_2H + CH_3CO_2H$$
cinnamic acid

The aldol reactions listed above are only a few of the very many known instances in organic chemistry where a carbonyl or similar electrophilic unsaturated carbon atom is attacked by an anion formed from a 'reactive' $\rangle$CH— or $\rangle$CH$_2$ group (that is, one rendered feebly acidic by neighbouring electronegative substituents).

The reactions so far considered can all be described in terms of attack by a nucleophilic reagent on the $\rangle$C$=$O group, followed by proton transfer and possibly by elimination of water. Certain carbonyl compounds undergo other reactions which again are initiated by nucleophilic reagents, but in which the subsequent stages are more complex. These are considered without discussion of mechanism in the following sections.

(6) The Cannizzaro reaction

As mentioned above, aldehydes with no α-hydrogen atoms cannot undergo the aldol condensation with themselves. In the presence of aqueous caustic alkali, such aldehydes disproportionate, two molecules of the aldehyde yielding one each of the corresponding primary alcohol and carboxylic acid anion. Thus, for example:

$$2HCHO + OH^{\ominus} \rightarrow HCOO^{\ominus} + CH_3OH$$
formaldehyde   formate ion   methanol

$$2C_6H_5CHO + OH^{\ominus} \rightarrow C_6H_5COO^{\ominus} + C_6H_5CH_2OH$$
benzaldehyde   benzoate ion   benzyl alcohol

Clearly, since the reaction involves the oxidation of one molecule of aldehyde to the corresponding acid, it cannot occur with ketones.

Organic Chemistry

(At one time, the view was widely held that the Cannizzaro reaction proceded via the combination of the two molecules of aldehyde to form an ester, which was then hydrolysed. This view is still sometimes put forward but it is no longer generally accepted.)

(7) The benzoin condensation

Aldehydes with —CHO attached directly to the benzene ring dimerize on refluxing with alcoholic potassium cyanide. Thus with benzaldehyde:

$$2C_6H_5CHO \xrightarrow{CN^\ominus} C_6H_5\text{—CH—C—}C_6H_5$$
$$\underset{\text{OH}}{|} \quad \underset{\text{O}}{\|}$$
'benzoin'

Compounds of this type (acyloins) are formed from aliphatic aldehydes under these conditions in small yields only. The cyanide ion is a specific catalyst for this reaction, which is historically interesting as one of the first organic reactions to be investigated kinetically with a view to elucidating its mechanism.

As with the aldol reaction, one molecule of the aldehyde has become added to another, but here it is not the α-carbon atom, but the carbon atom of the $>C=O$ group itself, which has become attached to the carbon atom of the second $>C=O$ group. Since this reaction clearly involves the loss of hydrogen from a CHO group, it is not applicable to ketones.

(8) Acetal formation

It has been mentioned above (p. 173) that aldehydes in alcoholic solution are in equilibrium with an 'alcoholate' formed by addition of the alcohol molecule across the double bond. (This is clearly nucleophilic attack of the alcoholic oxygen atom on the carbonyl carbon atom, followed by proton transfer):

$$>C=O \longrightarrow >C-O^\ominus \longrightarrow >C-OH$$
$$\overset{|}{R-O^\oplus-H} \qquad \overset{|}{R-O}$$
$$R\ddot{O}H$$

In the presence of strong acids as catalysts, further reaction occurs with another molecule of alcohol, leading to the overall result with, for example, acetaldehyde and ethanol:

$$CH_3CHO + 2C_2H_5OH \underset{HCl_{Aq}}{\overset{\text{dry HCl}}{\rightleftharpoons}} CH_3CH(OC_2H_5)_2 + H_2O$$

acetaldehyde
diethyl acetal
('acetal')

184

Aromatic aldehydes behave similarly, though often rather slowly. The products are known generally as *acetals*; an unfortunate name, since they are neither aldehydes (-als) nor do they in general contain any group related to acetic acid. Acetals are ether-type compounds, with two ether linkages attached to the same carbon atom. They are characteristically inert to aqueous alkali, but are rapidly hydrolysed by aqueous acid (the reverse of their formation, as indicated above), the rate of hydrolysis being closely proportional to the hydrogen ion concentration of the reagent.

The analogous derivatives of ketones (inconsistently called 'ketals') are known, but cannot in general be prepared by the direct action of alcohols on ketones, presumably since the initial addition reaction does not readily occur.

(9) Certain polymerizations of aldehydes

(*a*) *Acetaldehyde → paraldehyde.* The addition of a drop or two of concentrated sulphuric acid to acetaldehyde causes a rapid and exothermic polymerization to a trimer, *paraldehyde*, which has the structure shown below:

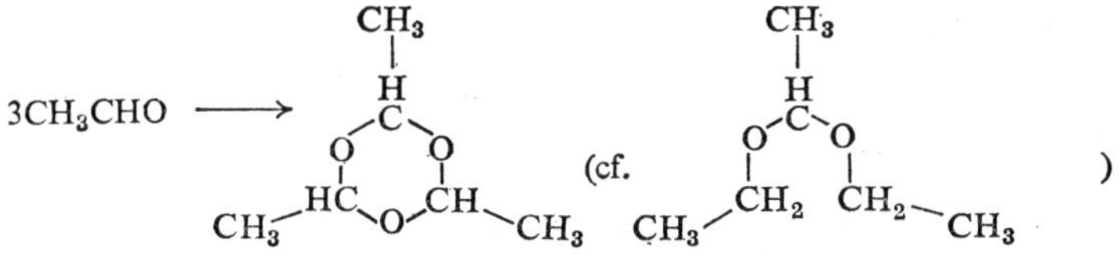

paraldehyde   acetal

Paraldehyde is thus a 'cyclic acetal' and like acetal itself is readily hydrolysed back to acetaldehyde by aqueous strong acids.

(*b*) *Acetaldehyde → metaldehyde.* Ice-cold acetaldehyde polymerizes to a tetramer, 'metaldehyde', in the presence of dry hydrogen chloride. This is a solid, used as a fuel ('meta-fuel') in some picnic stoves and for killing slugs. It is also toxic to humans.

(*c*) Formaldehyde polymerizes to a high molecular weight solid 'para-formaldehyde' on standing in aqueous solution: $HO(CH_2O)_nCH_2OH$.

(*d*) Formaldehyde polymerizes to trioxymethylene

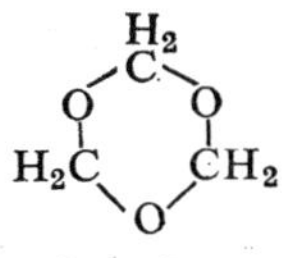

(cf. paraldehyde, above) at low temperatures.

Ketones and aromatic aldehydes do not undergo analogous polymerizations.

(10) The production of mesitylene from acetone

In addition to the base-catalysed aldol condensations discussed above in some detail, various acid-catalysed versions are known. The only one of interest to the elementary student is the effect of refluxing acetone with concentrated sulphuric acid. Among the products, 1,3,5-*trimethylbenzene* (mesitylene) is present in rather poor yield. The reaction is striking as one of the comparatively few in which an aromatic system is formed from an aliphatic one.

The symmetrical orientation of the three methyl groups can be deduced from the presumed symmetrical condensation of the three acetone molecules (see the equation); this agrees with the orientation deduced by other methods, as discussed on pp. 79–80.

The reaction is presumably a threefold aldol-type condensation, with elimination of water.

(11) The reduction of carbonyl compounds

Aldehydes and ketones are readily reduced to alcohols by gaseous hydrogen in the presence of metallic or other heterogeneous catalysts (the reverse of the catalytic dehydrogenation of alcohols) or by conventional 'nascent hydrogen' reagents such as sodium and ethanol, or sodium amalgam and water. More recent (and more costly) reagents include complex hydrides such as sodium borohydride $NaBH_4$ or lithium aluminium hydride $LiAlH_4$.

Aldehydes yield primary alcohols. Thus, formally:

$$CH_3CHO + 2H^\oplus + 2e \rightarrow CH_3CH_2OH$$
acetaldehyde   ethanol

and

$$C_6H_5CHO + 2H^\oplus + 2e \rightarrow C_6H_5CH_2OH$$
benzaldehyde   benzyl alcohol

while ketones yield secondary alcohols.

$$CH_3COCH_3 + 2H^\oplus + 2e \rightarrow CH_3CHOHCH_3$$
acetone   isopropyl alcohol

$$C_6H_5COCH_3 + 2H^\oplus + 2e \rightarrow C_6H_5CHOHCH_3$$
acetophenone   phenylmethylcarbinol

Reduction can also be carried out by the Ponndorf–Meerwein method (warming with aluminium isopropoxide in excess of isopropyl alcohol, followed by acidification); in effect, isopropyl alcohol is oxidized to acetone, and the other carbonyl compound reduced. Clearly the reaction is therefore reversible, and excess of the aluminium isopropoxide is required unless equilibrium is favourable without it. Overall:

$$3R.CO.R^1 + Al(OCH(CH_3)_2)_3$$
$$\rightarrow 3CH_3COCH_3 + Al(OCHRR^1)_3$$
$$\downarrow \text{acid}$$

$$\begin{array}{c} R \\ \diagdown \\ R^1 \diagup \end{array} CHOH$$

$LiAlH_4$, $NaBH_4$ and aluminium isopropoxide are all more or less specific reagents for reduction of carbonyl groups; thus they have the advantage that other reducible groups in the molecule (such as $-NO_2$ or $\diagup C = C \diagdown$) are left intact, whereas catalytic hydrogenation would attack these also. For example, crotonaldehyde $CH_3.CH=CH.CHO$ will yield butanol $CH_3CH_2CH_2CH_2OH$ on hydrogenation, but crotyl alcohol

$$CH_3CH=CHCH_2OH$$

with any of the three reagents named.

These three reagents may well act as sources of hydride ions $H^\ominus$, which may be in effect the reducing agent; that such might be the case is very obvious in the case of the two complex hydrides. As a reducing agent, the hydride ion is also a nucleophile. These reactions may therefore be added to the list of nucleophilic attacks on the carbonyl group, the essential step being

$$\begin{array}{c} \diagup \\ C = O \\ \diagup \\ :H^\ominus \end{array} \longrightarrow \begin{array}{c} \diagup \\ C - O^\ominus \\ | \\ H \end{array}$$

In addition to the reduction to the corresponding alcohol, certain carbonyl compounds undergo reduction to other products. Thus ketones and some aromatic aldehydes, on agitation with amalgamated zinc and concentrated hydrochloric acid, are reduced to the corresponding hydrocarbons; thus, formally:

$$\underset{\text{acetone}}{CH_3COCH_3} + 4H^\oplus + 4e \rightarrow \underset{\text{propane}}{CH_3CH_2CH_3} + H_2O$$

$$\underset{\text{acetophenone}}{C_6H_5COCH_3} + 4H^\oplus + 4e \rightarrow \underset{\text{ethyl benzene}}{C_6H_5CH_2CH_3} + H_2O$$

This is known as the Clemmensen reduction.

In the presence of metallic reducing agents, especially magnesium and sodium, ketones and certain aldehydes (especially those with —CHO attached to an aromatic ring, such as benzaldehyde) yield considerable quantities of the so-called 'pinacols'.

Thus acetone reacts with amalgamated magnesium:

$$\begin{matrix} (CH_3)_2CO \\ \\ (CH_3)_2CO \end{matrix} + Mg \rightarrow \begin{pmatrix} (CH_3)_2CO \\ | \\ (CH_3)_2CO \end{pmatrix} Mg$$

With aqueous acid, the magnesium derivative yields pinacol itself:

$$(CH_3)_2COH.COH(CH_3)_2$$

Benzaldehyde similarly yields appreciable quantities of hydrobenzoin, $C_6H_5CHOH.CHOHC_6H_5$, with metallic reducing agents. This type of reduction does not occur to an appreciable extent with acetaldehyde.

The Cannizzaro reaction (above, p. 183) is, of course, from one point of view a reduction of the carbonyl group.

(12) Replacement of oxygen by chlorine

Phosphorus pentachloride will convert the carbonyl group of aldehydes and ketones to a $>CCl_2$ group, thus, for example,

$$CH_3COCH_3 + PCl_5 \rightarrow CH_3CCl_2CH_3 + POCl_3$$
$$C_6H_5CHO + PCl_5 \rightarrow C_6H_5CHCl_2 + POCl_3$$

There remain a few reactions of aldehydes and ketones not ultimately affecting the carbonyl group (although its presence in the molecule is nevertheless essential to the reactions).

(13) Oxidation to carboxylic acids

Aldehydes, unlike ketones, are powerful reducing agents, and can be oxidized by a variety of reagents to carboxylic acids without loss of carbon from the molecule. $R.CHO+(O) \rightarrow R.CO_2H$

Aldehydes are comparatively readily oxidized by atmospheric oxygen (benzaldehyde notably so); this reaction is catalysed by manganous salts. Aldehydes readily reduce ammoniacal solutions of silver oxide to give silver mirrors (a well-known test) and aliphatic, though not aromatic aldehydes reduce Fehling's solution (an alkaline solution of a cupritartrate complex) and other alkaline cupric complexes to cuprous oxide. Aldehydes are, of course, readily oxidized to carboxylic acids by the usual conventional oxidizing agents (acid permanganate or dichromate, etc.).

This reaction depends on the presence of the hydrogen atom attached to the carbonyl group. Ketones, which do not possess this, can as a rule be oxidized only by vigorous and prolonged treatment. Oxidation occurs on one side or other of the $\diagdown$C$=$O group, yielding in general two carboxylic acids, or one carboxylic acid, water and carbon dioxide. For an example see the oxidation of cyclohexanone to adipic acid, p. 336.

(14) The halogenation of ketones and the haloform reaction

In the presence of bases, the bromination of acetone is known to proceed at a rate given by the equation

$$\text{rate} = k[CH_3COCH_3]\,[\text{base}]$$

and to be independent of $[Br_2]$. Such kinetics can be accounted for by assuming that the reaction depends on the slow formation of the anion from acetone (as discussed on pp. 173–4 above)

$$CH_3COCH_3 + B \rightleftharpoons \overset{\oplus}{B}H + \overset{\ominus}{C}H_2COCH_3$$

followed by a rapid reaction with bromine or a bromine-containing species such as HOBr.

$$\overset{\frown}{Br} - \overset{\frown}{Br} \quad :\overset{\ominus}{C}H_2COCH_3 \rightarrow \overset{\ominus}{Br} + CH_2BrCOCH_3$$

Certain details of the haloform reaction (see p. 136) can now be understood. Once the monohalogeno-ketone is formed, further loss of a proton is more likely to occur from the carbon atom carrying the bromine atom, since this latter is highly electronegative and will withdraw electrons.

$$Br \longleftarrow \overset{\overset{\displaystyle H}{\big\uparrow}}{\underset{\underset{\displaystyle H}{\big\uparrow}}{C}} - COCH_3$$

Hence reaction proceeds in the above pattern to form $CBr_3.COCH_3$, the same picture presumably applying to chlorination and iodination in these conditions. A ketone such as $CH_3.COCH_2CH_3$ is likely to be attacked at the α-CH$_3$ rather than at the α-CH$_2$, since the β-CH$_3$ acts effectively as a source of electrons (see p. 48) and *reduces* the tendency for the adjacent α-CH$_2$ to lose a proton to a base.

The trihalogenomethyl ketone finally obtained is so 'denuded' of electrons at the carbonyl carbon atom by the combined effect of three halogen atoms and the carbonyl oxygen

$$\begin{matrix} Br \\ Br \\ Br \end{matrix} \!\!\! \diagup\!\!\!\!\!\! C \longleftarrow \overset{\displaystyle C}{\underset{\underset{\displaystyle O}{\big\|}}{}} - R$$

that attack by a hydroxyl ion leads to C—C fission:

$$\underset{\underset{Br}{\overset{Br}{Br}}}{}C-\!\!\!-\!\!\!-\overset{\overset{:OH^{\ominus}}{|}}{\underset{\underset{O}{\|}}{C}}-R$$

Addition of a proton to the $\overset{\ominus}{C}Br_3$ ion (to form $CHBr_3$) and removal of a proton from the $R.CO_2H$ molecule (to form $R.CO_2^{\ominus}$) complete the reaction. (The student should appreciate why these two opposite steps occur in the same conditions; $CHBr_3$ is so weak an acid that its conjugate base is too strong to exist except in very small concentration, even in aqueous alkali, while the carboxylic acid is relatively so strong that only a very low concentration of it can persist in the presence of excess $OH^{\ominus}$ ion. Similar considerations, of course, determine the proton transfer steps in a number of the mechanisms outlined in this book.)

The action of a suspension of bleaching powder on acetone is the usual way of preparing chloroform. The overall reaction is

$$CH_3COCH_3 + 3OCl^{\ominus} \rightarrow CHCl_3 + CH_3CO_2^{\ominus} + 2OH^{\ominus}$$

but the yield is far from quantitative.

The reaction of a methyl ketone $CH_3CO.R$ with sodium hypobromite solution is often a good preparative method of oxidizing the ketone to obtain the acid $R.CO_2H$; the student might care to speculate on the basis of the above suggested mechanism why considerable amounts of carbon tetrabromide as well as bromoform are produced.

The iodoform version of the reaction is a reliable diagnostic test for the CH_3CO group in a ketone (or, of course, in acetaldehyde, the only aldehyde containing it). The conditions for the test are the same as those for alcohols (see p. 136).

Chloral (trichloroacetaldehyde)

The topics discussed in the last section throw some light on the special features of chloral.

Thus the abnormally electrophilic nature of the carbonyl carbon atom, resulting from the electron-attracting effects of the three chlorine atoms and the carbonyl oxygen atom, accounts for the exceptionally rapid attack of water, ethanol and ammonia, and the unusual stability of the addition products:

$$CCl_3.CH\diagup\begin{smallmatrix}OH\\\\OH\end{smallmatrix} \qquad CCl_3.CH\diagup\begin{smallmatrix}OH\\\\OC_2H_5\end{smallmatrix} \qquad CCl_3.CH\diagup\begin{smallmatrix}OH\\\\NH_2\end{smallmatrix}$$

(Reversal of these additions requires the action of concentrated sulphuric acid; contrast the instability of the diol of acetaldehyde itself.)

Chloral is rapidly hydrolysed by warm aqueous alkali; this is, of course, identical with the last step of the haloform reaction. Chloroform and a formate are obtained

$$CCl_3.CHO + OH^\ominus \rightarrow CHCl_3 + H.COO^\ominus$$

Chloral hydrate (often simply called 'chloral') is used as a sleeping drug.

- In spite of the unifying concept of nucleophilic attack on carbonyl carbon, the impression given by the diversity of the reaction details discussed in this chapter may be bewildering. The table on p. 192 summarizes the topics covered. A blank means that there has been no discussion under this head; it should not be taken as necessarily implying that no reaction occurs.

Introduction of the carbonyl group into organic molecules

(Methods of preparing aldehydes and ketones.)

(1) Oxidation of primary and secondary alcohols

Oxidation of primary alcohols yields aldehydes, for example,

$$CH_3CH_2OH - 2e \rightarrow CH_3CHO + 2H^\oplus$$

and of secondary alcohols yields ketones, for example,

$$CH_3CHOHCH_3 - 2e \rightarrow CH_3COCH_3 + 2H^\oplus$$

The conventional oxidizing agent is acidified dichromate solution.

Since ketones are oxidized only with difficulty, it is sufficient with secondary alcohols to ensure that the oxidizing agent is not strong enough to oxidize the ketone. Aldehydes, however, are very readily oxidized— more so than alcohols—so that, to obtain even a moderate yield of aldehyde from a primary alcohol, excess of oxidizing agent must be avoided, e.g. by dripping acidified dichromate into the heated alcohol, or for the lowest water-soluble alcohols, by dripping a mixture of alcohol and neutral aqueous dichromate into hot aqueous sulphuric acid, and the aldehyde (which has a lower boiling point than the alcohol) should be distilled off as formed. Even so, yields are not good.

Table of reactions of familiar $\rangle$C=O compounds

Reagent	HCHO	CH_3CHO	C_6H_5CHO	CCl_3CHO	CH_3COCH_3	$C_6H_5COCH_2$
H_2O alone	unstable diol in aq. solution	as HCHO		*stable* diol (hydrate)	no action	no action
C_2H_5OH alone	unstable alcoholate in ethanolic solution	as HCHO		*stable* alcoholate	no action	no action
$CN^{\ominus}$, $H^{\oplus}$	cyanohydrin	cyanohydrin	cyanohydrin ($CN^{\ominus} \to$ benzoin)		cyanohydrin	cyanohydrin
$Na^{\oplus}HSO_3^{\ominus}$	addition compound (water-soluble)	as HCHO	addition compound (water-insoluble)	addition compound	addition compound	no action
NH_2OH	oxime	oxime	oxime	addition compound which $\to$ oxime slowly	oxime	oxime
$C_6H_5NH.NH_2$ NH_3	Ph. hydrazone $(CH_2)_6N_4$	Ph. hydrazone initially, addition cpd.	Ph. hydrazone hydrobenzamide	Ph. hydrazone *stable* addition cpd.	Ph. hydrazone	Ph. hydrazone
$C_6H_5NH_2$; CH_3CHO, $OH^{\ominus}$; CH_3COCH_3, $OH^{\ominus}$; $(CH_3CO)_2O$, $CH_3COO^{\ominus}$			benzal-aniline Claisen condensation Perkin reaction $\to$ cinnamic acid	no action		
C_2H_5OH, $H^{\oplus}$ concentrated H_2SO_4	acetal	acetal	acetal (sulphonates C_6H_5—)	acetal	no action	no action (sulphonates C_6H_5—)
alkalis	Cannizzaro reaction	weak, $\to$ aldol strong, $\to$ resin	Cannizzaro reaction	$CHCl_3$, $HCOO^{\ominus}$	mesitylene (etc.) diacetone alcohol	no action
Various polymerizations	trioxymethylene paraformaldehyde	paraldehyde metaldehyde		metachloral	none	none
Reduction to alcohol	Yes	Yes	Yes	Yes	Yes	Yes
Amalgamated Zn HCl_{aq}	no hydrocarbon	no hydrocarbon	$C_6H_5.CH_3$	no hydrocarbon	$CH_3CH_2CH_3$	$C_6H_5CH_2CH_3$
Reduction to 'pinacol'	no	no	yes	no	yes	yes
Mild oxidation (e.g. $Ag^{\oplus}(NH_3)_2$)	$H.COOH$	$CH_3.COOH$	$C_6H_5.COOH$	$CCl_3.COOH$	no action	no action
Vigorous oxidation	CO_2, H_2O				$CH_3.COOH$, CO_2, H_2O	$C_6H_5.COOH$, CO_2, H_2O
PCl_5	no	>CCl_2	>CCl_2	>CCl_2	>CCl_2	>CCl_2

Alcohols may be catalytically *dehydrogenated* by passing the vapour over heated finely divided metals (e.g. copper).

$$CH_3CH_2OH \rightleftharpoons CH_3CHO + H_2$$

The reaction is reversible, and excess alcohol will be used, but this can be recycled. Oxidation of primary alcohols to the acid (which is a process requiring actual addition of oxygen atoms) is avoided. Secondary alcohols yield ketones.

Formaldehyde is manufactured by the catalytic dehydrogenation of methanol over heated silver.

The simple dehydrogenation reaction is endothermic, so the methanol vapour is mixed with air or oxygen and the hydrogen liberated is exothermically oxidized to steam, thus maintaining the catalyst temperature. It is probable, however, that oxidation as well as dehydrogenation of the methanol occurs.

(2) Oxidation and hydrolysis of aromatic side-chain halides

Benzaldehyde is obtained when benzyl chloride is refluxed with aqueous lead or copper (II) nitrate solution. The nitrate is reduced to oxides of nitrogen. The heavy metal ion presumably functions as a catalyst in some way.

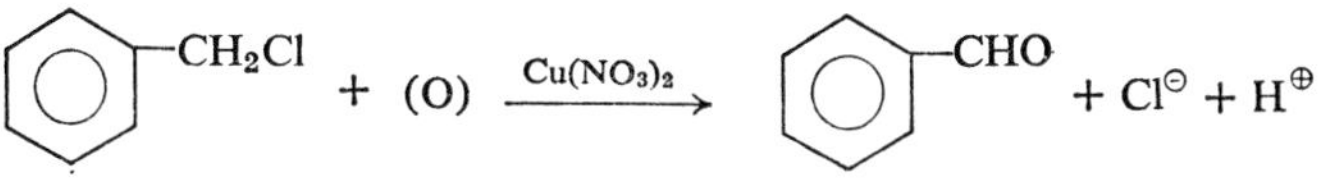

The reaction is equivalent to hydrolysis and oxidation in a single operation. Compare:

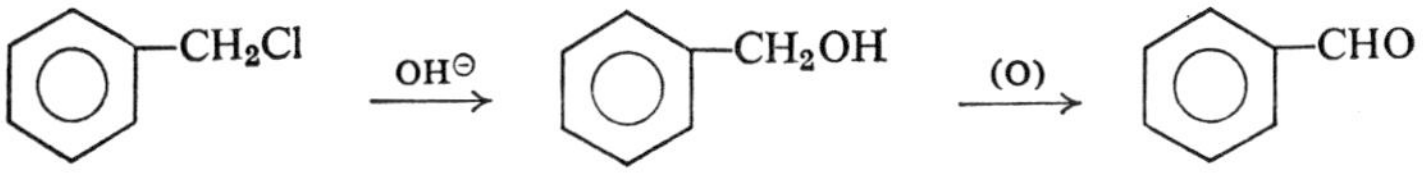

(3) Oxidation of aromatic side-chains

Toluene may be oxidized to benzaldehyde by a suspension of manganese dioxide in dilute sulphuric acid, or by chromyl chloride (CrO_2Cl_2). To carry out the latter (Etard's) reaction, a solution of toluene in chloroform is slowly added to a cooled solution of chromyl chloride in the same solvent. An addition product is formed, which with water yields benzaldehyde.

(4) Hydrolysis of *gem*-dihalides (i.e. *twin* dihalides—with two halogen atoms attached to one carbon atom)

Hydrolysis of $\begin{smallmatrix}R\\R^1\end{smallmatrix}{>}CCl_2$ on the analogy of the hydrolysis of monohalides to alcohols would lead to $\begin{smallmatrix}R\\R^1\end{smallmatrix}{>}C{<}\begin{smallmatrix}OH\\OH\end{smallmatrix}$. Since, as a rule, molecules with two OH groups attached to one carbon atom eliminate a water molecule, the product will instead be $\begin{smallmatrix}R\\R^1\end{smallmatrix}{>}C{=}O$. If $R^1{=}H$, this is an aldehyde; if R and R^1 are both alkyl or other groups it is a ketone.

Since aldehydes react with alkalis, either to yield an aldol or a resin or to undergo Cannizzaro's reaction, it is clear that boiling with caustic alkali will *not* produce aldehydes from dihalides. If the aldehyde has an α-hydrogen atom, heating with water under pressure will serve. Cannizzaro's reaction is more sluggish than the aldol reaction and requires more prolonged reaction with caustic alkali. For producing aldehydes without α-hydrogen atoms from dihalides, it may therefore be possible to use weak alkali such as a suspension of lead oxide in water, or even milk of lime (*ca.* M/40). A good reagent is a suspension of calcium *carbonate*. The method is technically applied to the production of benzaldehyde from benzylidene dichloride (from the side-chain chlorination of toluene):

$$C_6H_5CHCl_2 + H_2O \rightarrow C_6H_5CHO + 2HCl$$

The practicability of this method depends on the availability of the *gem*-dihalide. The simplest way of making this is often from the carbonyl compound, in which case the reaction is of little value for preparing the latter.

(5) The reduction of carboxylic acids and their derivatives

Carboxylic acids themselves are resistant to reduction and, under conditions which will reduce them (see p. 226), they usually yield primary alcohols rather than the half-way aldehyde. Certain derivatives of acids can be reduced to aldehydes. Thus, acyl chlorides are reduced catalytically to aldehydes by hydrogen in the presence of palladium (Rosenmund reaction), for example,

$$C_6H_5COCl + H_2 \rightarrow C_6H_5CHO + HCl$$
benzoyl chloride   benzaldehyde

To avoid further reduction to alcohols the catalyst is partly 'poisoned' by adding traces of sulphur-containing reagents.

(Strictly speaking, this reaction does not *introduce* the ${>}CO$ group, since it is present in a modified form in the acyl chloride.)

194

(6) The pyrolysis of salts of carboxylic acids, and allied reactions

If the calcium salt of an acid $R.CO_2H$ is heated, the ketone $R.CO.R$ is formed:

$$\begin{array}{c} R.CO_2^{\ominus} \\ \phantom{R.CO_2^{\ominus}}Ca^{2\oplus} \\ R.CO_2^{\ominus} \end{array} \rightarrow Ca^{2\oplus}CO_3^{2\ominus}+R.CO.R$$

Thus calcium acetate yields acetone, calcium benzoate, benzophenone $(C_6H_5.CO.C_6H_5)$, and calcium formate, formaldehyde.

A mixture of calcium salts of $R.CO_2H$ and $R^1.CO_2H$ yields the mixed ketone $R.CO.R^1$ as well as the two symmetrical ketones. In the special case where $R^1=H$ (i.e. when a mixture of calcium formate with another calcium carboxylate is heated), an aldehyde is formed, for example,

$$\begin{array}{c} CH_3CO_2^{\ominus} \\ \phantom{CH_3CO_2^{\ominus}}Ca^{2\oplus} \\ H.CO_2^{\ominus} \end{array} \rightarrow CH_3CHO+Ca^{2\oplus}CO_3^{2\ominus}$$

Yields are rarely good, and often extremely poor with many by-products. Acetone was once manufactured by the pyrolysis of calcium acetate, but the process has been totally obsolete for many years.

Better results as far as ketones (mixed or symmetrical) are concerned are obtained by passing the vaporized acid (or acids) over heated thoria on a pumice support.

(7) The Friedel–Crafts and allied reactions

(For a discussion of this reaction, see chap. 8.)

Ketones with the $>CO$ group attached to an aromatic ring can be prepared by acting on aromatic hydrocarbons with acyl chlorides or acid anhydrides in the presence of certain catalysts, pre-eminently anhydrous aluminium chloride, for example,

$$C_6H_6+CH_3COCl \rightarrow C_6H_5COCH_3+HCl$$
$$C_6H_6+(CH_3CO)_2O \rightarrow C_6H_5COCH_3+CH_3CO_2H$$
$$\text{acetophenone}$$

The preparation of aldehydes by this method would require the use of formyl chloride or formic anhydride, neither of which can be isolated. However, a mixture of carbon monoxide and hydrogen chloride reacts with aromatic hydrocarbons in the presence of aluminium chloride and cuprous chloride, behaving as if formyl chloride were present; for example, with toluene:

$$CO + HCl \rightleftharpoons HCOCl ?$$

$$+ \text{'HCOCl'} \longrightarrow \quad + \text{HCl} \quad (\text{and } o\text{-isomer})$$

The hydrogen chloride, though necessary, is not consumed in the reaction. (This is the *Gattermann–Koch* reaction.)

A reaction of similar type but limited application is the Reimer–Tiemann reaction for preparing certain phenolic aldehydes (see p. 103).

(8) The use of ethyl acetoacetate to prepare methyl ketones

(See p. 199.)

(9) The catalytic hydration of alkynes (acetylene and homologues)

Acetaldehyde can be manufactured by the hydration of acetylene, which is catalysed by aqueous sulphuric acid and mercuric salts. The overall reaction is simply

$$CH{\equiv}CH + H_2O \rightarrow CH_3CHO$$

but mercury complexes (which are readily formed by acetylenic compounds) are probably formed intermediately. Higher alkynes will form ketones, not aldehydes, as implied by the operation of Markovnikov's Rule. (Compare the addition of hydrogen bromide to alkynes.)

(10) The manufacture of acetone

Much acetone is obtained by the oxidation of cumene (isopropyl benzene) in the manufacture of phenol. This is outlined on p. 143.

Acetone has also been obtained from starch or other carbohydrate sources by fermentation with the bacillus *Clostridium acetobutylicum* (Weizmann's method). *Acetone* (about 20%) and *butanol* (about 75%) were the main products but the process is no longer operated industrially.

Acetone can also be made directly from propylene (as well as via preliminary conversion to cumene) by hydration to isopropyl alcohol, followed by oxidation or dehydrogenation.

$$CH_3-CH{=}CH_2 \xrightarrow{\;H_2O\;} CH_3-CHOH-CH_3 \longrightarrow CH_3COCH_3$$

$$O_2/PdCl_2/CaCl_2$$

The presence of $-C\begin{smallmatrix}H\\\\O\end{smallmatrix}$ **in aldehydes and of** $\rangle C{=}O$ **in ketones**

Formaldehyde (molecular formula CH_2O) can only be formulated as:

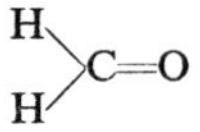

$$\begin{smallmatrix}H\\\\H\end{smallmatrix}\!\!\diagdown C{=}O$$

implying the presence of the $\rangle C{=}O$ group. The structural formula of acetaldehyde (C_2H_4O) can be established as follows:

(*a*) Chlorination yields ultimately trichloroacetaldehyde (chloral) C_2HOCl_3. This yields chloroform $CHCl_3$ on mild alkaline hydrolysis. Hence the three chlorine atoms in the chloral molecule must be present as $CCl_3{-}$. Chloral must hence be $(CCl_3)(CHO)$, which can only be formulated:

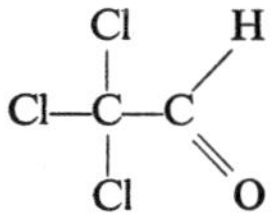

$$Cl\!-\!\underset{\underset{Cl}{|}}{\overset{\overset{Cl}{|}}{C}}\!-\!C\diagup^{H}_{\diagdown\!O}$$

Acetaldehyde must by analogy be formulated:

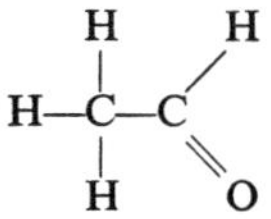

$$H\!-\!\underset{\underset{H}{|}}{\overset{\overset{H}{|}}{C}}\!-\!C\diagup^{H}_{\diagdown\!O}$$

(*b*) Acetaldehyde undergoes addition reactions with hydrogen and catalysts, hydrogen cyanide and sodium bisulphite. These are consistent with the presence of the $C{=}O$ double bond.

(*c*) The ready oxidation of aldehydes to carboxylic acids, which contain the $-OH$ group, can be formulated as

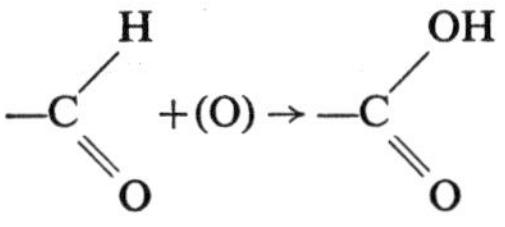

$$-C\diagup^{H}_{\diagdown\!O} \;+(O)\rightarrow -C\diagup^{OH}_{\diagdown\!O}$$

(*d*) Acetone and other ketones undergo many reactions attributable to the $\rangle C{=}O$ group in the same way as aldehydes, and are therefore formulated with this group, but cannot be oxidized to carboxylic acids without loss of carbon atoms from the molecule. Hence the $\rangle C{=}O$ group cannot be on the end carbon atom.

(*e*) Acetone is thus formulated as

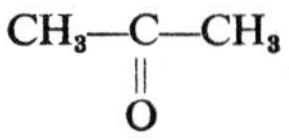

$$CH_3\!-\!\underset{\underset{O}{\|}}{C}\!-\!CH_3$$

197

and the isomeric propionaldehyde as

$$CH_3CH_2C{\overset{\displaystyle H}{\underset{\displaystyle O}{\Big<}}}$$

The presence of two methyl groups in acetone is confirmed by fission of the trihalogeno-acetones to haloform and acetate ion; the latter can be shown to contain a methyl group.

Preparation of ethyl acetoacetate

When sodium is added to ethyl acetate, slow evolution of hydrogen occurs. The reaction gradually becomes faster, and the sodium reacts almost completely. A brownish semi-solid mass is formed, consisting largely of the sodium derivative of ethyl acetoacetate suspended in unchanged ethyl acetate.

$$2CH_3COOEt + 2Na \rightarrow CH_3COCHNaCOOEt + EtONa + H_2\uparrow$$

The free ester is liberated by addition of aqueous acetic acid (a strong acid might bring about hydrolysis).

$$(CH_3COCHCOOEt)^{\ominus} + CH_3CO_2H \rightarrow CH_3COCH_2COOEt + CH_3COO^{\ominus}$$

The mechanism is as follows:

(*a*) The sodium forms sodium ethoxide with traces of ethanol in the original ester:

$$2EtOH + 2Na \rightarrow 2EtO^{\ominus}Na^{\oplus} + H_2.$$

(*b*) The ethoxide ion as a base causes some ionization of the ethyl acetate as a very weak acid:

$$EtO^{\ominus} + CH_3CO_2Et \longrightarrow EtOH + \left(\overset{\ominus}{C}H_2 - C{\overset{\displaystyle O}{\underset{\displaystyle OEt}{\Big<}}} \longleftrightarrow CH_2 = C{\overset{\displaystyle O^{\ominus}}{\underset{\displaystyle OEt}{\Big<}}} \right)$$

(i)

(*c*) The conjugate base of ethyl acetate, as a nucleophile, attacks a second molecule of ethyl acetate:

$$CH_3 - \overset{\displaystyle O}{\overset{\displaystyle \|}{C}} - OEt \longrightarrow CH_3COCH_2CO_2Et + EtO^{\ominus}$$

$$\overset{\ominus}{:}CH_2CO_2Et$$

(*d*) Proton transfer → $(CH_3COCHCOOEt)^{\ominus} + EtOH$

(ii)

Two molecules (i) and (ii) of ethanol are thus formed for every one used; if step (*b*) is assumed to be slow and dependent on [EtO$^\ominus$], this accounts for the speeding-up of the reaction. Step (*a*) is consistent with Claisen's claim that the reaction will not proceed with ethanol-free ethyl acetate.

Step (*c*) in reverse is then the likely first step of the so-called 'acid' hydrolysis of ethyl acetoacetate and its derivatives (see p. 200).

Syntheses with acetoacetic ester and allied compounds

It is pointed out on pp. 202–7, that the compound ethyl acetoacetate (acetoacetic ester) $CH_3COCH_2CO_2Et$ behaves as a weak acid, and with very strong bases, such as the ethoxide ion, forms the conjugate base $CH_3CO^\ominus CHCO_2Et$. This conjugate base has the ionic charge distributed over the carbonyl oxygen atoms as well as the carbon atom of the methylene group; nevertheless in many reactions it behaves as a nucleophilic reagent with available electrons on this carbon atom. Thus in particular it undergoes the usual type of displacement reaction with alkyl and similar halides, for example, with methyl iodide:

$$(CH_3COCHCO_2Et)^\ominus + CH_3I \rightarrow CH_3COCHCO_2Et + I^\ominus$$
$$\overset{|}{CH_3}$$

This product can again lose a proton in the same way as acetoacetic ester itself, and its conjugate base behaves as a nucleophilic reagent in the same way, for example, with ethyl iodide:

$$(CH_3CO.C.CO_2Et)^\ominus + C_2H_5I \rightarrow CH_3.CO.\overset{\overset{C_2H_5}{|}}{C}.CO_2Et + I^\ominus$$
$$\underset{CH_3}{|} \qquad\qquad \underset{CH_3}{|}$$

This product clearly has neither of the ionizable methylene hydrogen atoms of the parent ester.

In both of the above steps, a C—C link is formed between the alkyl group of the halide and the methylene carbon atom of the ester.

Acetoacetic ester and the alkylated derivatives obtained as above can undergo two types of hydrolytic fission.

(*a*) On refluxing with dilute aqueous alkali (or dilute mineral acid) hydrolysis occurs as with esters in general, but in addition decarboxylation occurs. This may be compared with the ready decarboxylation of trichloroacetic acid and nitroacetic acid (see p. 234 and p. 261).

$$CH_3COCH_2CO_2Et \xrightarrow[\text{aq}]{OH^\ominus} CH_3COCH_2CO_2{}^\ominus \xrightarrow[\text{aq}]{OH^\ominus} CH_3COCH_3 + CO_3{}^{2\ominus}$$
$$(+EtOH)$$

The products from acetoacetic ester itself are therefore ethanol, carbonate and acetone; mono-alkyl derivatives of acetoacetic ester will yield, instead of acetone, ketones of the general type CH_3COCH_2R, and dialkyl derivatives ketones of the type $CH_2COCHRR^1$. (Both substituent alkyl groups may of course be the same.) This type of fission is known as *ketonic hydrolysis*, from the type of organic product obtained.

(*b*) On refluxing with concentrated ethanolic alkali, acetoacetic ester yields ethanol and two molar proportions of acetate; this is in essence the reversal of the formation of the ester from two molecules of ethyl acetate, together with saponification:

$$CH_3COCH_2CO_2Et \xrightarrow[\text{EtOH}]{OH^\ominus} 2CH_3COO^\ominus + EtOH$$

Whereas ketonic hydrolysis results in fission of the C—C bond between the methylene group and the *ester* carbonyl group, this second type results in fission of the C—C bond between the methylene group and the *ketonic* carbonyl group.

Mono-alkyl derivatives of acetoacetic ester under these conditions yield one molar proportion of acetate and one of an acid anion of the general type $RCH_2CO_2{}^\ominus$; dialkyl derivatives yield acetate and an ion $RR'CH.CO_2{}^\ominus$. This type of fission is known as *acid hydrolysis*, from the type of organic product obtained (and not, of course, from the conditions employed, which are strongly alkaline).

The general procedure is to dissolve the acetoacetic ester in dry ethanol and to add an equimolar amount of sodium dissolved in dry ethanol (i.e. of ethoxide).

$$CH_3COCH_2CO_2Et + OEt^\ominus \rightarrow (CH_3COCHCO_2Et)^\ominus + EtOH$$

The suspension or solution of the sodium derivative of the ester thus obtained is refluxed with an equimolar amount of the requisite halide (preferably, with simple alkyl halides, the iodide, which will undergo the displacement reaction most readily). The resulting ethanolic solution can be worked up for the alkylated ester; the whole procedure can then be repeated if a dialkyl derivative is required. The product can then be subjected to ketonic or acid hydrolysis. To sum up therefore:

$$CH_3COCH_2CO_2Et \xrightarrow{OEt^\ominus} (CH_3COCHCO_2Et)^\ominus \xrightarrow{RI} CH_3COCHRCO_2Et$$

Then, optionally:

$$(\xrightarrow{OEt^\ominus} (CH_3COCRCO_2Et)^\ominus \xrightarrow{R^1I} CH_3COCRR^1CO_2Et)$$

Then:

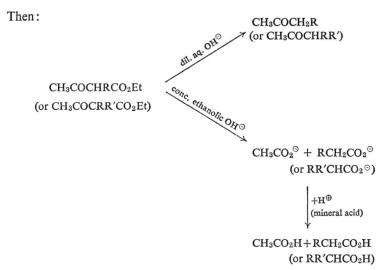

$$CH_3COCHRCO_2Et$$
$$(or\ CH_3COCRR'CO_2Et)$$

dil. aq. OH$^\ominus$ → CH_3COCH_2R
(or $CH_3COCHRR'$)

conc. ethanolic OH$^\ominus$ → $CH_3CO_2^\ominus + RCH_2CO_2^\ominus$
(or $RR'CHCO_2^\ominus$)

$+H^\oplus$
(mineral acid)

$CH_3CO_2H + RCH_2CO_2H$
(or $RR'CHCO_2H$)

(In practice, small amounts of ketone will of course be obtained under acid hydrolysis conditions, and some carboxylate anions under ketonic hydrolysis conditions.)

This basic scheme is open to many modifications. For example, dihalides will react with two molar proportions of the acetoacetic ester base yielding ultimately diketones or dibasic acids. (Amusingly, iodine itself will act as a dihalide leading to a direct linking of the methylene carbon atoms of two molecules of ester.) Other compounds with displaceable halogen may be used in place of simple alkyl halides, for example, the esters of α-halogeno fatty acids, such as ethyl α-bromopropionate, $CH_3CHBrCO_2Et$. (Clearly halogenated *acids* themselves must be avoided, since these would simply regenerate acetoacetic ester from its conjugate base.) Other β-keto esters such as benzoylacetic ester, $C_6H_5COCH_2CO_2Et$, can be made and behave in the same way.

Syntheses with malonic ester

Diethyl malonate $CH_2(CO_2Et)_2$ behaves as a weak acid in the same way as ethyl acetoacetate, forming a 'sodium derivative' which acts as a nucleophilic reagent under the same experimental conditions. Thus it can be used to form C—C links according to the general scheme:

$$CH_2(CO_2Et)_2 \xrightarrow{OEt^\ominus} [CH(CO_2Et)_2]^\ominus \xrightarrow{RI} RCH(CO_2Et)_2$$

then, optionally

$$(R.CH(CO_2Et)_2 \xrightarrow{OEt^\ominus} [RC(CO_2Et)_2]^\ominus \xrightarrow{R^1I} RR^1C(CO_2Et)_2$$

The mono- and di-alkyl substituted malonic esters so obtained may be saponified and the acids obtained; these, like malonic acid itself, lose carbon dioxide at or around their melting points, thus yielding a fatty acid:

$$R.CH(CO_2Et)_2 \xrightarrow[\text{Aq}]{OH^{\ominus}} R.CH(CO_2^{\ominus})_2 \xrightarrow[\text{(mineral acid)}]{H^{\oplus}\text{Aq}} R.CH(CO_2H)_2$$

(or $RR^1C(CO_2Et)_2$)   (or $RR^1C(CO_2^{\ominus})_2$)   (or $RR^1C(CO_2H)_2$)

$$\xrightarrow[\text{to m. pt.}]{\text{heat}} \begin{array}{l} RCH_2CO_2H \\ \text{(or } RR^1CH.CO_2H) \end{array}$$

The ultimate product is thus an acid *of the same general type* as those obtainable from acetoacetic ester. Since no ketonic product is possible malonic ester is usually preferable to acetoacetic ester for synthesizing such acids.

The malonic ester synthesis can be extended on the same lines as those with acetoacetic ester.

Keto–enol tautomerism

It was stated on p. 173, that aldehydes and ketones possessing an α-hydrogen atom were very feebly acidic:

$$\begin{array}{ccc} \overset{\displaystyle >}{C}H{-}\overset{\displaystyle }{C}{-} + B & \rightleftharpoons & BH^{\oplus} + \overset{\ominus}{>}C\overset{\curvearrowleft}{-}C \longleftrightarrow >C{=}C{-} \\ \parallel & & \parallel \\ O & & O \qquad\qquad O^{\ominus} \\ \text{base} & & \end{array}$$

mesomeric anion

yielding a mesomeric anion. The ionic charge of this is distributed between the carbonyl oxygen and the α-carbon. Should proton addition in the reverse reaction occur at the former instead of the latter site, an isomer $>C{=}C(OH){-}$ of the original carbonyl compound would be formed. This is known as the *enol* form of the compound (i.e. 'ene-ol', since it contains $>C{=}C<$ attached to —OH).

$$\begin{array}{ccccc} \overset{\ominus}{>}C{-}C{-} & \longleftrightarrow & >C{=}C{-} + BH^{\oplus} & \rightleftharpoons & >C{=}C{-} + B \\ \parallel & & \mid & & \mid \\ O & & O^{\ominus} & & OH \end{array}$$

The enols of the simple aldehydes and ketones cannot be isolated; it is supposed that they exist in minute traces in equilibrium with the ordinary or *keto*-form. In certain types of compound, however, a detectable or even predominant proportion of the enol is found. We then have a situation where two isomeric substances exist in equilibrium with one another as a result of a readily reversible isomerization reaction; such reversible isomerism is known as 'tautomerism' and the readily interconvertible isomers are called 'tautomers' or 'tautomeric' forms. The classical case of the keto-enol tautomerism is that of the β-keto ester *ethyl acetoacetate*:

$$CH_3COCH_2CO_2Et$$

and this will be discussed in some detail in the following pages.

Ethyl acetoacetate (or acetoacetic ester) is formed by the action of sodium on ethyl acetate, followed by addition of aqueous acid. This reaction is discussed on p. 198. Its formulation as the ester of a β-keto-acid is supported by the following evidence:

(*a*) Reduction yields ethyl β-hydroxybutyrate.

(*b*) It combines mole for mole with

(i) 2,4-dinitro phenylhydrazine to form a 2,4-dinitro phenyl-hydrazone,

(ii) semicarbazide to form a semicarbazone,

(iii) cyanide and hydrogen ions to form a cyanohydrin,

(iv) sodium bisulphite solution to form a bisulphite compound.

(Phenylhydrazine and hydroxylamine react to form nitrogen-containing ring compounds, no doubt by way of the phenylhydrazone and oxime, which cannot, however, be isolated.)

(*c*) On cautious hydrolysis at room temperature, the corresponding acid (or in alkaline conditions its anion) can be obtained, but this loses carbon dioxide (or carbonate ion) yielding acetone. This decarboxylation occurs slowly at room temperature, more rapidly on heating;

$$CH_3COCH_2CO_2H \rightarrow CH_3COCH_3 \text{ and } CO_2.$$

On the other hand, the following reactions are less easily reconciled with the keto-ester formulation.

(*d*) Rapid decolorization of bromine water.

(*e*) Formation in solution in water (in which the ester is sparingly but appreciably soluble) or ethanol of a deep red-purple colour on addition of ferric chloride.

(*f*) Formation with saturated copper (II) acetate solution of a copper (II) compound $(C_6H_9O_3)_2Cu$, which is readily soluble in chloroform.

(*g*) Formation in ethanolic solution with sodium or sodium ethoxide of a sodium compound $C_6H_9O_3Na$, which is obtained as a white solid on evaporating off excess ethanol.

An *enol*-type formula $CH_3C(OH){=}CHCO_2Et$ is consistent with these facts: (*d*) is explicable as olefinic addition of bromine; (*e*) as complex formation, the colour being comparable with that of, say, phenol with iron (III); (f) as the formation of an uncharged chelate copper (II) complex, thus:

$$\left(\begin{array}{c} CH_3 \\ | \\ C-O \\ \parallel \quad \diagdown \\ HC \qquad Cu \\ \diagdown \quad \diagup \\ C=O \\ | \\ OEt \end{array}\right)_2$$

(The sodium 'salt' formed in (g) was early formulated as

$$CH_3C(ONa)=CHCO_2Et$$

by analogy with the formation of, for example, sodium ethoxide from ethanol. The reasoning behind this explanation of (g) would be essentially, in nineteenth-century terms: 'hydrogen attached to carbon is not replaceable by metals, but is when attached to oxygen; acetoacetic ester has hydrogen replaceable by sodium, therefore it is probably an—OH compound'. As we shall see, in this crude form the argument is fallacious; nevertheless, it unquestionably played a major part in establishing the idea of the existence of an enol form.)

These two formulations were reconciled by assuming that the ester as normally obtained was a mixture of the two forms, keto and enol, in equilibrium:

$$CH_3.COCH_2CO_2Et \rightleftharpoons CH_3C(OH)=CHCO_2Et$$

On removing one or other form by an appropriate reaction, equilibrium is quite rapidly re-established, so that ultimately all the ester present will react as the keto-form with, say, sodium bisulphite, or as the enol with, say, saturated copper (II) acetate solution.

(A combination of (d) and (e) above is instructive. If ferric chloride solution is added to a saturated aqueous solution of acetoacetic ester a deep purple colour forms. If bromine water is added the colour fades and with excess bromine disappears completely to be replaced by the colour of the bromine. On standing the bromine colour fades and as it disappears the purple colour reappears and slowly increases to a definite intensity. The whole sequence can be repeated. For each successive addition of equal amounts of bromine, the disappearance of this and the reappearance of the purple are slower. In addition, an emulsion of the almost insoluble brominated product separates out. These results should be examined directly so that the hypothesis of a keto-enol equilibrium can be confirmed.)

The hypothesis of an equilibrium mixture of forms can be confirmed by isolating the two forms from the mixture, provided that conditions can be found at which equilibrium is re-established extremely slowly: this in turn implies low temperature and/or the absence of catalysts. This has been achieved with acetoacetic ester. By cooling a solution of the pure ester in light petroleum (i.e. a mixture of C_5 and C_6 paraffins) containing a little ethanol to about $-80°$ C, a crystalline form of m.p. $-39°$ separates out. This gives no immediate colour with ferric chloride solution and is believed to be the *keto*-tautomer. No separation of the two forms is achieved by fractional distillation in ordinary glass apparatus, because the tautomerism reactions are catalysed by bases, including ordinary soda glass. So-called 'aseptic' distillation in pure silica vessels is necessary. The more volatile enol distils off from the keto form. The enol form is also obtained when dry hydrogen chloride is passed into a suspension of the dry sodium derivative in light petroleum at about $-80°$. The precipitate of sodium chloride can be filtered off, and the petroleum ether evaporated off in a vacuum, all at low temperatures, and the *enol* remains as an oil which gives an instant intense purple colour, fading to a less intense one with ferric chloride solution. As normally prepared, acetoacetic ester contains about 93% keto form and about 7% enol.

It will be noticed that the enol form is *more* volatile and *lower* melting than the keto form, and readily soluble in paraffinic solvents; on the face of it, the contrary would be expected from a hydroxyl compound, on account of association by hydrogen bonding. The absence of associated behaviour can be accounted for by assuming *internal* hydrogen bonding within a single enol molecule, giving a cyclic structure, thus:

$$H_3C\diagdown{C}\!\!\!\underset{\diagdown{O}\diagdown{H\cdot}\diagdown{O}}{\overset{\overset{H}{C}}{\diagup}}\!\!\!{C}\diagup^{OEt}$$

The hydrogen-bonding powers of the —OH group are thus not available for linking molecules together, and the enol molecule becomes less and not more polar than the keto.

The interconversion of the keto and enol forms involves essentially the migration of a hydrogen atom from carbon to oxygen or vice versa:

$$-\overset{|}{C}\!\!(\!H\!)\!\!-\!\overset{|}{C}\!\!=\!O \quad\rightleftharpoons\quad -\overset{|}{C}\!\!=\!\overset{|}{C}\!\!-\!O\!(\!H\!)$$

with a corresponding shift of a double bond. Quite early in the investigation of tautomerism, it was realized that this hydrogen atom probably migrated as an hydrogen ion. Putting this in terms of current concepts, for keto–enol tautomerism to occur, a hydrogen atom attached to the α-carbon atom of the carbonyl compound must be appreciably ionizable, and thus be removable by the action of a base; the reasons for this 'abnormal' ionizability of a CH group are to be sought in the electron-withdrawing effect of the electronegative oxygen atom and in the stabilization of the anion by delocalization of its charge and double bond pair. The equations at the beginning of this section summarize this hypothesis. Wherever the reaction rates make observation possible, tautomerism is found to be subject to base catalysis, and much kinetic investigation has confirmed that this mechanism is consistent with the facts in the great majority of tautomerism reactions.

In the case of acetoacetic ester, the ionic charge of the mesomeric anion will be distributed not only over the oxygen and carbon atoms of the —CH$_2$CO— group, but also over the oxygen atom of the ester carbonyl group, in accordance with the following bond diagrams:

$$CH_3 \cdot C = CH - C \underset{OEt}{\overset{O}{\diagup}} \longleftrightarrow$$

$$CH_3 \cdot C - \overset{\ominus}{CH} - C \underset{OEt}{\overset{O}{\diagup}} \longleftrightarrow CH_3 \cdot C - CH = C \underset{OEt}{\overset{O^\ominus}{\diagup}}$$

This extra delocalization of the ionic charge and of the double bond pairs presumably accounts for the relatively greater stability of the anion *vis-à-vis* the parent molecule in acetoacetic ester as compared, say, with acetone: that is, for the greater acid strength of the β-keto-ester over the simple ketone.

Since enol and keto forms give rise to the same (mesomeric) anion on loss of a proton, there is clearly no simple structural sense in which the sodium compound is a derivative of the enol rather than of the keto form, as was at one time thought. The argument that the formation of a sodium derivative implies the presence of a hydroxyl group, as outlined above, is therefore fallacious; it is only because, in this molecular environment, hydrogen attached to carbon *is* ionizable that keto–enol tautomerism occurs. The fact remains that practically pure enol is obtained by the action of an acid (hydrogen chloride) on the sodium derivative as described above. This is explicable if it is assumed that the addition of a proton to oxygen (and its reverse) occurs much more rapidly than its addition to carbon; that is to say, the anion and an added acid reach equilibrium with the enol much more rapidly than with the keto. This equilibrium is metastable, and the enol largely reverts to the more stable keto as equilibrium between the anion and the latter slowly becomes established. This phenomenon is found in the tautomerism of nitro compounds (see p. 258), and indeed is quite general in tautomeric systems.

Recognition of the fact that the sodium compound is not specifically derived from the enol form, but has a mesomeric anion, helps to dispose of a problem which puzzled earlier workers in this field, namely, why it is that, in the alkylation reactions of sodio-acetoacetic ester, carbon-alkylation and not oxygen-alkylation is the general though not invariable rule. (These reactions are described on p. 199.) Clearly the anion is potentially capable of acting as a nucleophile either at a carbon or an oxygen site. Which behaviour predominates will depend on the relative electron availability at the two sites, the nature of the electrophilic reagent, and the solvent conditions. In fact, although nucleophilic reactivity is normally located at the carbon site, it was shown quite early on that reaction at the oxygen site could occur; for example, the main product with ethyl chloroformate $Cl.CO_2Et$ is $CH_3C{=}CHCO_2Et$. For the purpose of representing

$$\underset{\displaystyle O.CO_2Et}{|}$$

these reactions formally, it would seem reasonable to represent the anion simply as $(CH_3COCHCO_2Et)^{\ominus}$, avoiding any implications about the location of the charge; this convention has been adopted on pp. 198–201.

The equilibrium ratio of a given keto-enol pair is by no means an invariable quantity. In general, it will depend on temperature (though the effect in the case of acetoacetic ester is small) but also on the solvent, if any, since preferential solvation of one form will stabilize it relative to the other. Thus although in pure liquid acetoacetic ester there is 7% of enol this drops to 0·4% in water and rises to 46% in hexane. This confirms the view that the keto form is the *more* polar and thus the more readily solvated by polar solvents such as water. Similarly, the equilibrium content of enol in the vapour phase is said to be 49%. The student may like to consider why, as a preliminary to isolating the enol by aseptic distillation, it is advantageous to distil from a *glass* flask into a *silica* condenser and receiver.

Tautomerism is by no means confined to keto–enol pairs. It has been observed in other systems, as for example the following:

$$\underset{\displaystyle O}{\overset{\displaystyle \|}{-NH{-}C{-}}} \rightleftharpoons \underset{\displaystyle OH}{\overset{\displaystyle |}{-N{=}C{-}}}$$

$$-NH{-}N{=}N{-} \rightleftharpoons -N{=}N{-}NH{-} \text{ (see p. 270)}$$

$$HO{-}\langle\bigcirc\rangle{-}N{=}O \rightleftharpoons O{=}\langle\bigcirc\rangle{=}N{-}OH$$

The tautomerism of nitro-compounds is discussed on p. 258.

The table below shows the enol content of some familiar compounds.

Compound	Percentage of enol in liquid state
Acetone CH_3COCH_3	0·00025 %
Acetylacetone $CH_3COCH_2COCH_3$	80 %
Acetoacetic ester $CH_3COCH_2CO_2Et$	7 %
Phenol C_6H_5OH	Very nearly 100 %

15

The carboxyl group $-\mathrm{C}\begin{smallmatrix}\diagup\!\!\diagup \mathrm{O}\\ \diagdown \mathrm{OH}\end{smallmatrix}$ and allied functional groups

It has been pointed out in the preceding chapters that the properties and reactions associated with the presence of certain simple functional groups (halogen, —OH, —OR, $-NH_2$) are profoundly modified when these groups are attached to a carbonyl radical and that the reactions associated with the carbonyl group in aldehydes and ketones are similarly modified when the carbonyl group is attached to one of the above groups.

The combined groups are therefore conveniently regarded, as it were, as functional groups in their own right and since the *carboxyl* group $-\mathrm{C}\begin{smallmatrix}\diagup\!\!\diagup \mathrm{O}\\ \diagdown \mathrm{OH}\end{smallmatrix}$ can readily be converted into the others, and they in their turn readily reconverted to it, they can conveniently be considered in close association. Conventionally the carboxylic acids and carboxylate esters are formulated RCO_2H, RCO_2R' and these forms will be used in this book. The older forms —COOH or —CO.OH may be met. They are occasionally convenient when it is desirable to emphasize the relationship with compounds such as acid chlorides or amides.

Compounds containing the $-CO_2H$ group are known as *carboxylic acids*, and these containing the other groups are regarded as derivatives of the corresponding acid, thus:

$R.CO_2H$	the acid;
R.COCl	the acid chloride (or acyl chloride, the group R.CO being an 'acyl' group);
$R.CONH_2$	the amide;
$R.CO_2C_2H_5$	(e.g.) the ethyl ester of the acid;
$\begin{matrix}\mathrm{R.CO}\\ \quad\rangle\mathrm{O}\\ \mathrm{R.CO}\end{matrix}$	the anhydride of the acid.

Carboxylic acids in which the —CO_2H group is attached to an alkyl group (as for example, CH_3CO_2H acetic acid) are known as *fatty acids* from the fact that certain of the higher members of the series with un-branched carbon chains—e.g. stearic acid $C_{17}H_{35}.CO_2H$, occur as esters with the trihydric alcohol glycerol in natural fats. Systematically, the fatty acids are named after the paraffin or alkane with the same number of carbon atoms in the molecule. Formulae and names of some of the simpler and more familiar aliphatic and aromatic carboxylic acids are shown below.

$H.CO_2H$
formic acid
(methanoic acid)

$CH_3.CO_2H$
acetic acid
(ethanoic acid)

$CH_3CH_2.CO_2H$
propionic acid
(propanoic acid)

$CH_3CH_2CH_2·CO_2H$

n-butyric acid
(butanoic acid)

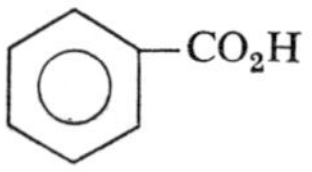

benzoic acid

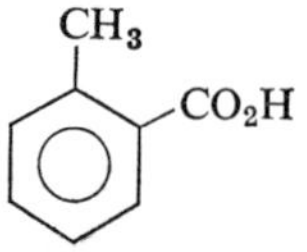

o-toluic acid

General properties. The lower fatty acids are liquids; the higher members are waxy solids. Formic, acetic and propionic acids are miscible with water; the higher members show diminishing solubility. Benzoic acid and its homologues are colourless crystalline solids, rather sparingly soluble in cold water. Acetic acid is the acidic constituent of vinegar (formed by the oxidation of the ethanol content of beer or wine). Formic acid, as its name implies, is present in ants. Benzoic acid has been used in small care-fully controlled quantities as a food preservative.

Physical properties. The carboxylic acids show the characteristic physical properties of hydroxyl compounds. Thus, as already mentioned, the lower members are completely miscible with water, presumably on account of hydrogen bonding (which can occur not only between the —OH groups, but between the —OH of the water molecules and $>C{=}O$ of the acids). They also have relatively high boiling points (e.g. acetic acid 118° C; compare the isomeric ester methyl formate, which contains no —OH group, with b.p. 32° C). The carboxylic acids, however, show a special type of association; in hydrocarbon solvents, and others which undergo hydro-gen bonding to a negligible extent, the acids are present as double mole-cules, as shown both by colligative properties (such as elevation of boiling point and depression of freezing point) and partition experiments. This is believed to be due to hydrogen bonding between pairs of —CO_2H groups, thus, for example,

210

$$\text{CH}_3.\overset{\displaystyle O\text{---}H\text{---}O}{\underset{\displaystyle O\text{---}H\text{---}O}{C}}\text{C---CH}_3$$

The vapour density of acetic acid, for example, immediately above its boiling point shows that this association persists somewhat in the vapour phase.

In solvents which can form hydrogen bonds with the —OH group of the acids (e.g. other hydroxylic solvents or ethers) this association does not occur; in a large excess of solvent molecules, solvation to form such species

as $\text{CH}_3\text{—C}\overset{\displaystyle O\text{---}HOH}{\underset{\displaystyle O\text{—}H\text{---}O\overset{H}{\underset{H}{}}}{}}$ will clearly predominate over the dimeric associa-

tion of the acid molecules. The student should satisfy himself that in dilute solution this will lead to no increase in the molecular weight as calculated from colligative property measurements.

Reactions

(1) Acid behaviour

As their name implies carboxylic acids are conspicuously acidic in aqueous solution. For acetic acid, the conventional dissociation constant K_A for the equilibrium

$$CH_3CO_2H + H_2O \rightleftharpoons CH_3CO_2^{\ominus} + H_3O^{\oplus}$$

is $1 \cdot 7_6 \times 10^{-5}$. Formic acid is noticeably stronger ($K_A 1 \cdot 7_7 \times 10^{-4}$). The higher homologues are slightly weaker than acetic acid, for example K_A for n-butyric acid is $1 \cdot 5_1 \times 10^{-5}$ and for octanoic acid $1 \cdot 2_8 \times 10^{-5}$; the effect of ascending the series is therefore small after the first step. That is to say, fatty acids are typical weak electrolytes in aqueous solution; the degree of ionization of $0 \cdot 1$N acetic acid is about $1 \cdot 4 \%$.

Aromatic acids such as benzoic acid, are noticeably stronger than fatty acids (K_A for benzoic acid $= 6 \cdot 5 \times 10^{-5}$). The difference is much smaller than that between an alcohol and a phenol. (All the above dissociation constants are quoted for a temperature of $25°$ C.)

Carboxylic acids therefore form well-defined salts with all the common bases, both metallic and nitrogenous; normal formates and acetates (i.e. as opposed to basic salts) are more or less readily soluble in water. The carboxylate salts of the most electropositive metals (e.g. sodium and potassium) are of course strong electrolytes, a point of importance in the evolution of the physical chemistry of electrolytes, since it leads to the evaluation of Λ_∞ for the acids themselves by the application of Kohlrausch's Law of Independent Mobilities, and hence to the evaluation of their dissociation constants. The acetates of heavy metals may show complex formation between acetate and metal ions.

The great increase in acid strength on passing from alcohols to carboxylic acids can be attributed to two factors. First, the electronegative oxygen of the carboxyl group will tend to withdraw electrons from the carbon atom, and this effect 'relayed' inductively through the molecule will withdraw the electron pair bonding the oxygen and hydrogen atoms away from the hydrogen atom, thus making it more likely to be lost to a base. Secondly, there is a resonance or electron delocalization effect. The carboxylic acid group itself may be written

and the carboxylate ion

The greater symmetry of and absence of charge separation in the anion compared with acid implies an increased stabilization of the former. That is, taking the two effects, there is in, say, acetic acid as compared with ethanol a greater tendency of the hydrogen of the —OH group to be lost as a proton to a base, and a greater reluctance of the anion so formed to recombine with a proton.

(2) Base behaviour

Like water or indeed any other compound of bi-covalent oxygen the carboxylic acids are capable of acting as bases in the presence of sufficiently strong acids. Thus the depression of freezing point of concentrated sulphuric acid by dissolved acetic acid is twice that obtained with the same concentration of a non-ionized solute (such as sulphuryl chloride) presumably because of the formation of *two* new particles by the reaction:

$$CH_3CO_2H + H_2SO_4 \rightleftharpoons (CH_3CO_2H_2)^\oplus + HSO_4^\ominus$$

A problem arises as to the structure of this 'acetoxonium' ion. In general, ROH will form the conjugate acid $\left(R - O\!\!\begin{smallmatrix}H\\H\end{smallmatrix}\right)^\oplus$ but with acetic acid

a more symmetrical and more probable structure results from the addition
of a proton to the non-hydroxylic oxygen atom, to give the structure

$$CH_3 \cdot C \overset{\overset{\oplus}{\underset{}{O-H}}}{\underset{O-H}{}} \quad \longleftrightarrow \quad CH_3 \cdot C \overset{\overset{\cdot \cdot}{O-H}}{\underset{\underset{\oplus}{O-H}}{}}$$

and this presumably predominates over $CH_3 \cdot C \overset{O}{\underset{\overset{\oplus}{OH_2}}{}}$

As well as ionizing as a base in strongly acid solvents, acetic acid will itself
act as an ionizing (and therefore basic) solvent for stronger acids than
itself. For example, a solution of perchloric acid in water-free acetic acid is
a valuable reagent for titration of a number of organic base types in acetic
acid solution; the acetic acid acts as a base towards the perchloric acid in
the same way that water does in aqueous acid solutions.

Since the carboxylic acids are able to function both as acids and bases,
it is to be expected that in the pure liquid acids, molecules will perform both
functions and, as with water, ionization will occur to a small extent by
autoprotolysis. The extent of this in formic acid

$$2H \cdot CO_2H \rightleftharpoons (HCO_2H_2)^{\oplus} + H \cdot CO_2^{\ominus}$$

is believed to be about the same as in water; in acetic acid somewhat less.

Except in these circumstances, of course, the basic behaviour of the
$-CO_2H$ group is not evident in the ordinary chemistry of carboxylic acids;
nevertheless, the fact that the group (and allied functional groups) can
gain as well as lose protons can be important in the mechanism of its
reactions.

Reactions involving the replacement of —OH in —CO₂H by other groups

These are the reactions by which the carboxyl group is converted to the
related groups mentioned above. The —OH group may be replaced by
—OR, —NH₂, —NRR¹ (R and R¹ can of course be the same) or a halogen
atom. Elimination of water between two carboxyl groups would yield
—CO.O.CO—, and such anhydrides can be made, though only in special
circumstances by the direct dehydration of the acid.

(3) Esterification

This reaction has been outlined in chapter 4. Alcohols (and in suitable
cases, phenols) and carboxylic acids react reversibly to form esters, the

reaction being catalysed by acids. For example

$$C_2H_5OH + CH_3CO_2H \rightleftharpoons CH_3CO_2C_2H_5 + H_2O$$

(The elementary student should satisfy himself that he understands the structural difference implied by the conventional formulae of, for example, ethyl acetate and methyl propionate respectively:

$$CH_3CO_2C_2H_5 \quad \text{i.e.} \quad CH_3.C\underset{OCH_2CH_3}{\overset{O}{<}}$$

$$C_2H_5.CO_2CH_3 \quad \text{i.e.} \quad CH_3CH_2.C\underset{OCH_3}{\overset{O}{<}})$$

It is clear from the above equation that the reaction could be either a replacement of the ionizable hydrogen of the acid by the alkyl group of the alcohol, or a replacement of the —OH of the carboxyl group by the alkoxyl (or analogous) group of the alcohol. That the latter is in fact the process occurring has been shown in several cases by the use of reagents with 'labelled' oxygen; that is, having the oxygen in certain positions in the molecule enriched in the isotope ^{18}O. Thus for example if benzoic acid is esterified with methanol enriched with ^{18}O, it is found that the heavy oxygen appears in the *ester*, and not in the water, formed by the reaction:

$$C_6H_5.CO_2H + CH_3{}^{18}OH \rightarrow C_6H_5CO.^{18}OCH_3 + H_2O$$

There is no doubt that this is the normal way in which the reaction proceeds in the esterification of simple carboxylic acids by alcohols.

(4) Amide formation

If the ammonium salt of a carboxylic acid is heated, preferably with excess of the acid, water is lost and the amide is formed. For example

$$CH_3CO_2{}^{\ominus}\overset{\oplus}{N}H_4 \rightarrow CH_3CONH_2 + H_2O$$
$$\text{acetamide}$$

Although in the ammonium salt itself the ions $NH_4{}^{\oplus}$ and $CH_3CO_2{}^{\ominus}$ are present, proton transfer can occur—ammonium salts dissociate into ammonia and the acid on vaporization—so that the reaction may well in fact take place between ammonia and the free acid:

$$CH_3CO_2H + NH_3 \rightarrow CH_3CONH_2 + H_2O$$

The reaction can be carried out by allowing the excess of acid and the water formed to distil from the top of a long column.

Yields from this method are often poor, much of the salt being simply converted to the acid with loss of ammonia. Heating in a sealed vessel will eliminate this, but at the cost of leaving the water in the reaction mixture. Since the reaction is reversible, equilibrium will be established.

(5) Reaction with amines

Primary and secondary amines may react in the same way as ammonia yielding substituted amides. Thus if aniline and acetic acid are refluxed together, *N*-phenyl acetamide (acetanilide) is formed:

$$CH_3CO_2H + C_6H_5NH_2 \rightarrow CH_3CONH.C_6H_5 + H_2O$$
$$\text{acetanilide}$$

(For the use of the prefix *N*-, see p. 152.)

Anilides are crystalline solids with sharp melting points and the reaction can be used to characterize acids by conversion to their anilides.

Since the final effect from the point of view of the amine is a replacement of hydrogen attached to nitrogen by an acyl group, tertiary amines cannot undergo this reaction.

(6) Acid chloride formation

The hydroxyl group of carboxylic acids can be replaced by chlorine by reaction with such reagents as phosphorus trichloride, phosphorus oxychloride, phosphorus pentachloride or thionyl chloride.

(a) $\qquad$ $3CH_3CO_2H + PCl_3 \rightarrow 3CH_3COCl +$ $\qquad$ H_3PO_3
$\qquad\qquad\qquad\qquad\quad$ acetyl chloride $\quad$ phosphorous acid

When this reaction is carried out in the laboratory, considerable evolution of hydrogen chloride occurs, although none is shown in the conventional equation. This may partly come from adventitious moisture, and it may also partly be due to side reactions, including perhaps the condensation of the orthophosphorous acid, with in effect elimination of water which would attack the PCl_3 and thus liberate hydrogen chloride:

(b) $\qquad$ $3CH_3CO_2H + POCl_3 \rightarrow 3CH_3COCl + H_3PO_4$

(c) $\qquad$ $CH_3CO_2H + PCl_5 \rightarrow CH_3COCl + HCl + POCl_3$

(d) $\qquad$ $CH_3CO_2H + SOCl_2 \rightarrow CH_3COCl + SO_2 + HCl$

The choice of reagent is largely empirical. Factors affecting it include the problem of separating the acid chloride from excess of reagent or from the other products, especially the phosphorus oxychloride, if the boiling points are too close. Acyl bromides and iodides can be made by analogous methods.

Unlike alcohols, carboxylic acids cannot be converted into the corresponding halides by the action of the halogen hydracids.

(7) Anhydride formation

Direct dehydration of the carboxylic acids by conventional reagents such as phosphorus pentoxide is of little practical value. (Formic acid is dehydrated to carbon monoxide by concentrated sulphuric acid, but acetic acid is unaffected by it, except as in (2) above.)

The traditional laboratory method of arriving at the anhydride of a carboxylic acid is to distil its anhydrous sodium salt with its acid chloride, for example,

$$CH_3CO_2^{\ominus} + CH_3COCl \rightarrow CH_3CO.O.COCH_3 + Cl^{\ominus}$$

Modifications of this were once used industrially, but acetic anhydride is now manufactured by passing *ketene* into acetic acid.

$$CH_2{=}C{=}O + CH_3CO_2H \rightarrow CH_3CO.O.COCH_3$$

(In effect, the acetic acid molecule adds as CH_3CO_2— and H— across the ethylenic bond of the ketene.)

Ketene is made by the thermal cracking of acetone:

$$CH_3COCH_3 \rightarrow CH_2{=}C{=}O + CH_4$$

If ketene is passed into an excess of a carboxylic acid other than acetic the ultimate effect is to produce the anhydride of the other acid and free acetic acid. Presumably the 'mixed' anhydride is first formed, for example,

$$CH_2{=}C{=}O + C_2H_5CO_2H \rightarrow CH_3CO.O.COC_2H_5$$

which then undergoes a metathesis with the other acid:

$$CH_3CO.O.COC_2H_5 + C_2H_5CO_2H \rightleftharpoons (C_2H_5CO)_2O + CH_3CO_2H$$

the excess acid displacing the equilibrium to the right. The net result is dehydration of the propionic acid by the ketene.

As well as being readily obtainable from the acids, the compounds prepared by the reactions 3 to 6 above can be readily reconverted into the corresponding acids (or their salts) and can furthermore to a large extent be converted into one another. In view of the great general similarity between most of these changes, they can be considered at this stage before certain other changes of the carboxylic acids and their salts are discussed.

Reactions of esters

(8) Hydrolysis of esters

Esters may be hydrolysed by refluxing with aqueous acid, for example,

$$CH_3.CO_2C_2H_5 + H_2O \rightleftharpoons CH_3CO_2H + C_2H_5OH$$

This is manifestly the reverse of the esterification reaction (the excess of water displacing the equilibrium in favour of the free acid and alcohol), and like the forward reaction, has been shown by labelling with ^{18}O to proceed with fission of the bond between the *acyl* radical and the attached oxygen atom.

Esters are also hydrolysed by refluxing with aqueous alkali, for example,

$$CH_3CO_2C_2H_5 + OH^\ominus \rightarrow CH_3CO_2^\ominus + C_2H_5OH$$

Since the ultimate product is the anion of the acid, which does not react appreciably with the alcohol, this proceeds to completion and not to an intermediate equilibrium state.

The alkaline hydrolysis of esters is often referred to as 'saponification' (literally, making into soap), since the technical production of soap by the boiling of fats with aqueous alkali is from the chemical point of view alkaline hydrolysis of the glyceryl esters of higher carboxylic acids; for example,

$$
\begin{array}{lll}
CH_2O.CO(CH_2)_{16}CH_3 & CH_2OH & \\
| & | & \\
CHO.CO(CH_2)_{16}CH_3 + 3Na^\oplus OH^\ominus \rightarrow CHOH & +3CH_3(CH_2)_{16}CO_2^\ominus Na^\oplus \\
| & | & \text{sodium stearate} \\
CH_2O.CO(CH_2)_{16}CH_3 & CH_2OH & \text{(a soap)} \\
\text{glyceryl tristearate} & \text{glycerol} & \\
\end{array}
$$

(the main constituents of mutton fat).

The name has then been extended to alkaline hydrolysis of any ester.

(9) Alcoholysis of esters

When an ester of one alcohol is refluxed with a different alcohol in the presence of small amounts of strong acid, an equilibrium mixture of two esters is obtained. This reaction has been dealt with on p. 132. As an example:

$$CH_3CO_2C_2H_5 + CH_3OH \rightleftharpoons CH_3CO_2CH_3 + C_2H_5OH$$

(10) Ammonolysis of esters

Esters react with ammonia forming the corresponding amide and alcohol, for example,

$$CH_3CO_2C_2H_5 + NH_3 \rightarrow CH_3CONH_2 + C_2H_5OH$$

This is clearly analogous in its effect to the hydrolysis of an ester, with ammonia and —NH$_2$ taking the place of water and —OH. The reaction of esters with ammonia has been shown to be reversible, further emphasizing its analogy with ester hydrolysis. The equilibrium however normally favours the amide, even in alcoholic solution. The reaction is often slow; it can be hastened by heating the reagents in an autoclave.

(11)   Reaction with amines

Aliphatic primary and secondary amines behave in the same way as ammonia; thus for example with ethylamine and ethyl acetate, *N*-ethyl acetamide would be formed:

$$CH_3.CO_2C_2H_5 + C_2H_5NH_2 \rightarrow CH_3.CONHC_2H_5 + C_2H_5OH$$

Aniline and other aryl amines, however, have little or no effect on ethyl acetate and similar esters.

Reactions of amides

(12)   Hydrolysis of amides

Amides are converted to the corresponding acid (or its salts) by heating with aqueous acid or aqueous alkali, for example,

$$CH_3CONH_2 + H_2O \rightarrow CH_3CO_2H + NH_3$$

In strongly acid conditions, the products will be the free carboxylic acid and the ammonium ion; in strong alkali, the anion of the carboxylic acid and free ammonia. (Other reactions of amides which bear less directly upon the analogy with the behaviour of carboxylic acids and their other derivatives are given below.)

Reactions of acyl chlorides

(13)   Hydrolysis

Aliphatic and side-chain aromatic acyl chlorides are rapidly hydrolysed by water:

$$CH_3COCl + H_2O \rightarrow CH_3CO_2H + HCl$$

$$C_6H_5CH_2COCl + H_2O \rightarrow C_6H_5CH_2CO_2H + HCl$$
phenylacetyl chloride   phenylacetic acid

Benzoyl chloride and its homologues in which the —COCl group is attached to the aromatic ring are much more slowly hydrolysed, and can persist for some time even in the presence of aqueous alkali. It is this property which makes possible the Schotten–Baumann procedure for benzoylation (see pp. 133 and 159).

(14)   Reaction with alcohols and phenols: acylation of —OH

Alcohols react rapidly, phenols somewhat less rapidly, with acyl chlorides to form esters. The reaction of phenols with benzoyl chloride and its homologues can be carried out in the presence of aqueous alkali. These reactions have been discussed on pp. 132–3. For examples,

$$C_2H_5OH + CH_3COCl \rightarrow CH_3CO_2C_5H_5 + HCl$$
ethyl acetate

$$C_6H_5OH + CH_3COCl \rightarrow CH_3CO_2C_6H_5 + HCl$$
phenyl acetate

$$C_6H_5O^\ominus + C_6H_5COCl \rightarrow C_6H_5CO_2C_6H_5 + Cl^\ominus$$
phenyl benzoate

(15)   Ammonolysis

Acyl halides react rapidly with ammonia to form amides and ammonium chloride; for example, acetyl chloride yields acetamide:

$$CH_3COCl + 2NH_3 \rightarrow CH_3CONH_2 + \overset{\oplus}{N}H_4Cl^\ominus$$

(The essential reaction is the attack of ammonia on the acetyl chloride, as discussed in detail below; the ammonium ion results from combination of a second ammonia molecule with the $H^\oplus$ ion liberated in the main reaction.)

Since they are only slowly hydrolysed, benzoyl chloride and its homologues will perform this reaction efficiently with concentrated aqueous ammonia:

$$C_6H_5COCl + 2NH_3 \rightarrow C_6H_5CONH_2 + \overset{\oplus}{N}H_4Cl^\ominus$$
benzamide

(16)   Reaction with amines: acylation of —NH₂ and —NH—

Primary and secondary amines behave in the same way as ammonia.

This reaction has been discussed under the head of acylation of amines p. 157. Again, benzoyl chloride can be used in the presence of water or aqueous alkali. For examples,

$$C_6H_5NH_2 + CH_3COCl \rightarrow C_6H_5NH.COCH_3 + HCl$$
acetanilide

$$C_6H_5NH_2 + C_6H_5COCl \rightarrow C_6H_5NH.COC_6H_5 + HCl$$
benzanilide

The aliphatic acyl chlorides are somewhat vigorous, even violent reagents for the acylation of amines, alcohols and phenols and are often conveniently replaced by the anhydrides, which are less violently reactive but

219

undergo precisely analogous reactions. Benzoyl chloride and its homologues, on the other hand, are convenient and effective reagents; benzoic
anhydride, etc., are therefore much less often required.

Reactions of acid anhydrides

In view of the close analogy with the acyl chloride reactions, these may
be listed very briefly. In each case, a molecule of carboxylic acid (or a salt
thereof) appears as the other product instead of hydrogen chloride or a
salt of it.

(17) Hydrolysis

This is slow in the cold, rapid in hot water.

$$(CH_3CO)_2O + H_2O \rightarrow 2CH_3CO_2H$$

(18) Reaction with alcohols and phenols: acylation of —OH

(See also p. 132.)

$$(CH_3CO)_2O + C_2H_5OH \rightarrow CH_3CO_2C_2H_5 + CH_3CO_2H$$
$$(CH_3CO)_2O + C_6H_5OH \rightarrow CH_3CO_2C_6H_5 + CH_3CO_2H$$

(19) Ammonolysis

Dry ammonia passed into, for example, acetic anhydride, converts it
rapidly to the amide.

$$(CH_3CO)_2O + 2NH_3 \rightarrow CH_3CONH_2 + CH_3CO_2^{\ominus}\overset{\oplus}{N}H_4$$

(Clearly free acetic acid will not be formed in the presence of ammonia.)

(20) Reaction with amines: acylation of —NH$_2$ and —NH—

(See also p. 157.)

$$2CH_3NH_2 + (CH_3CO)_2O \rightarrow CH_3CONHCH_3 + CH_3CO_2^{\ominus}\overset{\oplus}{N}H_3CH_3$$
N-methylacetamide

$$C_6H_5NH_2 + (CH_3CO)_2O \rightarrow CH_3CONHC_6H_5 + CH_3CO_2H$$
acetanilide

(If the second reaction is carried out in the presence of excess aqueous
sodium acetate solution, acetic acid and not phenylammonium acetate will
be the other product, since the acetate ion is about as strong a base as
aniline.)

Since acetic anhydride and its homologues are only slowly hydrolysed
by cold water, amines may be acylated by them in the presence of water.

The interconversions of a carboxylic acid and its derivatives by the above reactions are shown diagrammatically below. (Certain reactions of less immediate interest have been omitted; for example the action of phosphorus halides and similar compounds on all except the acid itself.)

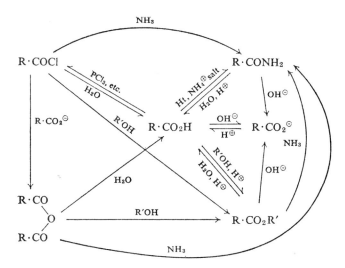

The ionization of the acid and its reaction with phosphorus halides have been included because of their practical importance in the picture of the acid and its derivatives. All the other reactions shown form a clearly related group of changes, which we are now in a position to view as a whole, having previously met them piecemeal under a number of heads.

First, they all conform with certain provisos to the general schematic equation:

$$R.COX + Y \, (\rightleftharpoons) \, R.COY + X$$

the provisos being that X and Y may be of various charge types, and that at some stage or other in the overall change X or Y or both may either gain or lose a hydrogen atom, presumably as a proton from some acid or to some base present in the reaction system. For example, if we suppose that the Schotten–Baumann benzoylation of phenol follows the equation given above, viz:

$$C_6H_5COCl + C_6H_5O^{\ominus} \rightarrow C_6H_5CO_2C_6H_5 + Cl^{\ominus}$$

then X ($Cl^{\ominus}$) and Y ($C_6H_5O^{\ominus}$) are in the free state negative ions, and the reaction step involves no process of proton addition or removal. On the other hand, in the saponification of ethyl acetate;

$$CH_3CO_2C_2H_5 + OH^{\ominus} \rightarrow CH_3CO_2^{\ominus} + C_2H_5OH$$

221

the $OH^\ominus$ ion at some stage loses a proton, ultimately being left attached to the acyl group as $-O^\ominus$, while the $-OC_2H_5$ group ultimately gains a proton to appear as the alcohol molecule. Further variants can be seen in the following changes:

$$CH_3COCl+NH_3(+NH_3) \rightarrow CH_3CONH_2+Cl^\ominus(+\overset{\oplus}{N}H_4)$$

$$CH_3CO_2H+C_2H_5OH \rightleftharpoons CH_3CO_2C_2H_5+H_2O$$

Furthermore, the fact that this last is acid-catalysed strongly suggests that, apart from the proton transfers implied in the stoichiometric equation, the reversible addition and removal of a proton originating from the catalyst is part of the mechanism. These 'protolytic' steps should not however obscure the fundamental similarity of all these changes.

In all these reactions X and Y have unshared pairs of electrons. The general equation above strongly resembles that for the displacement reactions of the halides (see p. 110). In carboxyl derivatives, the carbon atom of the $\rangle C{=}O$ group is attached to two atoms, both of which are more electronegative than carbon (e.g. in an amide the carbon is attached to oxygen and nitrogen). The electron density in the neighbourhood of this carbon atom will therefore be lowered, and it will be the likely point for attack by the unshared electron pair of a nucleophilic reagent. Unlike the alkyl halides, however, the carboxyl derivatives have a pair of electrons (that formally represented as the second bond of the $\rangle C{=}O$ group) which could be wholly transferred to the carboxyl oxygen to 'accommodate' the unshared pair of the reagent. On these considerations, the basic reaction picture emerges thus:

A

(Charge changes on X and Y have been omitted. Clearly in this simple scheme, Y has in effect lost an electron in forming the Y—C bond, and X has gained one in taking both electrons of the C—X bond.)

Such a basic scheme is essentially reversible; to what extent it is practically so will depend on the relative vigour of Y and X as nucleophilic reagents. Moreover, this aspect of it can be materially changed by the addition or removal of protons at intermediate stages, since in general the conjugate base of X or Y will be more nucleophilic and the conjugate acid less nucleophilic than X or Y itself. Such a picture, subject to experimental tests, offers a powerful aid to unifying of the diverse facts of carboxyl derivative reactions.

Let us consider the acetylation of a primary amine such as ethylamine from this point of view. As pointed out on p. 157, the practically available reagents for this are in descending order of vigour: acetyl chloride, acetic anhydride, acetic acid and an ester such as ethyl acetate. Y in our scheme is the amine, so the first step becomes:

$$C_2H_5NH_2 + \overset{\displaystyle O}{\overset{\displaystyle \|}{\underset{\displaystyle \underset{CH_3}{|}}{C}}}-X \rightleftharpoons C_2H_5\overset{\oplus}{N}H_2-\overset{\displaystyle O^{\ominus}}{\underset{\displaystyle \underset{CH_3}{|}}{\overset{|}{C}}}-X$$

Intermediate *A*

The course of the reaction depends on the subsequent steps. If the nitrogen atom regains the electron pair, no reaction occurs. If, however, X is lost as $X^{\ominus}$, then the reformation of the $>C{=}O$ bond, the loss of a proton from the nitrogen atom and normally the addition of a proton to $X^{\ominus}$ complete the reaction (not necessarily in that order). For example if X is OH, and we are using acetic acid as an acetylating agent, we have

$$C_2H_5\overset{+}{N}H_2-\overset{\displaystyle O^{\ominus}}{\underset{\displaystyle \underset{CH_3}{|}}{\overset{|}{C}}}-OH \rightarrow C_2H_5\overset{\oplus}{N}H_2-\overset{\displaystyle O}{\underset{\displaystyle \underset{CH_3}{|}}{\overset{\|}{C}}} \;+OH^{\ominus}$$

$$-H^{\oplus} \downarrow \qquad \downarrow +H^{\oplus}$$

$$C_2H_5NH-\overset{\displaystyle O}{\underset{\displaystyle \underset{CH_3}{|}}{\overset{\|}{C}}} \;+H_2O$$

N-ethylacetamide

It is immediately striking that the descending order of vigour of the acetylating agents is the descending order of strength of the acid HX liberated in the reaction $(HCl > HOCOCH_3 > HOH > HOC_2H_5)$ and therefore to the *increasing* strength as bases of the conjugate anions

$$(Cl^{\ominus} < CH_3COO^{\ominus} < OH^{\ominus} < C_2H_5O^{\ominus}),$$

which will also be roughly the order of their increasing vigour as nucleophilic reagents. This immediately suggests the consideration that a major factor in the reaction is the probability that the intermediate *A* in the above equation will lose $X^{\ominus}$ (this leading to acetylation) rather than $C_2H_5NH_2$ (reverting to the initial molecules); a process which is plausibly the more likely to occur, the *smaller* the tendency of the extruded $X^{\ominus}$ to share its unshared electron pairs.

Now let us examine the reversible esterification of acetic acid by ethanol. The first step becomes:

$$C_2H_5OH + \underset{\underset{CH_3}{|}}{\overset{\overset{O}{\|}}{C}} - OH \rightleftharpoons \underset{\underset{A}{}}{\underset{\underset{CH_3}{|}}{\overset{\overset{O^{\ominus}}{|}}{C_2H_5\overset{\oplus}{O} - \underset{H}{|} - C}}} - OH$$

It would seem that the loss of the strongly nucleophilic $OH^{\ominus}$ rather than the weakly nucleophilic C_2H_5OH from A would here be unlikely, and that esterification would be difficult. But the reaction is acid-catalysed; if we suppose that at some stage A has acquired a proton from the catalyst to form B:

$$\underset{\underset{B}{}}{\underset{\underset{CH_3}{|}}{\overset{\overset{O^{\ominus}}{|}}{C_2H_5\overset{\oplus}{O} - \underset{H}{|} - C - \overset{\oplus}{O}H_2}}}$$

then we have an intermediate species which can lose either C_2H_5OH or H_2O, molecules not markedly different in nucleophilic strength. Loss of H_2O, followed by loss of a proton and reformation of the $\diagup\!\!\!\diagdown C\!=\!O$ bond as in the previous example complete the reaction process:

$$B \rightarrow \underset{\underset{CH_3}{|}}{\underset{H}{\overset{\overset{O}{\|}}{C_2H_5\overset{\oplus}{O} - C}}} + H_2O$$

$$-H^{\oplus} \downarrow$$

$$\underset{\underset{CH_3}{|}}{\overset{\overset{O}{\|}}{C_2H_5O - C}}$$

There has been no net loss or gain of protons in the process, hence the catalytic nature of the added acid.

Such a picture is well-adapted to the facts. If the reaction to form B is slow and the subsequent events fast, the reaction rate will depend on the strength and concentration of the acid catalyst, as it indeed does. The mechanism is manifestly and facilely reversible, since B may lose either of two very similar and equally viable molecules. It is striking that although the *velocity* constants of esterification of various acids by a given alcohol, or of a given alcohol by various acids, may vary by factors of several powers of ten, the *equilibrium* constants within either set of processes differ comparatively little. Finally, it is consistent with the fact already mentioned, that esterification and its reverse (except in certain very abnormal cases) involves fission of the acyl–oxygen bond of the acid or ester, and the incorporation of the oxygen of the alcohol or the water in the corresponding product.

Many subtler variations on this general scheme are possible. Thus in the type equation

$$\text{Y:} \quad \underset{\underset{R}{|}}{\overset{\overset{O}{||}}{C}}-X \quad \underset{(1)}{\rightleftharpoons} \quad \text{Y}-\underset{\underset{R}{|}}{\overset{\overset{\ominus}{O:}}{C}}-X \quad \underset{(2)}{\rightleftharpoons} \quad \text{Y}-\underset{\underset{R}{|}}{\overset{\overset{O}{||}}{C}} + :X$$

$$A$$

either step (1) or (2) may be fast or slow; A may be a molecule capable of temporary independent existence, or may be a mere 'transition' complex, and the transfer of electrons $>C=O$ may only be partial; step (2) may precede step (1), so that the intermediate becomes an acylium ion $R-\overset{\oplus}{C}=O$; proton addition or removal may occur at various stages. These variations are susceptible of experimental investigation by kinetic or other methods, but this lies beyond the scope of the present book; the unity of the basic picture remains. The student may care to speculate on the application of the general scheme to the other reactions of carboxylic acid derivatives listed above, or on such matters as why ethyl acetate does not effectively acetylate aniline, and why anhydrous sodium acetate appears to catalyse the acetylation of alcohols and phenols by acetic anhydride, always bearing in mind that such speculations, until they have been subjected to experimental tests, remain at best intelligent hypotheses.

Other reactions of carboxylic acids and their derivatives

In the foregoing we have reviewed the related reactions which can be collectively called acylations (the hydrolysis of acyl derivatives being in effect acylation of water). There remains a miscellaneous collection of other reactions to review.

Reduction of carboxylic acids and their derivatives

Since carboxylic acids are obtained by the oxidation of primary alcohols via aldehydes, these latter types are potentially reduction products of the acids. In fact, classical laboratory methods failed to achieve this reduction, though some of the derivatives are more easily reducible.

Carboxylic acids can be reduced to primary alcohols

(a) By catalytic hydrogenation at about $300°$ C and 200 atm. pressure over a 'copper chromite' catalyst.

$$R . CO_2H + 2H_2 \rightarrow RCH_2OH + H_2O$$

(b) By the action of lithium aluminium hydride in ethereal solution.

The product will contain such substances as lithium aluminium alkoxides, from which the primary alcohol is liberated by acid after destroying the excess of reducing agent with water or ethyl acetate (see below).

Some *amides* can be reduced to primary amines by lithium aluminium hydride. (Reduction by the Bouveault–Blanc method used for esters and given below, converts amides to primary alcohols and ammonia, but ineffectively.)

Acyl chlorides can be reduced to aldehydes by hydrogenation over palladium catalysts. By longer contact with active catalysts and hydrogen, primary alcohols are formed. By supporting the catalyst on a sulphur containing support (e.g. barium sulphate) the catalyst is sufficiently 'poisoned' to confine the reduction to the first stage (Rosenmund reaction). For example,

$$C_6H_5COCl + H_2 \overset{Pd}{\rightarrow} C_6H_5CHO + HCl$$

Acyl chlorides can also be reduced by lithium aluminium hydride to primary alcohols, as can acid anhydrides.

Esters may be reduced to primary alcohols by sodium and ethanol (Bouveault and Blanc reaction). This is the only one of the methods given here which does not rely on either catalytic hydrogenation or a reagent of comparatively recent development, e.g. LiAlH$_4$. The reducing reagent is of course the sodium, which is oxidized to Na$^\oplus$; it is unlikely that hydrogen, once liberated as molecules from the ethanol, has any reducing effect. The formal reduction equation is

$$R . CO_2Et + 4H^\oplus + 4e \rightarrow R . CH_2OH + EtOH$$

Apart from this reduction of the carbalkoxyl group, there are other reactions which suitable esters may undergo with sodium. One of these, the formation of ethyl acetoacetate from ethyl acetate, is described on p. 198.

Esters, like acids, may be reduced catalytically with hydrogen, or like acids, acyl chlorides and anhydrides, by lithium aluminium hydride. Primary alcohols are again obtained.

Some other points in the chemistry of carboxylic acids and their salts

(1) Decarboxylation of carboxylic acids

This is the name given to any reaction which achieves the replacement of —CO_2H by hydrogen, such as might be represented formally by:

$$R.CO_2H \rightarrow RH + CO_2$$

In fact, this reaction only occurs in special circumstances as a direct thermal decomposition of the carboxylic acid or its salts; see the reactions of malonic acid (p. 290), acetoacetic acid (p. 199) and the preparation of nitromethane (p. 261).

The simpler monobasic carboxylic acids may be decarboxylated by heating their anhydrous sodium or potassium salts with soda lime or other solid alkalis, for example,

$$CH_3CO_2{}^\ominus + OH^\ominus \xrightarrow[\text{soda-lime}]{\text{heat}} CH_4 + CO_3{}^{2\ominus}$$

$$C_6H_5CO_2{}^\ominus + OH^\ominus \longrightarrow C_6H_6 + CO_3{}^{2\ominus}$$

(2) Pyrolysis of the salts of carboxylic acids

The dry distillation of the calcium salts of acids yields ketones, for example, calcium acetate yields acetone:

$$(CH_3CO_2{}^\ominus)_2Ca^{2\oplus} \rightarrow (CH_3)_2CO + Ca^{2\oplus}CO_3{}^{2\ominus}$$

Calcium formate in these circumstances will yield formaldehyde.

Yields range from moderate to very poor and by-products of various kinds are also formed.

Mixtures of calcium salts yield the 'mixed' ketone together with the two possible simple ketones:

$$\begin{matrix} R.CO_2{}^\ominus \\ \phantom{R.CO_2{}^\ominus}Ca^{2\oplus} \\ R^1.CO_2{}^\ominus \end{matrix} \rightarrow R.CO.R^1 + Ca^{2\oplus}CO_3{}^{2\ominus}$$

If one of the salts is calcium formate, then the 'mixed' product will be an aldehyde:

$$\begin{matrix} R.CO_2{}^\ominus \\ \phantom{R.CO_2{}^\ominus}Ca^{2\oplus} \\ H.CO_2{}^\ominus \end{matrix} \rightarrow R.CHO + Ca^{2\oplus}CO_3{}^{2\ominus}$$

Small quantities of aldehydes are indeed found in the distillates, but the method is hardly a practicable one.

Much better results are obtained by passing the vapour of the acid (or the mixed acids) over heated thorium dioxide on a pumice support, or over supported manganous oxide. The effect is catalytic elimination of carbon dioxide; the reaction is probably related to the traditional salt pyrolysis method. For example:

$$CH_3CO_2H + C_6H_5CH_2CO_2H \xrightarrow[\text{hot ThO}_2]{\text{vapours over}} C_6H_5CH_2COCH_3 + CO_2 + H_2O$$

(together with acetone and dibenzyl ketone).

(3)   Electrolysis of carboxylic acid salts (Kolbé reaction)

The electrolysis of solutions of sodium or potassium salts of simple carboxylic acids yield a hydrocarbon and carbon dioxide at the anode; for example, sodium acetate solution yields ethane:

$$2CH_3CO_2{}^{\ominus} - 2e \rightarrow CH_3.CH_3 + 2CO_2$$

The electrolyte must be kept cool, and it is often advantageous to have free acid present in the solution; otherwise oxygen from the electrolysis of the water is the main anode product.

(4)   Ferric chloride test

Neutral solutions of salts of the lower fatty acids including formates, acetates, propionates and some of their derivatives (including mono-chloroacetates) give a deep brownish red colour with ferric chloride solution. On warming a brown precipitate of a basic ferric salt appears. This is a well known test.

Some further points of amide chemistry

(1)   Action of nitrous acid on amides

Amides react with nitrous in acid solution to yield nitrogen and the carboxylic acid, for example,

$$CH_3CONH_2 + HNO_2 \rightarrow CH_3CO_2H + N_2\uparrow + H_2O$$

The result is replacement of —NH$_2$ by —OH; compare the reactions of primary amines with nitrous acid (p. 160).

(2)   Dehydration of amides

On distillation with phosphorus pentoxide, amides are dehydrated to the corresponding nitrile, for example,

$$2CH_3CONH_2 + P_4O_{10} \rightarrow 2CH_3CN + 4HPO_3$$
acetonitrile
(methyl cyanide)

Technical dehydration can be carried out by catalytic methods; the dehydration of adipamide (the amide of the dibasic adipic acid) to adiponitrile:

$$H_2NCO.(CH_2)_4CONH_2 \xrightarrow{-2H_2O} N\equiv C-(CH_2)_4-C\equiv N$$

adipamide   adiponitrile

is an important step in the manufacture of 66 nylon (see p. 336).

(3) The Hofmann reaction

Amides can be converted with the loss of the carbonyl group to primary amines containing one less carbon atom

$$RCONH_2 \rightarrow RNH_2$$

by treatment with bromine and alkali, followed by heating with excess of alkali. The stages are as follows, using acetamide as an example:

(*a*) *N*-bromination of the amide

$$CH_3CONH_2 + HOBr \rightarrow CH_3CONHBr + H_2O$$
N-bromoacetamide

(*b*) formation of the conjugate base of the *N*-bromamide

$$CH_3CONHBr + OH^\ominus \rightarrow CH_3CO\overset{\ominus}{N}Br + H_2O$$

(*c*) loss of bromide ion and subsequent rearrangement of the product

$$CH_3.C\overset{\displaystyle O}{\underset{\overset{\displaystyle \diagdown}{NBr}}{\diagup}} \rightarrow CH_3N=C=O + Br^\ominus$$

(*d*) alkaline hydrolysis of the alkyl isocyanate

$$CH_3N=C=O + 2OH^\ominus \rightarrow CH_3NH_2 + CO_3^{2\ominus}$$

The pecularity of this reaction lies in the molecular rearrangement at stage (*c*).

Both aliphatic and aromatic amides undergo this reaction; thus benzamide $C_6H_5CONH_2$ yields aniline.

(4) Basic behaviour of amides

Although, like primary amines, they contain the $-NH_2$ group, amides are negligibly basic in aqueous solution. The pair of electrons which is unshared in the amines, and which is donated to a proton when the amine acts as a base, is in the amides partly involved in the bonding of the

229

nitrogen atom to the adjacent carbon atom (see p. 231) and is therefore less readily available for donation to a proton. In non-aqueous media, acetamide can act as a base; for example, its hydrochloride is formed when hydrogen chloride is passed into a solution of acetamide in benzene:

$$CH_3CONH_2 + HCl \rightarrow CH_3CO\overset{\oplus}{N}H_3Cl^{\ominus}$$

The cation will act as a strong acid in water—that is, the salt will be totally hydrolysed to acetamide and hydrochloric acid:

$$CH_3CO\overset{\oplus}{N}H_3 + H_2O \rightarrow CH_3CONH_2 + H_3O^{\oplus}$$

(5) Acidic behaviour

Again, in aqueous solution, acetamide is negligibly acidic. In liquid ammonia, however, it ionizes as a weak acid, much as acetic acid does in water:

$$CH_3CONH_2 + NH_3(l) \rightleftharpoons CH_3CO\overset{\ominus}{N}H + \overset{\oplus}{N}H_4$$

A sodium salt of acetamide $CH_3CO\overset{\ominus}{N}HNa^{\oplus}$ can be isolated; in water, it is totally hydrolysed.

$$CH_3CO\overset{\ominus}{N}H + H_2O \rightarrow CH_3CONH_2 + OH^{\ominus}$$

In fact then, water is too strong a base for the conjugate acid of acetamide to exist in it and too strong an acid for the conjugate base of acetamide to exist in detectable quantities.

The structure of the carboxyl and related groups, and the behaviour of the carbonyl group

It has been pointed out above that the carboxyl group is inadequately represented by the conventional formula or bond diagram:

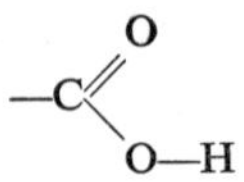

since the unshared electron pairs of the —OH oxygen atom implied by this formula are in fact involved in the adjacent C—O bond.

The same is clearly true of a greater or lesser extent of acyl halides, anhydrides, amides and esters, all of which possess electron pairs in the same situation:

(both carbonyl oxygen atoms will be involved in this case)

In contrast to this, the groups to which the $\!>\!C\!=\!O$ is attached in aldehydes and ketones (viz. hydrogen, alkyl or similar groups) have no electron pairs which can be involved in this way. Although the conventional formulae of all these compounds show the $\!>\!C\!=\!O$ group, in fact this group in the carboxylic acids and their derivatives is substantially modified.

Nevertheless, the frequently made statement that carboxylic acids, etc. differ from aldehydes and ketones in sharing none of the characteristic carbonyl reactions of addition and condensation, although true in a superficial sense, needs some modification. It is true that none of the ultimate reaction products of carbonyl addition (with or without elimination of water) such as bisulphite compounds, cyanohydrins, oximes and phenyl hydrazones can be formed from the carboxyl class of compounds. Nevertheless the initial step of nucleophilic attack on the carbon atom of the carbonyl group is essentially the same in acylations as in carbonyl additions; it is the subsequent history of the addition product which is different. This can be appreciated more clearly by considering a case where the same reagent attacks compounds of both types to give well-defined products. Hydroxylamine attacks not only ketones and aldehydes to yield oximes (see p. 178) but acyl chlorides, anhydrides, esters and amides to yield hydroxamic acids; e.g.

$$CH_5.C\!\!\begin{array}{c}O\\OEt\end{array} + NH_2OH \rightarrow CH_3.C\!\!\begin{array}{c}O\\NHOH\end{array} + EtOH$$

This clearly follows the general pattern of acylation; were an aldehyde or a ketone to follow this pattern, rather than forming an oxime, the reaction would require the extrusion of a hydride ion $H^\ominus$ or an alkyl anion—unlikely events under these conditions.

Preparation of carboxylic acids, methods of introducing —COOH into a molecule

Oxidative methods

(1) Carboxylic acids are obtained by the oxidation of primary alcohols or of the intermediate aldehydes:

$$R.CH_2OH \rightarrow R.CHO \rightarrow R.CO_2H$$

These reactions have been discussed on pp. 135 and 188.

The reactions can be carried out by conventional agents such as acidified permanganate or dichromate; to ensure complete oxidation, an excess of oxidant can be used and the mixture refluxed. Aldehydes can also be oxidized to acids by atmospheric oxygen. The reaction is catalysed by (among other things) manganous salts.

(2) Carboxylic acids are obtained by the drastic oxidation of ketones, where fission of the C—C bond on one side or other of the carbonyl group occurs, yielding in general two molecules of acid (the same or different) from the ketone molecule. This reaction has value in diagnosing the position of the carbonyl group in the ketone molecule by identifying the acids formed.

(3) The higher paraffins can be oxidized to carboxylic acids by passing air through the molten paraffin in the presence of manganous soaps (e.g. manganous stearate) which become dispersed in the paraffin.

This reaction was used during the second world war in Germany to eke out the limited supply of natural fatty acids. The acids so formed were converted both into sodium salts (for use in soap) and glyceryl esters (for use in margarine).

(4) Carbon chains attached to a benzene or similar aromatic nucleus may be oxidized by more or less prolonged treatment with vigorous oxidizing agents (e.g. refluxing with alkaline permanganate, chromic anhydride or concentrated nitric acid). The ultimate product has —CO_2H where the side chain was attached, whether this was a methyl group or a chain of several atoms. Thus toluene and ethyl benzene both yield benzoic acid,

$$C_6H_5.CH_3 + 3(O) \rightarrow C_6H_5CO_2H + H_2O$$

$$C_6H_5.C_2H_5 + 5(O) \rightarrow C_6H_5CO_2H + CO_2 + 2H_2O$$

while *p*-xylene yields terephthalic acid:

$$\text{CH}_3\text{-C}_6\text{H}_4\text{-CH}_3 + 6(O) \longrightarrow \text{CO}_2\text{H-C}_6\text{H}_4\text{-CO}_2\text{H} + 2H_2O$$

This reaction was used in one of the classical determinations of the orientation of substituents in disubstituted benzene derivatives (see p. 78). It is used in the manufacture of terephthalic acid for Terylene production (see p. 336).

Other methods

(5) Carboxylic acids are obtained by the alkaline and acidic hydrolysis of cyanides:

$$\text{CH}_3\text{CN} \to \text{CH}_3\text{CONH}_2 \to \text{CH}_3\text{CO}_2\text{H} + \text{NH}_3$$

With alkali, a salt of the carboxylic acid and free ammonia are obtained; with acid, the free acid and an ammonium salt. It is not usually possible to isolate the intermediate amide, since this is hydrolysed much more rapidly than the cyanide. It is this relation between the cyanide and the acid which leads to the alternative 'nitrile' nomenclature: thus methyl cyanide is acetonitrile.

The cyanides can be obtained from alkyl halides (p. 110) or from diazonium salts (p. 266).

(6) Grignard reagents react rapidly and smoothly with carbon dioxide, giving products which yield carboxylic acids on acidification. For example,

$$\text{C}_6\text{H}_5\text{MgBr} + \text{CO}_2 \to \text{C}_6\text{H}_5\text{CO}_2^{\ominus}\text{Mg}^{2\oplus}\text{Br}^{\ominus}$$

CO_2 reacts similarly with alkali metal alkyls but these are more inconvenient to prepare and as a rule have no advantage over the Grignard reagent.

Both methods 5 and 6 lead to the formation of the acid $R.CO_2H$ if the halide $R.Hal$ (or the aromatic amine RNH_2) is used for preparing the cyanide or the Grignard reagent; in each case an additional carbon atom is introduced.

(7) The group $-CCl_3$ will yield $-CO_2^{\ominus}$ on alkaline hydrolysis. (This would be predicted by assuming that $-Cl$ was replaced by $-OH$ and that water was then eliminated,

$$-CCl_3 \to -C(OH)_3 \to -C\underset{\text{OH}}{\overset{\text{O}}{\lessgtr}}$$

but this scheme must be regarded strictly as a mnemonic, and not as a likely mechanism. Quite apart from other considerations, it is highly unlikely that the implied intermediate —CCl(OH)$_2$ would await the displacement of the third —Cl before eliminating water.)

Chloroform on alkaline hydrolysis yields a formate

$$CHCl_3 + 4OH^{\ominus} \rightarrow HCO_2^{\ominus} + 3Cl^{\ominus} + 2H_2O$$

and benzotrichloride yields a benzoate:

$$C_6H_5CCl_3 + 4OH^{\ominus} \rightarrow C_6H_5CO_2^{\ominus} + 3Cl^{\ominus} + 2H_2O$$

Hence benzoic acid can be obtained technically by the complete side-chain chlorination of toluene, followed by hydrolysis with alkali and subsequent acidification.

When —CCl$_3$ is attached directly to $>$C$=$O (whether in chloral, trichloromethylketones or trichloroacetic acid) alkaline hydrolysis causes rapid C—C fission: thus the trichloroacetate ion yields not an oxalate but chloroform and a carbonate.

$$CCl_3.CO_2^{\ominus} + OH^{\ominus} \rightarrow CHCl_3 + CO_3^{2\ominus}$$

This is analogous (or, in the cases of chloral and trichloromethyl ketones, identical) with the last step of the haloform reaction.

(8) Carboxylic acids of the general type RR′CH.CO$_2$H (R and R′ alkyl or side-chain aromatic groups, e.g. benzyl) can be made from acetoacetic ester or malonic ester by the methods given on pp. 200–2.

The presence of —C$\underset{\displaystyle OH}{\overset{\displaystyle O}{\Big\langle}}$ in carboxylic acids

The structural formula of acetic acid (molecular formula C$_2$H$_4$O$_2$) can be established by arguments such as the following:

(1) It is a monobasic acid. (Its equivalent weight by ignition of the silver salt or by titration with standard alkali is 60, which is also its molecular weight.) Therefore (C$_2$H$_3$O$_2$)H.

(2) Chlorination yields successively C$_2$H$_3$O$_2$Cl, C$_2$H$_2$O$_2$Cl$_2$ and C$_2$HO$_2$Cl$_3$, all of which are monobasic acids.

(3) Acetic acid and the three chlorinated acids all yield acid chlorides with phosphorus trichloride: C$_2$H$_3$OCl, C$_2$H$_2$OCl$_2$, C$_2$HOCl$_3$ and C$_2$OCl$_4$. Here chlorine has replaced oxygen and hydrogen, hence the acids all contain the —OH group. Since trichloroacetic acid contains no other hydrogen atom, the ionizable hydrogen atom must be that in the OH group.

(4) Trichloroacetic acid yields chloroform $CHCl_3$ on heating with dilute aqueous alkali; hence all three chloride atoms are attached to the same carbon atom. It must therefore be formulated:

$$(CCl_3)CO(OH)$$

and acetic acid correspondingly as:

$$(CH_3)CO(OH)$$

The only bonding arrangement possible with normal valencies is:

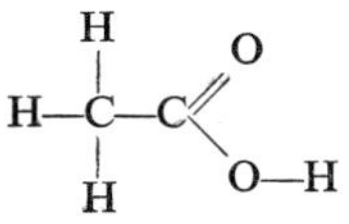

This establishes the conventional formula of the carboxyl group, but offers no positive evidence for the presence of the carbonyl group $>C=O$. This group is present in aldehydes $-C\begin{subarray}{l}\diagup H \\ \diagdown O\end{subarray}$, which yield carboxylic acids on oxidation.

Soaps and other detergents

Soaps in the layman's sense are the sodium salts or potassium salts of long-chain fatty acids or similar acids; for example, sodium stearate $CH_3(CH_2)_{16}CO_2^{\ominus}Na^{\oplus}$ or potassium oleate

$$CH_3(CH_2)_7CH=CH(CH_2)_7CO_2^{\ominus}K^{\oplus}.$$

These soaps dissolve as colloids in water; chemically the word is extended to include *insoluble* metallic salts of such acids, for example, aluminium stearate $(C_{17}H_{35}CO_2)_3Al$, calcium palmitate $(C_{15}H_{31}CO_2)_2Ca$.

The cleansing action of soaps and the various synthetic detergents which have been introduced in recent decades is probably due largely to their effect of reducing the interfacial tension between water and oily organic substances. The smaller the surface tension of a liquid, the less work is required to increase its surface area, for example, by breaking it up into smaller drops; thus oils are more easily emulsified (i.e. broken up into a more or less stable dispersion of droplets) by aqueous detergent solutions than by water itself, and thus more easily removed from greasy surfaces, together with adhering dirt, and flooded away.

Detergent molecules characteristically have a strong electrolyte 'head', with an attraction for the polar water molecules (hydrophilic), and a long-chain hydrocarbon 'tail' with no attraction for water (hydrophobic). In soaps, the head is the carboxylate ion group $—CO_2^{\ominus}$, and the tail a long *n*-alkyl or similar group.

The corresponding free long-chain fatty acids themselves and their salts with most other metals (including calcium and magnesium) are insoluble in water; soaps are therefore ineffective in acid conditions, or in hard water or in the presence of many metal ions. Soaps are also 'salted-out' of solution by substantial sodium ion concentrations; this is used to separate them from the aqueous product of fat hydrolysis, but makes them ineffective in seawater.

Synthetic detergents overcome these drawbacks by using other strong electrolyte substituents in place of the carboxylate group. Most of these have soluble calcium salts; many are strong acids or sodium salts thereof. They are thus effective in hard water and acid conditions. Some also resist salting-out (in some cases because they contain no sodium ions, and suffer no 'common ion' precipitation with brine, though this is not the only effect operating); they can therefore be used in salt water.

The so-called 'biologically-soft' detergents have unbranched chains in place of branched ones. These are more readily destroyed by bacterial action.

The following types are among those that have been used as detergents:

Higher alkane sulphonic acids $R.SO_3H$ and their salts;

Sulphonic acids of long-chain molecules with other functional groups;

Aromatic sulphonic acids with a long alkyl side-chain $R.C_6H_4SO_3H$;

Long-chain alkyl hydrogen sulphates $R.OSO_2OH$ and their salts;

Long-chain alkyl quaternary ammonium salts $R.\overset{\oplus}{N}(CH_3)_3X^{\ominus}$.

Formic acid

The first member of an homologous series sometimes differs more from the higher members than these do among themselves. This is particularly so when the functional group contains carbon, as this will then be attached to hydrogen in the first member, rather than to alkyl as in higher members.

Formic acid differs from acetic acid and its higher homologues in the following points:

(*a*) It is a stronger acid (K_A about 10 times greater).

(*b*) It is fairly readily oxidized (to water and carbon dioxide). Formally, formic acid contains the $—C{\overset{H}{\underset{O}{\big\langle}}}$ group, though this is modified by electron delocalization, and its reducing action can be compared with that of an aldehyde. Formic acid (or formates) reduce acid and alkaline permanganate and ammoniacal silver ion solutions on warming; acetic acid (or acetates) do not.

(c) It is less stable thermally. Formic acid decomposes on heating in the vapour state, especially in the presence of metal catalysts:

$$H.CO_2H \rightarrow H_2 + CO_2$$

(d) Formic acid is dehydrated by warm concentrated sulphuric acid to carbon monoxide. Acetic acid can be distilled unchanged from sulphuric acid.

(e) Formyl chloride cannot be isolated. Reagents which would convert the higher fatty acids to acyl chlorides therefore yield hydrogen chloride and carbon monoxide with formic acid.

Manufacture of formic acid

Carbon monoxide at about 10 atmospheres and 200° C is absorbed by concentrated sodium hydroxide solution to yield sodium formate:
The solution can be acidified and fractionated to yield formic acid.

Manufacture of acetic acid

Acetic acid is manufactured by oxidizing acetaldehyde (from ethanol or acetylene) by air in the presence of manganese acetate.

It can also be made from aqueous ethanol by atmospheric oxidation in the presence of the micro-organism *Acetobacter aceti*. Applied to beer, cider or wine, this is the manufacture of vinegar; it can also be used technically, and the acetic acid concentrated by fractionation.

The liquid-phase oxidation of C_5—C_7 paraffins at high temperatures and pressure yields a mixture of shorter chain-length carboxylic acids, including acetic, formic and propionic acids.

16

Organic derivatives of hydrogen cyanide; the cyanide $-C\equiv N$ and isocyanide $-\overset{\oplus}{N}\equiv\overset{\ominus}{C}$ groups

Two isomeric series of compounds are known of molecular formula RCN—the *cyanides* and the *isocyanides*. Their reactions and methods of formation are reviewed in this chapter, and taken together these leave no doubt that in cyanides the CN group is attached by carbon to the rest of the molecule, while in isocyanides it is attached by nitrogen. Ordinary valency rules therefore lead to the formulation of, for example, methyl cyanide as:
$$CH_3-C\equiv N$$
and methyl isocyanide as:
$$CH_3-N\equiv C \quad \text{or} \quad CH_3-\overset{\oplus}{N}\equiv\overset{\ominus}{C}$$

The lower alkyl cyanides and isocyanides are volatile liquids (the lowest miscible with water); the higher members are crystalline solids at ordinary temperatures. Phenyl cyanide is a liquid, *p*-tolyl cyanide a solid. Isocyanides have somewhat lower boiling points than the isomeric cyanides (e.g. CH_3CN.b.p., 81·6° C; CH_3NC, 59° C). This may seem surprising in view of the formulation of isocyanides with a dative bond, but the high polarity implied by this will be opposed by the fact that nitrogen is more electronegative than carbon, and in fact the cyanide molecule is the more polar of the two. Isocyanides are more toxic than cyanides (though neither are as toxic as hydrogen cyanide itself) and have much more unpleasant smells.

Reactions of cyanides

(1)   Reduction

Reduction of cyanides with sodium and ethanol yields a primary amine as the principal product. Thus methyl cyanide yields ethylamine.
$$Na \rightarrow Na^{\oplus}+e$$
$$C_2H_5OH \rightarrow C_2H_5O^{\ominus}+H^{\oplus}$$
$$CH_3CN+4e+4H^{\oplus} \rightarrow CH_3CH_2NH_2$$
Reduction by the action of acid stannous chloride solution on an ethereal solution of the cyanide, however, yields an aldehyde, presumably via the intermediate *aldimine* which is then hydrolysed:

$$SnCl_4{}^{2\ominus}+2Cl^{\ominus} \rightarrow SnCl_6{}^{2\ominus}+2e$$
$$CH_3CN+2H^{\oplus}+2e \rightarrow CH_3CH{=}NH$$
$$CH_3CH{=}NH+H_2O+H^{\oplus} \rightarrow CH_3CHO+NH_4{}^{\oplus}$$

In both types of reduction product, the carbon atom of the cyanide group remains attached to the alkyl radical; in the primary amine, the nitrogen atom must be at the end of the chain. This confirms the assumptions made about the structure of cyanides.

(Together with the primary amine RCH_2NH_2, varying amounts of the secondary amine $(RCH_2)_2NH$ and ammonia are formed, especially when catalytic hydrogenation or acid 'nascent hydrogen' reducing agents are used.)

(2) Hydrolysis

Cyanides are hydrolysed by refluxing with either aqueous alkali or aqueous strong acid, yielding ammonia and a carboxylate ion in alkaline conditions, or their corresponding conjugate acids in acid conditions:

$$CH_3CN+OH^{\ominus}+H_2O \rightarrow CH_3CO_2{}^{\ominus}+NH_3$$
$$CH_3CN+H^{\oplus}+H_2O \rightarrow CH_3CO_2H+NH_4{}^{\oplus}$$

The carbon atom of the CN group carries a partial positive charge and the nitrogen atom a negative one (nitrogen being more electronegative than carbon); these hydrolyses are therefore probably essentially similar to the alkaline and acid hydrolyses of carboxylic acid derivatives. Thus with alkali the initial step is presumably attack of the powerful nucleophilic $OH^{\ominus}$ on the carbon atom:

$$HO^{\ominus} \quad \overset{R}{\underset{}{C}}{\equiv}N \rightarrow HO{-}\overset{R}{\underset{}{C}}{=}\overset{\ominus}{N}$$

followed by proton transfers

$$\rightarrow O{=}\overset{R}{\underset{}{C}}{-}NH_2$$

thus yielding an amide.

With acid, the proton addition to the nitrogen atom is a likely initial step, thus denuding the carbon atom still more of electrons, and rendering it more open to the attack of the weaker nucleophile water.

$$\overset{R}{\underset{}{C}}{\equiv}N+H^{\oplus} \rightarrow \overset{R}{\underset{}{C}}{\equiv}\overset{\oplus}{N}{-}H$$

$$\begin{matrix}H\\ \diagdown \\ \diagup \\ H\end{matrix}O+\overset{R}{\underset{}{C}}{\equiv}\overset{\oplus}{N}H \rightarrow \begin{matrix}H\\ \diagdown \\ \diagup \\ H\end{matrix}O{-}\overset{R}{\underset{}{C}}{=}NH$$

Again, proton transfer gives the amide $O{=}\overset{R}{\underset{}{C}}{-}NH_2$, once more.

Since amides themselves are readily hydrolysed by aqueous alkali or acid (see p. 218), it is rarely possible to halt the hydrolysis of cyanides at the amide stage, and the ultimate products are those noted above. Amides, however, have been isolated when hydrolysis is carried out by small amounts of water in excess of concentrated sulphuric acid; different intermediates may then be involved.

Again, in the hydrolysis product, the carbon atom of the cyanide group remains attached to the alkyl group as the CO_2H group, thus once again confirming the accepted structure of the cyanides.

(3) Alcoholysis

It is sometimes practically important to convert a cyanide group to the ester of the corresponding carboxylic acid rather than the acid itself. This is achieved by refluxing the cyanide with excess alcohol in the presence of some water and sulphuric acid or hydrogen chloride.

$$R—C\equiv N + R'OH + H_2O \xrightarrow{H^\oplus} R.CO_2R' + NH_4^\oplus$$

If the conditions are completely anhydrous—if, for example, dry hydrogen chloride is passed into an anhydrous ethanolic solution of the cyanide —a reaction analogous to acid-catalysed hydrolysis will occur, the product being the so-called imido-ester hydrochloride:

$$\underset{Et—O—C=\overset{\oplus}{N}H_2Cl^\ominus}{\overset{\displaystyle R}{\vert}}$$

(The reader should satisfy himself why in this case the amide cannot be formed as it is in hydrolysis.) In the presence of any water, however, whether in the reagent or arising from other reactions proceeding simultaneously with other functional groups, the intermediate is rapidly hydrolysed with the elimination of ammonia, yielding the ethyl ester

$$\underset{EtO—C=O}{\overset{\displaystyle R}{\vert}}$$

Thus when cyanoacetic acid is refluxed with ethanol and sulphuric acid, water eliminated in the esterification of the carboxyl group ensures the conversion of the cyanide to an ester, so that ethyl malonate is formed:

$$CH_2 \overset{\displaystyle CN}{\underset{\displaystyle CO_2H}{\diagup \diagdown}} \xrightarrow[H_2SO_4]{EtOH} CH_2(CO_2Et)_2$$

Similarly, when acetone cyanohydrin is refluxed with methanol and sulphuric acid, elimination of water to form an olefinic bond occurs (see chapter 11, p. 134), and hence the cyanide is again converted to an ester:

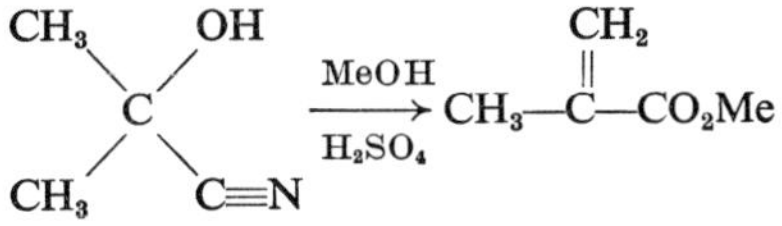

$$\underset{\underset{CH_3}{|}}{\overset{\overset{CH_3}{|}}{C}}\underset{C\equiv N}{\overset{OH}{\diagup}} \quad \xrightarrow[H_2SO_4]{MeOH} \quad CH_3-\overset{\overset{CH_2}{\|}}{C}-CO_2Me$$

The product is methyl methacrylate, the monomer of the plastic 'Perspex'.

Aryl cyanides in general carry out the above reactions, but hydrolysis proceeds comparatively slowly in either acid or alkaline conditions. The use of fairly concentrated sulphuric acid may cause some sulphonation. Since the aryl cyanides are very sparingly soluble in water, aqueous-ethanolic rather than aqueous alkali is often used in alkaline hydrolysis.

Formation of cyanides

(1) By refluxing alkyl halides with aqueous-ethanolic solutions of potassium cyanides, cyanides are formed together with small amounts of isocyanides. For example,

$$CH_3I + CN^\ominus \rightarrow CH_3CN + I^\ominus$$
$$\text{(and } CH_3NC)$$

This reaction has been discussed on p. 110, chapter 10.

Owing to the great difficulty of displacing halogen attached to the benzene ring, aryl cyanides cannot be made in this way in the laboratory though it is claimed that the reaction can be performed at about 200° C and the appropriate pressure and in the presence of Cu(I) compounds (cf. p. 111, chapter 10).

(2) Cyanides are formed by the drastic dehydration of amides (or of the ammonium salts of carboxylic acids, which yield amides on loss of water). The stock laboratory method is to distil the amide with phosphorus pentoxide. Thus acetamide yields methyl cyanide

$$CH_3CONH_2 \xrightarrow{P_2O_5} CH_3CN$$

and benzamide, phenyl cyanide.

The technical dehydration of adipamide, $H_2NCO(CH_2)_4CONH_2$ to $N\equiv C(CH_2)_4C\equiv N$ and the subsequent reduction of this to hexamethylenediamine $H_2N(CH_2)_6NH_2$ are important stages in one process for the manufacture of 66 nylon (see p. 336).

(3) Cyanides are also formed by the dehydration of aldoximes, for example, by warming with acetic anhydride or thionyl chloride

$$C_2H_5CH{=}NOH \xrightarrow{-H_2O} C_6H_5CN$$

(4) Aryl cyanides can be obtained by the Sandmeyer reaction of a cuprocyanide solution on aryl diazonium salts. This reaction is discussed on p. 266. For example,

$$C_6H_5N_2{}^{\oplus} \xrightarrow[\text{in } KCN_{Aq}]{CuCN} C_6H_5CN$$

Small amounts of isocyanide are formed simultaneously.

(5) Aryl cyanides are obtained when the sodium salt of the corresponding sulphonic acid is fused with potassium cyanide. The reaction is of little practical importance.

$$C_6H_5SO_3{}^{\ominus}+CN^{\ominus} \rightarrow C_6H_5CN+SO_3{}^{2\ominus}$$

The preparation of cyanides by the dehydration of $RCONH_2$ and of $RCHN{=}OH$ (methods 2 and 3 above) further confirm their accepted structure.

Alternative nomenclature

As well as being regarded as compounds of the cyanide group with an alkyl or other group, and named accordingly, cyanides can be regarded as derivatives of the carboxylic acids which they yield on hydrolysis, and from whose corresponding amides they are formed by dehydration. From this point of view, they are called *nitriles* and named after the corresponding acid; thus methyl cyanide is called *acetonitrile* and phenyl cyanide is *benzonitrile*. Both names are acceptable.

Reactions of isocyanides

(1) Reduction

Catalytic hydrogenation of isocyanides yields methyl secondary amines. Thus, for example, ethyl isocyanide will yield methyl ethylamine.

$$C_2H_5NC \xrightarrow[\text{Pt}]{H_2} C_2H_5NH.CH_3$$

This confirms that the nitrogen atom is attached to the alkyl or similar group in the isocyanide.

'Nascent hydrogen' agents may also be used.

(2) Hydrolysis

Isocyanides are very rapidly hydrolysed by dilute aqueous strong acids. The products are the conjugate acid of the primary amine, and formic acid. Thus:

$$CH_3NC + 2N_2O + H^{\oplus} \rightarrow CH_3\overset{\oplus}{N}H_3 + H.CO_2H.$$

They are scarcely attacked, if at all, by aqueous alkali.

Again, the structure is confirmed by the fact that the carbon atom is lost (as formic acid) while the nitrogen atom remains attached to the alkyl group in the product.

(3) Isomerization

On heating to fairly high temperatures (round about 200° C), isocyanides are largely converted to the isomeric cyanides.

Formation of isocyanides

(1) An isocyanide rather than a cyanide is the main product when an alkyl halide is reflexed with silver cyanide; for example,

$$CH_3I + AgCN \rightarrow CH_3NC + AgI$$

This method is not available for aryl isocyanides owing to the low reactivity of the aryl halides.

(2) An isocyanide is obtained when a primary amine is warmed with chloroform and ethanolic caustic alkali. For example,

$$C_6H_5NH_2 + CHCl_3 + 3OH^{\ominus} \rightarrow C_6H_5NC + 3Cl^{\ominus} + 3H_2O$$

This is the well-known *carbylamine* reaction often given as a test for primary amines. The unpleasant smell of the isocyanide confirms the presence of the primary amine in the reaction mixture.

Alternative nomenclature

Isocyanides are sometimes known as carbylamines; thus the product shown in (2) above can be called phenyl carbylamine. They have also been called 'iso-nitriles' but, since unlike the nitriles they are in no sense derivatives of the carboxylic acids, this cannot logically be used as a method of naming them.

Hydrogen cyanide

Hydrogen cyanide is a colourless liquid, of b.p. $26°$ C at 760 mm., m.p. $-13°$ C. It is miscible with water in all proportions. It has a remarkably high dielectric constant (194 at its freezing point, and 116 at $20°$ C; compare water, about 80). It is a moderate solvent for ionic solids though not nearly so effective as water, in spite of its greater dielectric constant. In aqueous solution it is a very weak acid (hydrocyanic or 'prussic' acid) with K_A at $25°$ C about 5×10^{-10}—that is, of the same order of strength as phenol or the ammonium ion.

Since the cyanide ion has an unshared electron pair on both the carbon and the nitrogen atom, hydrogen cyanide might be expected to exist as a tautomeric equilibrium mixture of cyanide and isocyanide forms. Thus:

$$\text{H—C}{\equiv}\text{N} \rightleftharpoons \text{H}^{\oplus} + (:\text{C}{\equiv}\text{N}:)^{\ominus} \rightleftharpoons \overset{\ominus}{\text{C}}{\equiv}\overset{\oplus}{\text{N}}\text{—H}$$

There is, however, no real evidence of the presence of appreciable quantities of the isocyanide form in hydrogen cyanide.

Hydrogen cyanide could be regarded as the first member of the homologous series of fatty acid nitriles ('formonitrile'). In accordance with this, it is hydrolysed in aqueous solution especially in the presence of mineral acid, to formic acid and ammonium ions.

$$\text{HCN} + 2\text{H}_2\text{O} \xrightarrow{\text{H}^{\oplus}} \text{H}.\text{CO}_2\text{H} + \text{NH}_4{}^{\oplus}$$

It is reduced by 'nascent hydrogen' agents such as zinc and hydrochloric acid to the methylammonium ion

$$\text{HCN} + 4e + 5\text{H}^{\oplus} \rightarrow \text{CH}_3\text{NH}_3{}^{\oplus}$$

Hydrogen cyanide can be prepared in the laboratory by warming potassium cyanide or complex cyanides such as potassium ferrocyanide with moderately concentrated aqueous strong acid (e.g. 60% sulphuric acid). The vapour evolved is condensed; water may be removed by phosphorus pentoxide. (If near-concentrated sulphuric acid is used, carbon monoxide is the main product, at any rate with ferrocyanides—presumably because the hydrogen cyanide is rapidly hydrolysed to formic acid, which is then dehydrated.) For the chemistry of metallic cyanides and cyanide complexes textbooks of inorganic chemistry should be consulted.

Cyanogen (CN)$_2$

Cyanogen is a colourless, inflammable, highly toxic gas (b.p. $-21°$ C at 760 mm).

Just as hydrogen cyanide can be regarded as formonitrile, so cyanogen is oxalonitrile.

$$\begin{array}{ll} C\equiv N & CO_2H \\ | & | \\ C\equiv N & CO_2H \\ \text{cyanogen} & \text{oxalic acid} \end{array}$$

Aqueous solutions of cyanogen deposit a brown precipitate on standing, but some ammonium oxalate is formed.

Ethanolic hydrogen chloride yields the expected imido-ester hydrochloride:

$$\begin{array}{l} EtO-C\overset{\oplus}{=}NH_2Cl^{\ominus} \\ | \quad \overset{\oplus}{=} \\ EtO-C=NH_2Cl^{\ominus} \end{array}$$

With alkalis, however, cyanogen behaves as a 'pseudo-halogen', and forms an equimolecular mixture of cyanide and cyanate.

$$(CN)_2 + 2OH^{\ominus} \rightarrow CN^{\ominus} + OCN^{\ominus} + H_2O$$

Cyanogen is obtained when mercuric cyanide is heated (Gay-Lussac's original preparation).

It is also obtained when cyanide ions are oxidized by warming with a Cu(II) salt solution (compare the analogous behaviour of iodides):

$$2CN^{\ominus} + 2Cu^{2\oplus} \rightarrow 2Cu^{\oplus} + (CN)_2\uparrow$$

As oxalonitrile, it is obtained when oxamide or ammonium oxalate are heated with phosphorus pentoxide.

In certain respects, the cyanide group has analogies with a halogen atom. Thus potassium cyanide has a cubic lattice, like potassium chloride; hydrogen cyanide is an acid, though a very weak one. The above reactions of cyanides with cupric salts, and of cyanogen with alkali, and the analogy of behaviour of cuprohalides and cuprocyanides in the Sandmeyer reaction (see p. 266) are other examples. Nevertheless, the picture of the cyanide group as a 'pseudo-halogen' is misleading if pressed too far. In particular, it should be clear from this chapter that alkyl cyanides *do not* behave chemically as alkyl halides; contrast, for example, their behaviour on alkaline hydrolysis.

17

The sulphonic acid group $-\overset{\overset{\displaystyle O}{\|}}{\underset{\underset{\displaystyle O}{\|}}{S}}-OH$ and allied functional groups

The sulphonic acids contain the functional group $-\overset{\overset{\displaystyle O}{\|}}{\underset{\underset{\displaystyle O}{\|}}{S}}-OH$, usually written as SO_3H. The alternative SO_2OH is occasionally convenient when it is desired to emphasize the relationship between sulphonic acids and their derivatives. They may therefore be regarded as derivatives of sulphuric acid $HO-\overset{\overset{\displaystyle O}{\|}}{\underset{\underset{\displaystyle O}{\|}}{S}}-OH$ in which one —OH group has been replaced by an organic radical. The sulphur–oxygen bonds present the same problem in sulphonic acids, sulphuric acid and sulphuryl chloride SO_2Cl_2, and an analogous problem to that presented by the phosphorus–oxygen bonds in phosphoric acid, the organic phosphonic acids, phosphoryl chloride and the organic phosphine oxides R_3PO. For a full discussion of this problem, text-books of general chemistry should be consulted; sufficient here to say that the bond lengths and, where measurable, the bond polarities suggest that the formulations $S \rightarrow O$, $P \rightarrow O$ are inadequate. The bond is probably multiple in some way; the double bond representation used here should, however, be regarded as a convention and not as an accurate representation of the bond order.

Sulphonic acids show some formal analogies with carboxylic acids, having formally sexacovalent sulphur in place of quadricovalent carbon, and like the carboxylic acids give rise to a series of derivatives, thus:

R.SO$_3$H   or   R.SO$_2$OH   the sulphonic acid

R.SO$_2$Cl   the sulphonyl chloride

R.SO$_2$NH$_2$ the sulphonamide

R.SO$_3$C$_2$H$_5$ or   R.SO$_2$OC$_2$H$_5$ (e.g.)   the ethyl ester.

The sulphonic acids should be clearly distinguished from the acid esters of sulphuric acid, which contain the group —O—SO$_2$.OH, and a carbon-oxygen as opposed to a carbon sulphur bond. Contrast, for example,

C$_2$H$_5$—O.SO$_2$.OH   C$_2$H$_5$—SO$_2$.OH

ethyl hydrogen sulphate   ethanesulphonic acid

Nomenclature

The sulphonic acid group is treated as a substituent replacing an hydrogen atom of the parent hydrocarbon, to which the group name 'sulphonic acid' is suffixed. Thus:

CH$_3$SO$_3$H   methanesulphonic acid

p-toluenesulphonic acid

General properties

The aromatic sulphonic acids, which are the only ones the elementary student will meet in the laboratory, are crystalline solids, highly soluble in water, from which they often crystallize as hydrates. The sulphonamides are much less water soluble. Sulphonyl chlorides and the lower alkyl esters are liquids or low melting solids, more or less insoluble in water. The sulphonyl chlorides have highly characteristic, rather unpleasant sickly smells.

Chemical behaviour of the acids

(1) Acidity

The sulphonic acids, both aliphatic and aromatic, behave as *strong* monobasic acids in aqueous solution. In this they differ markedly from the carboxylic acids, which are weak in aqueous solution. The greater strength of the sulphonic acids can be referred (*a*) to the fact that sulphur is more electronegative than carbon, leading to a greater withdrawal of electrons from the neighbourhood of the hydrogen atom, and (*b*) to the possibility of spreading the ionic charge of the sulphonate ion over three sites rather than the two of the carboxylate ion, with consequent greater stabilization of the ion *vis-à-vis* the free acid. Thus:

$$
\begin{array}{ccc}
\overset{\displaystyle O}{\underset{\displaystyle O}{\overset{\|}{\underset{\|}{-S}}}}-O^{\ominus} & \overset{\displaystyle O^{\ominus}}{\underset{\displaystyle O}{\overset{|}{\underset{\|}{-S}}}}=O & \overset{\displaystyle O}{\underset{\displaystyle O^{\ominus}}{\overset{\|}{\underset{|}{-S}}}}=O
\end{array}
$$

The sodium salts of simple arylsulphonic acids can be isolated, not only by conventional neutralization, but by adding excess of saturated brine to the aqueous acid—a clear indication that (e.g.) benzenesulphonic acid and hydrochloric acid are of comparable strength in water. The arylsulphonates, both of metallic ions and of the conjugate acids of nitrogenous bases, are well-defined crystalline salts.

In contrast to the sulphates the barium, strontium and calcium salts are readily soluble in water.

(2) Conversion to chlorides

The free acids or their sodium salts react with phosphorus halides and similar substances to yield sulphonyl chlorides. This is comparable with the behaviour of carboxylic acids, for example,

$$C_6H_5SO_3H + PCl_5 \rightarrow C_6H_5SO_2Cl + POCl_3 + HCl$$

or

$$C_6H_5SO_3^{\ominus} + PCl_5 \rightarrow C_6H_5SO_2Cl + POCl_3 + Cl^{\ominus}$$

The other derivatives (amides and esters) are more readily and conveniently obtained from the sulphonyl chlorides than from the acids themselves.

(3) Hydrolysis

The sulphonation of aromatic hydrocarbons is reversible. Thus benzenesulphonic acid on refluxing with aqueous mineral acid, or heating with steam under pressure, yields benzene:

$$C_6H_5SO_3H + H_2O \rightarrow C_6H_6 + H_2SO_4$$

As an example of the use of this reaction, *m*-xylene can be separated from a mixture of xylenes by relying on its fairly rapid sulphonation with cold concentrated sulphuric acid to yield 2,4-dimethylbenzenesulphonic acid, which can easily be separated from the largely unchanged *o*- and *p*-xylenes and hydrolysed.

248

Alkanesulphonic acids cannot be hydrolysed in this way.

Sulphonic acids of the aromatic series undergo certain displacement reactions with nucleophilic reagents.

(4) Fusion with alkali

The alkali metal salts of the arylsulphonic acids yield the sodium salt of a phenol on fusion with caustic alkalis. This is the basis of the old-established method of making phenol from benzene.

$$C_6H_5SO_3^{\ominus}+OH^{\ominus} \rightarrow C_6H_5OH+SO_3^{2\ominus}$$

$$\downarrow OH^{\ominus}$$

$$C_6H_5O^{\ominus}$$

Aqueous alkali under pressure may in some cases be used.

(5) Heating with cyanide

An intimate mixture of a metal sulphonate and solid potassium cyanide yields the corresponding nitrile on pyrolysis. Yields are rarely good. For example,

$$C_6H_5SO_3^{\ominus}+CN^{\ominus} \rightarrow C_6H_5CN+SO_3^{2\ominus}$$

Reactions of the sulphonyl chlorides

(1) Hydrolysis

Like the aromatic aryl chlorides, such as benzoyl chloride, aromatic sulphonyl chlorides are not readily attacked by water, and can be handled even in the presence of aqueous alkali. They are, however, gradually hydrolysed to the sulphonic acid (or its anion) and chloride ion:

$$C_6H_5SO_2Cl+H_2O \rightarrow C_6H_5SO_3^{\ominus}+2H^{\oplus}+Cl^{\ominus}$$

(2) Alcoholysis

Alcohols (or, where these are ineffective, a suspension of alkali alkoxide in ether) convert sulphonyl chlorides to sulphonate esters. For example:

(3) Ammonolysis

Aqueous ammonia readily converts sulphonyl chlorides to sulphonamides. For example,

$$C_6H_5SO_2Cl + NH_3 \rightarrow C_6H_5SO_2NH_2 + Cl^\ominus + H^\oplus$$

$$\downarrow NH_3$$

$$NH_4^\oplus$$

Amines behave similarly. If necessary, the reaction can be performed in Schotten–Baumann conditions as with aromatic acyl chlorides; that is, in the presence of aqueous alkali. In that case, if the amine is primary, the substituted sulphonamide will dissolve as its conjugate base (see below).

(4) Reduction

Aromatic sulphonyl chlorides are reduced by zinc dust and aqueous strong acids to thiophenols:

$$C_6H_5SO_2Cl + 3Zn + 5H^\oplus \rightarrow C_6H_5SH + 2H_2O + 3Zn^{2\oplus} + Cl^\ominus$$

Since thiophenols contain no oxygen, they must have a C—S link; this reaction therefore confirms the presence of such a link in sulphonic acids and their derivatives.

Reactions of sulphonamides

(1) Acid behaviour

Unlike carboxyamides, sulphonamides are appreciably though weakly acidic in aqueous solution; thus the sparingly soluble sulphonamides and *N*-alkyl or *N*-aryl sulphonamides dissolve in aqueous alkali to form their conjugate bases.

$$C_6H_5SO_2NH_2 + OH^\ominus \rightarrow C_6H_5SO_2\overset{\ominus}{N}H + H_2O$$

$$C_6H_5SO_2NHC_6H_5 + OH^\ominus \rightarrow C_6H_5SO_2\overset{\ominus}{N}C_6H_5 + H_2O$$

This property is made use of in the Hinsberg separation of primary, secondary and tertiary amines from a mixture such as would arise, for example, in the action of an alkyl halide on ammonia. The method may be summarized as follows: the mixture is treated with benzene or *p*-toluenesulphonyl chloride (if necessary, in the presence of aqueous alkali);

$$R_3N \quad \text{no reaction}$$
$$R_2NH \rightarrow C_6H_5.SO_2NR_2 \quad \text{non-acidic; insoluble in NaOH}_{aq}$$
$$RNH_2 \rightarrow C_6H_5.SO_2NHR \quad \text{acidic; soluble in NaOH}_{aq}.$$

Clearly the three materials, tertiary amine (probably a fairly volatile liquid), *NN*-dialkylsulphonamide (crystalline water—insoluble solid of low volatility) and *N*-alkylsulphonamide anion (water-soluble electrolyte) can readily be separated physically. The amines can be regenerated by hydrolysing the sulphonamides. One of the groups R may be aryl.

The acidity of the sulphonamides contrasts with the negligible acidity of carboxyamides in water. It is analogous with the difference in strength of the corresponding acids, and can be explained on precisely analogous grounds. The similarity of the sulphonamides with phthalimide in this respect is noteworthy; the anionic charge of the phthalimide anion can be distributed over three sites

as can that of the benzenesulphonamide anion, thus leading to analogous strength in the conjugate acids.

(2) Hydrolysis

Sulphonamides and *N*-substituted sulphonamides are slowly hydrolysed by boiling with aqueous mineral acid. The reaction with aromatic sulphonamides is particularly slow; thus, for example, the acetyl group can be removed from the compound

by hot hydrochloric acid while leaving the sulphonamide group intact.

(3) Halogenation

Hypochlorite solutions effect *N*-chlorination of sulphonamides. For example,

Chloramine-T

Chloramine-T is a useful antiseptic, probably because it slowly liberates hypochlorous acid in water by the reverse of the above reaction. It has also been used as a decontaminating agent for removing 'mustard gas' $(ClCH_2.CH_2)_2S$, which it oxidizes to $(ClCH_2.CH_2)_2SO$ and other harmless products.

This halogenation can be compared with the first step of the Hofmann reaction (see p. 229).

Reactions of sulphonic esters

(1) Hydrolysis

The alkyl esters of aromatic sulphonic acids are fairly easily hydrolysed; for example, slowly by water in the cold.

$$C_6H_5SO_2OCH_3 + H_2O \rightarrow C_6H_5SO_3H + CH_3OH$$

(2) Ammonolysis and allied reactions

Towards ammonia and amines, sulphonic esters behave like alkyl halides, that is to say, alkyl-oxygen fission occurs. They therefore act as alkylating agents, in strong contrast to carboxy esters, which are mild acylating agents, undergoing acyl-oxygen fission. Thus, for example, methyl *p*-toluenesulphonate and methylamine yield a dimethyl ammonium salt:

$$C_6H_5SO_2OCH_3 + NH_2CH_3 \rightarrow C_6H_5SO_3^{\ominus} \overset{\oplus}{N}H_2(CH_3)_2$$

Contrast

$$CH_3.COOCH_3 + NH_2CH_3 \rightarrow CH_3CONH.CH_3 + CH_3OH$$

Presumably the presence of the relatively electronegative sulphur atom and an additional oxygen atom causes a greater withdrawal of electrons from the α-carbon atom of the ester alkyl group, thus rendering it a likely site for nucleophilic attack.

This property makes an ester like methyl *p*-toluenesulphonate a useful methylating agent, cheaper than methyl iodide and less toxic than dimethyl sulphate.

Preparation of sulphonic acids and their derivatives

(1) Sulphonation with sulphuric acid

Aromatic hydrocarbons are sulphonated by concentrated sulphuric acid or, more rapidly, by oleum. Benzene itself needs refluxing for many hours with the former, but reacts fairly rapidly in the cold with the latter. Homologues of benzene, owing to the presence of the ortho–para directing alkyl groups, react more rapidly than benzene itself and, where two such groups reinforce one another, as in *m*-xylene, sulphonation may occur smoothly and rapidly in the cold.

Sulphonation is reversible (see p. 92) and, in the technical sulphonation of benzene, the reaction water is removed continuously by allowing benzene and water to distil out, separating the water and recycling the benzene.

Since the —SO_3H group is characteristically meta-directing, further sulphonation requires more drastic conditions; for example, effective disulphonation of benzene requires oleum at over 200 °C.

Alkanes below hexane cannot be sulphonated directly; higher alkanes do however react with oleum to give sulphonic acids.

$$C_6H_{14}+H_2SO_4 \rightarrow C_6H_{13}SO_3H+H_2O$$

Alkyl groups in other aliphatic compounds can sometimes be sulphonated fairly readily; discussion of these cases is beyond the scope of this book.

(2) Sulphonation with chlorosulphonic acid

Chlorosulphonic acid $HO.SO_2.Cl$ is an effective sulphonating agent, yielding sulphonic acids with both aromatic and aliphatic compounds. If larger quantities of chlorosulphonic acid are used, a *sulphonyl chloride* is obtained; this is inevitably present as a by-product even when the acid is the main product.

$$RH+HOSO_2Cl \rightarrow R.SO_2OH+HCl$$
$$R.SO_3H+HOSO_2Cl \rightarrow R.SO_2Cl+H_2SO_4$$

The manufacture of sulphanilamide and saccharin (see below) illustrate the use of chlorosulphonic acid.

(3) From alkyl halides

Alkyl halides react with aqueous sodium sulphite solutions when heated in closed vessels, yielding sodium salts of the alkanesulphonic acids. For example,

$$C_2H_5Br+SO_3^{2\ominus} \rightarrow C_2H_5SO_3^{\ominus}+Br^{\ominus}$$

This is yet another example of the alkyl halide displacement type of reaction discussed in chapter 10, p. 110, and is often the most effective route to the simple alkanesulphonic acids.

Technical uses of sulphonation and sulphonic acids

Sulphonation and sulphonic acids are of considerable technical importance. Sulphonated long-chain aliphatic compounds are used as detergents, either as the sodium salts or as the free acid; they have the characteristic strong electrolyte 'head' and long-chain 'tail' of all detergents and have the advantage over the traditional soaps of being effective in acid conditions (since free sulphonic acids, unlike carboxylic acids, are strong electrolytes and water-soluble) and in hard water (since the calcium salts, unlike calcium soaps, are water-soluble). Similar surface-active properties are shown by aromatic sulphonic acids with long alkyl side-chains; the dodecyl benzene sulphonic acids $C_{12}H_{25}.C_6H_4SO_3H$ are manufactured as detergents.

Miscellaneous sulphonated compounds both aliphatic and aromatic are used as emulsifying and wetting agents. 'Twitchell's reagent', used in the manufacture of long-chain fatty acids from fats, is a typical example. It is made from benzene, oleic acid and concentrated sulphuric acid, and a small quantity is added to a fat–water mixture, through which steam is blown. The reagent acts both as an emulsifying agent, increasing the area of contact of the reactants, and as a strong acid catalyst for the ester hydrolysis.

Aromatic sulphonic acids can be used as intermediates in the manufacture of phenols (see p. 140). *p*-Aminobenzenesulphonic acid (sulphanilic acid) and other aromatic aminosulphonic acids are used as intermediates in azo-dye manufacture (see p. 268).

The industrial synthesis of two well-known materials, (*a*) saccharin and (*b*) sulphanilamide (the prototype 'sulfa' drug) are summarized below. They illustrate the use of chlorosulphonic acid, and a number of other points mentioned in this and other chapters.

(*a*)

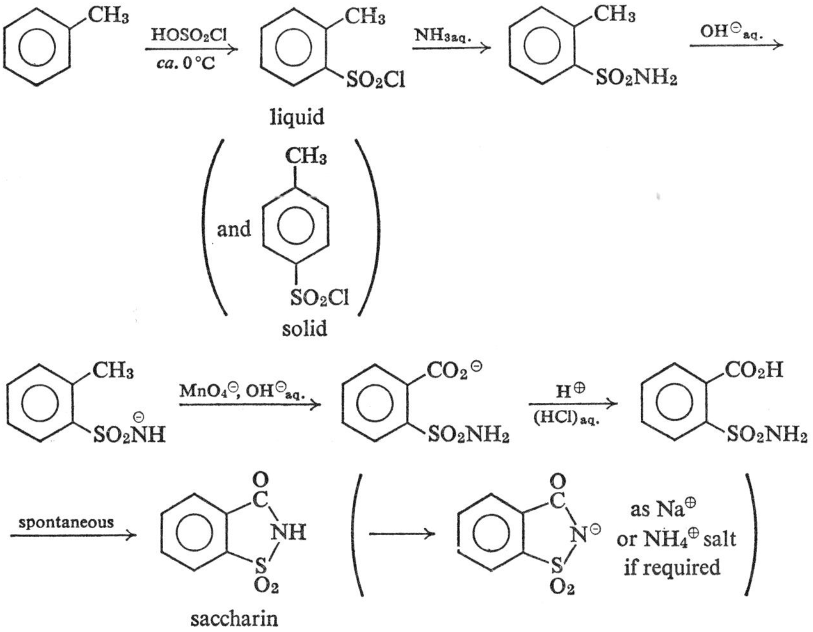

(*b*)

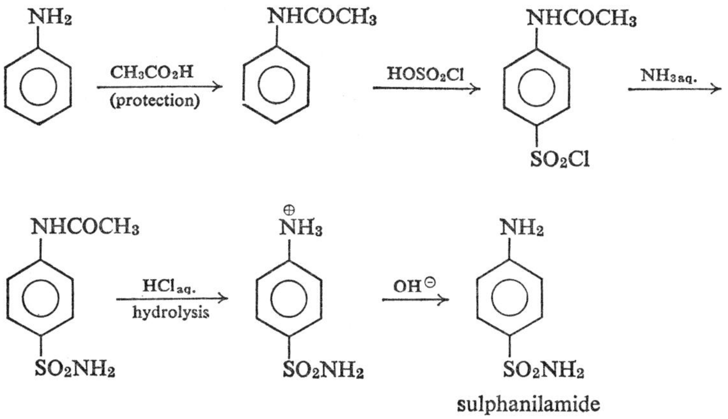

sulphanilamide

Other 'sulfa' drugs are obtained by replacing the ammonia in the third step by organic amines such as α-aminopyridine:

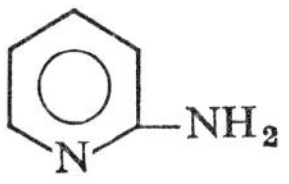

18

The nitro group –NO₂

Compounds in which the group NO_2 is attached to carbon of an aliphatic or aromatic group are known as *nitro-compounds*. Conventionally, nitro-compounds are formulated thus

$$R-N\overset{O}{\underset{O}{\lesseqgtr}} \quad \text{or} \quad R-\overset{\oplus}{N}\overset{\overset{\ominus}{O}}{\underset{O}{\lesseqgtr}}$$

(compare nitric acid $H-O-N\overset{O}{\underset{O}{\lesseqgtr}}$) but there can be no distinction between the two nitrogen–oxygen bonds. The electron pair represented by the second link of the double bond is delocalized and distributed over the whole group, and each oxygen atom will carry an equal partial negative change. The group is therefore symmetrical.

Nitromethane and the other lower nitroparaffins are colourless liquids at ordinary pressures and temperatures. (B.p. of CH_3NO_2, 101° C; $C_2H_5NO_2$, 114° C.) Their boiling points are much higher than those of the less polar isomeric alkyl nitrites (b.p. of CH_3ONO, 12° C.) Nitrobenzene is a high-boiling yellowish liquid b.p. 211° C, with a characteristic almond smell, almost indistinguishable from that of benzaldehyde.

In accordance with their formulation, nitro compounds are highly polar, and they are useful solvents for polar and ionic compounds, especially in the handling of substances attacked by water or hydroxylic solvents. Thus, for example, the behaviour of nitrogen pentoxide (nitronium nitrate $NO_2^{\oplus}NO_3^{\ominus}$) has been studied in nitromethane, and that of phosphorus pentachloride ($PCl_4^{\oplus}PCl_6^{\ominus}$) in nitrobenzene.

Reactions of nitro-compounds

Reduction

Both aliphatic and aromatic nitro-compounds can be reduced to a variety of products. In particular, strong reducing agents in acid conditions (e.g. tin or iron and hydrochloric acid) reduce them to primary amines

$$R-NO_2 + 7H^\oplus + 6e \rightarrow R.\overset{\oplus}{N}H_3 + 2H_2O$$
$$\downarrow OH^\ominus$$
$$R.NH_2$$

This is a technical method for obtaining both alkyl and, especially, aryl amines, and has been dealt with on p. 164, chapter 13.

With other reducing agents and in less acidic or even alkaline conditions, other less completely reduced products are formed. These are summarized below, but will not be discussed further.

$$R.NO_2 \xrightarrow[\text{NH}_4\text{Cl}_{\text{Aq}}]{\text{Zn dust}} R.NHOH$$

yielding *N*-alkyl- or *N*-aryl-hydroxylamines.

Aromatic nitro-compounds only (e.g. nitrobenzene) react as follows:

Tautomerism of nitroalkanes

The marked polarity of the nitro group will exert a considerable inductive effect on the attached alkyl group, tending to withdraw electrons from it towards the positively charged nitrogen.

$$R \rightarrow \overset{\oplus}{N}\!\!\!<\genfrac{}{}{0pt}{}{\overset{\ominus}{O}}{O}$$

Where the α-carbon atom carries one or more hydrogen atoms, this withdrawal of electrons renders these atoms feebly ionizable, so that the nitro-paraffin *slowly* dissolves in aqueous alkali, and from the solution a solid alkali metal salt can be obtained on evaporation. For example,

$$CH_3\!-\!NO_2 + OH^\ominus \rightarrow (CH_2NO_2)^\ominus + H_2O$$

The nitroalkane anion is clearly mesomeric in structure (a resonance hybrid), quite apart from the mesomerism of the nitro group itself

$$^\ominus CH_2\!-\!\overset{\oplus}{N}\!\!\!<\genfrac{}{}{0pt}{}{O^\ominus}{O} \quad \longleftrightarrow \quad CH_2\!\!=\!\!\overset{\oplus}{N}\!\!\!<\genfrac{}{}{0pt}{}{O^\ominus}{O^\ominus}$$

On adding an equimolar quantity of strong mineral acid to an aqueous solution containing the nitroalkane anion a homogeneous solution of high conductivity is formed, from which the nitroalkane separates, often quite slowly, with a fall in conductivity of the solution to that of the inorganic ions left in it.

We may account for this by supposing that the protons of the strong acid can add to the nitroalkane anion at both sites bearing the negative charge (which we may suppose to be mainly on the oxygen, since it is more electronegative than carbon).

The equilibrium

$$(CH_2NO_2)^\ominus + H^\oplus \rightleftharpoons CH_2\!\!=\!\!\overset{\oplus}{N}\!\!\!<\genfrac{}{}{0pt}{}{O^\ominus}{OH}$$

(water-soluble)

is rapidly established, but is well to the left, so that the solution still has a fairly high $H^\oplus$ concentration. However, the equilibrium

$$(CH_2NO_2)^\ominus + H^\oplus \rightleftharpoons CH_3\!-\!\overset{\oplus}{N}\!\!\!<\genfrac{}{}{0pt}{}{O^\ominus}{O}$$

(sparingly soluble in water)

is slowly established, thus removing the $H^\oplus$ ions as the practically insoluble and almost non-acidic nitroalkane separates out.

On this hypothesis, the nitroalkane exists in tautomeric forms, the ordinary nitro compound and the quite strongly acidic so-called '*aci*' form, whose structure

$$
\begin{array}{c} \diagup \\ \diagdown \end{array} C = \overset{\oplus}{N} \begin{array}{c} O^{\ominus} \\ \diagup \\ \diagdown \\ OH \end{array}
$$

may be compared with that of the nitric acid molecule

$$
O = \overset{\oplus}{N} \begin{array}{c} O^{\ominus} \\ \diagup \\ \diagdown \\ OH \end{array}
$$

The *aci*-form is itself mesomeric;

$$
CH_2 = \overset{\oplus}{N} \begin{array}{c} O^{\ominus} \\ \diagup \\ \diagdown \\ OH \end{array} \leftrightarrow \overset{\ominus}{CH_2} - \overset{\oplus}{N} \begin{array}{c} O \\ \diagup \\ \diagdown \\ OH \end{array}
$$

The *aci*-forms of nitroalkanes have never been isolated, but Hantzsch succeeded in isolating a *crystalline solid* from a freshly acidified solution of the phenylnitromethane anion. This substance was quite strongly acidic in aqueous solution but on keeping (alone or in solution) gradually reverted to ordinary *liquid* phenylnitromethane. The solid was presumably therefore the *aci*-form.

$$
\langle O \rangle - CH_2NO_2 \xrightarrow{\text{slow}} \left(\langle O \rangle - CHNO_2 \right)^{\ominus} + H^{\oplus} \xrightarrow{\text{rapid}}
$$

$$
\langle O \rangle - CH = \overset{\oplus}{N} \begin{array}{c} O^{\ominus} \\ \diagup \\ \diagdown \\ OH \end{array}
$$

The reader may speculate for himself on the role of the benzene ring in stabilizing the *aci*-form sufficiently to permit its isolation.

Nitro groups in aromatic compounds

The marked meta-directing and deactivating effect of the nitro group on the benzene ring has already been mentioned. Two other related effects are familiar enough to be briefly discussed.

Nitrophenols are considerably stronger acids than phenol itself; compare the following values for K_A at 25° C.

phenol	$1 \cdot 3 \times 10^{-10}$
o-nitrophenol	$6 \cdot 8 \times 10^{-8}$
m-nitrophenol	$5 \cdot 3 \times 10^{-9}$
p-nitrophenol	7×10^{-8}.

Clearly there are two effects operating: first, a general withdrawal of electrons by the nitro group, rendering the hydroxyl hydrogen more readily ionizable, and second, in the case of the ortho- and para-isomers but *not* the meta-, a stabilization of the conjugate base *vis-à-vis* the free phenol by mesomerism. For example,

(This increased mesomerism is associated with a change in colour; *p*-nitrophenol is almost colourless, but in alkaline solution it is deep yellow. Indeed, it can be used as an acid–base indicator. The colour of *o*-nitrophenol, which is yellow, darkens on addition of alkali.)

It has been presumed that *o*- and *p*-nitrophenols are therefore tautomeric, existing not only as phenols but as *aci*-forms such as

but these have never been isolated.

With three nitro groups occupying all possible ortho- and para-sites, the acidity is even more enhanced, and 2, 4, 6-trinitrophenol (picric acid) is similar in strength to trichloracetic acid, and is over 90 % ionized in saturated aqueous solution (about 0·006 M at 20° C).

o-Nitrophenol is markedly more volatile than the *m*- or *p*-isomer, and it is separated from the latter by steam distillation when working up the product of the nitration of phenol. This difference is accounted for by supposing that hydrogen bonding occurs between the —OH and —NO$_2$ groups, thus:

This hydrogen bonding *within* the molecule to a large extent prevents the usual association of an —OH compound by hydrogen bonding *between* molecules. In the *meta-* and *para-*isomers, the —NO$_2$ and —OH groups are too far apart for this *intra*molecular hydrogen bonding to occur, and their volatility will be reduced by *inter*molecular hydrogen bonding in the usual way.

Although chlorobenzene itself is very resistant to the attack of nucleophilic reagents such as OH$^\ominus$ (see p. 111), *o-* and *p-*nitrochlorobenzenes are considerably more readily hydrolysed, while 2,4,6-trinitrochlorobenzene (picryl chloride) is comparable in reactivity with an acyl chloride, and is hydrolysed by warm water. The bond diagram (*a*) shows the 'spreading' of the negative charge of the intermediate on to the NO$_2$ group, an effect not possible in the hydrolysis of chlorobenzene itself. This will favour attack by the OH$^\ominus$. Thus:

(*a*)

This effect makes possible the preparation of other di- and tri-nitro compounds by methods not applicable to the parent substance; for example, the useful reagent 2,4-dinitrophenylhydrazine can be made by the direct action of hydrazine on 2,4-dinitrochlorobenzene.

Preparation of nitro-compounds

(1) Aromatic nitro-compounds are made by the nitration of the parent compound by mixed concentrated nitric and sulphuric acids (or, in the case of phenol, by aqueous nitric acid). This reaction has been fully dealt with in chapter 8.

(2) Aliphatic nitro-compounds are made by the action of alkyl halides on silver nitrite. This is dealt with in chapter 10.

(3) A useful method of preparing nitroalkanes is to boil together sodium nitrite and the sodium salt of a α-halogeno fatty acid in aqueous solution. Thus sodium nitrite and sodium monochloroacetate yield nitromethane, which distils off in the steam. Presumably the α-nitroacetate ion is formed, which is spontaneously decarboxylated, on account of the electron-

withdrawing effect of the —NO_2 group; this is exactly comparable with the formation of chloroform from the trichloroacetate ion.

$$(NO_2)^\ominus + CH_2Cl.CO_2{}^\ominus \rightarrow CH_2NO_2.CO_2{}^\ominus + Cl^\ominus$$

$$\downarrow{\scriptstyle H_2O}$$

$$CH_3NO_2 + HCO_3{}^\ominus$$

(4) Methane, ethane and propane can be technically nitrated by heating the alkanes with nitric acid vapour (or, rather, its breakdown products) at 400° C. The lowest nitroalkanes could therefore be available in industrial quantities as intermediates for making other organic compounds (e.g. amines) if required.

19

The diazonium ion group $-\overset{\oplus}{N}\equiv N$

Diazonium salts, formed by the action of nitrous acid on salts of aromatic primary amines, were discovered by Griess in 1858. Since they contained *two* nitrogen atoms per benzene ring where the parent amine had one, they became known as '*diazo*-compounds' (from the Graeco–French name 'azote' for nitrogen). They are, however, salts and strong electrolytes, neutral in solution, and analogous in this respect with quaternary ammonium salts such as phenyltrimethyl ammonium halides. To express this the original name was modified to '*diazonium* salts'. A nitrogen atom carrying a positive ionic charge must be four-covalent, and hence for example the salt benzene diazonium chloride, formed from aniline and hydrochloric and nitrous acids, will be formulated

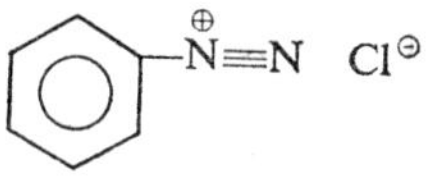

Compare phenyltrimethylammonium chloride:

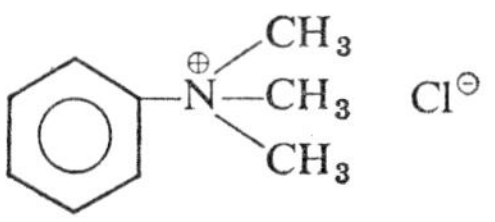

Diazonium salts are colourless crystalline solids, readily soluble in water. They are unstable, and explosive when dry; in normal laboratory and industrial practice, however, they are never isolated, being prepared in aqueous solution and used more or less immediately.

The only known diazonium salts are those in which the $-\overset{\oplus}{N}\equiv N$ *group is attached directly to the carbon of an aromatic ring.* No diazonium salts with $-N_2^{\oplus}$ attached to aliphatic or side-chain aromatic carbon atoms can be isolated, although such diazonium ions have been postulated as possible highly unstable intermediates in the reaction of amides and aliphatic and side-chain aromatic primary amines with nitrous acid.

This exceptional stability of aryl diazonium ions is one of the most striking features of aromatic systems. It is presumably due to partial involvement of the aromatic ring electrons in the carbon–nitrogen bond. Thus

and so on for the two other possible diagrams.

Nomenclature of diazonium salts

'Diazonium' is treated as a substituent replacing hydrogen and the ion is named accordingly, with 'diazonium' as a suffix after the name of the parent compound. Thus:

is the 2,4-dimethylbenzenediazonium (or 4,*m*-xylenediazonium) ion.

This replaces the 'radical' nomenclature, based on the naming of ammonium ions, in which the above example would be the 2,4-dimethyl-phenyldiazonium or 4,*m*-xylenyldiazonium ion. The older name (especially for the phenyldiazonium ion) may still be met. (Names such as 'diazo-benzene chloride' are totally obsolete and should not be used.)

Reactions of diazonium salts

These can be divided into (*a*) displacement-type reactions, in which the diazonium ion group is evolved as gaseous nitrogen, other atoms or groups becoming attached to the ring in its place, and (*b*) reactions in which the nitrogen atoms remain in the organic product.

Reactions in which $-\overset{\oplus}{N}\equiv N$ is eliminated as nitrogen

(1) Hydrolysis

If an aqueous diazonium salt solution is heated, a phenol is produced. Thus benzenediazonium salts yield phenol itself.

$$C_6H_5\overset{\oplus}{N}_2 + H_2O \rightarrow C_6H_5OH + H^\oplus + N_2\uparrow$$

To obtain the best yields, the solution should be strongly acidic, to avoid the 'coupling' of the phenol with the unchanged diazonium ion leading to tarry by-products. (For coupling, see (6) below.) The presence of halide ions should be avoided to prevent the formation of halogenation by-products (see (4) below) and the amine should therefore be diazotized in sulphuric rather than hydrochloric acid.

(2) Alcoholysis

If an amine is diazotized in alcoholic rather than aqueous solution, and the product is warmed, the corresponding phenol ether is obtained. The reaction is analogous with (a), for example,

$$C_6H_5\overset{\oplus}{N}_2 + CH_3OH \rightarrow C_6H_5OCH_3 + H^\oplus + N_2\uparrow$$

With alcohols higher than methanol, reduction of the diazonium ion [see (3) below] is an important side-reaction; the extent to which it occurs depends principally on the structure of the diazonium ion. Thus with ethanol and higher primary alcohols benzenediazonium salts yield largely the ether and only minor quantities of benzene.

(3) Reduction

Suitable reducing agents replace the $-\overset{\oplus}{N}_2$ of diazonium ions by hydrogen. The most effective reagent seems to be excess hypophosphorous acid, which works in the cold, thereby minimizing hydrolysis with the production of phenols and tarry by-products.

$$C_6H_5\overset{\oplus}{N}_2 + H^\oplus + 2e \rightarrow C_6H_6 + N_2\uparrow$$
$$(H_3PO_2 + H_2O \rightarrow H_3PO_3 + 2H^\oplus + 2e)$$

Other possible reagents are stannite solutions (which may be hazardous, since diazonium salts may form explosive intermediates in alkaline solution) and ethanol. As mentioned in (2), the main product with ethanol is often an aryl ethyl ether, but with some substituted aryldiazonium ions, reduction predominates. For example, 2,4,6-tribromobenzenediazonium salts give good yields of 1,3,5-tribromobenzene.

$$+ C_2H_5OH \longrightarrow + H^\oplus + CH_3CHO + N_2\uparrow$$

Diazotization of an amine followed by reduction in this way leads to replacement of —NH$_2$ by —H, and is therefore an effective way of *deaminating* primary aromatic amines. By using the powerful *ortho–para*-directing effect of the NH$_2$ group (either as such, or 'protected' by acetylation; see p. 158), and then deaminating the product, substituted benzenes can be made with the substituents in positions they would not take up in direct substitution, as in the case of the tribromobenzene mentioned above.

(4) Replacement of —$\overset{\oplus}{N}_2$ by halogen and analogous groups

As mentioned in (1) above, if diazonium salt solutions containing chloride or bromide ions are warmed, chloro- or bromo-compounds are formed as well as the phenol. Thus benzenediazonium chloride solutions yield appreciable quantities of chlorobenzene.

$$C_6H_5\overset{\oplus}{N}_2 + Cl^\ominus \rightarrow C_6H_5Cl + N_2\uparrow$$

Even with excess of halide, however, yields of chloro- and bromo-benzene are low. They can be considerably increased by adding precipitated copper (from zinc dust and Cu(II) salt solution) which catalyses the reaction (the *Gattermann* reaction). If potassium *iodide* is added to a diazonium salt solution and the mixture is warmed, the iodo-compound is the main product.

$$C_6H_5\overset{\oplus}{N}_2 + I^\ominus \rightarrow C_6H_5I + N_2\uparrow$$

This is the best way of making iodobenzene and its homologues. No catalyst need be added.

As an alternative to the Gattermann procedure, the *Sandmeyer* reaction may be used. In this procedure, the aqueous diazonium salt solution is added to a heated solution of a Cu^I complex. For examples:

$$C_6H_5\overset{\oplus}{N}_2 \xrightarrow{\text{CuCl in conc. HCl}_{aq}} C_6H_5Cl$$
$$\xrightarrow{\text{CuBr in conc. HBr}_{aq}} C_6H_5Br$$
$$\xrightarrow{\text{CuCN in excess KCN}_{aq}} C_6H_5CN$$

Since cyanides can be hydrolysed to carboxylic acids (see p. 233), this last method gives an effective method for the replacement of —NH_2 attached to an aromatic ring by —CO_2H.

The above reactions by no means exhaust the reactions in which —$N_2^{\oplus}$ can be replaced by other groups; —NO_2, —F, —$AsO(OH)_2$, —N=C=O, $>$S and —SH are among those that can be introduced in this way. The diazonium salts might therefore be compared in aromatic chemistry with the alkyl halides in aliphatic chemistry as intermediates in the introduction of functional groups.

Mechanism of diazonium salt reactions

The decomposition of diazonium salts in dilute aqueous solution by reaction (1) above is a first-order reaction which can be followed by the rate of evolution of nitrogen; that is, Rate $\propto$ $[ArN_2^{\oplus}]$. This in itself is not very informative, since water is present in large excess, and its participation in the rate-controlling step would not be revealed. However, as the reaction rate is independent of the concentration of, for example, chloride ions, even when these enter quite appreciably into the reaction product, it is deduced that the rate-controlling step is the slow heterolytic fission of the diazonium ion:

$$C_6H_5\overset{\oplus}{\overset{\diagup}{N}}{\equiv}N \longrightarrow C_6H_5^{\oplus} + N_2 \uparrow$$

and this being followed by rapid attack of water, $Cl^{\ominus}$, etc., on the phenyl cation.

Reactions in which nitrogen is not eliminated

(1) Reduction

Diazonium salt solutions are reduced by stannous chloride in hydrochloric acid to aryl hydrazines

$$C_6H_5N_2^{\oplus} + 4H^{\oplus} + 4e \rightarrow C_6H_5 . N\overset{\oplus}{H}NH_3$$
$$(Sn^{II}Cl_4^{2\ominus} + 2Cl^{\ominus} \rightarrow Sn^{IV}Cl_6^{2\ominus} + 2e)$$

Thus benzenediazonium salts yield phenylhydrazine as its conjugate acid; the free base is liberated by the addition of alkali.

Sodium sulphite, followed by acid, achieves the same result, though in this case the reaction proceeds via definite and isolable intermediate compounds.

This is the way in which the valuable reagent phenylhydrazine, which Emil Fischer used as 'the key to unlock the carbohydrates', is made.

(2) Coupling reactions

Diazonium ions couple with phenols and tertiary amines to give highly coloured 'azo' compounds. Thus with phenol, benzenediazonium salts yield *p*-hydroxyazobenzene:

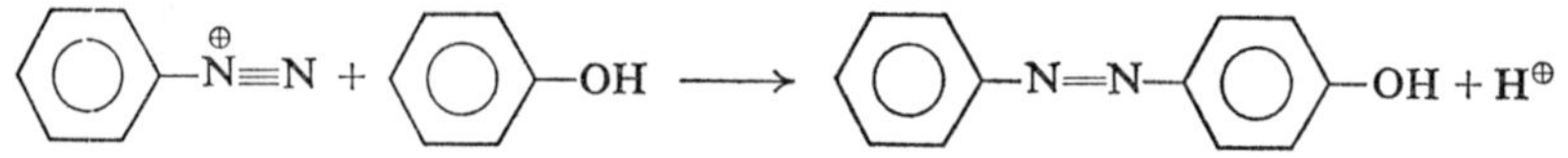

$$\text{C}_6\text{H}_5-\overset{\oplus}{\text{N}}\equiv\text{N} \; + \; \text{C}_6\text{H}_5-\text{OH} \longrightarrow \text{C}_6\text{H}_5-\text{N}=\text{N}-\text{C}_6\text{H}_4-\text{OH} + \text{H}^{\oplus}$$

and with *NN*-dimethylaniline, *p*-dimethylaminoazobenzene:

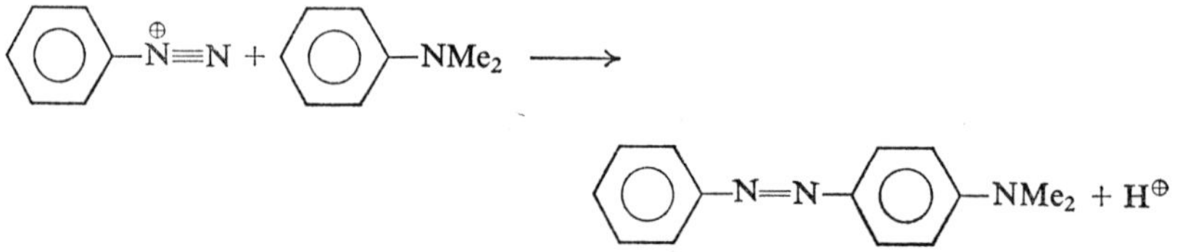

$$\text{C}_6\text{H}_5-\overset{\oplus}{\text{N}}\equiv\text{N} \; + \; \text{C}_6\text{H}_5-\text{NMe}_2 \longrightarrow$$

$$\text{C}_6\text{H}_5-\text{N}=\text{N}-\text{C}_6\text{H}_4-\text{NMe}_2 + \text{H}^{\oplus}$$

Excess of strong acid hinders the reaction. A possible explanation is that the effective reagents are respectively the phenoxide (phenate) ion and the free amine; acid, by combining with the amine and suppressing the ionization of the phenol, therefore reduces the concentration of the reactants. Coupling normally occurs in the *para*-position of the phenol or tertiary amine, but if this is occupied by a substituent, *ortho*-coupling will occur.

Phenols couple best in the presence of a *small* excess of alkali; too much would react with the diazonium ions (see (3) below), but sufficient is required to dissolve the phenol and to neutralize the excess of acid present in the diazonium salt solution as normally prepared.

The brilliant red coupling compound with *β*-naphthol is often used as a test for benzenediazonium ion and its homologues, and hence for aniline and the homologous amines from which they are made.

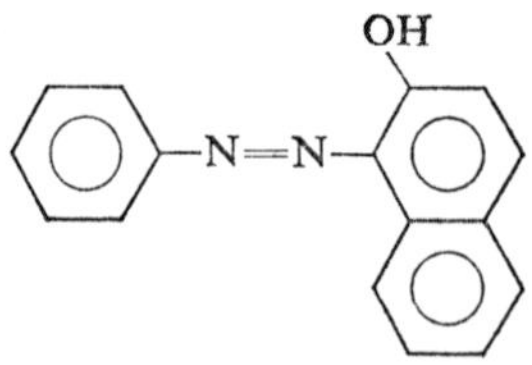

benzene-azo-*β*-naphthol

Many azo-compounds with substituents in various positions in the rings are manufactured as dyestuffs ('azo-dyes'), and the diazotization of amines is therefore carried out on a technical scale in dyestuffs manufacture. A few well-known azo-compounds are shown below.

$$\text{HO}_3\text{S} - \langle\bigcirc\rangle - \text{N=N} - \langle\bigcirc\rangle - \text{NMe}_2$$

methyl orange

$$\langle\bigcirc\rangle - \text{N=N} - \langle\bigcirc\rangle - \text{NMe}_2$$
$$\overset{|}{\text{CO}_2\text{H}}$$

methyl red

$$\text{HO}_3\text{S} - \langle\bigcirc\rangle - \text{N=N} - \langle\bigcirc\rangle$$
HO

Orange II (β-naphthol orange)

Diazonium ions also couple with primary and secondary amines, but the coupling then occurs principally between the diazonium and the amine nitrogen atom, yielding the so-called diazoamino compounds. Thus aniline and benzenediazonium ions yield diazoaminobenzene:

$$\langle\bigcirc\rangle - \overset{\oplus}{\text{N}} \equiv \text{N} + \text{H}_2\text{N}\langle\bigcirc\rangle \rightleftharpoons \langle\bigcirc\rangle - \text{N=N} - \overset{\oplus}{\text{N}}\text{H}_2 - \langle\bigcirc\rangle$$

$$\rightleftharpoons \langle\bigcirc\rangle - \text{N=N} - \text{NH} - \langle\bigcirc\rangle + \text{H}^\oplus$$

diazoaminobenzene

The reaction is reversible; it is clear that acid conditions will disfavour coupling, both by increasing $[\text{H}^\oplus]$ and by decreasing $[\text{C}_6\text{H}_5\text{NH}_2]$ by conversion to the conjugate acid. The importance of *avoiding* this reaction during diazotization has been discussed on p. 161.

A much slower but effectively irreversible coupling at the para-carbon atom (as with tertiary amines) occurs also; hence diazoaminobenzene slowly changes to *p*-aminoazobenzene if suspended in acid solution.

$$\langle\bigcirc\rangle - \overset{\oplus}{\text{N}} \equiv \text{N} + \langle\bigcirc\rangle - \text{NH}_2 \longrightarrow \langle\bigcirc\rangle - \text{N=N} - \langle\bigcirc\rangle - \text{NH}_2 + \text{H}^\oplus$$

p-aminoazobenzene

Diazoamino compounds show tautomerism, by the transfer of $H^\oplus$ from one nitrogen atom to another:

$$-N{=}N{-}NH{-} \rightleftharpoons -NH{-}N{=}N{-}$$

Thus the product of combining *p*-toluenediazonium ions with aniline is indistinguishable from that obtained from benzenediazonium ions and *p*-toluidine.

(3) Action of alkalis

Although diazonium ions are analogous in structure with ammonium ions, they do not form crystalline hydroxides analogous with the quaternary ammonium hydroxides, such as $C_6H_5\overset{\oplus}{N}Me_3OH^\ominus$. Instead, the hydroxyl ion combines with the diazonium ion: thus benzenediazonium ions yield a compound of the formula

$$C_6H_5{-}N{=}N{-}OH$$

which is acidic (a 'diazoic acid') and therefore reacts further with alkali to yield a diazotate ion:

$$C_6H_5{-}N{=}N{-}O^\ominus$$

For the chemistry and stereoisomerism of these substances more advanced text-books must be consulted.

Appreciable concentration of diazonium ions cannot therefore persist in alkaline conditions.

Preparation of diazonium salts

For use in preparing other compounds, diazonium salts are almost invariably made in aqueous solution by adding aqueous sodium nitrite to a cooled strongly acidic solution of the appropriate aromatic amine. The conditions for this and the reasons for adopting them have been fully discussed on p. 161.

Crystalline diazonium salts have been prepared by working in anhydrous ethanol as solvent, and using a readily hydrolysed ester of nitrous acid (such as amyl nitrite) as the diazotizing agent.

SECTION III

20

Compounds with more than one functional group

Introductory

In the previous chapters, the chemical behaviour of the principal functional groups in organic chemistry has been reviewed. In the course of this a number of compounds have been met whose molecules contain more than one such group, whether the same, as, for example, in m-dinitrobenzene $mC_6H_4(NO_2)_2$ and ethylene dibromide $CH_2Br.CH_2Br$, or different, as in aldol $CH_3CHOHCH_2CHO$ and salicylic acid, o-$C_6H_4(OH)CO_2H$.

In the present chapter, the chemistry of a few important classes and examples of such 'compounds of multiple function' will be reviewed in more detail. In studying such compounds, the following principles will have to be borne in mind:

(a) To a first approximation, each functional group will exert its ordinary behaviour independently of the other. Thus, choosing examples from those quoted above, both nitro groups in m-dinitrobenzene can be reduced to amino groups, and this can be done successively by a suitable choice of reagents. Aldol as an alcohol can be dehydrated to the olefinic compound crotonaldehyde; as an aldehyde it will reduce argentous ammine solutions, or form a phenylhydrazone.

(b) In detail, however, the presence of one functional group may somewhat modify the behaviour of the other. Thus salicylic acid is stronger than benzoic; m-dinitrobenzene is reduced to m-nitroaniline by hot aqueous alkaline polysulphide solution, a reagent which does not reduce nitrobenzene; aldol loses water extremely readily and under conditions where, say, butan-2-ol would not.

(c) It may be impossible to obtain certain reactions of one functional group without affecting the other. Thus the addition of aqueous alkali to salicylic acid is bound to form the anion of the more strongly acidic carboxyl group before removing protons from the phenolic OH, and it is impossible to obtain $o\text{-}C_6H_4\begin{smallmatrix}O^{\ominus}\\CO_2H\end{smallmatrix}$ in significant amounts. One would not expect to be able to prepare aminoacetyl chloride CH_2NH_2COCl by acting on glycine $CH_2NH_2CO_2H$ with, say, thionyl chloride, since amines react far too readily with acid chlorides, and hence the NH_2 groups will be attacked both by the reagent and by the hypothetical product, if any were formed.

(*d*) Finally, although the compound with two functional groups may be isolated, in some cases the functional groups may react with one another under suitable conditions. Thus hydroxyacetic or glycollic acid

$$CH_2OHCO_2H$$

can be readily isolated, but potentially the alcohol and the carboxylic acid functional groups can interact in an esterification reaction and, on heating, glycollic acid loses water to form a cyclic compound, glycollide, in which mutual esterification of the molecules has occurred in pairs.

glycollide

With these points and the chemical behaviour of the single functional groups in mind, the student should have no difficulty in understanding and, indeed, to a large extent predicting, the behaviour of multi-functional compounds.

In the following sections, some of the more familiar compounds with two or more functional groups are reviewed, and some of their more obvious properties, reactions and uses are summarized. The discussion and descriptions are not meant to be exhaustive.

Polyhalogen compounds

Ethylene dibromide (1,2-dibromoethane) $CH_2Br.CH_2Br$

Prepared from ethylene and bromine (see p. 56).

Colourless liquid, denser than water.

Both halves of the molecule will normally undergo the usual alkyl halide displacement reactions; for example, cyanide yields $\begin{smallmatrix}CH_2CN\\|\\CH_2CN\end{smallmatrix}$; the sodium derivative of malonic ester yields $\begin{smallmatrix}CH_2.CH(CO_2Et)_2\\|\\CH_2.CH(CO_2Et)_2\end{smallmatrix}$; etc.

On refluxing with ethanolic alkali, it yields acetylene.

$$CH_2Br.CH_2Br + 2OH^\ominus \rightarrow CH\equiv CH + 2Br^\ominus + 2H_2O$$

Ethylidene dibromide (1,1-dibromoethane) CH₃CHBr₂

Best obtained by the addition of hydrogen bromide to acetylene (see p. 66). Like ethylene dibromide, it yields acetylene when refluxed with ethanolic alkali.

The different behaviour of the two dibromoethanes on hydrolysis is discussed on p. 51.

Chloroform (trichloromethane) CHCl₃

In principle, obtained by carrying out the haloform reaction (see p. 136) with a hypochlorite on any compound of the types $CH_3.CHOH.R$ or $CH_3.CO.R$. Practically worthwhile yields are only obtainable from acetone and a bleaching powder suspension; even so, the yield is much less than the theoretical.

Colourless liquid, denser than water. Well-known anaesthetic, introduced by Simpson in 1847; largely supplanted by other substances.

Useful solvent.

Reactions. 1. Hydrolysis. Rapid with warm ethanolic alkali to yield *formate*:

$$CHCl_3 + 4OH^\ominus \rightarrow H.COO^\ominus + 3Cl^\ominus + 2H_2O$$

2. A Williamson-type reaction yields orthoformic esters; for example,

$$CHCl_3 + 3OEt^\ominus \rightarrow HC(OEt)_3 + 3Cl^\ominus$$
ethyl orthoformate

3. Carbylamine reaction; yields isocyanides on warming with primary amines and ethanolic alkali; for example,

$$C_6H_5NH_2 + CHCl_3 + 3OH^\ominus \rightarrow C_6H_5NC + 3Cl^\ominus + 3H_2O$$

4. Reimer–Tiemann reaction: yields salicylaldehyde with phenol and alkali; see p. 103.

5. Oxidation in air and light yields phosgene; see p. 294.

Carbon tetrachloride

Manufactured by the action of chlorine on carbon bisulphide (obtained by the direct combination of carbon and sulphur vapour) in presence of ferric chloride.

$$CS_2 + 3Cl_2 \rightarrow CCl_4 + S_2Cl_2$$

Colourless liquid, denser than water. Used as a fire-extinguisher fluid. (It volatilizes readily (b.p. 77° C) to a dense vapour which 'blankets' the fire. The vapour is toxic and carbon tetrachloride extinguishers should never be used in closed spaces.) Useful solvent (e.g. for removing greases).

Chemically, extremely inert. Unattacked by water (contrast the rapid hydrolysis of silicon tetrachloride) and exceedingly slowly hydrolysed by boiling aqueous alkali. Since the electron-withdrawing effect of four chlorine atoms should render the carbon atom more rather than less open to the attack of nucleophilic reagents, this inertness is presumably a steric effect, the four large chlorine atoms shielding the carbon atom from nucleophilic attack.

Di- and tri-hydric alcohols

Ethylene glycol (ethane-1,2-diol) $CH_2OH.CH_2OH$. 'Glycol'

Manufacture. In principle, ethylene glycol is obtained by the hydration and oxidation of ethylene. Formally:

$$CH_2=CH_2+H_2O+(O) \rightarrow CH_2OH.CH_2OH$$

Various routes have been proposed and operated, including the following:

$$CH_2=CH_2 \xrightarrow[\text{Ag catalyst}]{\text{air}} CH_2-CH_2$$

Ethylene oxide

$$\xrightarrow{H_2O,H^\oplus} CH_2OH.CH_2OH$$
glycol

'Glycol' is used as a generic term for dihydric alcohols with the —OH groups attached to adjacent carbon atoms. Glycols arise from the oxidation of the corresponding olefins by cold aqueous permanganate.

Propylene glycol ($CH_3CHOH.CH_2OH$) is produced technically from propylene by methods analogous to those used for ethylene glycol.

Ethylene glycol is a rather viscous colourless liquid, miscible with water. It is sweetish to the taste (hence the name, from the Greek γλυκυς, sweet) but is toxic. It is extensively used as an anti-freeze in car radiators, and in the manufacture of Terylene (see p. 336).

Reactions. The ethylene glycol molecule consists of two primary alcohol groups directly linked, and all the usual reactions of this group can be carried out with glycol, usually in two stages. There are five possible oxidation products (other than carbon dioxide and water):

CH_2OH	CH_2OH	CHO	CHO	CO_2H
CHO	CO_2H	CHO	CO_2H	CO_2H
glycollic aldehyde	glycollic acid	glyoxal	glyoxylic acid (or glyoxalic acid)	oxalic acid

274

Glycerol (propane-1,2,3-triol) $CH_2OH.CHOH.CH_2OH$ 'glycerine'

Manufacture. Natural fats and oils are the glyceryl esters of long-chain carboxylic acids, and glycerol is a by-product of their saponification (see p. 217). It can also be synthesized from propylene by the following scheme:

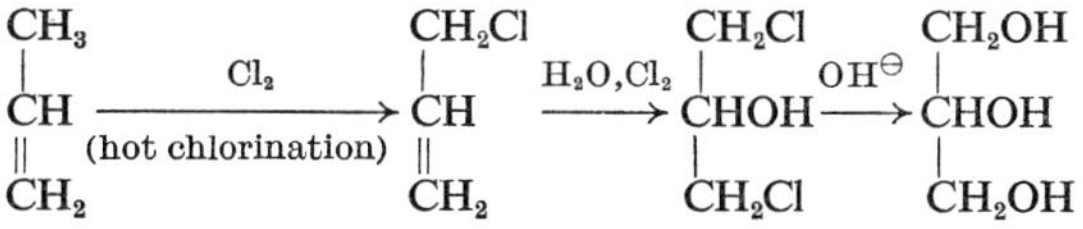

$$\begin{array}{ccccccc}
CH_3 & & CH_2Cl & & CH_2Cl & & CH_2OH \\
| & \xrightarrow{\ Cl_2\ } & | & \xrightarrow{\ H_2O,Cl_2\ } & | & \xrightarrow{\ OH^{\ominus}\ } & | \\
CH & \text{(hot chlorination)} & CH & & CHOH & & CHOH \\
\| & & \| & & | & & | \\
CH_2 & & CH_2 & & CH_2Cl & & CH_2OH
\end{array}$$

It can be made by the fermentation of sucrose in the presence of sodium sulphite, though this is not operated commercially. Acetaldehyde and glycerol are intermediates in alcoholic fermentation and, by combining with the former, the sulphite 'blocks' the reaction step which removes the glycerol.

Glycerol is a viscous colourless liquid, miscible with water and practically insoluble in diethylether—signs of its polyhydroxy character. It is sweet (hence its name) and, unlike glycol, non-toxic.

Technically, glycerol is converted to glyceryl trinitrate

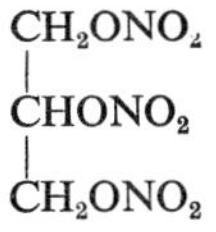

$$\begin{array}{l}
CH_2ONO_2 \\
| \\
CHONO_2 \\
| \\
CH_2ONO_2
\end{array}$$

by a mixture of concentrated sulphuric acid and nitric acids. This is known as 'nitration' and the product is the explosive 'nitroglycerine'; both terms are in the strict sense misnomers. Nitroglycerine is prone to detonation by shock and cannot be safely handled or transported in bulk but, absorbed in kieselguhr or similar materials, it forms the invaluable blasting explosive 'dynamite'.

Glycerol may be esterified with phthalic anhydride to yield 'glyptal' resins (see p. 344).

Halogeno-acids

Halogen atoms may be introduced in place of hydrogen in alkyl groups or other hydrocarbon residues attached to the carboxyl group, thus giving rise to halogeno-acids. A few of the most familiar halogenated fatty acids are reviewed briefly below.

Monochloroacetic acid CH$_2$Cl . CO$_2$H

Preparation. Direct chlorination of acetic acid by passing chlorine into acetic acid at about 100° C in the presence of about 5 % of red phosphorus as a catalyst.

$$CH_3CO_2H + Cl_2 \rightarrow CH_2ClCO_2H + HCl$$

Iodine and sulphur also catalyse the reaction; all three elements no doubt function via the formation of their halides. Monochloroacetic acid is a white crystalline solid, readily soluble in water.

Reactions. Monochloroacetic acid shows the reactions of a carboxylic acid and an alkyl halide. As a carboxylic acid it reacts:

(1) with alkalis, etc. yielding salts containing the chloroacetate ion CH$_2$Cl . CO$_2^\ominus$;

(2) with alcohols in the presence of strong acids yielding esters, for example, ethyl chloroacetate CH$_2$Cl . CO$_2$C$_2$H$_5$;

(3) with phosphorus trichloride and similar reagents to yield chloro-acetyl chloride CH$_2$Cl . COCl.

Chloroacetamide CH$_2$Cl . CONH$_2$ can be obtained by ammonolysis of the esters. Conditions must be such as to avoid reaction (5) below.

As a halide, chloroacetic acid undergoes readily the characteristic displacement reactions discussed on p. 110. The following list summarizes some simple examples of preparative importance, dealt with in more detail on other pages. Since the nucleophilic reagents which effect these reactions are more or less basic in character, the reaction has frequently to be carried out not with the free acid, but the chloroacetate ion; the importance of this in the case of reaction with cyanide is obvious.

(4) $CH_2Cl . CO_2^\ominus \xrightarrow{OH^\ominus} CH_2OH . CO_2^\ominus$ glycollate ion (p. 280);

(5) $CH_2Cl . CO_2^\ominus \xrightarrow{NH_3} CH_2\overset{\oplus}{N}H_3CO_2^\ominus$
$\quad\quad\quad\quad\quad\quad\quad \updownarrow \quad$ glycine (p. 283);
$\quad\quad\quad\quad\quad CH_2NH_2CO_2H$

(6) $CH_2Cl . CO_2^\ominus \xrightarrow{CN^\ominus} CH_2CN . CO_2^\ominus$ cyanoacetate ion (p. 290);

(7) $CH_2Cl . CO_2^\ominus \xrightarrow{NO_2^\ominus} CH_2NO_2 . CO_2^\ominus \xrightarrow{H_2O} CH_3NO_2$ (p. 261).
$\quad\quad\quad\quad\quad\quad\quad\quad\quad\quad$ spontaneous   nitromethane
$\quad\quad\quad\quad\quad\quad\quad\quad\quad\quad$ decarboxylation

By raising the reaction temperature and prolonging the reaction time, acetic acid may be further chlorinated to *dichloroacetic acid* CHCl$_2$. COOH, and at yet higher temperatures (about 160° C) to *trichloroacetic acid* CCl$_3$. COOH.

Dichloroacetic acid may also be made by heating chloral hydrate with aqueous cyanide and calcium carbonate; a peculiarly empirical procedure.

Trichloroacetic acid is conveniently made by oxidizing chloral.

The following values of K_A at 25° C for acetic acid and the three chloro-acids

CH_3CO_2H $1\cdot8 \times 10^{-5}$ $CHCl_2.CO_2H$ $3\cdot3 \times 10^{-2}$
$CH_2Cl.CO_2H$ $1\cdot4 \times 10^{-3}$ $CCl_3.CO_2H$ about 2×10^{-1}

show the effect of successive replacements of hydrogen by Cl in increasing the tendency of the —CO_2H to lose a proton to a base. This may be referred to the electron-withdrawing effect of the chlorine atom in reducing the electron density in the neighbourhood of the acidic hydrogen atom, thus rendering it more susceptible to removal by a base.

$$Cl\!\leftarrow\!\!\underset{H}{\overset{H}{C}}\!\leftarrow\!C\!\underset{\diagdown O\!\leftarrow\!H}{\overset{\diagup O}{}}$$

This effect increases with the number of chlorine atoms, and trichloro-acetic acid approaches a strong electrolyte in character in aqueous solution.

Hydrolysis of di- and trichloroacetic acids

(1) With hot water under pressure, dichloroacetic acid yields glyoxylic acid

$$\underset{CO_2H}{\overset{CHCl_2}{|}} + H_2O \rightarrow \underset{CO_2H}{\overset{CHO}{|}} + 2HCl$$

(normal hydrolysis of gem-dihalide; cf. ethylidene dihalides, p. 194).

With alkali, a Cannizzaro reaction will follow (see p. 183):

$$2\,\underset{COO^\ominus}{\overset{CHO}{|}} + OH^\ominus \rightarrow \underset{COO^\ominus}{\overset{CH_2OH}{|}} + \underset{COO^\ominus}{\overset{COO^\ominus}{|}}$$

$$\text{glycollate} \qquad \text{oxalate}$$

(2) Trichloroacetates are decarboxylated to chloroform and carbonate on boiling in dilute alkaline solution.

$$\underset{COO^\ominus}{\overset{CCl_3}{|}} + OH^\ominus \rightarrow CHCl_3 + CO_3^{2\ominus}$$

Compare the last step of the haloform reaction (p. 189).

The halogenation of the higher fatty acids by the direct action of chlorine or bromine and red phosphorus proceeds in the α-position only; the α-monobromo fatty acids (or, with larger amounts of phosphorus and bromine, the α-monobromo-acid bromides) are especially easily and smoothly prepared, for example,

$$C_2H_5.CO_2H + Br_2 \xrightarrow{P} CH_3CHBr.CO_2H + HBr$$

$$\alpha\text{-bromopropionic acid}$$

The bromoacyl halides arise from the action of the phosphorus bromides formed from excess phosphorus and bromine.

β-Halogeno-acids have usually to be prepared by indirect routes.

The effect of the halogen atom in increasing the acid strength is much weaker in the β-position as shown by the following K_A values (at 25° C).

$$CH_3CH_2CO_2H \quad 1\cdot34 \times 10^{-5}$$
$$CH_3CHClCO_2H \quad 1\cdot4 \times 10^{-3}$$
$$CH_2ClCH_2CO_2H \quad 1\cdot0 \times 10^{-4}$$

This is consistent with the above interpretation.

Sodium $\alpha\alpha$- and $\beta\beta$-dichloropropionates are used as herbicides; the β-compound destroys monocotyledonous plants (grasses, etc.), the α-dicotyledons.

Hydroxy-acids

Compounds derived from fatty acids or other types of aliphatic acid by introducing OH in place of hydrogen attached to carbon are known as hydroxy-acids, for example,

CH_2OHCO_2H hydroxyacetic acid (glycollic acid)

$CH_3CHOHCO_2H$ α-hydroxypropionic acid (lactic acid)

$CH_2OHCH_2CO_2H$ β-hydroxypropionic acid (hydracrylic acid)

$CH(OH)CO_2H$
$|$
$CH(OH)CO_2H$ $\alpha\alpha'$-dihydroxysuccinic acid (tartaric acid).

These compounds may thus be expected to combine the functional behaviour of an alcohol and a carboxylic acid.

The introduction of the electronegative oxygen atom increases the acid strength; compare the K_A values at 25° C: acetic acid $1\cdot76 \times 10^{-5}$; glycollic acid $1\cdot48 \times 10^{-4}$ and propionic acid $1\cdot34 \times 10^{-5}$, lactic acid $1\cdot37 \times 10^{-4}$. The effect, predictably, becomes weaker as the oxygen atom is more remote from the carboxyl group; K_A for β-hydroxypropionic acid is $3\cdot1 \times 10^{-5}$.

Aromatic carboxylic acids in which a hydrogen atom of the benzene ring has been replaced by —OH are also hydroxy-acids, but since the hydroxyl group here will show phenolic behaviour, they are usually known as phenolic acids. The best known, and the only one the elementary student is likely to meet, is o-hydroxybenzoic or salicylic acid:

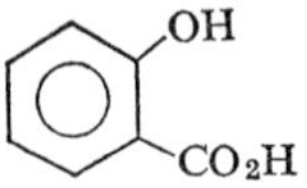

The behaviour of a simple aliphatic α-hydroxy acid towards the more familiar reagents is summarized in tabular form on p. 279.

Reactions of α-hydroxyacid (e.g. glycollic acid)

Reagent	Reaction with —OH	Reaction with —CO₂H	Net effect
Aqueous alkali	no action	$-CO_2H + OH^\ominus \to -CO_2^\ominus + H_2O$	Salt formation (e.g. $CH_2OH.CO_2H \xrightarrow{NaOH_{Aq}} CH_2OH.CO_2^\ominus Na^\oplus$) sodium glycollate
Metallic sodium	$-OH \to -O^\ominus Na^\oplus,\ H_2\uparrow$	$-CO_2H \to -CO_2^\ominus Na^\oplus,\ H_2\uparrow$	$CH_2OH.CO_2H \to CH_2O^\ominus Na^\oplus.CO_2^\ominus Na^\oplus$ (water on this → $CH_2OH.CO_2^\ominus Na^\oplus$ + alkali)
Alcohol (e.g. ethanol) + acid catalyst	no action	$-CO_2H \to -CO_2Et$	esterification e.g. $CH_2OH.CO_2H \to CH_2OH.CO_2Et$ ethyl glycollate
Concentrated HBr_aq	$-OH \to -Br$	no action	$CH_2OH.CO_2H \to CH_2Br.CO_2H$ monobromoacetic acid
Phosphorus halides, etc. (e.g. PCl₅, SOCl₂)	$-OH \to -Cl$	$-CO_2H \to -COCl$	$CH_2OH.CO_2H \to CH_2Cl.COCl$ monochloroacetyl chloride (which $\xrightarrow{cold\ H_2O} CH_2Cl.CO_2H$)
Acylating agents, e.g. acetic anhydride	$-OH \to -O.COCH_3$	no action	$CH_2OH.CO_2H \to CH_2O(COCH_3).CO_2H$ acetylglycollic acid
Heat	functional groups interact (mutual esterification of two molecules)		$2CH_2OHCO.OH \to$ [ring structure] glycollide
Oxidation	$-CH_2OH \to -CHO \to -CO_2H$; $\diagdown CHOH \to \diagdown C{=}O$	no action	$CH_2OH.CO_2H \to CHO.CO_2H \to (CO_2H)_2$ glyoxylic acid oxalic acid ; $CH_3.CHOH.CO_2H \to CH_3CO.CO_2H$ pyruvic acid

β-hydroxyacids such as hydracrylic acid do not as a rule undergo mutual esterification of the functional groups on heating, but rather lose water to form unsaturated acids; thus hyracrylic acid yields acrylic acid:

$$CH_2OHCH_2CO_2H \rightarrow CH_2{=}CHCO_2H + H_2O$$

γ- and δ-hydroxyacids can undergo mutual esterification of the functional groups within a single molecule, forming cyclic esters known as *lactones*, with 5- and 6-membered rings.

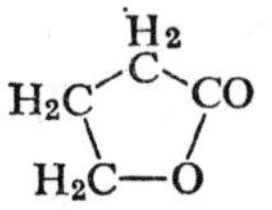

a γ-lactone   a δ-lactone

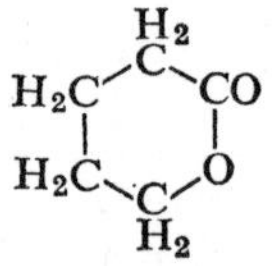

Methods of preparation

α-Hydroxyacids can most effectively be prepared by two general methods:

(1) Acid hydrolysis of aldehyde or ketone cyanohydrins (see p. 176); thus acetaldehyde cyanohydrin yields lactic acid.

(2) Alkaline (or, in some case, neutral aqueous) hydrolysis of α-halogeno-acids; thus chloroacetic acid yields glycollic acid (or its conjugate base) on refluxing with aqueous alkali or (more slowly) with water.

Test. The conjugate bases of the lower α-hydroxyacids in neutral solution give with dilute ferric chloride solution a fairly marked yellow colour, conspicuously more intense than that of dilute ferric chloride solution itself.

Salicylic acid occurs naturally as a glucoside (see p. 330) of its methyl ester. Methyl salicylate itself is known as 'oil of wintergreen'.

The acid can be made by the Reimer–Tiemann reaction (see p. 103), or by the Kolbé reaction (see p. 103), which is operated commercially.

Salicylic acid behaves as both carboxylic acid and phenol. It is therefore just dibasic in aqueous conditions; its first (carboxylic) dissociation constant is fairly high ($K_1 = 1 \cdot 1 \times 10^{-3}$ at 25° C) and its second (phenolic) much lower ($K_2 = 4 \times 10^{-14}$).

It may be esterified in the usual way; its esters with the lower aliphatic alcohols have a very characteristic smell.

It may be acetylated with acetic anhydride or acetyl chloride to yield acetylsalicylic acid:

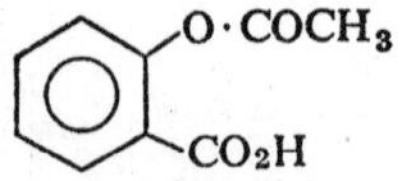

universally familiar as the febrifuge drug, 'aspirin'. Neutral or *slightly* acidic solutions of the salicylate ion give a strong purple colour with ferric chloride. This is characteristically phenolic, though not all phenolic acids give it.

Methyl salicylate and the other esters of salicylic acid still retain the phenol functional group. Thus for example they react at once with aqueous sodium hydroxide to give a sparingly soluble sodium salt; refluxing with excess alkali brings about saponfication of the ester.

Apart from its use in the manufacture of aspirin, salicylic acid and its methyl ester have a limited use as antiseptics.

Amino-acids

These contain —NH_2 in place of hydrogen attached to carbon in the parent acid. For examples, in the aliphatic series:

$$CH_2(NH_2)CO_2H \quad \text{aminoacetic acid (glycine)}$$
$$CH_3CH(NH_2)CO_2H \quad \alpha\text{-aminopropionic acid (alanine)}$$
$$CH_2NH_2CH_2CO_2H \quad \beta\text{-aminopropionic acid}$$

and in the aromatic:

o-aminobenzoic acid (anthranilic acid).

α-amino aliphatic acids form the basic units from which natural protein molecules are built up; consequently the term 'amino-acid', as well as having the above general sense, is often used in suitable contexts to mean simply the protein amino-acids. In all these except glycine itself, the α-carbon atom is asymmetrically substituted. These acids can therefore show optical activity and exist in (+) and (−) forms. All natural α-amino-acids except glycine are optically active, and nearly all belong to the L-series, L in this context meaning 'having the same configuration of the groups round the α-carbon atom as L-(−)-serine', which in turn has the same configuration as L-glyceraldehyde, as shown.

(see also p. 322 for the use of the prefixes D- and L-). Nearly all the natural α-amino-acids have trivial names ending in -ine; a more comprehensive book must be consulted for their names and structures.

Amino-acids are functionally both primary amines and carboxylic acids; that is, they contain one characteristically basic and one acidic functional group. In accordance with this, they are amphoteric in behaviour (see

p. 284). Nitrogen is a relatively electronegative element, and as an acid aminoacetic acid itself might be expected to be stronger than acetic, just as glycollic acid is. Nevertheless an aqueous solution of glycine is practically neutral because of the combined basic and acidic effects of the $—NH_2$ and $—CO_2H$ groups. Such a solution will in fact contain *four* organic species in equilibrium, thus:

$$
\begin{array}{ccc}
A & -H^{\oplus} & B \\
CH_2.NH_2.CO_2H & \rightleftharpoons & CH_2.NH_2.CO_2^{\ominus} \\
\text{aminoacetic acid} & +H^{\oplus} & \text{amino acetate ion}
\end{array}
$$

$$
\begin{array}{ccc}
+H^{\oplus} \big\| -H^{\oplus} & & +H^{\oplus} \big\| -H^{\oplus} \\
\overset{\oplus}{C}H_2\overset{}{N}H_3CO_2H & \underset{+H^{\oplus}}{\overset{-H^{\oplus}}{\rightleftharpoons}} & CH_2\overset{+}{N}H_3CO_2^{\ominus} \\
D & & C \\
\text{glycinium cation} & & \text{glycine zwitterion}
\end{array}
$$

In high $H^{\oplus}$ concentrations, (D) will greatly predominate; in low $H^{\oplus}$ concentrations, (B), and in neutral aqueous solutions, (A) and (C). This last represents a type of compound we have not previously discussed, in which, as a result of the $—NH_2$ and $—CO_2H$ groups having exerted their respective basic and acidic functions, two oppositely charged ionic groups are present in a single molecule. Such a species is picturesquely known as a zwitterion, from the German 'Zwitter' = a hermaphrodite; that is, a creature with both male and female sex-organs (e.g. a slug). Glycine and its homologues in the solid state have simple physical properties much closer to those of ionic solids than otherwise comparable organic substances, suggesting that they exist as the zwitterion in the crystal. Thus glycine has a much higher melting point (*ca.* 230° C with decomposition) than either acetic or glycollic acid (17 and 63° C respectively) and is sparingly soluble in methanol and practically insoluble in diethyl ether; properties consistent with the assumption that the crystal is held together by interionic forces.

The behaviour of glycine, as typical α-amino-acid, towards the more familiar reagents is summarized in table form on pp. 284 and 285.

The amino-acids are relatively sensitive substances, and easily form indefinite tarry condensation products. They cannot be distilled, even at very low pressures; concentrated sulphuric acid cannot be used with them as an esterification catalyst. Separation of the mixtures of amino-acids obtained by the hydrolysis of proteins was first achieved by the Fischer–Speier esterification, followed by fractional distillation at low pressures; under these conditions, interaction between $—NH_2$ and $—CO_2Et$ can be avoided. The esters can then be saponified and the acids regenerated.

The reaction with formaldehyde is the basis of Sörensen's method for estimating amino-acids; the stronger acids formed by the action of excess formalin on amino-acids (both previously made 'neutral' to phenolphthalein by appropriate addition of aqueous alkali) can be titrated with standard alkali, with phenolphthalein as indicator.

Amino groups in amino-acids and various other NH_2 compounds can also be estimated by the Van Slyke nitrogen method; although various organic products are formed when nitrous acid acts on amino-compounds, the evolution of nitrogen is practically quantitative—one mole (i.e. 22·4 litres at n.t.p.) per mole of NH_2 present initially.

Preparation of α-amino-acids

(1) Strecker synthesis from aldehyde or ketone, cyanide, ammonium ion (see p. 177); thus acetaldehyde yields alanine $CH_3CH(NH_2)CO_2H$.

(2) Ammonolysis of α-halogeno-acids; for example, monochloroacetic acid and excess aqueous ammonia yield glycine on standing at room temperature. (Excess ammonia avoids $NH(CH_2CO_2H)_2$.)

$$CH_2Cl.CO_2H + 2NH_3 \rightarrow CH_2NH_2.CO_2H + NH_4^{\oplus}Cl^{\ominus}$$

Separation from ammonium chloride after concentration: either

(a) Extract solid with methanol–pyridine mixture; glycine *less* soluble; or

(b) Precipitate copper glycine (see p. 284); suspend in water, pass hydrogen sulphide:

$Cu + H_2S \rightarrow 2CH_2NH_2.CO_2H + CuS\downarrow$

Filter off copper sulphide, concentrate filtrate.

(3) Gabriel synthesis (see p. 162). Essentially a modification of (2); for example, chloroacetate yields glycine.

(Compare (1) and (2) with syntheses of α-hydroxy acids, p. 280.)

Reactions of α-amino acid (e.g. glycine)

Reagent	Reaction with —NH₂	Reaction with —CO₂H	Net effect
Aqueous strong acid	$-NH_2 + H^{\oplus} \rightarrow -NH_3^{\oplus}$	no action	forms conjugate acid; i.e. salt formed with strong acid: $CH_2NH_2CO_2H + HCl \rightarrow (CH_2NH_3CO_2H)Cl^{\ominus}$ 'glycine hydrochloride'
Aqueous alkali	no action	$-CO_2H + OH^{\ominus} \rightarrow$ $-CO_2^{\ominus} + H_2O$	forms conjugate base; i.e. salt formed with alkali: $CH_2NH_2CO_2H + Na^{\oplus}OH^{\ominus} \rightarrow CH_2NH_2CO_2^{\ominus}Na^{\oplus} + H_2O$ sodium aminoacetate
Copper hydroxide, acetate, carbonate	acts as ligand in complex (cf. NH_3)	$-CO_2H \rightleftharpoons -CO_2^{\ominus} + H^{\oplus}$ (removed by bases e.g. $CO_3^{2\ominus}$) $-CO_2^{\ominus}$ acts as ligand in complex	Sparingly soluble uncharged chelate complex formed; e.g. copper glycine
Alcohol (e.g. ethanol) + dry HCl	$-NH_2 + HCl$ $\rightarrow -NH_3Cl^{\ominus}$	$-CO_2H \xrightarrow{HCl} -CO_2Et$ ('Fischer–Speier' Esterification)	forms salt of ester; e.g $(CH_2NH_3CO_2Et)Cl^{\ominus}$ 'glycine ester hydrochloride' Alkali on this → free ester $CH_2NH_2.CO_2Et$
Alkylating agents, e.g. MeI	$-NH_2 + MeI$ $\rightarrow -NH_2MeI^{\ominus}$ $(\rightarrow -NHMe_2$ $\rightarrow -NMe_3)$	no action	N-alkylamino acids formed; e.g. glycine → N-methylglycine $CH_2NH(CH_3)CO_2H$ and further methylated glycines

Acylating agents: (i) (e.g.) acetic anhydride;	$-NH_2 \rightarrow -NH.COCH_3$	acyl derivatives formed; **e.g.** $CH_2NH(COCH_3)CO_2H$ acetylglycine
(ii) (e.g.) benzoyl chloride+NaOH$_{aq}$ (Schotten–Baumann)	$-NH_2 \rightarrow -NH.COC_6H_5$ no action $-CO_2H+OH^\ominus$ $\rightarrow -CO_2^\ominus+H_2O$	conjugate base of acyl derivative formed; **e.g.** $CH_2NH(COC_6H_5)CO_2^\ominus$ benzoyl glycine anion (hippurate ion) Mineral acid liberates free acid, benzoylglycine (hippuric acid)
Aqueous formaldehyde	$-NH_2+H\!\!>\!\!C\!=\!O$ (H) $\rightarrow$ various condensation products no action	condensation products are stronger acids; see text i.e. Sörensen's method
Heat with soda-lime	no action $-CO_2H+2OH^\ominus \rightarrow -H$ $+CO_3^{2\ominus}+H_2O$	Decarboxylation $\rightarrow$ amine, e.g. $CH_2NH_2CO_2H \rightarrow CH_3NH_2$ (and other products) methylamine
Nitrous acid	$-NH_2+HONO \rightarrow -OH$ $+N_2\!\uparrow+H_2O$ (etc.) no action	$CH_2NH_2CO_2H \rightarrow CH_2OH.CO_2H, N_2\!\uparrow$ glycollic acid
Heat	functional groups interact (mutual amidation of two molecules)	$2CH_2NH_2CO_2H \rightarrow$ $\begin{array}{c} \quad CH_2 \\ NH \quad\quad CO \\ CO \quad\quad NH \\ \quad CH_2 \end{array}$, etc. 'diketopiperazine'

Proteins and the peptide link

Proteins are complex naturally occurring substances, the main organic constituents of skin, hair, nails and claws, muscles and generally of the body tissues as opposed to the skeletons of living organisms. On hydrolysis with aqueous mineral acid, proteins yield a fairly complex mixture of α-amino-acids; over forty such protein amino-acids have been recognized, and upwards of twenty occur widely. They were originally separated by the esterification method outlined above; other methods are now available, and the separation and characterization by paper chromatography of the principal amino-acids in a protein hydrolysate is an elementary exercise.

It is thought that the amino-acid residues in a protein molecule are joined by an amide-type link, in which the —NH_2 of one amino-acid has condensed with the —CO_2H of the other; for example,

$$NH_2CH_2.CO_2H + H_2N.\overset{\overset{\displaystyle CH_3}{|}}{C}H.CO_2H$$

$$\rightarrow H_2N.CH_2.\underline{CONH}.\overset{\overset{\displaystyle CH_3}{|}}{C}H.CO_2H + H_2O$$

This link is known as the *peptide* link, and compounds of two or more amino-acids so joined are called peptides. Thus the above example is a dipeptide, glycylalanine. Compounds containing two or more such links, including proteins and most of their intermediate hydrolytic degradation products, give the so-called 'biuret' test; that is to say, give colours ranging from violet to pink with aqueous alkali and small quantities of a Cu(II) salt solution (see also pp. 290 and 296). Methods have been devised for building up quite complex polypeptides; basically, the problem is to bring about interaction of the two functional groups under mild enough conditions not to destroy the amino-acids, to protect where necessary the functional groups which are not to interact, and to remove any protecting group without breaking the peptide link. For information about these methods, more advanced books must be consulted.

Proteins are thus complex polypeptides; they range in molecular weight from about 17,000 to over 6,000,000, and therefore contain anything from about 200 to over 60,000 amino-acid units. In addition to the polypeptide chains, a protein may contain non-peptide residues linked to these; such substances are called 'conjugated proteins'. Furthermore, the polypeptide chain of a so-called 'globular' protein (as opposed to a fibrous one) is coiled up upon itself, and held in this form by hydrogen-bonding between —NH— and —CO— groups. The elucidation of the structure of a protein involves therefore discovering (*a*) what amino-acid residues are present and in what relative numbers, (*b*) their sequence in the chain, (*c*) the conformation of the chain. Some relatively simple protein-like substances (notably the hormone insulin) have been synthesized.

Proteins which are water-soluble (e.g. gelatin, egg albumen, casein) behave in solution as amphoteric colloidal electrolytes. The amphoteric character is not solely due to the terminal—NH_2 and —CO_2H groups of the polypeptide chain; a number of the amino-acids present in proteins have other acidic groups (—CO_2H, phenolic —OH) or other amino groups besides those involved in the peptide link, and these are present in the branches of the protein chain and give it its amphoteric character. A few such acids are shown below.

$$\begin{array}{c} CHNH_2CO_2H \\ | \\ CH_2CO_2H \end{array}$$
aspartic acid

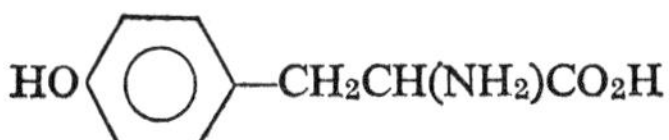

$$HO\!\!-\!\!\langle\bigcirc\rangle\!\!-\!\!CH_2CH(NH_2)CO_2H$$
tyrosine

$$NH_2(CH_2)_4CH(NH_2)CO_2H$$
lysine

At a certain pH (different for different proteins) the extents of the ionization of any particular protein as base and as acid will be equal, and the average net charge on the molecules will be zero. This pH value is known as the *iso-electric point* of the protein; the solubility of the protein in water is usually a minimum at this pH.

Proteins, carbohydrates and fats form the three basic types of food material. Animals have no biochemical mechanism for synthesizing many essential amino-acids, and must obtain these directly or indirectly by eating plants. The digestive tracts of animals contain proteolytic enzymes, which progressively break down the food proteins to single amino-acids or very small peptides, in which form they are absorbed into the blood stream and then reassembled into proteins. Animals (including man) normally eat more protein than they require for growth or replacement of bodily wear and tear; the amino-acids of the excess are *deaminated* in the liver. That is to say, the amino group is removed and converted into some non-toxic material (in mammals, urea) which is transported in the blood stream and excreted; the rest of the amino-acid molecule is oxidized and supplies energy. For further information on these points, a text-book of bio-chemistry must be consulted.

Dicarboxylic acids and some of their derivatives

Oxalic acid $\begin{array}{c} CO_2H \\ | \\ CO_2H \end{array}$

So named from its occurrence in wood sorrel (*oxalis*). Also in spinach, rhubarb leaves. Poisonous.

Preparation. (1) Heat on sodium formate yields sodium oxalate, hydrogen

$$2H.CO_2^{\ominus} \rightarrow H_2 + (CO_2^{\ominus})_2$$

Precipitate oxalate as insoluble $Ca^{2\oplus}$ or $Ba^{2\oplus}$ salt; treat this with equivalent of dilute sulphuric acid, which precipitates $Ca^{2\oplus}$ or $Ba^{2\oplus}$ as sulphate and leaves oxalic acid in solution.

(2) Oxidation of sucrose, cellulose (e.g. sawdust) or other carbohydrates with concentrated nitric acid. Isolate oxalic acid as in (1).

(3) Oxalic acid (or oxalate ion) is formed by the following typical —CO_2H preparation methods:

(*a*) as an oxidation product of ethylene glycol $CH_2OH.CH_2OH$;

(*b*) as one product of the slow hydrolysis of cyanogen $(CN)_2$, on standing in aqueous solution;

(*c*) by the action of carbon dioxide on metallic sodium at $360°C$ (compare action on sodium alkyls $\rightarrow$ fatty acid salts).

Properties. Colourless crystalline solid, obtainable anhydrous; water-soluble; crystallization from water yields $(CO_2H)_2.2H_2O$. Used as a primary standard in alkalimetry where the highest accuracy is not required.

Stronger than fatty acids; $K_1 = 5.9 \times 10^{-2}$, $K_2 = 6.4 \times 10^{-5}$ at 25° C. In addition to normal and acid salts, yields *quadroxalates*, for example, $KHC_2O_4.H_2C_2O_4.H_2O$. Alkali and ammonium salts water-soluble. Most others (including $Ca^{2\oplus}$ salt—contrast fatty acids) sparingly soluble. Oxalate ion acts as a bidentate ligand, forming chelate complexes with many transition metal ions; for example,

$$[Cr^{III}(C_2O_4)_3]^{3\ominus}$$

Owing to intermediate acid strength of oxalic acid calcium oxalate is insoluble in aqueous acetic acid, soluble in aqueous hydrochloric or nitric (hence test).

Reactions. The elementary student may meet the following:

(1) Esterification. Anhydrous oxalic acid refluxed with excess methanol or ethanol yields esters without need of stronger acid as catalyst; for example,

$$(CO_2H)_2 + 2EtOH \rightarrow (CO_2Et)_2 + 2H_2O.$$

(2) Amide formation. Ammonium oxalate yields some oxamide on heating:

$$(CO_2NH_4)_2 \to (CONH_2)_2 + 2H_2O.$$

(3) Acid chloride formation. Oxalyl chloride (b.p. 64° C) is obtained by the action of phosphorus pentachloride and similar reagents on oxalic acid.

$$(CO_2H)_2 + 2PCl_5 \to (COCl)_2 + 2POCl_3 + 2HCl$$

(4) Alkali metal oxalates on heating with soda-lime yield hydrogen and a carbonate. Formally at any rate, this curious reaction is analogous with the decarboxylation of other carboxylic acids by this method.

$$\begin{matrix} CO_2^\ominus \\ | \\ CO_2^\ominus \end{matrix} + 2OH^\ominus \xrightarrow[\text{dry}]{\text{heat}} 2CO_3^{2\ominus} + H_2$$

The above reactions are more or less typical carboxylic acid behaviour. Oxalic acid does not form an anhydride.

(5) On heating with concentrated sulphuric acid, oxalic acid and oxalates are dehydrated to an equimolar mixture of carbon monoxide and dioxide:

$$(CO_2H)_2 - H_2O \to CO + CO_2$$

This and the behaviour of calcium oxalate (above) are the familiar elementary tests for oxalic acid and oxalates.

Esters of oxalic acid

Dimethyl oxalate

Colourless crystalline solid, slightly soluble in water. (One of the few familiar esters which is solid at ordinary temperatures.)

Reactions. (1) Hydrolysis. More rapid than with fatty acid esters; hence aqueous solution rapidly becomes acidic and gives oxalate ion reactions. Fairly rapid with cold aqueous alkali (hence if this is coloured with phenolphthalein and dimethyl oxalate added, colour is fairly rapidly discharged).

$$(CO_2Me)_2 + 2OH^\ominus \to (CO_2^\ominus)_2 + 2MeOH$$

(2) Ammonolysis. With aqueous ammonia, *rapid* (contrast fatty acid esters) to yield *precipitate* of oxamide:

$$(CO_2Me)_2 + 2NH_3 \to (CONH_2)_2 + 2MeOH$$

(3) Concentrated sulphuric acid decomposes it to carbon monoxide and dioxide (and presumably methyl hydrogen sulphate, etc.).

Dimethyl oxalate is easily mistaken for oxalic acid by the elementary student. Distinguishable by: lower solubility in water, greater volatility; appreciable smell; reaction (2) above. (Under parallel conditions, oxalic acid yields the moderately soluble ammonium oxalate; no precipitate except with fairly concentrated solutions.)

Diethyl oxalate

Colourless liquid. Reactions as dimethyl oxalate, though hydrolysis rather slower.

Oxamide $(CONH_2)_2$

White, highly insoluble in water (*contrast* other lower aliphatic amides). Sublimes on heating.

Preparation. From esters and aqueous ammonia, as above.

(1) Hydrolysis by boiling aqueous alkali:

$$(CONH_2)_2 + 2OH^\ominus \rightarrow (CO_2{}^\ominus)_2 + 2NH_3.$$

(2) Dehydration: with phosphorus pentoxide, yields cyanogen ('oxalo-nitrile') $(CONH_2)_2 + P_4O_{10} \rightarrow (CN)_2 + 4HPO_3$

These are the expected amide reactions.

(3) 'Biuret' test. Oxamide in aqueous alkali suspension gives a pink coloration with dilute copper (II) salt solutions.

Malonic acid $CH_2{\Big\langle}{\,}^{CO_2H}_{CO_2H}$

Synthesis.

$$CH_2Cl.CO_2{}^\ominus \xrightarrow[\text{evaporate}]{CN^\ominus_{Aq}} CH_2CN.CO_2{}^\ominus \xrightarrow[\text{reflux}]{H^\oplus,\,H_2O} CH_2{\Big\langle}{\,}^{CO_2H}_{CO_2H} \quad (+NH_4{}^\oplus)$$

Colourless water-soluble solid. Forms esters, malonamide, malonyl-chloride, but no normal anhydride.

Reactions. (1) Loses carbon dioxide at melting point (about 130° C) forming acetic acid. $CH_2(CO_2H)_2 \rightarrow CH_3CO_2H + CO_2$

(General reaction of dibasic acids with two —CO_2H groups attached to the same carbon atom).

(2) Dehydration. On heating in vacuo at *ca.* 150° with phosphorus pentoxide, yields carbon suboxide $O{=}C{=}C{=}C{=}O$. This substance bears the same relation to malonic acid that ketene $CH_2{=}C{=}O$ does to acetic acid.

Syntheses using diethyl malonate are discussed on p. 201.

290

Succinic acid:
$$\begin{matrix} CH_2 . CO_2H \\ | \\ CH_2 . CO_2H \end{matrix}$$
(ethane 1, 2-dicarboxylic acid)

So called from occurrence in amber (Latin, *succinum*).

Synthesis.

$$CH_2 = CH_2 \xrightarrow{Br_2} CH_2Br . CH_2Br \xrightarrow{CN^{\ominus}} CH_2CN . CH_2CN \xrightarrow[H_2O]{H^+} \begin{matrix} CH_2CO_2H \\ | \\ CH_2CO_2H \end{matrix} (+2NH_4^{\oplus})$$

Colourless water-soluble solid. Used as a primary standard in alkalimetry. Succinic acid yields esters, an amide, succinyl chloride; it also forms an anhydride and an imide.

Reactions. On refluxing with acetic anhydride, succinic acid loses water to form *succinic anhydride*, a cyclic compound with a 5-membered ring.

$$\begin{matrix} CH_2 . CO_2H \\ | \\ CH_2 . CO_2H \end{matrix} + (CH_3CO)_2O \rightarrow \begin{matrix} CH_2 . CO \\ | \qquad \diagdown \\ \qquad \quad O \\ | \qquad \diagup \\ CH_2 . CO \end{matrix} + 2CH_3CO_2H$$

Two carboxyl groups on adjacent carbon atoms are favourably placed to interact with loss of water in this way, and such acids readily form a cyclic anhydride (see maleic acid, p. 311, and phthalic acid, p. 292).

Succinic anhydride is easily hydrolysed by boiling water to succinic acid.

An analogous nitrogen compound, *succinimide*, $\begin{matrix} CH_2 . CO \\ | \qquad \diagdown \\ \qquad \quad NH \\ | \qquad \diagup \\ CH_2 . CO \end{matrix}$ is obtained by heating succinic anhydride in dry ammonia

$$\begin{matrix} CH_2 . CO \\ | \qquad \diagdown \\ \qquad \quad O \\ | \qquad \diagup \\ CH_2 . CO \end{matrix} + NH_3 \rightarrow \begin{matrix} CH_2 . CO \\ | \qquad \diagdown \\ \qquad \quad NH \\ | \qquad \diagup \\ CH_2 . CO \end{matrix} + H_2O$$

or by heating succinamide (made, for example, by ammonia on succinyl chloride):

$$\begin{matrix} CH_2CONH_2 \\ | \\ CH_2CONH_2 \end{matrix} \rightarrow \begin{matrix} CH_2 . CO \\ | \qquad \diagdown \\ \qquad \quad NH \\ | \qquad \diagup \\ CH_2 . CO \end{matrix} + NH_3$$

Phthalic acid

$$\begin{array}{c} \text{CO}_2\text{H} \\ \text{CO}_2\text{H} \end{array}$$

benzene *o*-dicarboxylic acid

Manufacture. Oxidation of na*phthal*ene (now catalytic; formerly by concentrated sulphuric acid); hence name. The anhydride is formed:

$$\text{naphthalene} + 4\tfrac{1}{2}\,\text{O}_2 \xrightarrow[\text{catalyst}]{\text{V}_2\text{O}_5} \text{phthalic anhydride} + 2\text{CO}_2 + 2\text{H}_2\text{O}$$

from which the acid can be obtained by hydrolysis (see below). Also by oxidation of *o*-xylene (cf. p. 82).

Colourless crystalline solid, sparingly soluble in water. Potassium hydrogen phthalate is used as a primary standard in alkalimetry.

Reactions. (1) Dehydration. Phthalic acid loses water on heating a little above its melting point to form phthalic anhydride. (For the importance of this in orienting disubstituted benzene derivatives, see p. 78).

$$\begin{array}{c} \text{CO}_2\text{H} \\ \text{CO}_2\text{H} \end{array} \rightleftharpoons \begin{array}{c} \text{CO} \\ \text{O} \\ \text{CO} \end{array} + \text{H}_2\text{O}$$

Phthalic anhydride is hydrolysed back to the acid with warm water.

(2) Phthalic anhydride on heating with ammonium carbonate yields *phthalimide*. Essentially:

$$\begin{array}{c} \text{CO} \\ \text{O} \\ \text{CO} \end{array} + \text{NH}_3 \longrightarrow \begin{array}{c} \text{CO} \\ \text{NH} \\ \text{CO} \end{array} + \text{H}_2\text{O}$$

Phthalimide is also formed by loss of ammonia from phthalamide on heating.

Phthalimide behaves as a weak acid and, though sparingly soluble in water, dissolves in aqueous alkali.

$$\begin{array}{c} \text{CO} \\ \text{NH} \\ \text{CO} \end{array} + \text{OH}^{\ominus} \longrightarrow \begin{array}{c} \text{CO} \\ \text{N}^{\ominus} \\ \text{CO} \end{array} + \text{H}_2\text{O}$$

For its use in Gabriel's amine synthesis, see p. 162.

(3) Phthalic anhydride forms *phthaleins* with phenols; see p. 104.

(4) The esters of phthalic acid with aliphatic monohydric alcohols are colourless liquids with (exceptionally among esters) little or no smell. They have industrial use as plasticizers. *Dimethyl phthalate* is a well-known active constituent of midge-repellant creams. *Dibutyl phthalate* has a very

low vapour pressure at ordinary temperatures, and is used as a manometer and gas flowmeter fluid, since it will not contaminate the gas stream or be lost by evaporation into it.

(5) Phthalic acid (or anhydride) forms high-molecular-weight resinous esters with glycerol; see p. 344.

In addition to the derivatives described above, dibasic acids can clearly, in general, yield derivatives in which only one carboxyl group has reacted. Thus apart from the acid salts already mentioned, acid esters such as ethyl hydrogen succinate $HO_2C.CH_2.CH_2CO_2Et$ and half-amides such as the oxamates $(H_2N.CO.CO_2^{\ominus})$ are known. The elementary student is unlikely to meet them in the ordinary course of laboratory work, but should realize the possibility of their existence and be able to predict their more obvious properties.

Carbonic acid and its derivatives

Water dissolves roughly its own volume of carbon dioxide at ordinary temperatures. The solution is feebly acidic (saturated aqueous carbon dioxide at ordinary temperatures has a pH of about 3·8), and is believed to contain a small equilibrium concentration of carbonic acid.

$$CO_2+H_2O \rightleftharpoons O=C\begin{cases} OH \\ OH \end{cases}$$

The free acid cannot be isolated. The practical value of K_1 (i.e. of $\dfrac{[H^{\oplus}][HCO_3^{\ominus}]}{[CO_2, H_2CO_3]}$) is $4\cdot3 \times 10^{-7}$, so that carbonic acid is always thought of as very weak but, since only a small fraction of the dissolved carbon dioxide is converted to carbonic acid, the true value of K_1 $\left(\text{i.e. o }\dfrac{[H^{\oplus}][HCO_3^{\ominus}]}{[H_2CO_3]}\right)$ must be much larger. Indeed, one would expect replacement of hydrogen in formic acid by OH, giving carbonic acid, to lead to an increase in strength. K_2 (the acid dissociation constant of the bicarbonate ion) is $5\cdot6 \times 10^{-11}$; aqueous solutions of alkali metal carbonates are therefore quite strongly alkaline and, of bicarbonates, rather weakly so. Conventionally, the behaviour of the salts of carbonic acid falls within the scope of inorganic chemistry, and they will not be further dealt with here.

Although carbonic acid itself cannot be isolated, some of its characteristic derivatives as a carboxylic acid can be. Thus esters (e.g. ethyl carbonate $CO(OEt)_2$) acid esters (e.g. ethyl hydrogen carbonate $HO.CO.OEt$), carbonyl chloride $COCl_2$, the amide urea $CO(NH_2)_2$ and salts and esters of the half amide carbamic acid $NH_2.CO.OH$ (not itself known free) are all known. Of the general preparative methods for these functional types, those involving isolating the free acid are not available; those general reactions which normally lead to the free acid will instead yield carbon dioxide and water.

Carbonyl chloride (phosgene) $COCl_2$

Preparation. Direct combination of carbon monoxide and chlorine over active carbon (reversible)

$$CO + Cl_2 \underset{800°}{\overset{200°}{\rightleftharpoons}} COCl_2$$

Properties. Colourless gas, readily liquified. Highly poisonous (used as poison gas in World War 1).

Reactions. Carbonyl chloride shows the characteristic behaviour of an acid chloride; it is often possible to obtain 'half-way' products by the replacement of only one chlorine atom in the molecule.

(1) Hydrolysis.
$$COCl_2 + H_2O \rightarrow CO_2 + 2HCl$$

(2) Ester formation:

$$COCl_2 + EtOH \rightarrow Cl.COOEt + HCl$$
(ethyl chloroformate)

$$COCl_2 + 2EtOH \rightarrow CO(OEt)_2 + 2HCl$$
diethyl carbonate

(3) Amide formation

$$COCl_2 + NH_3 \rightarrow NH_2.CO.Cl + HCl$$
carbamyl chloride
(effectively, by heating ammonium
chloride in phosgene)

$$COCl_2 + 2NH_3 \rightarrow NH_2.CO.NH_2 + 2HCl$$
urea $\downarrow$
$(2NH_4Cl)$

(4) Similar reactions with amines yield alkyl and aryl ureas, for example,

$$COCl_2 + 2C_6H_5NH_2 \rightarrow CO(NH.C_6H_5)_2 + 2HCl$$

(5) Friedel–Crafts reaction; for example, with benzene and aluminium chloride:
$$2C_6H_6 + COCl_2 \rightarrow (C_6H_5)_2CO + 2HCl$$
benzophenone

Urea (carbamide) $CO(NH_2)_2$

So called from occurrence in mammalian urine (end-product of nitrogen metabolism).

Preparation. (1) From carbonyl chloride, as above.

(2) Evaporation of solutions containing ammonium and cyanate ions

$$NH_4^{\oplus} + CNO^{\ominus} \rightleftharpoons CO(NH_2)_2$$

Urea is less soluble than ammonium cyanate, and crystallizes out, thus displacing the equilibrium. (Wöhler's original urea synthesis.)

(3) From ammonia and carbon dioxide (technical). Dry, these combine to form ammonium carbamate (reversible):

$$CO_2 + 2NH_3 \rightleftharpoons NH_4^{\oplus}(O.CONH_2)^{\ominus}$$

On heating under pressure, urea is formed (cf. acetamide from ammonium acetate):

$$NH_4^{\oplus}(O.CONH_2)^{\ominus} \rightleftharpoons CO(NH_2)_2 + H_2O$$

Properties. Colourless water-soluble solid. Non-toxic.

Reactions. (1) Basic properties. Unlike fatty acid amides, urea acts as a weak mono-acid base even in presence of water:

$$CON_2H_4 + H^{\oplus} \rightarrow CON_2H_5^{\oplus}$$

In water, the effect on pH is negligible, but those salts which have low solubilities can be isolated by precipitation on mixing urea and acid in fairly concentrated solution; the nitrate and oxalate are best-known:

$$(CON_2H_5)^{\oplus}NO_3^{\ominus};\ (CON_2H_5)_2^{\oplus}C_2O_4^{2\ominus}$$

It has been shown by X-ray diffraction studies that the urea cation in the crystalline salts is an oxonium-type ion, with the proton added to the oxygen atom. This is stabilized by considerable delocalization of the ionic charge:

(2) Action of heat. Urea melts at 132° C; on further gentle heating it loses ammonia, re-solidifying to 'biuret':

$$2CO(NH_2)_2 \rightarrow NH_2.CO.NH.CONH_2 + NH_3$$
biuret

Some cyanuric acid: $(NHCO)_3$, possibly

$$O:C \overset{\overset{H}{N}}{\underset{\underset{C}{\underset{O}{\parallel}}}{}} C:O$$
$$HN \qquad NH$$

is also formed.

Biuret with aqueous alkali and a few drops of a copper (II) salt solution gives a purplish-pink colour (the 'biuret test'). Similar colours, ranging from purple to pink, are given by proteins and their partial hydrolysis products (see p. 286) and oxamide (p. 290).

(3) Hydrolysis. Normal behaviour as carbamide with aqueous acid or alkali:

$$CO(NH_2)_2 + 2OH^\ominus \rightarrow CO_3^{2\ominus} + 2NH_3$$
$$CO(NH_2)_2 + H_2O + 2H^\oplus \rightarrow CO_2 + 2NH_4^\oplus$$

(4) Alcoholysis. Urea can be recrystallized from hot ethanol. At higher temperatures and pressures, alcoholysis yields carbamic esters

$$CO(NH_2)_2 + EtOH \rightarrow NH_2.CO.OEt + NH_3$$

(5) Reaction with nitrous acid. Nitrous acid decomposes urea.

$$CO(NH_2)_2 + 2HNO_2 \rightarrow 2N_2 + 3H_2O + CO_2$$

(6) Reaction with sodium hypobromite. A reaction analogous to the Hofmann amide-to-amine reaction takes place (see p. 229)

$$CO(NH_2)_2 + OBr^\ominus + 2OH^\ominus \rightarrow CO_3^{2\ominus} + Br^\ominus + N_2H_4 + H_2O$$

but the hydrazine is immediately oxidized to nitrogen and water.

$$N_2H_4 + 2OBr^\ominus \rightarrow N_2 + 2H_2O + 2Br^\ominus$$

21

Optical activity and mirror-image isomerism; geometrical isomerism

(In this section it is assumed that the student is familiar with the elementary concepts of light as a transverse wave motion and of plane polarization as the confining of the transverse vibrations to a single plane, and with the production of plane polarized light by such devices as the Nicol prism.)

Many chemical substances have the power of rotating the plane of polarization of plane polarized light. That is, if such substances are placed in the path of a beam of monochromatic plane polarized light, the plane to which the oscillations are confined is twisted or rotated. The magnitude of the angle of rotation is directly proportional to the length of the path of the beam through the substance in question (assuming it is homogeneous). In the case of substances in solution, the angle of rotation also depends on the concentration of the solution; it also depends on the wavelength of the light employed. Such substances are said to be *optically active*. (The student should appreciate that this apparently vague phrase has this precise meaning, and does not apply to any other optical effects of chemical substances.)

Optical activity is detected and measured by means of a polarimeter. Light from a suitable source (e.g. a sodium vapour lamp) is polarized by a Nicol prism (the 'polarizer'). Another rotatable Nicol prism is placed coaxially with the polarizer in the path of the polarized beam. This second prism is attached to an angular scale. If, when this prism (the 'analyser') is set to transmit the maximum (or minimum) intensity, an optically active material is placed between the prisms, the analyser will have to be rotated through a certain angle to restore maximum (or minimum) intensity of the transmitted light. This is the angle through which the plane of polarization has been rotated by the interposed substance. If, from the point of view of the observer looking *towards* the light source from the remote side of the analyser, this last has to be rotated *clockwise*, the optically active substance is said to be *dextro*-rotatory; if anti-clockwise, *laevo*-rotatory. In practice, an adjustment as outlined above would be extremely insensitive, and various optical devices are incorporated in laboratory polarimeters to give a sensitive setting of the 'extinction' position; that is, the setting at which the analyser extinguishes the polarized beam. A description of these devices will be found in suitable text-books of optics.

Some substances are optically active in the crystalline state, but lose their activity on melting or dissolving; an example of such a substance is sodium iodate. Many others, on the other hand, retain their activity in the fused or dissolved state; ordinary cane sugar, for example, is optically active in solution. In the crystal, molecules or ions are arranged in a regular pattern, whereas in the fused state and (especially) in dilute solution the molecules approximate more or less closely to a random arrangement. It is thus logical to deduce that substances which *lose* their optical activity on melting or passing into solution owe that activity to some feature of their *crystal lattice*, whereas substances which *retain* their activity in solution owe it to some feature of their *molecular structure*. Many organic substances are of this latter type, and it is with these only that we are concerned here.

Optical activity in solution, then, is a consequence of some structural feature of the molecule, and the principal interest of organic chemists in optical activity has been in its importance as a diagnostic of such structural features. It is therefore of prime importance to deduce what are the structural features which confer optical activity in solution.

It has been shown that *optically active substances exist in isomeric pairs*; one member of the pair is *dextro*-rotatory, the other *laevo*-rotatory, and their specific rotatory powers are equal and opposite. (The specific rotatory power of a material is the constant α in the expression

$$\theta = \alpha l c,$$

where θ is the angle of rotation produced by a path length l in a solution of concentration c. By convention, l is expressed in *decimetres*, c in g per cm³. α must be quoted for a specific wavelength of light and a specific temperature: thus α_D^{25} means the specific rotatory power at 25° C to light of the sodium D line wavelength). In all other physical respects (such as density or solubility) and in all chemical respects not involving the participation of other optically active materials (such as acid dissociation constants, nature *and rate* of reaction with optically inactive compounds) the two isomeric forms are identical. Their separation therefore involves special techniques, which are outlined below on p. 304. The structural feature or features of the molecule which confer optical activity must therefore be such as to give rise to two recognizably different types of molecule; those of the *dextro*-rotatory, or (+)-isomer and of the *laevo*-rotatory or (−)-isomer. Yet the differences between these types of molecule must not be such as to confer any differences in spacing or energy in the crystal lattice, in molecular cohesion generally, or in chemical reactivity. The two different molecules must therefore be alike in shape and their functional groups must be in chemically identical molecular environments. Such conditions are fulfilled if one type of molecule is a mirror-image of the other but not identical with it. Van't Hoff therefore suggested in 1874 *that the molecules of an optically active isomeric pair are related as object and non-superposable mirror image.*

The image in a plane mirror of an object, all of which lies in a single plane, is superposable on that object; that is to say, if we imagine that we can take the image from behind the mirror and bring it into contact with the object, then, however complicated the shape of the object, a suitable rotation of the image through 180° will enable image and object to be fitted together at all points. The mirror-image of a three-dimensional object, however, will only be superposable on the object if this possesses one or more of certain features of symmetry. These are for practical purposes: (*a*) a plane of symmetry; that is, a plane dividing the object so that all unique features lie in the plane, while the parts of the object on either side of the plane are related as object and mirror image; (*b*) a centre of symmetry; that is, a point such that any unique feature of the object lies at this point, while all other features are duplicated in such a way that features lying on the same straight line through the point and equidistant from it are identical.

An object—and hence a molecule—possessing none of these features is non-superposable on its mirror image. We therefore conclude that the *molecules of any optically active substance must have such a structure that they possess neither plane nor centre of symmetry.* Such a substance is said to show '*molecular dissymmetry*'. Furthermore, it is clear from what has been said about planar objects that the molecules of optically active substances at least, and therefore presumably many others too, must have appreciable extension in three dimensions; hence the title (translated) of Van't Hoff's treatise 'Chemistry in Space' which earned him such derision from the more conservative of his contemporaries.

Van't Hoff observed that all the fairly numerous optically active substances whose constitutions were known at the time had molecules of the general type:

$$\begin{array}{c} W \\ | \\ Z-C-X \\ | \\ Y \end{array}$$

that is, contained at least one carbon atom linked to four different groups. No substance which did not contain at least one carbon atom so linked had been obtained in optically active isomeric forms. Thus for example α-hydroxypropionic acid (lactic acid) $CH_3\boxed{C}HOH \cdot CO_2H$, with four different groups attached to the carbon atom $\boxed{C}$, is known as a pair of isomers of equal and opposite rotatory powers, whereas neither propionic acid $CH_3CH_2 \cdot CO_2$ nor β-hydroxypropionic acid $CH_2OH \cdot CH_2 \cdot CO_2H$ can be obtained optically active. He therefore concluded that the valency bonds of the carbon atom were distributed in space in such a way that when, and only when, they were attached to four different groups, the resulting molecule lacked both plane and centre of symmetry. (Such a carbon atom is known as an 'asymmetric carbon atom', though it is not the atom itself so much as its molecular environment which is asymmetric.) The equivalence of the four hydrogen atoms of methane (as shown, for example by the fact that whichever is replaced, the same methyl compound is formed) requires a symmetrical distribution of the carbon valencies. The only simple symmetrical arrangement which confers molecular dissymmetry on a molecule containing an asymmetric carbon atom is one in which the carbon atom is at the centre of a regular tetrahedron, and the attached groups occupy the four apices. Van't Hoff therefore drew this conclusion: *the four valencies of a saturated carbon atom are directed towards the corners of a regular tetrahedron with the carbon atom at its centre.*

(This at once raises the problem of indicating the three-dimensional aspects of molecules in two dimensions on paper; a useful convention is to use a 'perspective' representation of bonds as thicker at the end nearer the reader, and thinner at the further end.)

With three groups different and two identical, the molecule has a plane of symmetry containing C, X and Y and bisecting the edge ZZ of the tetrahedron at right angles. Such a molecule exists in one form only, being identical with its mirror image.

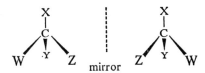

With four different groups attached to the carbon atom, the molecule has neither plane nor centre of symmetry, and can exist in two non-superposable mirror-image forms.

We may summarize the discussion so far as follows:

(1) Optical activity in solution must be a consequence of molecular structure.

(2) Optically active substances exist as isomeric pairs, one member differing from the other solely in the *sign* of its optical rotatory power.

(3) The molecules of such isomers must therefore be distinguishable, yet identical in all respects affecting molecular cohesion and chemical reactivity, and are therefore presumed to be non-superposable mirror images one of the other.

(4) These molecules must therefore be three-dimensional structures lacking both plane and centre of symmetry; possessing, in fact, molecular dissymmetry.

(5) Many simple optically active substances contain an asymmetric carbon atom, whereas similar substances with no asymmetric carbon atom are not optically active.

(6) A single asymmetric carbon atom therefore confers molecular dissymmetry.

(7) The only plausible valency bond arrangement to account for this is a tetrahedral distribution of the four valency bonds of the carbon atom.

This argument represents the pre-electronic-theory basis for assuming the truth of point (7); it is therefore of the highest importance in the development of theories of molecular structure.

When a substance capable of optical activity (that is, one showing molecular dissymmetry) is prepared from optically inactive reagents (that is with molecules possessing one or more of the above-mentioned elements of symmetry), it can readily be seen that there is statistically an equal chance of obtaining either of the two mirror-image forms, so that what we may call left-handed and right-handed molecules are bound to be formed in equal numbers. Two examples will illustrate this.

If propionic acid is brominated to yield α-bromopropionic acid, the probabilities of replacing one or other of the α-hydrogen atoms by bromine are equal; one replacement will yield, say, a (+)-α-bromopropionic acid molecule, the other a molecule of the (−)-acid.

When a cyanide ion (followed by a proton) is added to the planar molecule of acetaldehyde, a molecule of (+)-acetaldehyde cyanohydrin or one of the (−)-compound will be formed, according to which side of the molecule is attacked by the approaching cyanide ion.

In accordance with this, it is found in practice that, when a compound with dissymmetric molecules is synthesized from optically inactive materials, the product is always optically inactive, though it is usually separable into (+)- and (−)-isomers by the methods given on p. 304.

Furthermore, synthetic products of this kind, containing equal numbers of the two mirror image molecules, often crystallize as a single crystalline material, containing both types of molecule in equal numbers in the crystal lattice. Such a substance is known as a *racemic form* or *racemate*, for historical reasons given on p. 303. Since the crystal lattice contains two types of molecule, it will not in general be identical with the lattice of the (+)- and (−)-isomers; nor will molecular cohesion forces be the same in a mixture of two types of molecule as when all the molecules are alike. In accordance with this, racemic forms are found in general to have different *physical* properties from those of the (+)- and (−)-isomers, although they are chemically identical. Except in the solid state (in solution, for example) a racemate is identical with a mixture of the appropriate equal weights of the $(+)$- and $(-)$-isomers.

A racemate is comparable in this last respect with a double salt such as ferrous ammonium sulphate. In solution, this is identical with a solution of equimolar amounts of ferrous sulphate and ammonium sulphate; in the solid state the double salt exists as a separate species, with $Fe^{2\oplus}$, $NH_4^{\oplus}$, $SO_4^{2\ominus}$ ions and H_2O molecules in a characteristic lattice, and is different from an equimolar mixture of solid ferrous and ammonium sulphates.

The reader may find it helpful to think of $(+)$, $(-)$ and racemic crystal lattices in terms of the following analogy. A pile of left-handed gloves, placed palm to back with thumbs and fingers superimposed, is structurally identical with a similar pile of right-handed gloves; one pile is the mirror image of the other, being made up from mirror-image units. If, however, equal numbers of left- and right-handed gloves are piled, then the result is structurally different; if the thumbs and fingers are to be superimposed then they must be stacked alternately palm to palm and back to back.

The existence of racemic forms accounts for the statement that an optically active substance such as lactic acid exists in *three* forms; these are the two optically active isomers $(+)$-lactic acid and $(-)$-lactic acid, and the racemic form $(\pm)$-lactic acid. (Formerly, the prefixes *d*-, *l*- and *dl*- were used instead of $(+)$, $(-)$ and $(\pm)$. As, however, these could be confused with the prefixes D- and L-, whose use is explained on p. 322, they have been discarded.)

Resolution of racemic mixtures

To establish the cardinal fact that optically active substances occur in $(+)$ and $(-)$ isomeric pairs, differing only in the sign of their rotatory power, it was necessary to separate $(+)$- and $(-)$-isomers from natural or synthetic $(\pm)$-compounds. The first such separation was effected by Pasteur in 1848. He was investigating the salts of tartaric acid, a *dextro*-rotatory dibasic organic acid formed in wine-making, and had observed that the crystals of its salts showed so-called 'hemihedral' facets—that is, facets sited in such a way as to render the crystal form dissymmetric and non-superposable on its mirror image. He believed this feature to be associated with the optical activity. Another substance, *racemic acid* (from the Latin *racemus* = a bunch of grapes) is also formed in wine-making. It appears to be an isomer of tartaric acid and chemically identical with it, but optically inactive. Pasteur prepared the sodium ammonium salt of racemic acid, expecting to find that its crystals differed from those of sodium ammonium tartrate in having no hemihedral facets. To obtain well-formed crystals, he grew them slowly at about room temperature. On inspecting the crystal crop, he was surprised to find hemihedral facets present, but still more surprised when he realized that while some of his crystals had them placed in the same sense as those of sodium ammonium tartrate and seemed identical with this, others had them placed in the mirror image arrangement. He picked out and separated the two types of crystal, dissolved them separately in water and examined them in a polarimeter. The one batch of crystals proved *dextro*-rotatory and identical in optical rotatory power with sodium ammonium tartrate; the second batch was *laevo*-rotatory, with equal and opposite rotatory power to the first. Pasteur had separated or 'resolved' racemic acid, which is in fact ($\pm$)-tartaric acid, into (+)-tartaric acid and the previously unknown (−)-tartaric acid. It is from this research which Pasteur carried out that the term 'racemic' has come to apply to all ($\pm$)-substances and not just to ($\pm$)-tartaric acid.

Pasteur had in fact observed a case of *spontaneous resolution* of a racemic substance into (+)- and (−)-isomers, where, owing to the lower solubility of the (+)- and (−)-forms, the two types of molecule become segregated into separate crystals of these instead of coming together and crystallizing as the more soluble ($\pm$)-substance. Had Pasteur crystallized his salts above 28° C, where the racemate becomes *less* soluble than the (+)- and (−)-forms, he would have obtained one type of crystal only, those of sodium ammonium ($\pm$)-tartrate.

Spontaneous resolution is unusual, and even when it occurs the hand-picking of the two types of crystal from the crop is excessively laborious. (No separation by preferential crystallization of one form will occur, since the (+)- and (−)-members of an isomeric pair have identical solubilities.) Other methods of resolution have therefore been devised. The most widely used involves combining the ($\pm$)-substance with an equivalent quantity of an already available optically active material. (As a rule, naturally occurring optically active compounds are found in nature in only one of the two isomeric forms; such natural compounds can therefore be used for resolutions by this method.) Suppose, for example, we combine ($\pm$)A with (−)B, we shall have formed the compounds (+)A(−)B and (−)A(−)B. These are *not* mirror image forms; the mirror image of (+)A(−)B is (−)A(+)B, and no (+)B is present. In general they will have different physical properties including different solubilities and therefore may be separated by fractional crystallization. The separated compounds may then be decomposed to yield the required isomers (+)A and (−)A.

The method is widely applicable, though it has snags and limitations. Clearly A must have a suitable functional group to combine with B; it would be difficult to resolve a paraffin such as

$$CH_3CH_2CH(CH_3)CH_2CH_2CH_3$$

by this method. If many laborious recrystallizations are to be avoided, B must be chosen to give as large a difference as possible between the two solubilities; this is largely a matter of trial and error. By far the largest number of applications of this method have been in resolving racemic acids by the use of naturally occurring optically active bases such as strychnine, cinchonine, brucine or nicotine (so-called alkaloids), or racemic bases by optically active acids such as camphorsulphonic acid (made from the naturally occurring optically active ketone, camphor). In these cases, strictly speaking, there is no segregation of $(+)$A and $(-)$A into separate compounds by combination with, say, $(-)$B until the actual crystallization of the salt, since in solution A and B will be present as ions of a strong electrolyte; the separation is therefore a matter of the different solubilities of the ionic solids, say, $(+)A^{\oplus}(-)B^{\ominus}$ and $(-)A^{\oplus}(-)B^{\ominus}$. The principle remains the same.

(There is no certainty that the ions will not crystallize as a single substance $(+)A^{\oplus}(-)A^{\oplus}[(-)B^{\ominus}]_2$, a so-called 'partial racemate', but this is comparatively infrequent.)

Another method depends on the fact that living organisms almost invariably metabolize one isomer of a $(+)$ $(-)$ pair much faster and more completely than the others. By growing, say, a suitable mould on a racemic material, one isomer will be destroyed and the remaining one can be recovered. The method obviously involves the loss of one half of the racemic substance, and often more, as the living organism rarely discriminates absolutely between the isomers. The human body metabolizes $(+)$-glucose but, it is said, not $(-)$-glucose; there seems no reason other than aesthetic why a chemist wishing to isolate $(-)$-glucose from synthetic $(\pm)$-glucose should not eat the lot and recover the unmetabolized $(-)$-glucose from the waste products of metabolism in the urine.

Structural causes of molecular dissymmetry

It should be clear from the preceding that the presence of an asymmetric carbon atom in the molecule is not a fundamental requirement for optical activity of a compound but merely the most common and obvious source of the fundamental requirement, which is molecular dissymmetry.

The stock example of a compound with a single asymmetric carbon atom is the already-quoted case of lactic acid, the two forms of the molecule being as shown.

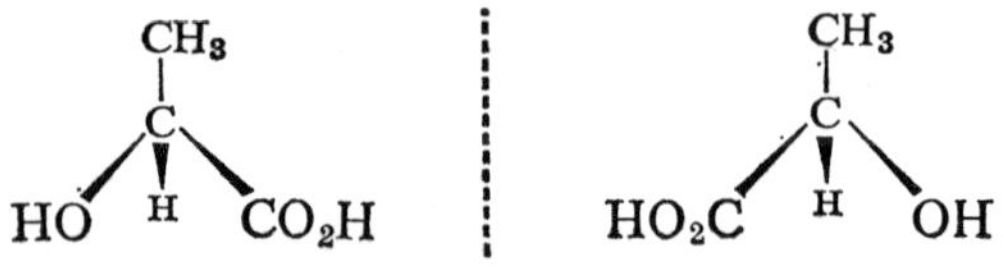

The asymmetrically substituted atom need not be carbon; any 4-covalent atom with a tetrahedral valency distribution will serve as a *centre of asymmetry*. Thus, for example, quaternary ammonium ions of the type $(NR^1R^2R^3R^4)^{\oplus}$ exist as $(+)$- and $(-)$-isomeric pairs. This was first shown for the allylbenzylmethylphenylammonium ion:

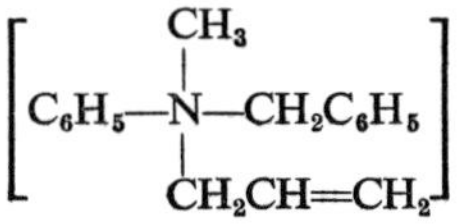

$$\left[\begin{array}{c} CH_3 \\ | \\ C_6H_5-N-CH_2C_6H_5 \\ | \\ CH_2CH=CH_2 \end{array} \right]$$

Molecular dissymmetry can arise with suitable substitution of atoms with covalencies other than 4, notably with 6 covalencies octahedrally distributed; for a discussion of such cases, more advanced text-books should be consulted.

Some compounds show a molecular dissymmetry which is not referable to a specific asymmetric atom; three examples are shown below. One form only is shown; the student can construct the mirror image and confirm the non-superposability of the two forms.

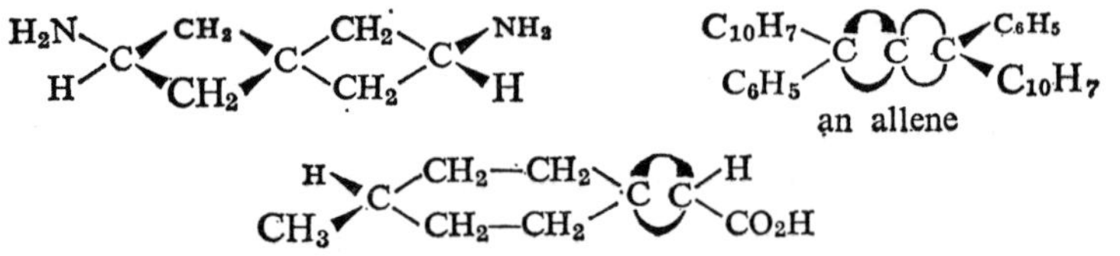

an allene

An interesting case is that of the derivatives of diphenyl where sufficiently bulky substituents in the 2,2′ and 6,6′ positions confine the rotation of one ring relative to the other to an arc of less than 180°, thus giving rise to molecular dissymmetry. For example

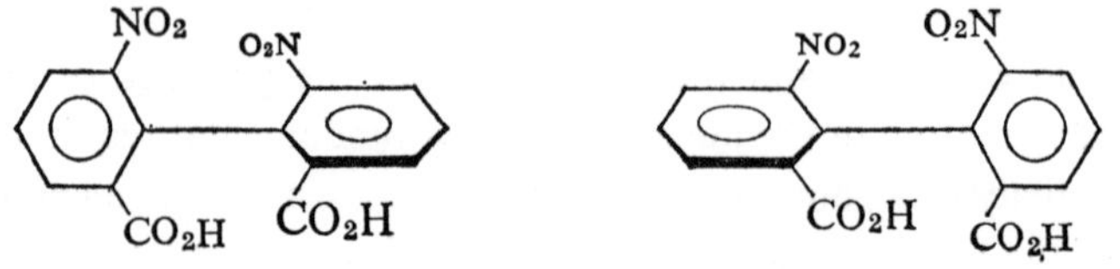

(Rotate this whole molecule through 90° about the horizontal; it will be seen that though one substituted ring is superposable on the mirror image, the other is not.)

Substances with more than one asymmetric centre

If a molecule has more than one asymmetric centre, then in general each centre can possess one or other of the mirror-image arrangements independently of the others. For n such centres, all different, there will therefore be 2^n different arrangements of the molecule, in $2^{(n-1)}$ mirror-image pairs. For example, the molecule of α-bromo-α′-hydroxy succinic acid $HO_2C.CHBr.CHOH.CO_2H$ can exist in four forms, leading to two pairs of $(+)$ and $(-)$ mirror-image isomers. Thus:

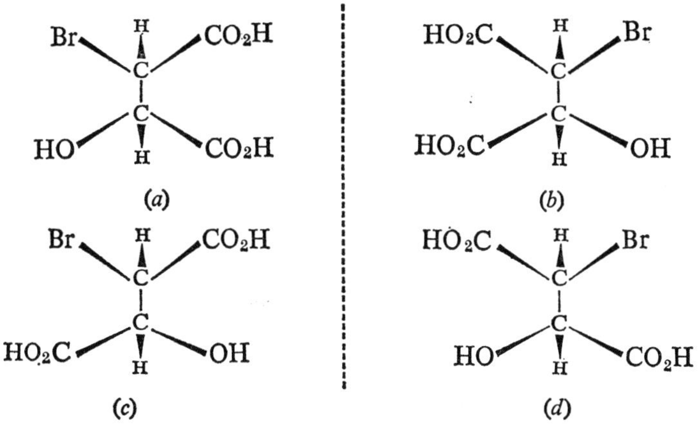

$$
\begin{array}{cc}
\text{(a)} & \text{(b)} \\
\text{(c)} & \text{(d)}
\end{array}
$$

(a): Br, H, CO$_2$H on top carbon; HO, H, CO$_2$H on bottom carbon.
(b): HO$_2$C, H, Br on top carbon; HO$_2$C, H, OH on bottom carbon.
(c): Br, H, CO$_2$H on top carbon; HO$_2$C, H, OH on bottom carbon.
(d): HO$_2$C, H, Br on top carbon; HO, H, CO$_2$H on bottom carbon.

The relation between (a) or (b) on the one hand and (c) or (d) on the other merits consideration. (a) is, of course, an isomer of (c), but is not related to it as object and mirror image, and the spatial relationships of the groups in the two molecules are different; for example if, as in the diagram, the α-hydrogen atoms lie in the same plane as their attached atoms and as near together as possible, then the carboxyl groups are closer in (a) than in (c). We accordingly find that the substances represented by these two formulae, though very similar, are different in physical and chemical properties; for example, their solubilities and their acid dissociation constants are different and their optical rotatory powers differ in magnitude. Such substances are known as 'diastereoisomers'. These are in all six crystalline substances all describable as α-bromo-α-hydroxysuccinic acid; two pairs of $(+)$ and $(-)$ isomers, and a racemic $(\pm)$ form corresponding to each pair. These would be described as $(+)$, $(-)$ and $(\pm)$ forms of two chemically different, diastereoisomeric compounds.

If the two asymmetric centres are identically substituted, then the number of forms becomes less. For example, take the case of $\alpha\alpha'$-dihydroxy-succinic or tartaric acids. By writing —OH in place of —Br in the above diagrams, it will be seen that the arrangements corresponding to (c) and (d) still form a non-superposable mirror-image pair.

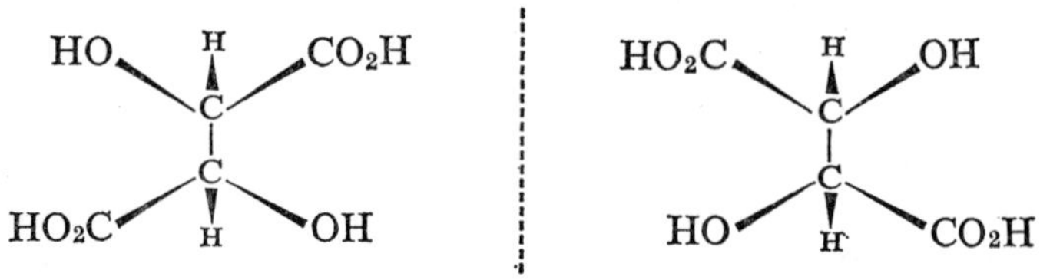

but those corresponding to (a) and (b) give a structure with a plane of symmetry:

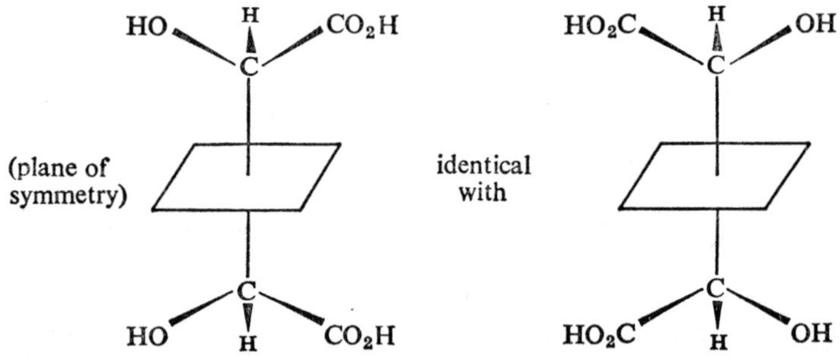

and thus become identical. (Rotate one molecule through 180° about an axis perpendicular to the plane of the page.)

We accordingly find *four* crystalline tartaric acids; (+)-tartaric acid, (−)-tartaric acid and (±)-tartaric acid, as investigated by Pasteur, and a diastereoisomeric substance, *meso*-tartaric acid, which is optically inactive, non-resolvable and chemically somewhat different from the other three. Compare:

	(+), (−), (±) tartaric acids	*meso*-tartaric acid
K_1	$1 \cdot 04 \times 10^{-3}$	6×10^{-4}
K_2	$4 \cdot 55 \times 10^{-5}$	$1 \cdot 53 \times 10^{-5}$
(at 25° C)		

A precisely analogous situation arises with the 1,1′-dibromosuccinic acids or any other set of isomers with two identically substituted asymmetric centres in the molecule. The 1,1′-dibromination of succinic acid will yield (+)-, (−)- and *meso*-1,1′-dibromosuccinic acids; the first two will necessarily be formed in equal quantities, but the quantity of the *meso*-form will bear no simple relation to these, since once one α-bromine atom has been introduced, the two α'-hydrogen atoms are no longer in chemically identical situations, and hence the probabilities of forming a (+)- or (−)-molecule on the one hand or a *meso*-molecule on the other are not equal.

If the above formulae for the various tartaric acid molecules are imagined as cut in half through the central C—C bond, and the lower halves turned through 180° about an axis perpendicular to the page, it will be seen that the two halves of one dissymmetric form are identical and are mirror-images of the two halves of the other. The two halves of the *meso*-molecule, on the other hand, are mirror-images one of the other, as indeed is obvious from the definition of a plane of symmetry; thus one half has the configuration of the asymmetric centres of the (+)-form, and the other half, of the (−). *Meso*-forms are therefore sometimes spoken of as 'internally compensated', as if within the molecule the effect of the (+) half cancelled the effect of the (−) half; racemic forms are by contrast called 'externally compensated'. This view is, however, somewhat arbitrary. Optical activity in solution is the statistical effect of a large number of more or less randomly oriented molecules. Since there is free rotation of the asymmetric centres about the C—C bond joining them, it is highly unlikely that at any instant any particular *meso*-molecule will be in the eclipsed arrangement shown in the diagram, with its plane of symmetry, or in the arrangement below, with a centre of symmetry:

Individual *meso*-molecules, therefore, at any instant are likely to be dissymmetrically arranged, and there is no *a priori* reason why the effect of a single molecule on the plane of polarization (if such a concept is meaningful) should be nil. In a large random assembly of *meso*-molecules (or of any others capable of a symmetrical configuration), the effect of such deviations from the symmetrical configurations will be cancelled by opposite deviations, and the total effect will be nil. This will not be so if the molecules are all left-handedly or all right-handedly dissymmetric.

Nothing has been said about why molecular dissymmetry leads to optical activity, nor has any indication been given of which of the mirror-image arrangements of, say, the lactic acid molecule belongs to the (+) and which to the (−)-isomer. The second problem, long thought insoluble, has recently been solved, but a discussion is beyond the scope of this book, and there is little point in the elementary student trying to memorize the answer. Attacks have been made on the first problem with some success but again the topic is beyond the scope of this book. Neither point is relevant to the argument developed here.

An elegant experimental model of optical rotation has been developed. Closely equal lengths of uniform copper wire are wound into short spirals and mounted with axes parallel in a simple cubic lattice in holes in an expanded polystyrene block. The assembly when placed in the path of a beam of plane-polarized radio micro-waves (of wavelength about 3 cm) rotates the plane of polarization in one direction or the other, depending on whether the copper spirals are left or right-handedly wound. If left- and right-handed spirals in equal numbers are mounted alternately in the lattice, there is no rotation. Furthermore, if the spirals are enclosed in polystyrene spheres, and shaken to give a random arrangement of their axes, then the assembly still has a rotatory effect if spirals of one kind only are used. while if equal numbers of left- and right-handed spirals are shaken together, the rotatory effect is very small. (A zero rotation would only be expected on statistical grounds if a very large number of spirals was used.)

Geometrical or *cis–trans* isomerism

It is pointed out on p. 52 that even a primitive 'model' of ethylene and its derivatives based on the concept of directed valency bonds leads to the idea that a double bond would prevent the free rotation of the carbon atoms linked by it. This in turn suggests that 1,2-disubstituted ethylene derivatives should exist in isomeric forms; for example, for dibromo-ethylene:

These conclusions have been confirmed by experiment. Such substances are said to show *geometrical isomerism*; the two types of molecule contain the same atoms linked to one another by the same types of bond, but the lack of free rotation about the double bond leads to a different geometry of the molecule in the two cases. It is therefore regarded as a type of stereoisomerism rather than of structural isomerism. In many simple cases of geometrical isomerism, the terms *cis* (on the same side) and *trans* (on the opposite side) can be applied to distinguish the two arrangements of the molecule, as indicated above; this is clearly not applicable to isomers of the types:

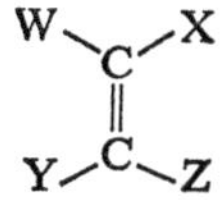

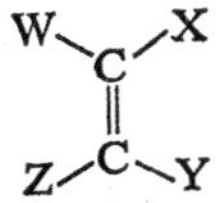

W—C—X, Y—C—Z (first structure)   W—C—X, Z—C—Y (second structure)

The classical case of *cis–trans* isomerism is that of the ethylene-1,2-dicarboxylic acids $HO.CO.CH=CH.CO.OH$. Two isomeric acids of this constitution are obtainable, for example, from the dehydration of hydroxy-succinic or malic acid $HO.CO.CH(OH).CH_2.CO.OH$; they are called maleic and fumaric acids. These two acids can be made to lose water under various conditions to yield an anhydride $C_2H_2\left(\begin{array}{c}CO\\ \diagup\diagdown O\\ CO\end{array}\right)$; both acids yield the *same* anhydride, but under different conditions. The most informative differences are:

(*a*) on heating to 100° C with acetyl chloride, maleic acid forms the anhydride. Under these conditions fumaric acid remains unchanged; it forms the anhydride on heating with acetyl chloride at 140° C.

(*b*) on heating alone *in vacuo* (so that any water formed is removed) maleic acid yields the anhydride at 100° C; fumaric acid is unchanged under these conditions, and only forms the anhydride above 200° C.

(*c*) The anhydride with cold water slowly yields maleic acid.

(*d*) On heating in the presence of water in a sealed tube at about 200° C, maleic acid is largely converted to fumaric acid (with some malic acid as a result of hydration of the double bond).

From (*a*) and (*b*) we may say that maleic acid forms the anhydride a great deal more easily than fumaric acid, and from (*c*) it follows that the anhydride is related more closely to maleic acid than to fumaric. (The anhydride is therefore called *maleic* anhydride.)

These facts are consistent with the conclusion that maleic acid is the *cis* isomer and fumaric acid the *trans*:

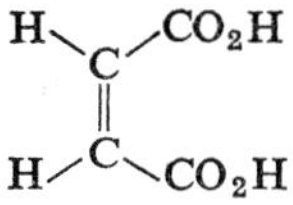

H—C—CO₂H, H—C—CO₂H (maleic acid)   H—C—CO₂H, HOCO—C—H (fumaric acid)

maleic acid 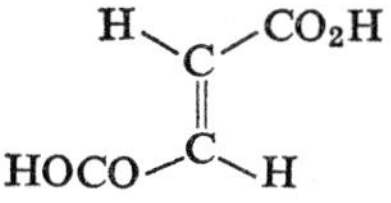   fumaric acid

and that loss of water to form the cyclic anhydride:

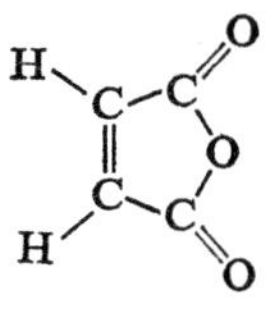

requires the carboxyl groups to be in the close, *cis* arrangement. To form the anhydride from fumaric acid, conditions have to be drastic enough to supply the energy required to overcome the resistance to rotation imposed by the double bond.

The facts that maleic acid is largely converted to fumaric acid on heating under non-dehydrating conditions, and that hydrolysis of the anhydride with aqueous hydrochloric acid (as opposed to water alone) yields a mixture of the two acids, with fumaric predominating, make it clear that the phrase 'lack of free rotation' by no means implies total resistance to rotation. The two isomers are interconvertible; moreover, fumaric acid appears from the above to be the more stable form, and this is confirmed by thermo-chemical data. The energy relationships between the two forms can be summarized graphically as shown (not to scale), where θ is the angle between the planes of the two H—C—CO₂H groups.

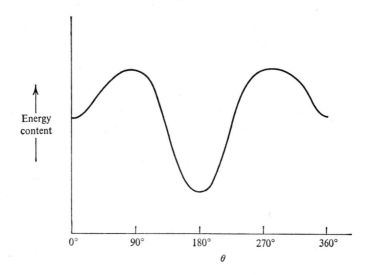

The greater stability of fumaric acid can be explained from the fact that in the *trans* arrangement, the polar —CO.OH groups are arranged far apart in a position of minimum potential energy, whereas in the *cis* arrangement they are closer and the force of repulsion between them will be at a maximum.

The addition of bromine to fumaric acid yields *meso- αα'*-dibromo-succinic acid; addition of bromine to maleic acid yields (±)-dibromo-succinic acid (see p. 308). These results clearly imply *trans* addition of bromine; see p. 57.

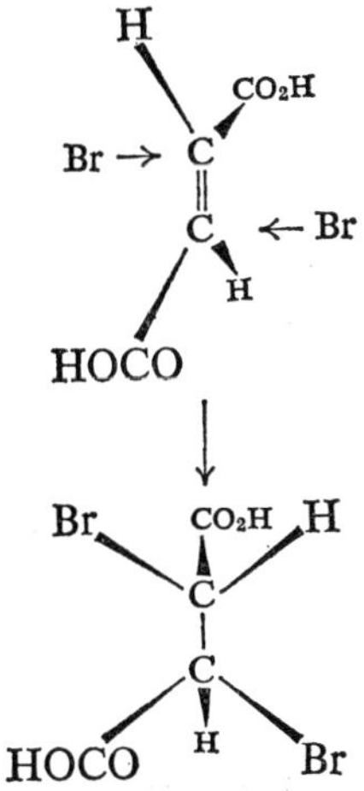

(Rotation of one
—$CHBrCO_2H$ group through
120° in the appropriate
direction relative to
the other will reveal
the plane of symmetry.)

meso-dibromosuccinic acid

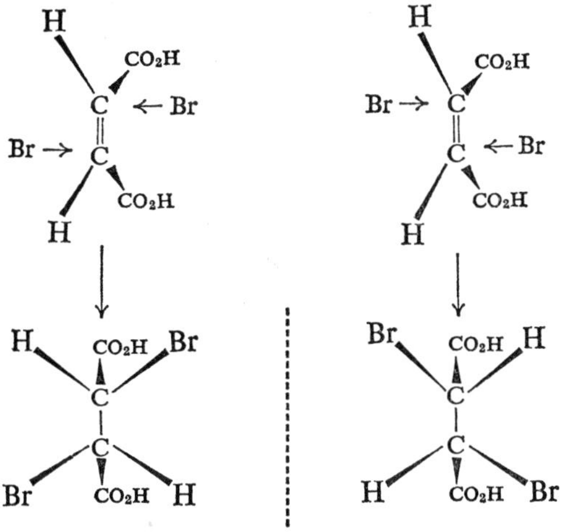

Non-identical mirror-image forms of (+)- and (−)-dibromosuccinic acid.

The oxidation of fumaric acid by aqueous permanganate, on the other hand, yields (±)-tartaric acid while oxidation of maleic acid yields *meso*-tartaric acid. In contrast to bromine addition, therefore, the two —OH groups are added on the *same* side of the unsaturated molecule in this reaction.

Geometrical isomerism is not confined to olefinic compounds. A closed ring offers an obstacle to the rotation of the atoms composing it, so that *cis–trans* isomerism occurs as, for example, in the cyclohexane-1,4-dicarboxylic acids:

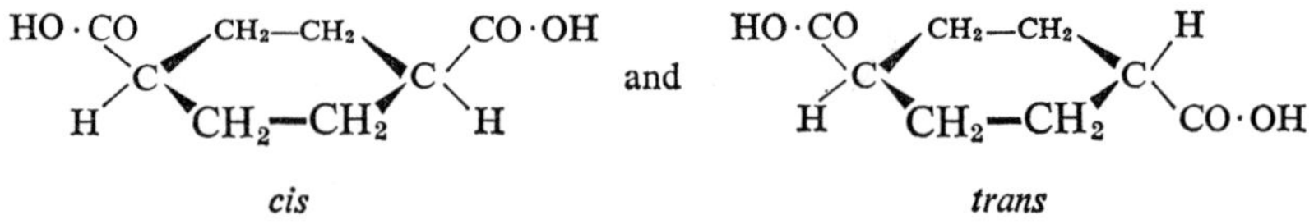

HO·CO   CH₂—CH₂   CO·OH   HO·CO   CH₂—CH₂   H

and

cis   trans

Geometrical isomerism also occurs in oximes of the general type RR'C=NOH. This implies that the molecules are planar, having C=N and N—O bonds at an angle of less than 180° with lack of free rotation about the C=N bond:

Isomerism essentially geometrical in character will occur where, for example, an atom has four valency bonds directed to the corners of a square. This arrangement was rejected by van't Hoff in the case of the carbon valencies since no such isomerism is found, but it occurs in, for example, four-co-ordinate platinum compounds; thus, isomeric compounds are known of the configurations:

314

Carbohydrates

From both plants and animals we can isolate a number of compounds of the type familiarly known as '*sugars*'—white crystalline solids, readily soluble in water and sweet in taste. These organisms also contain other compounds which are clearly closely related to the sugars, since they form them as a result of simple chemical reactions, such as (especially) hydrolysis. Such substances include *starch, cellulose* (the main constituent of vegetable fibres) and the starch-like compounds *inulin* (found in artichoke and dahlia tubers) and *glycogen* (found in animal livers). All of the above-mentioned compounds contain carbon, hydrogen and oxygen only; their empirical formulae can all be represented by the general type $C_m(H_2O)_n$. They therefore become known early on as hydrates of carbon or *carbohydrates*. It should be clearly understood that this is a purely descriptive name, and has no structural significance. Many compounds (for example acetic acid $C_2H_4O_2$; lactic acid $C_3H_6O_3$) have empirical or molecular formulae fitting the above general formula yet are not carbohydrates, since they are neither sugars nor closely related to them. Moreover, a number of substances—such as *glucosamine* $C_6H_{13}O_5N$, *chitin* (the hard material of the exoskeletons of crustaceans and insects, $C_8H_{13}O_5N$ empirically) and *ascorbic acid* or vitamin C $C_6H_8O_6$—though not strictly carbohydrates according to the original sense of the term, are regarded nowadays as coming within the scope of carbohydrate chemistry on account of their close structural and chemical relationship with the simple sugars. The compounds dealt with in this chapter will, however, all be within the scope of the definition of a carbohydrate as a compound of empirical formula $C_m(H_2O)_n$ which is either a sugar in the everyday sense of the word or closely related in chemistry and structure to a sugar.

Classification of carbohydrates

The commonest simple sugars—that is, sugars whose molecules cannot be further broken down by hydrolysis—have the general molecular formula $C_6H_{12}O_6$; the best known of these is glucose. The essential chemical characteristics of a simple sugar are found in other compounds of molecular formulae $C_3H_6O_3$, $C_4H_8O_4$ and $C_5H_{10}O_5$. Simple sugars are therefore classified according to the number of carbon atoms in the molecule, as trioses, tetroses, pentoses and hexoses. Of these, the pentoses and hexoses are by far the most important both biochemically and industrially.

Besides the simple sugars, other substances of larger molecular weight are known, which yield one or more simple sugars on hydrolysis. Some of these are sugar-like themselves, and have compositions and molecular weights which indicate that their molecules are formed by a few—most commonly two—simple sugar molecules uniting with loss of water. These are known as *oligosaccharides* (from the Greek roots for 'a few' and 'sugar') or, specifying the number of simple sugar molecules which unite, *di-*, *tri-*, or *tetra-saccharides*. (The simple sugars are thus *monosaccharides*.) Others, however, are clearly of much larger molecular weight, tasteless, and dispersing in water, if at all, as colloids. These are therefore known as *polysaccharides*. The following table illustrates these classifications with a few examples:

	Pentose series	Hexose series
Monosaccharides	ribose⎫ xylose⎭ $C_5H_{10}O_5$	glucose⎫ fructose⎭ $C_6H_{12}O_6$
Disaccharides (the commonest oligosaccharides)		maltose⎫ sucrose⎭ $C_{12}H_{22}O_{11}$
Polysaccharides	xylan $(C_5H_8O_4)n$ and other 'pentosans'	starch⎫ cellulose⎭ $(C_6H_{10}O_5)n$

It will have become obvious that all sugars are given names ending in -ose. Polysaccharides can be named, using the termination -an, after the monosaccharide to which they break down on hydrolysis; thus starch and cellulose could be (but rarely are) classed as *glucosans*.

Other subdivisions of these classifications, based on the detailed chemical character of the sugars, are dealt with in the course of this chapter.

Glucose

To bring out the chemical character and structure of a monosaccharide, we can take *glucose*, the most abundant and familiar of them, as a typical example.

316

Occurrence and general properties

Glucose occurs in fruit juices, notably in grapes (whence the old name, 'grape-sugar'), and in human and other mammalian blood, being the normal form in which ingested carbohydrate is transported to the tissues. It is obtained by the hydrolysis of starch (from cereal grains or potato tubers) and cellulose (in the form of plant fibres) by dilute mineral acids. With an equimolecular proportion of its isomer fructose, it forms the bulk of honey, and the same mixture is obtained by the acid hydrolysis of cane sugar, or sucrose. It is a colourless crystalline solid, highly soluble in water, sparingly soluble in ethanol and practically insoluble in ether. On heating, it decomposes with charring, and has no sharp melting point. Naturally occurring glucose is optically active and *dextro*-rotatory—hence another old name, 'dextrose'.

Reactions of glucose

(1) Glucose behaves in many ways as a *carbonyl compound*. Thus it is reduced to the compound sorbitol $C_6H_{14}O_6$ by sodium amalgam and water. It adds hydrogen cyanide to form glucose cyanohydrin; and forms an oxime with hydroxylamine. A phenylhydrazone can also be obtained, though glucose and its isomers react in a characteristic way with excess phenylhydrazine to yield compounds known as *osazones*; this reaction is discussed later in this chapter.

We could provisionally formulate these reactions thus:

$$(C_5H_{12}O_5)CO + 2H^\oplus + 2Na \rightarrow (C_5H_{12}O_5)CHOH + 2Na^\oplus$$

$$+ H^\oplus + CN^\ominus \rightarrow (C_5H_{12}O_5)C{\overset{\displaystyle OH}{\underset{\displaystyle CN}{<}}}$$

$$+ NH_2OH \rightarrow (C_5H_{12}O_5)C{=}NOH + H_2O$$

$$+ C_6H_5NH.NH_2 \rightarrow (C_5H_{12}O_5)C{=}N.NHC_6H_5 + H_2O$$

(2) Glucose further behaves in such a way as to show that the carbonyl group is present as an *aldehyde* rather than a ketone group.

All hexose monosaccharides are oxidized by warming with a solution of silver oxide in aqueous ammonia (Tollen's reagent), a silver mirror being formed. This does not of itself indicate an aldehyde structure, since some of the hexoses (for example, fructose) form a mixture of C_2 and C_4 acids on oxidation with this reagent, suggesting that they are readily oxidized ketones. Glucose, however, is oxidized to a C_6 acid, *gluconic acid*, which we can provisionally formulate as $(C_5H_{11}O_5)CO_2H$, glucose being the corresponding aldehyde $(C_5H_{11}O_5)CHO$. Bromine water also oxidizes glucose to gluconic acid. Nitric acid, however, oxidizes it to *saccharic acid*, a dibasic acid $(C_4H_8O_4)(CO_2H)_2$.

Unlike the simple aliphatic aldehydes, glucose is stable to atmospheric oxidation, and does not form a bisulphite addition compound.

(3) Glucose is acetylated to a pentacetyl glucose by refluxing with acetic anhydride and anhydrous zinc chloride. The composition of this compound can be established as follows:

(*a*) Its molecular weight, as determined by colligative property methods, is 390, corresponding to the replacement of 5H by $5CH_3CO$.

(*b*) It is hydrolysed by aqueous mineral acids to glucose and acetic acid, and if a known weight is refluxed with a known excess of standard acid, and the product titrated with alkali, it is found that one mole of the acetylated glucose yields five moles of acetic acid.

(*c*) If glucose is acetylated with excess of acetic anhydride, and the unchanged anhydride is hydrolysed with water, it is clear that the total number of moles of acetic acid present will be less than that obtainable from the original weight of anhydride by the number of moles of acetyl groups that have become attached to glucose. If a known weight of glucose is refluxed with a known weight (excess) of acetic anhydride in pyridine (which acts as solvent and catalyst), and the product is titrated with standard alkali, it is found that, for each mole of glucose, about five moles of acetyl groups become combined.

We may therefore provisionally regard glucose as *a pentahydric alcohol*, and formulate it thus: $(C_5H_6)(OH)_5CHO$.

(4) The structure of the carbon skeleton of glucose can be established in two ways.

(*a*) Sorbitol, obtained by the reduction of glucose, is reduced by hydriodic acid to 2-iodo hexane, $CH_3(CH_2)CHICH_3$.

(*b*) Glucose cyanohydrin on hydrolysis with aqueous mineral acid yields an acid which on reduction with hydriodic acid and red phosphorus yields heptanoic acid (*n*-heptylic acid). Thus:

$$(C_5H_{12}O_5)C\!\!\begin{array}{c}OH\\ \diagdown\\ CN\end{array} \rightarrow (C_5H_{12}O_5)C\!\!\begin{array}{c}OH\\ \diagdown\\ CO_2H\end{array} \rightarrow CH_3(CH_2)_5CO_2H$$

(Kiliani's cyanohydrin synthesis)

From both of these pieces of evidence, the glucose molecule has an unbranched chain of six carbon atoms; furthermore, (*b*) shows that the —CN group of the cyanohydrin is at the end of the chain, and confirms that glucose behaves as an aldehyde and not as a ketone.

Putting these points together, and assuming that only one —OH group can be attached to one carbon atom, glucose can be formulated as a straight-chain pentahydroxy-aldehyde:

1. CHO
2. CHOH
3. CHOH
4. CHOH
5. CHOH
6. CH$_2$OH

The carbon atoms are numbered as shown in naming derivatives.

Certain points in the chemical behaviour of glucose are, however, not adequately explained by this structure. The failure to form a bisulphite compound and the resistance to atmospheric oxidation have been mentioned; other points follow.

(5) Aldehydes in general yield acetals with alcohols and dry hydrogen chloride according to the general scheme:

$$\text{R.CHO} + 2\text{R}'\text{OH} \xrightarrow{\text{HCl}} \text{R.CH(OR}')_2 + \text{H}_2\text{O}$$

Glucose and methanol in these conditions do not react in this way, but yield two isomeric substances (*α- and β-methyl glucosides*) according to the scheme:

$$\text{C}_6\text{H}_{12}\text{O}_6 + \text{CH}_3\text{OH} \rightarrow \text{C}_6\text{H}_{11}\text{O}_6\text{CH}_3 + \text{H}_2\text{O}$$

Both isomers revert to glucose and methanol on acid hydrolysis. A reaction of the type:

$$-\text{OH} + \text{CH}_3\text{OH} \rightleftharpoons -\text{OCH}_3 + \text{H}_2\text{O}$$

is strongly indicated, but the easy acid hydrolysis suggests that an acetal-type compound rather than a simple ether is involved. A possible explanation is that the methyl glucosides *are* acetals, but that the second 'molecule' of alcohol involved is one of the alcoholic —OH groups of the glucose itself, leading to a ring formula. Thus, assuming the —OH group on carbon atom 5 reacts, thus giving a 6-membered ring, the suggested structure is:

OCH$_3$
|
^{1}CH
^{2}CHOH   O
|
^{3}CHOH ^{5}CH—^{6}CH$_2$OH
CHOH
4

It will be seen that carbon atom 1 has now become asymmetric; this accounts for the existence of two methyl glucosides.

(6) Glucose shows the phenomenon of *mutarotation*. A fresh solution of ordinary glucose has $\alpha_D = +113°$, but this decays in accordance with a first-order rate law to a final value of $+52°$. If the glucose is recovered from the solution and redissolved, the original α_D of $113°$ is restored.

Furthermore, if glucose is crystallized from a concentrated aqueous solution at 110 °C (or, more conveniently, from hot pyridine) a fresh solution of the product has $\alpha_D = +19°$, rising to $52°$.

The clear conclusion is that glucose, like the methylglucosides, exists in two isomeric forms, but that these are interconverted in aqueous solution, and reach equilibrium in a concentration ratio of (113–52): (52–19) of $\beta:\alpha$, where α indicates the form with the higher specific rotation and β the other.

A ring formula analogous to that proposed for the methyl glucosides:

$$\begin{array}{c} \text{OH} \\ | \\ {}^1\text{CH} \\ {}^2\text{CHOH} \quad \text{O} \\ | \qquad\qquad {}^6 \\ {}^3\text{CHOH} \quad {}^5\text{CH--CH}_2\text{OH} \\ \text{CHOH} \\ {}_4 \end{array}$$

accounts for these results.

The interconversion of the two isomeric forms (which arise from the asymmetry of carbon atom no. 1 in the ring form) then results from the reversible hydrolytic opening of the ring. In the open chain sugar (possibly in the gem-diol form) this asymmetry is absent: reclosure of the ring can thus lead to either configuration of the groups about carbon atom no. 1.

That the isomerism of glucose itself is indeed analogous to that of the methyl glucosides has been shown as follows. The hydrolysis of one methylglucoside is catalysed by the enzyme *maltase* (from yeast), and of the other by *emulsin* (from bitter almonds). If the hydrolysis is followed polarimetrically, it can be shown that the former (the α-glucoside) yields α-glucose on hydrolysis and the latter (the β-glucoside) β-glucose, the mutarotation reaction being slower than the enzymatic hydrolysis.

(7) In accordance with the existence of α- and β-glucoses, two pentacetyl derivatives are also known. One has been described; the other is obtained if anhydrous sodium acetate is used as acetylating catalyst in place of zinc chloride. The five OH groups acetylated are therefore presumably *not* on the 2, 3, 4, 5 and 6 sites as assumed above but on 1, 2, 3, 4 and 6 as in the ring structure.

We have assumed that a six-membered ring formula rather than a five-membered one is correct; this has been established for normal glucose by a number of arguments and methods. One way is to etherify the free OH groups (e.g. with methyl sulphate) and to show by degradation that it is carbon atom no. 5 that does not carry an —OMe group. Further discussion of this is beyond the scope of the present book. Under certain circumstances, however, it is believed that glucose and its derivatives do exist in five-membered ring forms.

The six-membered aromatic ring containing an oxygen atom (which can only exist in derivatives) is called *pyran* and the five-membered ring *furan*; six- and five-membered ring sugars can be regarded as derivatives of the totally hydrogenated derivatives of these:

$$
\begin{array}{cc}
CH_2 & \\
CH_2 \quad CH_2 & CH_2 - CH_2 \\
| \quad\quad | & | \quad\quad | \\
CH_2 \quad CH_2 & CH_2 \quad CH_2 \\
O & O
\end{array}
$$

and are therefore known respectively as *pyranoses* and *furanoses*.

On the above views, therefore, an aqueous solution of glucose is an equilibrium mixture of at least six types of molecule, viz. the α- and β-glucopyranoses and the α- and β-glucofuranoses, the open-chain aldehyde and the gem-diol. The first two, however, are believed to form by far the greatest part of the mixture.

Both the pyranose and furanose forms have the character of a cyclic hemiacetal, analogous for example to the substance $CH_3CH \begin{smallmatrix} OH \\ \\ OC_2H_5 \end{smallmatrix}$ which is believed to exist in equilibrium with acetaldehyde in ethanolic solution.

Stereochemistry of glucose

Examination of the open-chain aldehyde formula of glucose will show that carbon atoms 2, 3, 4 and 5 are asymmetric. There are therefore two possible configurations of the groups round each of them, and since no two of them are joined to precisely the same four groups, the total number of different molecules represented by this formula is 2^4, i.e. 16, in eight mirror-image pairs. One of the 16 is the natural (+)-glucose molecule; its mirror-image is *laevo*-rotatory (−)-glucose, which does not occur in nature. The other seven pairs represent seven other *aldohexose* sugars; all are known, and two of them, mannose and galactose, occur in one of the mirror-image forms in nature. Their stereochemical relationship has been fully worked out, and (+)-glucose is the isomer conventionally represented thus:

$$
\begin{array}{c}
\text{CHO} \\
|\\
\text{HCOH} \\
|\\
\text{HOCH} \\
|\\
\text{HCOH} \\
|\\
\text{HCOH} \\
|\\
\text{CH}_2\text{OH}
\end{array}
$$

To understand the meaning of this, we must start with glyceric aldehyde $CHO . CHOH . CH_2OH$. This is the simplest substance that can be said to have the general characteristics of an *aldose* sugar; it is in fact the only *aldotriose*. Carbon atom no. 2 in it is asymmetric, and glyceraldehyde exists in *dextro-* and *laevo-* rotatory forms. Imagine picking up a glyceraldehyde molecule and holding it so that (*a*) the hydrogen and OH groups project towards you, in a horizontal plane with the no. 2 carbon atom, (*b*) the CHO and CH_2OH groups project away from you, in a vertical plane with the no. 2 carbon atom, and (*c*) the CH_2OH is below the CHO. (The student is strongly advised to carry out all these operations with ball and spring models.) *By convention*, it was agreed that the OH group should be assumed to be to the right of the hydrogen atom in the molecule of (+)-glyceraldehyde and to the left in that of (−)-glyceraldehyde; these arrangements were respectively called D and L.

$$
\begin{array}{cc}
\text{CHO} & \text{CHO} \\
| & | \\
\text{H}\!\blacktriangleright\!\text{C}\!\blacktriangleleft\!\text{OH} & \text{HO}\!\blacktriangleright\!\text{C}\!\blacktriangleleft\!\text{H} \\
| & | \\
\text{CH}_2\text{OH} & \text{CH}_2\text{OH} \\
\text{(+)-glyceraldehyde} & \text{(−)-glyceraldehyde} \\
\text{a D-compound} & \text{an L-compound}
\end{array}
$$

(Fortunately, later work, outside the scope of this book, showed that this was in fact the correct assumption.)

If these formulae are now projected on to the plane of the paper, we get the conventional representation of D- and L-type molecules.

$$
\begin{array}{cc}
\text{CHO} & \text{CHO} \\
| & | \\
\text{H---C---OH} & \text{HO---C---H} \\
| & | \\
\text{CH}_2\text{OH} & \text{CH}_2\text{OH} \\
\text{D-glyceraldehyde} & \text{L-glyceraldehyde}
\end{array}
$$

Now pick up a (+)-glucose molecule, and first of all arrange that the successive C—C bonds have the tetrahedral angles between them all on the same side of the molecule, thus

and *not* zig-zag thus: ●\\●/●\\● in any place.

Now view the molecule as shown so that no. 5 carbon atom is arranged in the same way as the glyceraldehyde molecule above, hydrogen and OH towards you, CH_2OH at the bottom. You will find that the arrangement is D, not L. *Natural* (+)-*glucose is therefore said to belong to the* D *series of sugars.* (Most natural sugars and their derivatives belong to the D-series whether they are *dextro-* or *laevo-*rotatory; most L-sugars are laboratory arte-facts.) Now turn the glucose molecule as shown by the arrow so that carbon atoms 4, 3 and 2 are inspected in turn, each with the attached hydrogen and OH towards you, and plot the projected configurations, working upwards on the paper; the result will be the above formula. A convenient shorthand for this is:

$$+$$
$$-$$
$$+$$
$$+$$

L(−)-glucose on this convention is

$$
\begin{array}{c}
CHO \\
HOCH \\
HCOH \\
HOCH \\
HOCH \\
CH_2OH
\end{array}
$$

or

$$
\begin{array}{c}
- \\
+ \\
- \\
-
\end{array}
$$

The pyranose structure of glucose is sometimes represented as

$$
\begin{array}{c}
H\diagdown C \diagup OH \\
HCOH \\
HOCH \qquad O \\
HCOH \\
HC \\
CH_2OH
\end{array}
$$

in order to retain the above projection convention; on this system, all D-aldopyranoses will have the oxygen atom of the ring on the right. Such a formula, however, bears little relation to the shape of the glucose molecule, and perspective formulae such as

are now favoured. The following series of formulae should explain the relation between the two conventions without further comment.

(1)   (2)   (3)

(4)   α   (5)   β

It will be noticed that in the formula attributed to α-glucose, the −OH groups on carbon atoms 1 and 2 are on the same side of the ring, whereas in the β-form the −OH groups are alternatively above and below it, as are the remaining −OH groups of the α-form. This is in accordance with the observation that α-glucose, like glycerol and mannitol and other polyhydric alcohols with two −OH groups sterically placed to be able to co-ordinate with boron, increases the strength of boric acid in solution, whereas β-glucose does not.

Note that in the 'perspective ring' formulae, the angle between the CH and COH bonds is shown as 180° and not as 109½°; this is for ease of printing.

Formation of osazones

If glucose is heated with excess of phenylhydrazine in weakly acid aqueous solution, reaction proceeds beyond the formation of a phenyl-hydrazone to yield a handsome yellow crystalline solid known as *glucosazone*. Three moles of phenylhydrazine react with one mole of glucose; two become attached as phenylhydrazone residues to carbon atoms 1 and 2, while the third is reduced to ammonia and aniline. The following scheme is consistent with these facts:

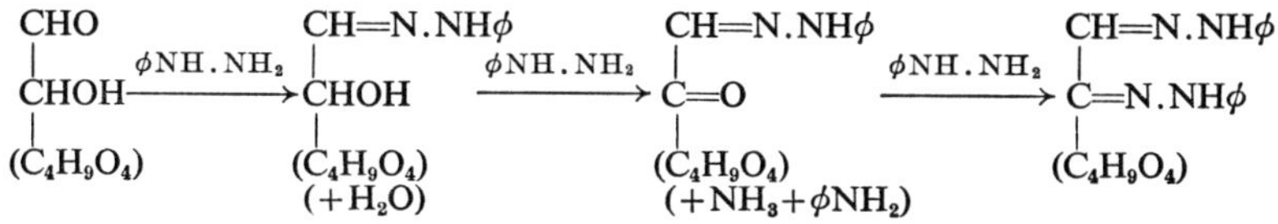

$$
\begin{array}{llll}
\mathrm{CHO} & \mathrm{CH{=}N.NH}\phi & \mathrm{CH{=}N.NH}\phi & \mathrm{CH{=}N.NH}\phi \\
| \quad\quad \phi\mathrm{NH.NH_2} & | \quad\quad \phi\mathrm{NH.NH_2} & | \quad\quad \phi\mathrm{NH.NH_2} & | \\
\mathrm{CHOH} \xrightarrow{\quad\quad} & \mathrm{CHOH} \xrightarrow{\quad\quad} & \mathrm{C{=}O} \xrightarrow{\quad\quad} & \mathrm{C{=}N.NH}\phi \\
| & | & | & | \\
\mathrm{(C_4H_9O_4)} & \mathrm{(C_4H_9O_4)} & \mathrm{(C_4H_9O_4)} & \mathrm{(C_4H_9O_4)} \\
& \mathrm{(+H_2O)} & \mathrm{(+NH_3+}\phi\mathrm{NH_2)} &
\end{array}
$$

but it cannot be considered satisfactory for two reasons. First, since some of the strongest reducing agents (such, for example, as titanium (III) salts) do not reduce phenylhydrazine, the second step seems most improbable. Secondly, the scheme offers no reason why the remaining CHOH groups remain unattacked. Further discussion of these points will be found in more advanced text-books; the above over-simple scheme will however serve as a mnemonic.

Since sugars are often difficult to crystallize, especially if impure, the markedly crystalline osazones proved invaluable for separating and characterizing them. In fact, phenylhydrazine has been colourfully but not undeservedly described as 'the key with which Emil Fischer unlocked the secret of the sugars'. It will be seen that two aldohexoses which differ only in the configuration of the no. 2 carbon atom will yield the same osazone; a valuable short cut to the structure of one if the other is known.

Fructose

Fructose, like glucose, occurs in fruit juices—hence its name. Its occurrence in honey and as part of the sucrose molecule has been mentioned on p. 317. Inulin is a fructosan present in artichoke and dahlia tubers, and can be used as a manufacturing source of fructose. Physically, fructose is very similar to glucose, but sweeter and more soluble in water; natural fructose is, however, *laevo*-rotatory (hence the old name 'laevulose'). Since α_D for fructose (in equilibrium solution) is $-90°$, numerically greater than the value for glucose, the equimolar mixture of glucose and fructose obtained by hydrolysing sucrose is *laevo*-rotatory, though sucrose itself is *dextro-*

325

rotatory; hence the term 'inversion of cane sugar', applied to this hydro-lysis, and the name 'invert sugar' of the mixture.

Reactions and structure

By reactions and arguments analogous to those for glucose, the fructose molecule can be deduced to possess a $>C=O$ and five OH groups. Fructose gives a silver mirror with Tollen's reagent (a reaction given by α-hydroxy ketones as well as by aldehydes), but the oxidation breaks down the mole-cule into C_2 and C_4 acids in equimolar proportions. Furthermore, Kiliani's cyanohydrin synthesis yields ultimately the acid:

$$\begin{array}{c} CH_3 \\ | \\ CH_3(CH_2)_3CH.CO_2H \end{array}$$

Fructose is therefore given the open-chain formula

$$\begin{array}{c} CH_2OH \\ | \\ CO \\ | \\ CHOH \\ | \\ CHOH \\ | \\ CHOH \\ | \\ CH_2OH \end{array}$$

and is an example of a *ketohexose*.

With phenylhydrazine, fructose yields the same osazone as glucose, though rather more rapidly. Its stereochemical formula is therefore:

$$\begin{array}{c} CH_2OH \\ | \\ CO \\ | \\ HOCH \\ | \\ HCOH \\ | \\ HCOH \\ | \\ CH_2OH \end{array}$$

In spite of being *laevo*-rotatory, it is therefore a D-sugar—D($-$)-fructose.

Fructose, like glucose, shows muta-rotation, and for analogous reasons is allotted a pyranose formula:

$$\begin{array}{c} CH_2OH \\ | \\ C-OH \\ \diagdown \\ CHOH \quad O \\ | \qquad | \\ CHOH \quad CH_2 \\ \diagdown \quad \diagup \\ CHOH \end{array}$$

(Note that it is therefore the 6 —OH group that forms the hemiacetal with the $>C=O$ group, and that the ring contains a CH_2 group).

In combination, however (as for example in sucrose or inulin) the fructose ring is invariably found in the furanose form:

$$
\begin{array}{c}
CH_2OH \\
| \quad OH \\
\underline{\quad} C < \\
CHOH \quad\quad O \\
\backslash \quad\quad / \\
CHOH—CH—CH_2OH
\end{array}
$$

Disaccharides

The most familiar disaccharides are *sucrose* (ordinary domestic 'sugar', obtained from the sugar-cane or sugar-beet), *maltose* (formed by the enzymatic hydrolysis of starch using malt or suitable fungi) and *lactose* (the sugar present in mammalian milk). Sucrose is an example of a *non-reducing* disaccharide, maltose and lactose of *reducing* disaccharides. The chief differences can be tabulated, thus:

Reducing (e.g. maltose, lactose)	Non-reducing (e.g. sucrose)
Reduce Fehling's solution and ammoniacal silver oxide	Do not
Muta-rotate	Do not
Form osazones	Do not

Both types undergo hydrolyses by dilute acids, 1 mole yielding two moles of monosaccharide.

Sucrose → glucose and fructose
Maltose → glucose only
Lactose → glucose and galactose

The two monosaccharide molecules are therefore probably joined by an 'acetal' type link.

We infer that in maltose and lactose, the 'potential' carbonyl group of one of the monosaccharide molecules is not involved in the link, and thus this part of the disaccharide can show the usual monosaccharide reactions, as above. In sucrose, on the other hand, the acetal link is between the two potential carbonyl groups themselves, and thus neither half of the molecule can show characteristic aldo- or keto-hexose behaviour.

The structures allotted to these three disaccharides are shown on p. 328. (It will be seen that the C—O—C link between the rings is represented as

$$
\begin{array}{c}
| \quad\quad | \\
>C \quad C< \\
\backslash\underline{\quad O\quad}/
\end{array}
$$

rather than $\rangle C\langle_O\rangle C\langle$. This is to preserve consistency with the '180°' convention mentioned on p. 324 above.) It will be seen that the sugar residue on the right-hand side is linked to the left-hand one in the same way that the methyl group is linked in the methyl glucosides.

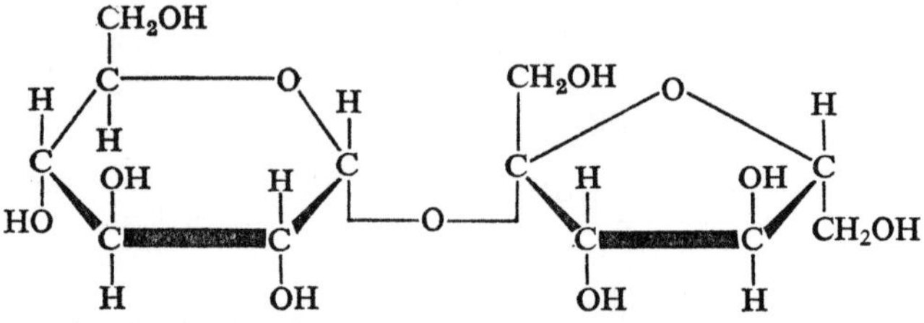

glucopyranose unit   fructofuranose unit

sucrose

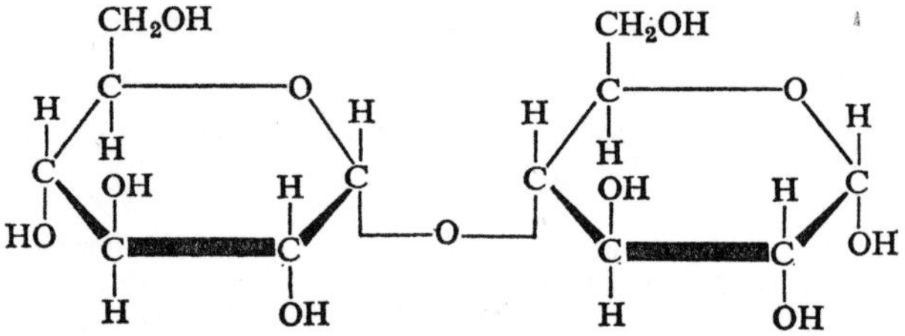

glucopyranose unit   glucopyranose unit

maltose (α-isomer)

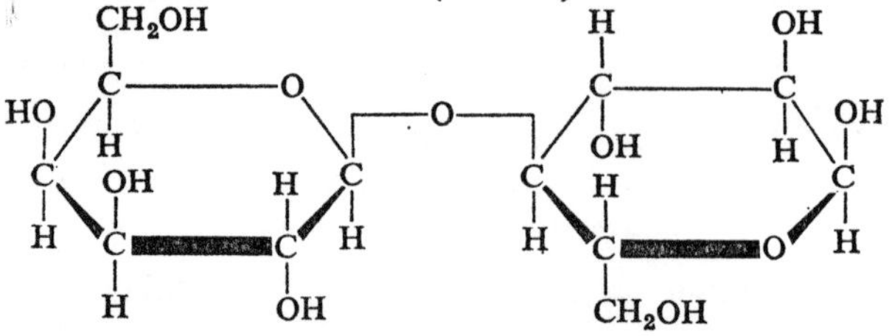

galactopyranose unit   glucopyranose unit

lactose (α-isomer)

The allocation of formulae such as the above involves the establishment by experiment of the following points:

(1) Which pair of carbon atoms is linked by the C—O—C bond. In a non-reducing sugar, these must be the two 'potential carbonyl' carbon atoms; in a reducing sugar, *one* of the carbon atoms must be elsewhere in the ring (but not both, otherwise the C—O—C link would be ether type rather than acetal type, and presumably much more resistant to hydrolysis, and the resulting molecule would have *two* potential carbonyl groups).

(2) Whether the monosaccharide unit linked by the potential carbonyl

carbon atom is in the α- or β-form (since these are no longer readily interconvertible in the glycoside, as opposed to the free monosaccharide). In a non-reducing sugar, this point will need settling for *both* carbon atoms of the C—O—C link.

Point (1) can be settled by methylation studies; on conversion of the free —OH groups to —OMe groups, and subsequent hydrolysis, the —OH group on the carbon atom involved in the C—O—C link remains unmethylated.

Point (2) can be settled by using the specificity of enzymes such as maltase and emulsin, which catalyse the hydrolysis of glucosides. These enzymes are known as *glucosidases* (or, more generally, where the substrates are derived from sugars other than glucose, as *glycosidases*). As mentioned above, maltase catalyses the hydrolysis of α-methylglucoside, emulsin that of β-methylglucoside. In general, the hydrolysis of any compound containing a glucoside-type link, including disaccharides, is catalysed by one or the other but not by both. Maltose is hydrolysed in the presence of maltase but not of emulsin; the link between the glucose units in it is therefore α-glucosidic in character.

Similar specificity is shown by other glycosidases. Lactase, which catalyses the hydrolysis of lactose, is a β-galactosidase, and the link binding the glucose unit to the galactose unit is therefore *β-galactosidic* in character.

In sucrose, where the link is both glucosidic and fructosidic (involving the 'potential carbonyl' groups of *both* units) enzyme studies show that the link is α-*glucosidic* and β-*fructosidic*.

Polysaccharides

Starch

Starch is separable into two fractions—about 20% is soluble in hot water ('amylose') and the remainder ('amylopectin') is not.

Enzymatic hydrolysis yields maltose from both, and both are believed to consist of chains of glucopyranose molecules, each linked to the next at C atom 4 by an α-glucoside link. Since amylase brings about complete hydrolysis of amylose, but not of amylopectin, it is believed that in the latter the chains are linked to each other at some other position than carbon atom 4, probably at carbon atom 6.

Amylose has a probable molecular weight about 10 000 to 50 000, amylopectin much higher (up to 1 000 000).

Organic Chemistry

Glycogen

Similar to amylopectin, but it has a shorter and a more highly branched chain.

Cellulose

Like starch and glycogen, cellulose is built up of glucose units but, unlike these, yields the disaccharide *cellobiose* on enzymatic hydrolysis. It differs from maltose in having a β- and not an α-type link between the glucose units. The cellulose chain thus differs structurally from amylose in being built up of β-glucose and not α-glucose molecules. This seemingly small difference makes an immense difference to the properties of the material. Whereas starch and glycogen molecules 'curl up' into more or less spherical shape, cellulose molecules aggregate into fibres, in which X-ray diffraction studies show a fair degree of parallel orientation of the long cellulose molecules. Whereas starch and glycogen are the forms in which plants and animals respectively store their reserves of carbohydrates, cellulose is essentially a structural material and forms the main constituent of plant cell walls.

Biological importance of carbohydrates

This is a very extensive topic which can only briefly be hinted at here. For further information the student should consult text-books of biochemistry.

The oxidation of carbohydrates forms one of the main energy sources of both plants and animals. Green plants, containing chlorophyll, can synthesize carbohydrates from carbon dioxide and water in the presence of sunlight (photosynthesis). Animals cannot do this, and depend on green plants, either directly in the case of herbivores, or indirectly in the case of carnivores, for their food supplies of carbohydrate.

Carbohydrates enter the blood as monosaccharides. Disaccharides, starch and glycogen in food are degraded to monosaccharides by the enzymes present in saliva and in the gut. Man and the other carnivores cannot utilize cellulose as a food carbohydrate, since they lack the enzymes needed for its degradation. Animals which chew the cud (ruminants) can do so, however, as their guts contain micro-organisms which degrade the cellulose to glucose and other products.

Many plants contain glycosides—for example, the amygdalin of almonds and other prunus kernels, which is a glycoside of benzaldehyde cyano-

330

hydrin and a disaccharide, gentiobiose. Plants normally contain enzymes capable of breaking down their own glycosides, and which will do so if the tissues are crushed, thus allowing enzyme and substrate to come into contact. It is probable that the function of the enzyme in the living plant is to catalyse the *formation* of the glycoside, and that the function of this is to convert otherwise toxic byproducts of the plant's metabolism into compounds harmless to the plant.

The fermentation of carbohydrates to ethanol has been briefly discussed on p. 141 and to acetone and butanol on p. 196.

The industrial importance of cellulose

Cellulose fibres are technologically the most widely used of all natural fibres. Cotton and linen are practically pure cellulose. Wood fibres are mainly cellulose, and although the fibres are too short for spinning, wood pulp is used in the manufacture of paper and of artificial fibres of cellulose and cellulose derivatives ('rayons'). Cellulose esters and ethers are also used as plastics. These artificial fibres and plastics from cellulose are dealt with in the following chapter.

Fibres and plastics

Fibres

Since mankind moved out of skins into woven clothing, natural fibres have been among the essential raw materials of civilization. In the twentieth century, the industrial organic chemist has been able to supplement these natural fibres with artificial ones.

The most widely used natural fibres consist of either cellulose (cotton, linen) or proteins (wool, silk). Chemically, fibres consist of long molecules, with a regular repeating structural unit, which may be comparatively simple, like the β-glucose unit of cellulose, or more complex, like the polypeptide units of fibroin (silk) or keratin (wool). Furthermore, X-ray diffraction studies show that in the fibre, these are regions where the long molecules run regularly parallel in an ordered way, and that these regions of crystallinity are themselves oriented with their axes more or less parallel. The production of artificial fibres therefore involves synthesizing suitable long molecules and orienting them in a way which will give the necessary fibre strength; the first stage is by-passed if naturally occurring long molecules are used, from fibrous materials which in their natural state are unsuitable for direct use in spinning and weaving.

Cellulose-based artificial fibres

Wood-pulp fibres and the short cotton fibres ('linters') remaining when the long fibres have been combed out cannot be spun into usable thread; these materials can be used as the bases of artificial fibres. The cellulose molecules need, as it were, 'sorting out' and reorienting; in order to do this the molecules must be got into solution. Cellulose does not dissolve without chemical change in any common solvent and it must be converted to a soluble derivative. If the solution so obtained is forced through small holes and the long molecules removed from solution, while the resulting thread is under tension the required orientation of the molecules is achieved and fibres of the necessary tensile strength can be formed. Two processes using these principles are commercially operated.

In the *viscose* processes, sheets of wood pulp are steeped in aqueous sodium hydroxide. Sodium and hydroxyl ions become incorporated in the structure of the fibres, which swell up, forming 'alkali cellulose'. This material, dried and shredded, is agitated with carbon bisulphide. Some of the —OH groups of the cellulose undergo the following reaction:

$$-OH + CS_2 + OH^\ominus \rightarrow -O-CS_2{}^\ominus + H_2O$$

the product being a half-ester, half salt, of dithiocarbonic acid $\begin{smallmatrix} HO \\ \\ HS \end{smallmatrix} \!\!\!\! \diagdown C{=}S$

known as cellulose *xanthate* (from its yellow colour). This substance, unlike cellulose itself, carries a large number of anionic charges on each molecule, and disperses in water to form a yellow-orange viscous colloidal solution. This is forced through the minute holes of a platinum 'spinneret' (shaped roughly like a small top-hat, approximately $\frac{1}{2}$ in. in diameter, with the holes in the crown) into aqueous sulphuric acid containing zinc salts and various other additives. Presumably these assist in coagulating the colloidal cellulose as it is thrown out of solution by acid hydrolysis of the xanthate. The threads are wound under tension onto bobbins. The process may be summarized:

$$\text{cellulose} \xrightarrow{\text{NaOH}_{Aq}} \text{alkali cellulose} \xrightarrow{\text{CS}_2} \text{cellulose xanthate}$$

$$\xrightarrow{\text{water}} \text{viscose solution} \xrightarrow{\text{H}_2\text{SO}_{4Aq}} \text{regenerated cellulose.}$$

The final product is therefore chemically the same as the raw material; no linking up to form larger molecules has occurred. (In fact, the average chain length of the molecules is less, owing to hydrolytic degradation of the cellulose during the processing.) The whole process is therefore directed essentially to 'remodelling', not the molecules, but the state of molecular aggregation.

(The old *cuprammonium* process, now obsolete, was similar in principle. The cellulose was dispersed in aqueous tetrammino copper (II) hydroxide (Schweitzer's Reagent) and regenerated by spinning into aqueous acid.)

In the *acetate* process, wood pulp or cotton linters are esterified by agitation with *acetic* anhydride in either glacial acetic acid or methylene dichloride as solvent, with a small amount of sulphuric acid as catalyst. The product is practically completely acetylated cellulose ('cellulose triacetate'). Since this is insoluble in acetone, the solvent to be used, it is allowed to stand in contact with aqueous acetic acid until hydrolysis has reduced the acetyl content to about two thirds of the original value ('cellulose diacetate'). This is then dried, dissolved in acetone and spun from spinnerets, the acetone being evaporated by warm air to leave a fibre of cellulose acetate. In contrast to the viscose process, therefore, the fibre consists of a derivative of cellulose and not of regenerated cellulose. In summary, the process is:

$$\text{cellulose} \xrightarrow{\text{(MeCO)}_2\text{O}} \text{cellulose triacetate} \xrightarrow{\text{H}_2\text{O}} \text{cellulose diacetate}$$

$$\xrightarrow{\text{acetone}} \text{'spinning dope'} \xrightarrow[\text{and evaporation}]{\text{spinning}} \text{acetate rayon fibre}$$

The viability of the cellulose acetate process depends on sedulously efficient recovery of the acetone (by charcoal absorption) and of the acetic acid liberated in the acetylation and hydrolysis steps.

Both types of fibre are known as 'rayons'; the obsolete term 'artificial silk' was properly frowned on by the manufacturers.

Viscose is extensively used in tyres as well as for clothing and other fabrics; acetate rayon is used for decorative clothing and furnishing fabrics.

Synthetic fibres

In truly synthetic fibres, the industrial chemist builds up 'tailored' long molecules by the controlled interaction of relatively small molecules. If two 'small' molecules each containing a single functional group interact, the resulting molecule will itself be a 'small' molecule. The same will be true if one of the two molecules contains two functional groups, each of which reacts with the single functional group of the other. (Thus for example, benzoic acid or phthalic acid react with methanol to yield esters of low molecular weight.) If, however, both molecules are bifunctional, then there is the possibility of forming chain molecules of indefinite length, since the initial product of reaction of two molecules will itself be bifunctional, and so on indefinitely. Thus extending the above example, the esterification of phthalic acid with ethylene glycol could (and does) form chains of the type:

$$-\text{OCH}_2 \cdot \text{CH}_2\text{O}-\text{CO} \quad \text{CO}-\text{OCH}_2 \cdot \text{CH}_2\text{O}-\text{CO} \quad \text{CO}-\text{OCH}_2 \cdot \text{CH}_2\text{O}-\text{CO} \quad \text{CO}-\text{OCH}_2 \cdot \text{CH}_2\text{O}-$$

(Ring formation is an alternative possibility—as for example in the reaction of two molecules of glycollic acid to form glycollide rather than a long-chain ester.)

334

The main types of reaction leading to long-chain molecules suitable for synthetic fibre manufacture are listed below:

Polymerization of olefins

$$C{=}C+C{=}C \rightarrow -C-C-C-C-$$

Polyester formation

$$HO-R-OH+HOCO.R'.COOH$$
$$\rightarrow -ORO-CO.R'.CO-$$

Polyamide formation

$$H_2N-R-NH_2+HOCO.R'.COOH$$
$$\rightarrow -NH.R.NH.CO.R'.CO-$$

or

$$H_2N-R-COOH \rightarrow -NH.R.CO.NH.R.CO-$$

Not all long molecules that can be made in these general ways are suitable for fibre production. Some of the most important processes in commercial operation are discussed in outline in the following sections of this chapter.

Acrylic fibres

The principal olefinic compound polymerized for fibre manufacture is acrylonitrile (vinyl cyanide) $CH_2{=}CH-C{\equiv}N$.

This is made either by the addition of hydrogen cyanide to ethylene oxide, followed by dehydration of the ethylene cyanohydrin, or by the catalysed addition of hydrogen cyanide to acetylene. The acrylonitrile is polymerized in part-solution, part-suspension in water. The polymer is spun from solution in much the same way as cellulose acetate.

$$C_2H_2 + HCN \longrightarrow$$
$$\text{or}$$
$$\underset{O}{CH_2{-}CH_2} + HCN \longrightarrow HOCH_2CH_2CN \longrightarrow CH_2{=}CH-CN \longrightarrow$$

$$\text{polyacrylonitrile} \xrightarrow{\text{solvent}} \text{spinning solution} \xrightarrow{\text{evaporation}} \text{acrylic fibre}$$

Various types of catalyst have been used for the polymerization step, including such characteristic olefin polymerization initiators as organic peroxides, other oxidizing agents and organic-metallic compounds. The probable function of these is discussed later in the chapter.

Polyacrylonitrile fibres are marketed under such names as 'Orlon', 'Acrilan' and 'Courtelle'.

Polyester fibres

The long-chain ester of terephthalic acid and ethylene glycol is widely used in fabrics under such trade-names as 'Terylene'.

Terephthalic acid is obtained by the oxidation of the side-chains of *p*-xylene. In practice it is found more effective not to esterify this directly with glycol, but to make the dimethyl ester and then 'trans-esterify' this with glycol. The polyester is then melted and spun from the melt through spinnerets, the thread resolidifying on cooling under tension. In summary, the process is:

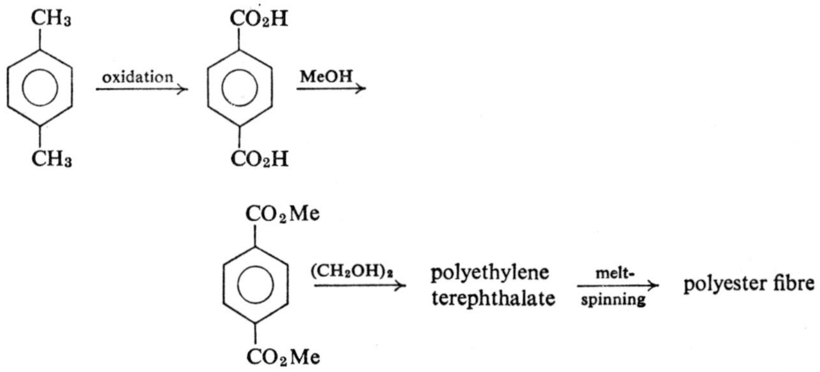

Polyamide fibres

N-substituted amides are obtained when a carboxylic acid (or a derivative) condenses in an acylation reaction with an organic amine. Thus a

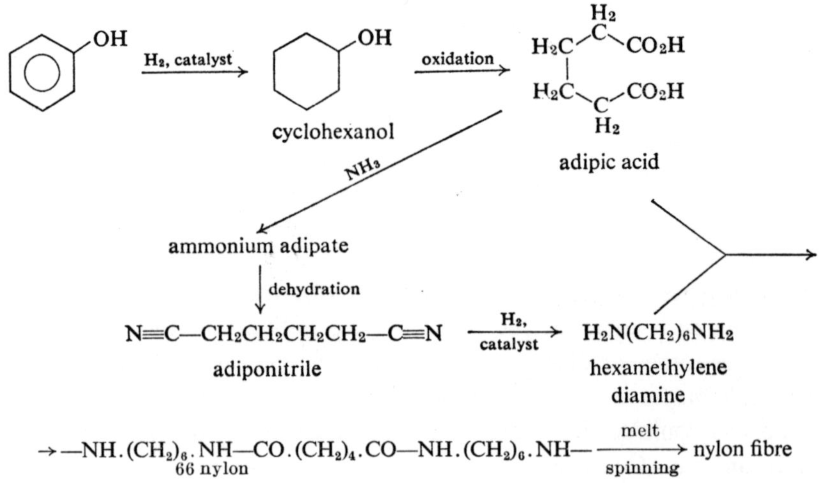

N≡C—CH₂CH₂CH₂CH₂—C≡N $\xrightarrow[\text{catalyst}]{\text{H}_2,}$ H₂N(CH₂)₆NH₂

adiponitrile   hexamethylene
                                                  diamine

→ —NH.(CH₂)₆.NH—CO.(CH₂)₄.CO—NH.(CH₂)₆.NH— $\xrightarrow[\text{spinning}]{\text{melt}}$ nylon fibre
                66 nylon

336

long-chain polyamide can be obtained by acylating a diamine with a dibasic acid, but the alternative of forming a chain molecule by the interaction of the —COOH and —NH$_2$ groups of an amino-acid is also operated commercially. Both types of products are known generically as 'nylons'.

'66 nylon' is made from adipic acid and hexamethylenediamine. A possible route using phenol as the initial raw material is summarized above, but adipic acid can be made from other materials, such as cyclohexane, and hexamethylenediamine from other sources than adipic acid.

The significance of '66' is that the —NH— groups link chains of 6 carbon atoms, which are alternately of two types, —(CH$_2$)$_6$— and —CO(CH$_2$)$_4$CO—.

'6' nylon is made in essence from 6-aminohexanoic acid, although this is mainly in the form of its internal cyclic amide or lactam, called caprolactam, a 7-membered ring compound:

$$\begin{array}{c} H_2 \\ H_2C{\overset{C}{\diagup}}^{\diagdown}CO \\ H_2C \quad\quad\quad NH \\ {\diagdown}C{-}CH_2 \\ H_2 \end{array}$$

(Caproic acid is the trivial name of hexanoic acid.)

Caprolactam can be made from the oxime of cyclohexanone by a well-known general reaction of oximes known as the Beckmann rearrangement.

cyclohexanone oxime

Formally, the polyamide chain is a strict polymer of this:

$$-CONH(CH_2)_5CONH(CH_2)_5CONH-$$

Its formation involves opening the lactam ring; this can be achieved by heating the lactam with a small amount of 6-aminohexanoic acid itself. A possible explanation would be a nucleophilic attack of the free —NH$_2$ of the acid on the $\rangle$C$=$O of the lactam, with consequent opening of the ring:

followed by proton transfers and repetition of the process.

The name '6-nylon' implies that all the C_6 units of the chain are alike. Both of the above nylons are melt-spun in the same way as Terylene.

Plastics

Plastics are materials which can be moulded to shape while in a pliable or plastic condition, but which can by suitable treatment acquire some degree of rigidity after shaping.

The great extension in the use of plastics, supplementing or replacing more traditional materials such as wood, metals and glass is one of the most striking contributions of the industrial organic chemist to the twentieth-century scene. (Glass, of course, can be regarded on the above definition as a plastic, though an inorganic one.) Chemically, plastic materials consist of large molecules; some of the materials used in artificial fibres can also be used as plastics. Thus nylons can be cast in moulds as well as extruded; to a limited extent, polyacrylonitrile softens on heating and can be moulded under pressure. Polyethylene terephthalate, cellulose esters and viscose can all be extruded through slot orifices to produce films as sheets or tapes rather than fibre. There are, however, a large number of high molecular weight materials not suitable for making fibres which are in commercial use as plastics, some of which are reviewed below.

Materials such as nylon, linear polyesters like terylene and other materials described below, which soften or melt on heating and can be moulded or cast in this state, and set again on cooling, are known as *thermoplastic* materials. Others are used in the forms of 'moulding powders' which on heating under pressure fuse and then harden irreversibly as a result of chemical change; these are *thermosetting* materials. Others again are converted from syrups to hard materials by 'curing' under the action of other reagents.

Polyolefin and polyvinyl plastics

The polymerization of compounds containing olefinic double bonds leads to some of the best known plastics. The main types are summarized below.

Polythene

Monomer: ethylene. Production of monomer: cracking of petroleum fractions in the presence of steam. Polymerization conditions: (*a*) heating at very high pressures (several tons per square inch) in the presence of a small amount of oxygen or organic peroxide; (*b*) (more recent) at moderate pressures in presence of *Ziegler* catalyst (organo-aluminium compounds and $Ti^{(III)}$ or $Ti^{(IV)}$ compounds). Basic structure of polymer:

$$-CH_2-CH_2-CH_2-CH_2-$$

Polythene is thermoplastic (softening above 100° C) and resistant to chemical attack, except by such vigorous reagents as hot concentrated nitric acid. It is familiar in domestic ware and laboratory sinks and waste-pipes, and as a film for packaging.

Polypropylene

Monomer: propylene from the cracking of petroleum. Manufacture and properties of the polymer: similar to polythene. Basic structure: $-CH(CH_3).CH_2-CH(CH_3).CH_2-$. Polypropylene has a higher softening point than polythene. It is used for miscellaneous plastic goods (suitcases, bottle crates, toys, laboratory ware) and for packaging film. Recently, fibres of polypropylene have been developed commercially.

Polystyrene

Monomer: styrene (vinylbenzene) $C_6H_5.CH{=}CH_2$. Production of monomer:

$$C_6H_6 + CH_2{:}CH_2 \xrightarrow{AlCl_3} C_6H_5.CH_2.CH_3 \xrightarrow[ZnO,\ 600°C]{-H_2} C_6H_5.CH{=}CH_2$$

Polymerization conditions: rapid on heating in presence of oxygen or peroxides. Basic structure:

$$-CH(C_6H_5)CH_2-CH(C_6H_5)CH_2-$$

Polystyrene is thermoplastic; it has outstandingly good electrical insulating properties. Styrene is co-polymerized (see below) with butadiene in some synthetic rubbers.

Polyvinyl chloride (P.V.C.)

Monomer: vinyl chloride (monochloroethylene) $CH_2{=}CH-Cl$. Production of monomer:

(*a*) $\qquad CH{\equiv}CH + HCl \xrightarrow{HgCl} CH_2{=}CH-Cl$ (see p. 66)

or (*b*) $\qquad CH_2{=}CH_2 + Cl_2 \longrightarrow CH_2Cl.CH_2Cl \xrightarrow{-HCl} CH_2{=}CH.Cl$
$\qquad\qquad\qquad\qquad\qquad\qquad\qquad\qquad\quad$ (alkali or heat)

Polymerization conditions: heat, peroxides or oxidizing agents. Basic structure:

$$-CH_2.CHCl-CH_2.CHCl-CH_2.CHCl-$$

P.V.C. is thermoplastic; its plasticity can be increased by incorporating 'plasticizers'—relatively low molecular weight organic materials—during moulding or extrusion. It is a very versatile material and can be used in sheets, pipes, in upholstery and for weatherproof outer clothing. Fibres of P.V.C. have been developed.

Polyvinyl acetate (P.V.A.)

Monomer: vinyl acetate $CH_3CO_2CH=CH_2$. Production of monomer: $CH\equiv CH + CH_3CO_2H \rightarrow CH_3CO_2CH=CH_2$ (see p. 66).

Polymerization conditions: heat, peroxide or oxidizing agents. Basic structure: $-CH(OCOCH_3)CH_2-CH(OCOCH_3).CH_2-$

Polyvinyl acetate is thermoplastic. It can be used in solution and in aqueous emulsions of solutions in adhesives and emulsion paints. A further range of polyvinyl plastics can be made by hydrolysing polyvinyl acetate in aqueous acid or alkali to yield polyvinyl alcohol:

$$-CHOH-CH_2-CHOH-CH_2-$$

(and acetic acid) and this in turn can be converted to polyvinyl acetals with aldehydes and acid catalysts; for example, with formaldehyde to :

Both types have specialized uses.

Polymethyl methacrylate ('Perspex')

Monomer: methyl methacrylate $CH_2=\underset{\underset{CH_3}{|}}{C}-CO_2CH_3$. Production of monomer:

Polymerization conditions: heat, peroxides. Basic structure:

Polymethylmethacrylate is a thermoplastic substance which can be cast into sheets, flat or shaped, of outstanding transparency (hence the trade-names 'Perspex', 'Luciglas') and resistance to weather, light and chemical action. It is also used for moulded articles and lacquers.

Polytetrafluoroethylene ('PTFE')

Monomer: tetrafluoroethylene $CF_2{=}CF_2$. Production of monomer: pyrolysis of CHF_2Cl (from metallic fluorides and HF on chlorinated methane). Polymerization conditions; peroxides, moderated by water. Basic structure: $-CF_2-CF_2-CF_2-$. Polytetrafluoroethylene is a relatively expensive material, but is practically inert to any type of chemical attack (a property of fully halogenated fluorocarbons) and can be used for electrical insulation, etc., where complete chemical inertness is essential. It is familiar in everyday life as the protective film in 'non-stick' cooking vessels.

The ubiquity of peroxides or other oxidizing agents as initiators for the polymerization of olefinic compounds is striking. Peroxides dissociate to form a pair of free radicals, one of which can be represented as $R\cdot$, with an unpaired electron. This reacts with an olefin molecule to form another free radical; for example,

$$R\cdot + CH_2{=}CH_2 \to R-CH_2-CH_2\cdot$$

which attacks yet another olefin molecule, and so on in a chain reaction. Reaction chains will be terminated by the combination of two free radicals; for example,

$$R(CH_2)_n\cdot + \cdot(CH_2)_m R \to R(CH_2)_{n+m}R$$

to form a normal molecule, which may contain as many as 1000 or more monomer units. Other oxidizing agents possibly operate to produce peroxides *in situ*. Organo-metallic compounds, which also appear as polymerization initiators, may also act as sources of free radicals.

Rubber is a natural polymer of the diolefin *isoprene* (2-methylbutadiene):

$$CH_2{=}C(CH_3)-CH{=}CH_2$$

The repeating chain unit is thus

$$-CH_2-C(CH_3){=}CH-CH_2-,$$

the isoprene molecules combining by the process of terminal addition typical of conjugated polyolefins (compare the addition of bromine to butadiene itself:

$$Br_2 + CH_2{=}CH-CH{=}CH_2 \to BrCH_2-CH{=}CH-CH_2Br)$$

341

Since the chains are still unsaturated, they can themselves polymerize; that is, *cross-linking* between chains can occur. This happens to some extent in the *vulcanization* of rubber, in which it is milled with small amounts of sulphur and 'accelerators'. The nature of the cross-linking is not fully understood, but it may involve both C—C and C—S—C links. Most *synthetic rubbers* resemble natural rubber in being polymers of conjugated diolefins. Instead of isoprene, the parent monomers are *chloroprene* CH_2=CCl—CH=CH_2 (in 'neoprene') and butadiene itself CH_2=CH—CH=CH_2 (in 'Buna' rubbers—so called because the polymerization of *bu*tadiene is initiated by sodium metal, or in German, *Na*trium). The preparation of chloroprene is dealt with on p. 66; butadiene is obtained by the catalytic dehydrogenation of butane.

Other unsaturated compounds can be incorporated by 'co-polymerization' in the rubber structure. Thus Buna-S rubbers contain styrene units and Buna-N rubbers acrylonitrile.

Rubber-like polymers are also made from isobutylene $(CH_3)_2C$=CH_2 mixed with a small amount of butadiene.

Polyurethanes

These plastics have become increasingly familiar in recent decades, especially as polyurethane foams.

A 'urethane' is an addition product of an organic isocyanate and an alcohol; for example,

$$C_6H_5N=C=O + C_2H_5OH \rightarrow C_6H_5NHC\overset{O}{\underset{OC_2H_5}{\diagup}}$$

(the urethane being therefore an ester of an *N*-alkyl or *N*-arylcarbamic acid). Dihydric alcohols and di-isocyanates will yield chain polyurethanes. The reaction can also be used to cross-link chain molecules containing —OH groups.

Thermosetting plastics

Two of the best-known types of plastics are based on the use of formaldehyde to bring about chain-formation and cross-linking. These are *phenolformaldehyde* plastics, known universally as Bakelite after their discoverer Baekeland, and *urea-formaldhyde* plastics, marketed under such names as 'Beetle'.

Bakelite

Phenol and formalin are heated together with sulphuric acid as catalyst, the water from the formalin and that released in the reaction being allowed to distil off at reduced pressure. The product, a viscous fluid, is run out into trays and set to a transparent pale brown resin. Up to this stage it is believed that phenol molecules have become linked by methylene groups attached to their ortho- and para-positions, but little if any cross-linking has occurred, and the product is thermoplastic, like the other chain-type polymers described above. The chain-forming reactions are probably of the type:

$$C_6H_5OH + HCHO \xrightarrow{H^{\oplus}} HO.C_6H_4.CH_2OH$$
$$(o \text{ and } p\text{-isomers})$$

$$HO.C_6H_4.CH_2OH + C_6H_5OH \rightarrow HO.C_6H_4.CH_2.C_6H_4.OH + H_2O$$
$$(o\text{- or } p\text{-linking})$$

Reaction with more formaldehyde at one of the unoccupied *o*- or *p*-sites and further condensation with phenol yields chains of the general type:

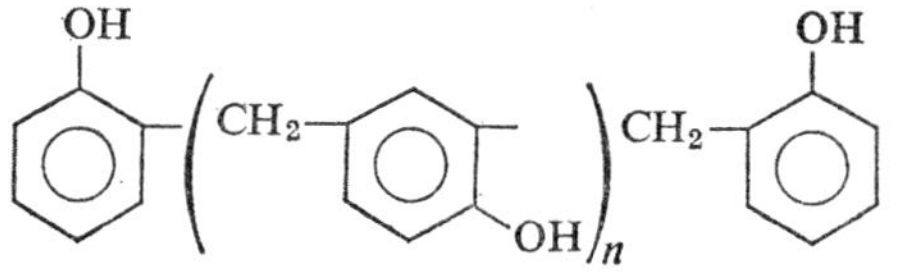

though the —CH$_2$—links need not be alternately *o*- and *p*-. These reactions are essentially of the Friedel–Crafts type. This material is crushed and powdered and mixed with pigments, 'fillers' (such as wood flour) and hexamethylenetetramine (the condensation product of formaldehyde and ammonia) to form a moulding powder. When this is heated in the mould the resin fuses, cross-linking occurs between the unoccupied *ortho*- or *para*-sites of the phenol residues, and resin sets to the final infusible, moulded product which is a three-dimensional macromolecule. The cross-links are probably partly —CH$_2$—, partly nitrogen-containing, in either case arising from the hexamethylenetetramine.

Bakelite was among the earliest commercially produced plastics. Bakelite articles, if pigmented, are usually made fairly dark and opaque, as the unpigmented resin is slightly coloured, and darkens with age.

Urea-formaldehyde and melamine plastics

Urea and formalin heated in the presence of a little ammonia give a thermoplastic intermediate which can be made into moulding powders and has thermosetting properties.

The probable reactions are of the type:

$$\underset{NH_2}{\overset{NH_2}{\diagup}}CO \quad +2HCHO \rightarrow \underset{NH.CH_2OH}{\overset{NH.CH_2OH}{\diagup}}CO$$

—CONH.CH$_2$OH + H$_2$N.CO— $\rightarrow$ —CONH.CH$_2$NH.CO— + H$_2$O

Cross-linking proceeds similarly, with the formation of tertiary nitrogen atoms with —CH$_2$— cross-links, forming a three-dimensional macro-molecule.

Unlike bakelite, urea-formaldehyde resins are colourless and can be coloured with pale pigments.

Similar resins are obtained by using *melamine* (a trimer of cyanamide):

in place of urea.

Alkyd or glyptal resins

If a trihydric alcohol such as glycerol is used instead of ethylene glycol to esterify a dibasic acid such as phthalic acid, the chain-polyester will have unesterified —OH groups, and the chains can therefore be cross-linked by esterifying these with further dibasic acid molecules. Glyptal or alkyd plastics are thermosetting polyesters of glycerol and phthalic acid: the final product will be a three-dimensional macromolecule with the basic structure:

Exercises

Chapter 1

1. Explain the terms: molecular formula; structural formula; isomer. Write out graphical structural formulae (i.e. with all atoms shown separately) for the isomers of molecular formula C_5H_{12}.

How many different substances do the following formulae represent? Comment.

$$CH_3.CH_2.CH_2.CH_2OH$$

2. Explain with examples the difference between structural isomerism and stereo-isomerism.

3. Explain the terms: paraffin; alkyl group; homologous series. Give an example (other than the paraffins) of a homologous series.

Chapter 2

1. Explain with simple examples, the terms: 'hydrogen bonding'; 'resonance hybrid'.

2. Explain the terms: 'heterolytic', 'homolytic' as applied to the breaking of a covalent bond, and 'nucleophilic', 'electrophilic' as applied to reagents. How are the last two terms related to the concepts of acids and bases?

Chapter 3

1. How are (*a*) nitrogen, (*b*) halogens, (*c*) sulphur detected in an organic compound?

2. Explain *in principle* how the carbon, hydrogen and halogen content of an organic substance can be determined.

3. 0·0291 g of an organic compound containing carbon, hydrogen and oxygen only gave 0·0581 g carbon dioxide and 0·0239 g water on combustion. In a Victor Meyer determination, 0·140 g of the compound on vaporizing displaced 39·5 cm³ of air, measured at 20° C, 740 mm. Calculate the molecular formula of the compound.

4. In a Dumas nitrogen determination, 0·0236 g of a compound gave 2·12 cm³ nitrogen measured at 15° C, 750 mm. In a cryoscopic molecular weight determination in benzene, 0·450 g depressed the freezing point of 20·5 g of benzene by 0·833° C. Calculate the number of nitrogen atoms in one molecule of the compound.

(Cryoscopic constant for benzene = 5·12° C per mol per kg benzene.)

5. 0·0214 g of an organic compound yielded on combustion 0·0225 g of carbon dioxide and 0·0031 g of water. In a Carius determination, 0·0171 g yielded 0·0254 g of silver bromide. Calculate the empirical formula of the compound.

6. 0·0251 g of an organic compound yielded on combustion 0·0371 g of carbon dioxide and 0·0177 g of water.

In a Kjeldahl determination, 0·105 g was digested with concentrated sulphuric acid and catalysts, and the product distilled with alkali. The ammonia evolved, on absorption in boric acid solution and titration with 0·05 M hydrochloric acid, gave a titre of 23·5 cm³. Calculate the empirical formula of the compound.

(C = 12, H = 1, O = 16, N = 14, Br = 80, Ag = 108.)

Alkanes (chapter 4)

1. How may (*a*) methane, (*b*) ethane, be obtained from acetic acid, and (*c*) ethane, (*d*) *n*-butane from ethyl iodide?

2. The name 'paraffin' implies 'unreactive'; is this justified? What reactions of paraffins (other than combustion) are technically feasible?

3. Give systematic names for the following alkanes:

$$CH_3.CH(CH_3).CH_2.CH_3 \qquad CH_3.C(CH_3)_2.CH_2.CH(CH_3).CH_3$$

$$\begin{array}{c} \quad\;\; CH_2CH_3 \quad CH_3 \\ \quad\quad\quad | \qquad\quad | \\ CH_3\!-\!\overset{\displaystyle |}{\underset{\displaystyle |}{C}}\!-\!CH_2\!-\!CH\!-\!CH_3 \\ \quad\;\; CH_3 \end{array}$$

4. 10 cm³ of a gaseous hydrocarbon was mixed with 100 cm³ of oxygen and exploded. 80 cm³ of gaseous product remained, which contracted to 50 cm³ on shaking with aqueous alkali. (All volumes were measured at laboratory temperature and pressure). Find the molecular formula of the hydrocarbon.

5. 10 cm³ of a mixture of methane and ethane was mixed with 60 cm³ oxygen and exploded. 48 cm³ of gaseous product remained, which contracted to 34 cm³ on shaking with aqueous alkali. (All volumes were measured at laboratory temperature and pressure.) Find the mole composition of the mixture.

Olefinic $\diagdown$C=C$\diagup$ (chapter 5)

1. What is an addition reaction? What are the principal addition reactions of ethylene and its homologues?

2. Calculate the heats of formation of the C—C bond in ethane and the C=C bond in ethylene as suggested on p. 54, and comment on the results.

3. What light is thrown on the reaction of bromine with olefinic compounds by (*a*) the reaction of ethylene with bromine in the presence of sodium chloride solution, (*b*) the stereochemistry of the reactions of bromine with maleic and fumaric acids?

4. How could the position of the double bonds in the following compounds be established?

$$CH_2\!=\!CH\!-\!CH\!=\!CH_2; \quad CH_3CH_2CH\!=\!C(CH_3)_2$$

5. Normal butyl alcohol was subjected to the following changes:

$$CH_3(CH_2)_3OH \rightarrow \underset{A}{C_4H_8} \rightarrow \underset{B}{C_4H_9HSO_4} \rightarrow \underset{C}{C_4H_9OH}$$

Give reagents and conditions for carrying out these changes, and write structural formulae for *A*, *B* and *C*, giving reasons for your answer.

6. After reading chapters 9, 12, 23 (on Petroleum, Ethers, Fibres and Plastics), write an account of the technical importance of compounds containing olefinic double bonds.

7. 0·214 g of a mixture of hexane and hexa-l-ene was added to 22 cm³ of $\frac{M}{10}$ Br₂ in carbon tetrachloride in a stoppered vessel. After a time, an excess of potassium iodide solution was added; the iodine set free by the remaining bromine required 26 cm³ of M/10 thiosulphate solution for titration. An excess of potassium iodate was then added to the titration flask. A further small amount of iodine was liberated, which required a further 2 cm³ of M/10 thiosulphate solution for titration. How do you account for these results, and what was the molar composition of the mixture?

Acetylenes (chapter 6)

1. How would you convert ethylene to (*a*) acetylene, (*b*) 1,2-dichloro-ethylene, (*c*) 1,1-dichloroethane, (*d*) trichloroethylene?

2. How can the following compounds be obtained from calcium carbide as starting material: (*a*) ethanol, (*b*) acetone, (*c*) neoprene rubber, (*d*) polyvinyl chloride? (see also chapter 23).

3. Carry out the calculation of the heat of formation of the C≡C bond in acetylene as suggested on p. 70. Compare the value with those for C—C in ethane and C=C in ethylene (see p. 54 and question 2, p. 347).

4. How would you distinguish chemically between the following isomers:
$$CH_2=CH-CH=CH_2; \quad CH_3.C\equiv C.CH_3; \quad CH_3CH_2.C\equiv CH?$$

Aromatic systems (chapter 7)

1. In what respects and to what extent does benzene show unsaturation? How does its behaviour in this respect differ from that of an open-chain unsaturated aliphatic hydrocarbon?

2. What is the 'Kekulé structure' for benzene? In what respects is it inadequate, and what modifications or further concepts are needed to give an acceptable structure for benzene?

3. From the data on p. 54 and from the further information:
$$C_6H_6 + 7\tfrac{1}{2}O_2 \longrightarrow 6CO_2 + 3H_2O$$
$$\Delta H = -3265 \text{ kJ mol}^{-1}$$

calculate the heat of formation of the aromatic carbon–carbon bond in benzene from free atoms, assuming the heat of formation of the CH bond in benzene is the same as in methane.

From the above data and

$$C_6H_{12}+9O_2 \longrightarrow 6CO_2+6H_2O$$
$$\text{cyclohexane} \qquad \Delta H = -3930 \text{ kJ mol}^{-1}$$

calculate ΔH for

$$C_6H_6+3H_2 \rightarrow C_6H_{12}$$

Comment on your results in the light of the ΔH values for aliphatic bonds and compounds (see pp. 54 and 69).

4. Explain the terms: 'ortho', 'meta', 'para', as applied to the orientation of substituents in derivatives of benzene. Explain how in suitable cases the orientation of such substituents has been experimentally established for di-derivatives of benzene.

5. Outline the principles involved in the isolation of aromatic hydrocarbons from coal tar.

6. Give three reactions in which aliphatic compounds are converted to benzene or benzene derivatives.

7. How may toluene be converted to (*a*) benzene, (*b*) benzyl chloride? What would you expect to be the aromatic product of prolonged oxidation with chromic acid of the following compound?

Benzene ring as a functional group (chapter 8)

1. What are the principal reactions leading to replacement of a hydrogen atom in benzene by other groups? Give the essential practical conditions for each reaction.

2. Do the reactions and reagents listed in question 1 show any common feature? Give a brief account of the accepted mechanisms of two of these reactions.

3. What is meant by the directing effect of a substituent group in an aromatic compound? What structural features determine the directing effect of a particular substituent? Discuss the directing effect of the groups

$$-CH_3; \quad -CO_2H; \quad -CCl_3; \quad -NO_2; \quad -NH_2; \quad -N(CH_3)_2; \quad -\overset{\oplus}{N}(CH_3)_3$$

to illustrate your answer.

4. How would you obtain from benzene and suitable reagents: (*a*) *m*-bromonitrobenzene; (*b*) *p*-chloronitrobenzene; (*c*) α-chlorotoluene (benzyl chloride); (*d*) *p*-chlorotoluene; (*e*) *m*-nitroacetophenone?

5. How does the presence of (*a*) an —OH group, (*b*) an —NH₂ group attached to a benzene ring modify the usual aromatic substitution reactions?

6. How may phenol be converted to (*a*) salicylic acid; (*b*) salicylaldehyde; (*c*) phenolphthalein?

Petroleum industry (chapter 9)

1. Explain the terms: cracking, polymerization, alkylation, isomerization, reforming, as applied in petroleum technology. Why are these processes important?

Halide function (chapter 10)

1. What reagents and conditions are required to obtain the following compounds from ethyl iodide? (*a*) C_2H_5CN; (*b*) C_2H_5OH; (*c*) C_2H_4; (*d*) $C_2H_5OCH_3$; (*e*) $C_2H_5NH_2$; (*f*) $C_2H_5O.COCH_3$; (*g*) C_2H_5NC? What difficulties, if any, would you anticipate in achieving analogous transformations of tertiary butyl iodide?

2. Discuss the mechanisms of the reactions involved in question (1) for both of the halides named.

3. What chemical reactions would you use to distinguish between unlabelled samples of the following pairs of isomers?

(*a*) CH_2BrCH_2Br and CH_3CHBr_2

(*b*) [benzene ring with CH₃ and Cl substituents] and [benzene ring with CH₂Cl substituent]

(*c*) [benzene ring with CH₂Cl and Br substituents] and [benzene ring with CH₂Br and Cl substituents]

4. What is a Grignard reagent? How may a Grignard reagent solution be prepared from ethyl bromide, and how may it be used to obtain

(*a*) $CH_3CH_2CH_2OH$;   (*b*) $CH_3CH_2CH_2CH_3$;   (*c*) $C_2H_5CO_2H$;

(*d*) $C_2H_5CHOHCH_3$;   (*e*) $(C_2H_5)_3COH$?

5. What reagents and conditions would you use to convert bromobenzene to (*a*) phenol; (*b*) aniline; (*c*) ethyl benzene; (*d*) benzoic acid; (*e*) triphenyl carbinol $(C_6H_5)_3COH$?

6. Devise methods involving the use of Grignard reagents at appropriate stages for the following syntheses:

(a) $(C_2H_5)_2COHCH_3$ — from ethanol
(b) $C_6H_5CH_2CHOHC_6H_5$ — from toluene
(c) $(CH_3)_2COHCH(CH_3)_2$ — from isopropyl alcohol
(d) $(CH_3)_2CHCO_2H$ — from acetone

(to be attempted after studying chapters 10 to 14).

7. 0·204 g of a compound of molecular formula $C_9H_{10}O_2$ was added to an excess of methyl magnesium iodide in dipentyl ether. 33·1 cm³ of gas, measured at 20° C, 750 mm was evolved. What conclusion do you draw about the compound?

—OH group (chapter 11)

1. Write the structural formulae and give systematic names for the isomeric alcohols $C_5H_{11}OH$.

2. How may ethanol be converted to (a) ethyl bromide, (b) ethylene, (c) diethyl ether, (d) acetaldehyde, (e) ethyl acetate?

3. Explain the terms primary, secondary and tertiary as applied to alcohols. How do these three types of alcohol differ in their behaviour towards (a) oxidizing agents, (b) strong mineral acids, (c) carboxylic acids?

4. Compare the reactions of the —OH group in ethanol and phenol.

5. Explain how you would use behaviour with oxidizing agents and the iodoform test to distinguish between the following isomers:

$CH_3(CH_2)_5OH$; $(CH_3CH_2)_2COHCH_3$; $CH_3(CH_2)_3CHOHCH_3$;
$CH_3CH_2CHOH(CH_2)_2CH_3$

6. Give *four* routes for making phenol from benzene, and discuss their advantages and drawbacks.

Ether group (chapter 12)

1. Write the structural formulae of the isomeric ethers of molecular formula $C_5H_{12}O$. How would you distinguish between samples of the isomers by chemical means?

2. Compare and as far as you can account for the simple physical characteristics, solvent properties and behaviour towards proton acids and bases of water, the lower aliphatic alcohols and the lower aliphatic ethers.

3. How is ethylene oxide made? How does it differ in chemical behaviour from an open-chain aliphatic ether such as dimethyl ether?

4. In a Zeisel determination, 0·0250 g of a compound of molecular weight 194 was digested with hydriodic acid. The methyl iodide liberated was passed into aqueous-ethanolic silver nitrate solution. After the addition of water, 0·0602 g of silver iodide was obtained. How many methoxyl groups were present in one molecule of the compound? (AgI = 235).

NH_2 group (chapter 13)

1. Explain the meaning of the terms primary, secondary and tertiary as applied to amines. How does this differ from the meaning of the same terms as applied to alcohols?

2. Write structural formulae for the isomers of molecular formula C_3H_9N. How far can these isomers be distinguished from one another by the action of (*a*) acetylating agents, (*b*) nitrous acid? What further steps would you suggest for their complete identification?

3. How do ammonia, methylamine and aniline differ in basic strength? What explanation can you offer for these differences?

4. How may aniline be acylated? What practical applications has the acylation of amines?

5. How does aniline react with (*a*) hydrochloric acid, (*b*) acetic acid, (*c*) methyl iodide, (*d*) bromine water?

6. What are the principal chemical differences between the isomers

$$CH_3-\!\langle\bigcirc\rangle\!-NH_2, \quad \langle\bigcirc\rangle\!-CH_2NH_2 \quad and \quad \langle\bigcirc\rangle\!-NHCH_3 \ ?$$

7. What is diazotization? Describe and account for the practical procedure for preparing from aniline a solution of a benzenediazonium salt.

8. List in sequence and account for the practical steps in the laboratory preparation of aniline from nitrobenzene.

9. Starting in each case with ethanol, how would you prepare (*a*) ethylamine (free from secondary and tertiary amines), (*b*) methylamine, (*c*) *n*-propylamine, (*d*) isopropylamine, (*e*) ethylmethylamine?

10. Hydrolysis of the neutral compound A $C_6H_{13}ON$ with hydrochloric acid, followed by evaporation, gave the crystalline compound B $C_4H_{12}NCl$, together with a volatile organic acid. When B was treated with sodium nitrite a product C $C_4H_{10}O$ could be isolated which was readily oxidized to D $C_4H_8O_2$.

Trace the reactions concerned and suggest any further experiments, synthetic or otherwise, which would distinguish between alternative structures for A. (*Cambridge Schol.* Group I, 1963)

11. The compound P C_8H_9NO gives with zinc and hydrochloric acid a substance Q $C_8H_{12}NCl$. When sodium nitrite is added to the solution of Q so obtained, an oil R separates. This when isolated and purified is found to have the composition $C_8H_{10}O$.

When added to a solution of iodine in water containing potassium hydroxide and a little methanol, R forms a second layer, which dissolves gradually on shaking. When a slight excess of concentrated hydrochloric acid is now added to the solution, a white precipitate appears, which on recrystallization from water yields pure S, $C_7H_6O_2$.

Account for these changes, giving structures for P, Q, R and S.

(*Cambridge Schol.* Group I, 1965, slightly reworded)

$>$C=O group (chapter 14)

1. What changes in chemical behaviour result from the successive replacement of hydrogen atoms by methyl groups in formaldehyde?

2. How do aldehydes and ketones react with (*a*) hydrogen cyanide (potassium cyanide and acid), (*b*) sodium bisulphite solution, (*c*) hydroxylamine, (*d*) 2,4-dinitrophenylhydrazine? Comment on the classification of these reactions as 'additions' or 'condensations'. What laboratory uses have these reactions and their products?

3. How would you expect the isomers

to differ in their behaviour towards (*a*) alkalis, (*b*) solutions of potassium cyanide, (*c*) Fehling's solution, ammoniacal silver nitrate solution and other oxidizing agents, (*d*) sodium hypobromite solution?

4. Discuss the proposition that, catalytic hydrogenation apart, reagents which yield addition products with simple olefines do not do so with aldehydes and ketones, and vice versa. Illustrate with two examples for each type of substrate ($>$C=C$<$ and $>$C=O) and give what explanation you can.

5. Give a general account of the various types of polymerization reaction undergone by simple aldehydes and ketones. (Include not only strict polymerizations, but 'polycondensations' also).

6. The following compounds can all be obtained by suitable reaction sequences from a single compound, which in turn, can ultimately be made from ethanol. Give the reactions by which you would carry out the preparations.

$CH_3CHOHCH_2CH_2OH$; $CH_3CH=CHCH_2OH$; $CH_3CH_2CH_2CHO$;
$CH_3CH_2CH_2CH_3$; $CH_2=CH-CH=CH_2$

7. How could acetone be converted to: (*a*) propylene, (*b*) methacrylic acid ($CH_2=C(CH_3)CO_2H$); (*c*) *m*-xylene; (*d*) monomethylacetylene (propyne); (*e*) 2,3-dimethylbutadiene ($CH_2=C(CH_3)-C(CH_3)=CH_2$)?

8. How could you convert propan-1-ol to (*a*) 1, 1-dichloropropane, (*b*) isopropylamine, (*c*) $(CH_3)_2CHCH_2CHOHCH_3$?

9. What is the iodoform reaction, and by what types of compound is it given? Which of the following compounds will give a positive iodoform reaction? (*a*) CH_3OH; (*b*) $CH_3CHOHCH_3$; (*c*) $CH_3CH_2CH_2OH$; (*d*) $CH_3CO.CO_2H$; (*e*) CH_3CO_2H; (*f*) $CH_3COC_6H_5$; (*g*) $CH_3CO_2C_6H_5$?
In the case of *one* suitable substance from the above, trace the steps of the reaction.

10. How could you distinguish by chemical tests between unlabelled samples of the isomers (*a*) $(C_2H_5)_2CO$, (*b*) $CH_3(CH_2)_3CHO$ and (*c*) $CH_3CO(CH_2)_2CH_3$? How would you try by chemical methods to decide between the given structure and the isomeric structure $CH_3COCH(CH_3)_2$ for (*c*)?

11. How can formaldehyde, acetaldehyde, acetone, benzaldehyde be made technically?

12. How from benzaldehyde and any other reagents required would you prepare the following:

$C_6H_5CO.COC_6H_5$; $C_6H_5CH_2CH_2CO_2H$; $C_6H_5CH=CH.CHOH.CH=CHC_6H_5$

13. How is chloral (trichloroacetaldehyde) prepared? How does it react with (*a*) water, (*b*) ammonia, (*c*) hydroxylamine, (*d*) ethanol, (*e*) aqueous alkali? How does its behaviour to these reagents differ from that of acetaldehyde, and how do you account for the differences?

14. What is keto–enol tautomerism? Illustrate your answer by reference to ethyl acetoacetate. What is the usual mechanism of tautomerism? Which of the following compounds would you expect to show *marked* keto–enol tautomerism?

$$CH_3COCH_2COCH_3; \quad CH_3COCH_2CH_2COCH_3;$$
$$CH_3COCO_2C_2H_5; \quad C_6H_5COCH_2CO_2C_2H_5$$

15. What experimental evidence is there of keto and enol forms in equilibrium in ethyl acetoacetate? What conditions determine the proportion of keto to enol in this compound? What is your answer to the problem posed on p. 207?

16. Which of the following compounds may be obtained from ethyl acetoacetate, and by what steps?

$$CH_3COCH_2CH_3; \quad CH_3COCH(CH_3)_2; \quad CH_3COC(CH_3)_3;$$
$$CH_3CH_2CH_2CO_2H; \quad HO_2C(CH_2)_4CO_2H$$

17. How would you obtain the following compounds from ethyl malonate?

$$CH_3CH_2CH_2CO_2H; \quad \begin{array}{c} CH_3 \\ \diagdown \\ C_6H_5CH_2 \end{array} CH.CO_2H; \quad \begin{array}{c} CH_2CO_2H \\ | \\ CH_2CO_2H \end{array};$$
$$HO_2CCH_2CH(CO_2H)_2$$

18. A phenol U, C_7H_8O, is reduced by hydrogenation to V, $C_7H_{14}O$, which is oxidized in two stages, first to a ketone W, $C_7H_{12}O$, and then to an acid X, $C_7H_{12}O_3$. The acid on reduction with hydrogen and a catalyst forms Y, $C_7H_{14}O_3$, which on dehydration gives Z, $C_7H_{12}O_2$. Both X and Z may be oxidized to acetic acid and glutaric acid $HOOC.(CH_2)_3.COOH$. Elucidate the reactions involved and write structural formulae for U, V, W, X, Y and Z.
(Cambridge Schol. Group II, 1965)

19. A compound A, C_5H_9BrO, undergoes the following series of reactions:

$$\underset{A}{C_5H_9BrO} \xrightarrow[\text{HCl gas}]{\text{EtOH, dry}} \underset{B}{C_9H_{19}BrO_2} \xrightarrow{\text{KOH}} \underset{C}{C_9H_{18}O_2}$$
$$\downarrow \text{ozonolysis}$$
$$\underset{F}{CHI_3} \xleftarrow[\text{KOH}]{I_2} \underset{F}{C_3H_6O} \xleftarrow[\text{and heat}]{\text{oxidize}} \underset{E}{C_4H_6O_2} \xleftarrow[\text{HCl}_{Aq}]{\text{dil.}} \underset{D}{C_8H_{16}O_3} + CH_2O$$

Suggest formulae for A → F and incorporate them in a reaction scheme as above.
(Cambridge Schol. Group III, 1959)

355

—CO₂H (chapter 15)

1. How and under what conditions does acetic acid react with ethanol? The early nineteenth-century chemists considered this reaction analogous with the neutralization of acetic acid by an alkali, and called the products 'ethereal salts'. Explain fully, giving experimental evidence, why these analogies are false.

2. How may acetic acid be converted to acetamide? How can acetamide be converted to (*a*) acetic acid, (*b*) acetonitrile, (*c*) ethylamine, (*d*) methylamine?

3. How may acetic acid be converted to (*a*) acetyl chloride, (*b*) acetic anhydride? How do these compounds react with (i) water, (ii) alcohols, (iii) ammonia, (iv) amines?

4. What is 'acetylation', and by what reagents may it be carried out? State which of the following compounds can readily be acetylated, and give the names and formulae of their acetylation products: (*a*) CH₃NH₂; (*b*) CH₃CONH₂; (*c*) CH₃CH₂OH; (*d*) CH₃CHO; (*e*) CH₃CO₂H; (*f*) CH₂OHCO₂H; (*g*) C₆H₅NH₂; (*h*) C₆H₅NHCH₃; (*i*) C₆H₅N(CH₃)₂.

5. What is 'acylation'? Discuss the benzoylation of phenol, the esterification of ethanol, the action of acetic anhydride on aniline and the hydrolysis of acetamide in terms of your answer.

6. By comparing the relevant reactions of ethanol and acetic acid, diethyl ether and ethyl acetate, ethyl acetate and acetic anhydride, ethyl chloride and acetyl chloride, and ethylamine and acetamide, show how attachment to $\ce{>C=O}$ instead of to $\ce{>CH_2}$ modifies the chemical behaviour associated with —OH, —OC₂H₅, —O.COCH₃, —Cl and —NH₂.

7. How may acetic acid be converted to (*a*) methane, (*b*) ethane, (*c*) acetone, (*d*) acetaldehyde?

8. What is the 'classical' experimental evidence for the formulation of

acetic acid as

$$\ce{H-\underset{\underset{H}{|}}{\overset{\overset{H}{|}}{C}}-C\overset{\diagup\diagup O}{\diagdown O-H}} \quad ?$$

9. 'Although carboxylic acids and their derivatives are formulated with a $\ce{>C=O}$ group, they show none of the reactions given by this group in aldehydes and ketones.' Illustrate and discuss.

10. Give an account of fats, soaps and detergents.

11. Discuss the following:

(*a*) A solution in pure acetic acid of hydrogen iodide has a higher electrical conductivity than one of hydrogen chloride of the same concentration, and both solutions are better conductors than pure acetic acid.

(*b*) The apparent molecular weight of acetic acid (from colligative property measurements) is about 120 in solution in benzene, about 60 in water and about 30 in 100% sulphuric acid.

12. Write structural formulae for the isomeric esters and acids of molecular formula $C_4H_8O_2$. How would you distinguish by chemical methods between these isomers?

13. A compound X containing only carbon, hydrogen and oxygen gave on analysis carbon 48·66% and hydrogen 8·11%. In the presence of sulphuric acid, X reacted with methyl alcohol to give a liquid Y, of empirical formula C_2H_4O. Y reacted with a concentrated solution of ammonia to give a solid Z of molecular formula C_3H_7ON.

Z reacted with nitrous acid to give X. Give structural formulae for X, Y and Z, and show by equations the reactions involved. (H = 1; C = 12; O = 16). (*Cambridge* Group II Entr., 1963)

—CN and —NC groups (chapter 16)

1. How may alkyl cyanides be prepared, and how do they react on (*a*) reduction, (*b*) hydrolysis? What light is thrown by the reactions you give on the structure of alkyl cyanides?

2. How may alkyl isocyanides be prepared, and how do they react on (*a*) reduction, (*b*) hydrolysis? What light is thrown by the reactions you give on the structure of alkyl isocyanides?

3. The cyanide group is sometimes called a 'pseudo-halogen'. Give examples in which analogous compounds containing respectively —CN and a halogen (*a*) behave in analogous ways, (*b*) behave differently.

4. How would you convert toluene to

(*a*) ⬡—$CH_2CH_2NH_2$;   (*b*) CH_3—⬡—CH_2NH_2;

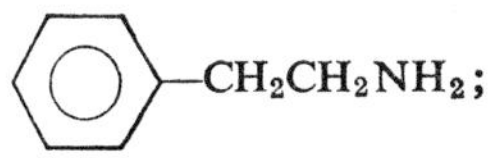

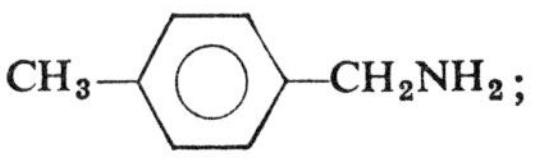

(*c*) CH_3—⬡—CHO ?

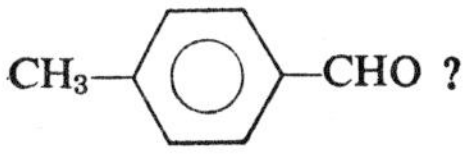

5. A compound U, C_4H_5N, which can be obtained in two stereoisomeric forms, is reduced by hydrogen and a catalyst to give V, $C_4H_{11}N$, which exists in one form only. The compound U undergoes the following reactions:

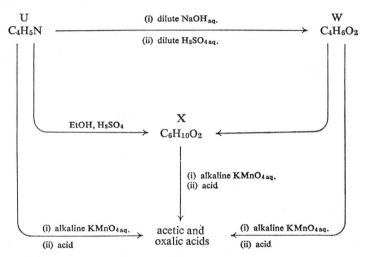

Elucidate the above reactions, and give structures for U, V, W and X.

—SO₃H and related groups (chapter 17)

1. How do (*a*) ethylene, (*b*) benzene react with sulphuric acid? What important structural difference is there between the types of product obtained, and what experimental evidence is there for this difference?

2. Compare and discuss the relative acid strengths of (*a*) benzoic acid and benzenesulphonic acid, (*b*) benzamide and benzenesulphonamide.

3. How is benzene converted to benzenesulphonic acid? How can benzenesulphonic acid be converted to (*a*) benzene, (*b*) phenol, (*c*) thiophenol, (*d*) benzonitrile?

4. 'Methyl acetate is an acetylating agent; methyl benzenesulphonate is a methylating agent'. Discuss this statement, illustrating it with examples.

5. List in sequence the practical operations you would use to separate the constituents of a mixture of aniline, *N*-methylaniline and *NN*-dimethylaniline by the use of benzenesulphonyl chloride. Explain the physicochemical basis of your procedure.

6. List the reaction steps in the preparation of saccharin from toluene (see p. 255) and comment on the points of interest at each reaction stage.

7. List the reaction steps in the preparation of sulphanilamide from aniline (see p. 255) and comment on the points of interest at each reaction stage.

—NO₂ group (chapter 18)

1. When ethyl iodide reacts with sodium nitrite, two isomeric products are formed; one, the lower boiling, is readily hydrolysed or reduced to ethanol, while the higher boiling isomer resists hydrolysis and can be reduced to ethylamine. Discuss the points raised by these statements.

2. How may nitromethane be obtained (*a*) technically, (*b*) from methyl iodide, (*c*) from chloroacetic acid? Give an account of the acidic behaviour and tautomerism of nitromethane.

3. Compare and discuss (*a*) the relative acid strengths of phenol and *p*-nitrophenol, (*b*) the relative ease of hydrolysis of chlorobenzene and *p*-chloronitrobenzene.

4. How would you distinguish between the following isomers?

(*a*) $CH_3-\langle\bigcirc\rangle-NO_2$ and $\langle\bigcirc\rangle-CH_2NO_2$

(*b*) $\overset{OH}{\langle\bigcirc\rangle}-NO_2$, $\overset{OH}{\langle\bigcirc\rangle}-NO_2$ and $HO-\langle\bigcirc\rangle-NO_2$

—N≡N group (chapter 19)

1. How would you prepare from aniline (*a*) methylphenylether, (*b*) iodobenzene, (*c*) benzylamine, (*d*) phenylhydrazine, (*e*) *p*-hydroxyazobenzene

$\left(HO-\langle\bigcirc\rangle-N{=}N-\langle\bigcirc\rangle \right)$?

2. Starting with benzene, and using diazonium salts as intermediates, how would you try to prepare (*a*) 1,3,5-tribromobenzene, (*b*) isophthalic acid (benzene-*m*-dicarboxylic acid), (*c*)

$\overset{CH_2NH_2}{\langle\bigcirc\rangle}_{NH_2}$?

3. Explain how diazotization can be used to give a simple laboratory test for distinguishing between nuclear and side-chain —NH₂ in aromatic compounds.

Compounds of multiple function (chapter 20)

1. How do acetic acid and mono-, di- and trichloroacetic acid differ in acid strength? How may these differences be explained? How and under what conditions do these compounds react with caustic alkalis?

2. How may ethylene glycol be prepared from ethylene? What possible products (other than carbon dioxide and water) can arise from the oxidation of ethylene glycol? Given unlabelled samples of glycol and all the possible oxidation products, how would you identify them?

3. Give an account of the preparation and uses of glycerol.

4. How may lactic acid be prepared from ethanol as starting material? How does lactic acid react (*a*) with phosphorus trichloride, (*b*) with hydrobromic acid, (*c*) with aqueous alkali and iodine, (*d*) on heating?

5. Explain and relate the terms: α-amino acid; peptide link; polypeptide; protein; iso-electric point.

6. How may alanine be prepared from (*a*) ethanol, (*b*) propanol as respective starting materials? How does alanine react (*a*) with acids, (*b*) with aqueous alkalis, (*c*) with ethanolic hydrogen chloride, (*d*) with benzoyl chloride in the presence of aqueous alkali, (*e*) on heating with soda-lime?

7. How would you distinguish chemically between the following? (*a*) chloroform and carbon tetrachloride; (*b*) oxalic acid and dimethyl oxalate; (*c*) sodium oxalate and sodium formate; (*d*) benzamide and phthalimide; (*e*) oxamide and urea.

8. How would you distinguish chemically between the following pairs of isomers?
(*a*) $CH_3CH(CO_2Et)_2$ and $(CH_2CO_2Et)_2$
(*b*) $HOCH_2CH_2CO_2H$ and $CH_3CHOHCO_2H$
(*c*) $H_2NCH_2CH_2COOH$ and $HOCH_2CH_2CONH_2$
(*d*) $\begin{array}{c}CO_2(CH_2)_3CH_3\\|\\CO_2(CH_2)_3CH_3\end{array}$ and $\begin{array}{c}CH_2CO_2(CH_2)_2CH_3\\|\\CH_2CO_2(CH_2)_2CH_3\end{array}$

9. How could you carry out the following syntheses?
(*a*) ethylene $\rightarrow \begin{array}{c}CHBrCO_2H\\|\\CHBrCO_2H\end{array}$
(*b*) acetone $\rightarrow (CH_3)C(NH_2)CONH_2$
(*c*) aniline $\rightarrow H_2NCONHC_6H_5$

10. How can urea be made, using as sources of carbon (*a*) potassium cyanide, (*b*) carbon monoxide, (*c*) carbon dioxide? How does urea react with (i) aqueous alkali, (ii) nitrous acid, (iii) nitric acid, (iv) sodium hypobromite solution, and (v) on heating?

11. What are the following substances, and how can they be obtained from carbon monoxide as sole source of carbon?

(*a*) $CH_2(OCH_3)_2$ (*b*) $CO(OCH_3)_2$ (*c*) $(CO_2CH_3)_2$

12. How far is it true to say that in compounds containing two functional groups, each group shows its characteristic behaviour independently of the other? Illustrate your answer with suitable examples.

13. A substance A, $C_2H_2OCl_2$ reacted with cold water to give B, $C_2H_3O_2Cl$, but on boiling with water gave C, $C_2H_4O_3$. With ethanol, A gave D, $C_4H_7O_2Cl$. C reacted with acetic anhydride to give E, $C_4H_6O_4$.

Elucidate these changes and write structural formulae for A, B, C, D and E.

14. A crystalline solid A, $C_4H_{10}O_2NCl$ gave on treatment with hot aqueous alkali and subsequent neutralization an amphoteric substance B, $C_3H_7O_2N$. B with nitrous acid gave C, $C_3H_6O_3$, which on mild oxidation gave D, $C_3H_4O_3$. C and D were both acids, and both reacted with aqueous alkali and iodine to give a yellow precipitate. The solutions remaining after filtering this off were acidified with acetic acid; both gave a white precipitate on the addition of calcium chloride solution.

Elucidate these changes and write structural formulae for A, B, C and D.

15. A compound A of molecular formula $C_8H_6N_2O$ undergoes the following reactions:

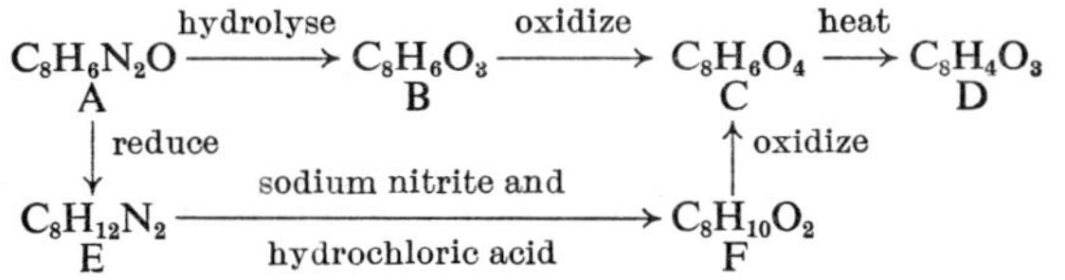

$$C_8H_6N_2O \xrightarrow{\text{hydrolyse}} C_8H_6O_3 \xrightarrow{\text{oxidize}} C_8H_6O_4 \xrightarrow{\text{heat}} C_8H_4O_3$$

A   B   C   D

A $\xrightarrow{\text{reduce}}$ $C_8H_{12}N_2$ (E) $\xrightarrow[\text{hydrochloric acid}]{\text{sodium nitrite and}}$ $C_8H_{10}O_2$ (F) $\xrightarrow{\text{oxidize}}$ C

Elucidate the above reactions and give structures for A, B, C, D, E and F.

(*Cambridge Schol.* Group II, 1961)

16. A hydrocarbon A, C_6H_{10}, absorbed one mole of hydrogen on catalytic reduction. With a special oxidizing agent it gave a product B, $C_6H_{10}O$, which on treatment with dilute hydrochloric acid gave a neutral compound C, $C_6H_{12}O_2$. C was oxidized by alkaline permanganate solution to an acid D, $C_6H_{10}O_4$, of which the calcium salt gave E, C_5H_8O, on heating.

A added bromine to give F, $C_6H_{10}Br_2$, which was converted into C with dilute aqueous sodium hydroxide solution, while hot concentrated alcoholic potash gave G, C_6H_8. Ozonolysis of G gave two acids, H, $C_2H_2O_4$ and I, $C_4H_6O_4$. On heating, I lost water and a neutral substance J, $C_4H_4O_3$, was produced.

Suggest structures for A–J and express the above results in the form of a reaction scheme. (*Cambridge Schol.* Group III, 1965)

Optical activity and mirror-image isomerism (chapter 21)

1. What is meant by 'optical activity' in a compound? It can be said that lactic acid (α-hydroxypropionic acid) and its salts exist in three isomeric forms, two of them optically active and one optically inactive. Explain the relation between these three forms, and give the principles of suitable methods for preparing them, starting from acetaldehyde.

2. Discuss critically the proposition that the presence of an asymmetric carbon atom in the molecule is essential for a compound to show optical activity.

3. Trace the argument from the existence of optical isomers to the assumption that the valencies of a saturated carbon atom are tetrahedrally disposed in space.

4. What is meant by an asymmetric centre in a molecule? Discuss the isomerism which arises when a molecule has *two different* asymmetric centres. How is this modified if the two asymmetric centres have the *same* groups attached to them?

5. Discuss critically the following proposition: 'optical activity results from molecular dissymmetry; since at any instant, practically all the molecules in a sample of acetic acid will be in dissymmetric arrangements, or configurations, one would expect a sample of acetic acid to be optically active'. How far is it justifiable to speak of meso-tartaric acid as 'optically inactive by internal compensation'?

6. What is *cis–trans* isomerism, and why does it arise? What is the experimental evidence that the isomerism of maleic and fumaric acids is of this type, and how does the evidence show which is the *cis* and which the *trans* isomer?

7. What isomers, if any, of the following structures would you expect to exist, and why?

$$C_6H_5CH_2CHOHCO_2H,$$
$$C_6H_5CH=CHCO_2H,$$
$$C_6H_5C\equiv CCO_2H.$$

How would you expect the isomers to differ in properties?

Carbohydrates (chapter 22)

1. Give the evidence leading to the open-chain formula for glucose, omitting stereochemistry. For what properties of glucose does this formula fail to account, and how may it be modified to account for them?

2. Answer question (1), substituting 'fructose' for 'glucose'.

3. Although natural glucose is *dextro*-rotatory and natural fructose *laevo*-rotatory, they both belong to the D-series of hexoses. Explain.

4. Some sugars of the formula $C_{12}H_{22}O_{11}$ reduce Tollen's reagent, others do not. Give an example of each kind, and explain this difference of behaviour in terms of their molecular structures. Give other differences in behaviour characteristic of these two types of sugar, and show how they are explained by the differences in structure.

5. What is a polysaccharide? Give three examples, and describe how they are related to simple monosaccharides.

Miscellaneous questions and revision exercises

1. Collect and classify as far as possible reactions in which carbon atoms become bonded together. Why are such reactions important?

2. Collect and classify as far as possible reactions in which bonded carbon atoms become separated.

3. Attachment of a functional group to an aromatic nucleus instead of to an aliphatic group often markedly modifies its behaviour. Collect cases of this. Can any generalizations be made?

4. Give an account of the formation and fission of C—O bonds.

5. Give an account of the formation and fission of C—N and C=N bonds.

6. Collect and classify as far as possible reactions in which carbon–halogen bonds are (*a*) formed, (*b*) broken.

7. How do the reactions associated with the presence of the —NH$_2$ group in an organic compound depend on the residue to which the group is attached?

8. How do the reactions associated with the presence of the —OH group in an organic compound depend on the residue to which the group is attached?

9. How do the reactions associated with the presence of a halogen atom in an organic compound depend on the residue to which the group is attached?

10. Give an account of the various ways in which sulphuric acid reacts with organic compounds.

11. Give an account of the reactions of organic compounds with metals.

12. Give an account of the reactions of bromine (with or without other inorganic reagents present) on organic compounds.

13. Give an account of the action of reducing agents on organic compounds.

14. Give an account of the action of oxidizing agents on organic compounds.

15. Compounds are believed to have the following structures. Show how in each case by suitable degradation or other reactions, the formula could be confirmed.

(i) $(CH_3)_2C\!=\!CHCO_2C_2H_5$

(ii) $(CH_3)_2C\!=\!C\diagup^{CO_2C_2H_5}_{\diagdown CONH_2}$

(iii) $CH_3CONHCH_2CO_2CH(CH_3)_2$

(iv) $CH_3CCH(CH_3)CO_2C_2H_5$ with $\underset{NOH}{\|}$

(v) $\underset{CO_2CH(CH_3)CH_2CH_3}{\overset{CONHC_2H_5}{|}}$

(vi) 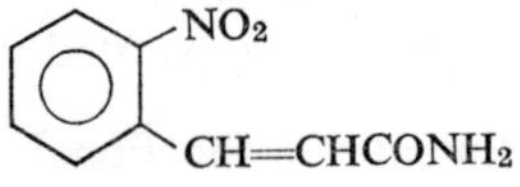 benzene ring with NO_2 and $CH\!=\!CHCONH_2$ substituents

(vii) 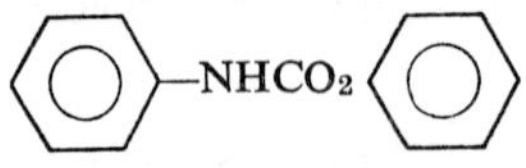 phenyl–$NHCO_2$–phenyl

(viii) CH_3O–phenyl–$CH\!=\!C(CH_3)CO_2CH_3$

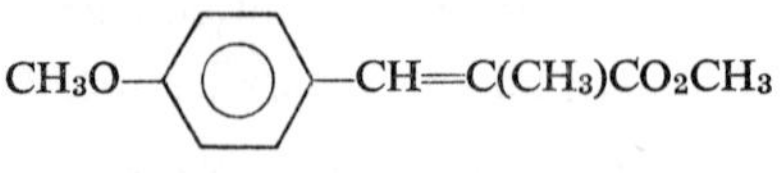

16. A compound A, $C_7H_6N_2$ reacted as shown.

$$C_7H_6N_2 \xrightarrow[\text{(ii) acid}]{\text{(i) NaOH aq}} C_7H_7O_2N \xrightarrow[\text{(ii) CuCN in KCN}_{aq}]{\text{(i) HNO}_2 \text{ at } 5°C} C_8H_5O_2N$$

A (below first) ; B (below second); C (below third)

$$\text{C}_8\text{H}_5\text{O}_2\text{N} \xrightarrow[\text{(ii) acid}]{\text{(i) NaOH}_{aq}} C_8H_6O_4$$

$$C_6H_6 \xleftarrow[\text{heat}]{\text{soda-lime}} C_8H_6O_4 \quad D$$

D on heating melted without change.

Elucidate these reactions

Write possible structures for A, B, C and D.

What other information is required for a complete identification of these substances?

17. An organic compound Z, $C_{13}H_{18}O_2$, was refluxed with alkali. On distilling the reaction product, a liquid A, $C_4H_{10}O$, was isolated from the distillate. The residue from distillation yielded on acidifying a sparingly soluble solid B, $C_9H_{10}O_2$. A and B gave the following reactions:

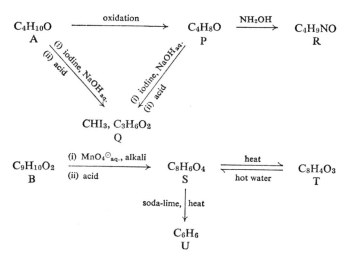

Elucidate these reactions and write structural formulae for Z, A, B, P, Q, R, S and T.

18. A compound C_9H_8O reacted as follows:

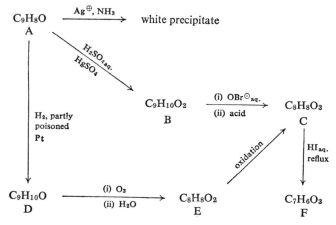

F proved identical with a sample of salicylic acid.

Elucidate these reactions and write structural formulae for A, B, C, D and E.

(*Cambridge Schol.* Group III, 1961, modified)

19. An aromatic compound A, C_9H_7N, was converted on heating with dilute sulphuric acid into B, $C_9H_8O_2$. Treatment of B with bromine yielded C, which contained 52 % of bromine. On heating C with alcoholic potash, followed by acidification, D, $C_9H_6O_2$, was obtained.

Write down a reaction scheme for the above changes, suggesting possible structures for A, B, C and D, and discuss their stereochemistry.

(Cambridge Schol. Group III, 1955)

20. A compound W, C_7H_7Cl, can be chlorinated under certain conditions to give X, $C_7H_6Cl_2$. On heating X with aqueous copper nitrate solution a compound Y, C_7H_5ClO, is produced, which forms Z, C_7H_6ClON, with hydroxylamine. Suggest formulae for W, X, Y and Z, and write equations for the reactions involved.

(Cambridge Schol. Group III, 1957)

21. (All the following formulae are empirical.) A neutral compound A, C_2H_2N, gave on boiling with hydrochloric acid an acid B, $C_2H_3O_2$. On treatment with acetic anhydride, B gave a neutral product C, $C_4H_4O_3$ which on boiling with water was reconverted to B. On reduction, A gave D, C_2H_6N, which with nitrous acid gave E, C_2H_5O. On oxidation, E gave B.

Elucidate the above reactions and outline a synthesis of A from ethyl alcohol. *(Cambridge Schol.* Group I, 1955)

22. An aliphatic compound, A, of molecular formula C_4H_7ON, undergoes catalytic reduction to B, $C_4H_{11}ON$, which readily gives a diacetyl derivative. Hydrolysis of A using aqueous sodium hydroxide yields a volatile product giving a positive iodoform reaction whilst the hydrolysis of A in dilute sulphuric acid solution and subsequent dehydration gives C, $C_4H_6O_2$, an acid whose ozonolysis gives D, $C_3H_4O_3$. Reduction of D under mild conditions gives E. This product can be resolved into optically active forms.

Deduce the structure of A and elucidate the reaction sequence.

(Cambridge Schol. Group I, 1960)

23. A colourless transparent glassy solid A on dry distillation gives a colourless liquid B, $C_5H_8O_2$, which on reduction with hydrogen and a catalyst leads to C, $C_5H_{10}O_2$. This on treatment with alcoholic ammonia gives D, C_4H_9NO, which with bromine and alkali yields a gas E, C_3H_9N. Both C and E alike give the same oxidation product F, C_3H_6O, with alkaline permanganate.

Incorporate structures for compounds A to F in a reaction scheme, using equations where possible.   (*Cambridge Schol.* Group. III, 1965)

24. An optically active acid A, $C_5H_8O_5$, on being heated, lost carbon dioxide to give another acid B, $C_4H_8O_3$, capable of being resolved into optical enantiomers. Treatment of B with sulphuric acid gave yet another acid C, whose ethyl ester in the presence of platinum and hydrogen gave D, $C_6H_{12}O_2$. D with concentrated ammonia solution gave E, C_4H_9ON, which with bromine and potassium hydroxide gave F, C_3H_9N.

Elucidate the above reactions and give structural formulae for A–F.

(*Cambridge Schol.* Group I, 1956)

25. An optically active compound A undergoes the following reactions

$$C_9H_{12}O \xrightarrow[\text{nitric acid}]{\text{dilute}} C_9H_{10}O \xrightarrow[\text{hypobromite}]{\text{sodium}} C_8H_8O_2$$
$$\underset{A}{} \qquad \underset{B}{} \qquad \underset{C}{}$$

$$\xrightarrow[\text{potassium permanganate}]{\text{alkaline}} C_8H_6O_4$$
$$\underset{D}{}$$

Compound D is unchanged on heating. Elucidate the above reactions and give structures for A, B, C and D.

Describe further experiments that you would carry out to confirm the structure of D.   (*Cambridge Schol.* Group II, 1963)

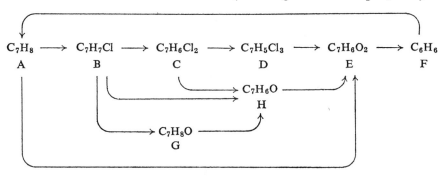

26. In the above series of chemical changes, each change can be achieved by a single reaction process.

Identify the compounds, giving names and structural formulae, and state briefly the reagents and conditions required for each step.

27. Chlorine was passed into a boiling organic compound A of molecular formula C_8H_{10}, to form B, $C_8H_8Cl_2$. When the liquid B was boiled with milk of lime a compound C, C_8H_8O, was formed, which reacted with chlorine to give a solid D, C_8H_7OCl. When D was warmed with sodium hypochlorite solution and this solution acidified, a solid E, $C_7H_6O_2$, was formed.

Elucidate these changes and give the equations for the reactions involved.

(*Cambridge Schol.* Group II, Entrance 1964)

28. A compound A, $C_4H_8O_2$ when heated, gave a compound B, C_4H_6O. On reduction A gave a compound C, $C_4H_{10}O_2$. When heated with concentrated sulphuric acid, C gave D, C_4H_6. B could be reduced to a compound E, $C_4H_{10}O$.

Deduce the nature of A, B and C and account for the above reactions.

(*Cambridge Schol.* Group II, 1956)

29. How would you synthesize the following compounds from readily available materials?

(i) $C_6H_5CHOHCHOHC_6H_5$; (ii) $H_2NCONHCH_2CH_3$;

(iii) $C_6H_5(CH_2)_2CO_2H$;   (iv) $CH_3O(CH_2)_2OH$;   (v) $H_2N(CH_2)_4NH_2$;

(vi) $CH_3NH(CH_2)_2NHCH_3$ (from ethanol and no other reagent containing carbon).

30. How would you distinguish chemically between the members of the following pairs?

(i) Ethylene and acetylene.

(ii) $(CH_3)COHCH{\Large\langle}^{CH_3}_{C_6H_5}$ and $CH_3CHOHC{\Large\langle}^{CH_3}_{C_6H_5}{\atop}$ ... $^{C_6H_5}_{CH_3}$

(iii) Acetone and acetaldehyde.

(iv) Diethylamine and *n*-butylamine.

(v) Diethylammonium chloride and tetramethylammonium chloride.

(vi) $HC{\equiv}CCH_2CH_3$ and $CH_3C{\equiv}CCH_3$.

(vii) $C_2H_5CONH_2$ and $C_2H_5CO_2NH_4$.

(viii) $C_2H_5NO_2$ and C_2H_5ONO.

(ix) $CH_3CO(CH_2)_2CO_2H$ and $CH_3COCH_2CO_2H$.

(x) $CH_3CHNH_2CO_2H$ and $CH_3CHOHCONH_2$.

(xi) 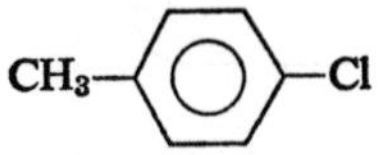 CH_3—⟨O⟩—Cl   and   ⟨O⟩—CH_2Cl

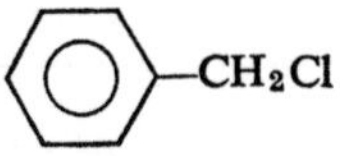

(xii) 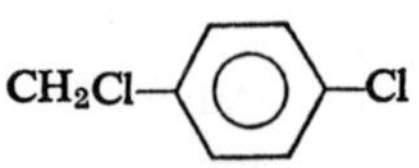 CH_2Cl—⟨O⟩—Cl   and   ⟨O⟩—$CHCl_2$

(xiii) CH_3—⟨O⟩—OH   and   ⟨O⟩—CH_2OH

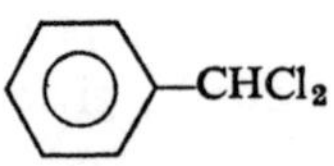

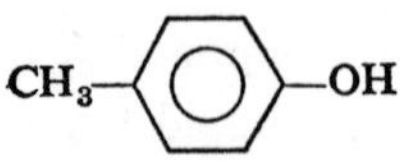

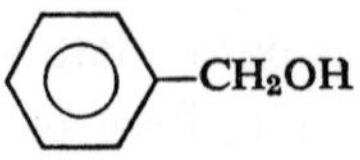

(xiv) $CH_3CH_2NHSO_2C_6H_5$ and $(CH_3)_2NSO_2C_6H_5$

Suggest a method other than simple physical fractionation for obtaining a sample of the first of each pair from a roughly equimolar mixture of the two.

31. Identify the following compounds as far as you can, and give equations for as many as possible of the reactions described:

(i) A colourless liquid A was immiscible with water and had a pronounced smell. When A was boiled with ethanolic potassium hydroxide, vapours were evolved and a white crystalline precipitate formed. The vapours, passed into an ammoniacal cuprous solution, gave a red precipitate. The white crystals were washed by decantation with ethanol. They were readily soluble in water, and the solution yielded with silver nitrate solution a cream precipitate which was insoluble in dilute nitric acid and scarcely soluble in aqueous ammonia.

(ii) A white crystalline solid, B, when heated strongly on a crucible lid left a colourless residue which evolved sulphur dioxide when warmed with dilute hydrochloric acid. An aqueous solution of B gave a deep yellow precipitate with a solution of 2,4-dinitrophenylhydrazine in dilute hydrochloric acid. When B was boiled with aqueous alkali, vapours were evolved which were condensed and added to a solution of iodine in aqueous potassium iodide. On adding a little aqueous alkali to this mixture, a pale yellow precipitate was rapidly formed.

(iii) A white crystalline solid C with a pronounced smell was quite soluble in water. A few drops of the solution gave a silver mirror when added to ammoniacal silver nitrate reagent. When C was warmed with dilute sodium hydroxide solution, a heavy colourless liquid with a pronounced smell separated as a lower layer. When C was stirred with excess of concentrated sulphuric acid, it dissolved, and an upper layer of colourless liquid appeared. This when separated off and mixed with a few drops of water gave a crystalline solid.

(iv) A white solid D left a white incombustible residue when heated on a crucible lid. D was soluble in water. The solution gave a white precipitate with sodium carbonate solution, but no precipitate with dilute sodium chromate solution; with a few drops of ferric chloride solution, it gave a reddish brown colour, and on heating the mixture a brown precipitate appeared. When D was heated dry, vapours were evolved which were condensed to a liquid distillate. This gave a yellow precipitate with 2,4-dinitrophenylhydrazine reagent. When a few drops of this distillate were added to iodine in aqueous potassium iodide, and the mixture was made alkaline with sodium hydroxide solution, a pale yellow precipitate appeared.

(v) A white crystalline solid E left a yellow residue when heated on a crucible lid. When E was warmed with concentrated sulphuric acid, a gas was evolved which burnt with a blue flame and had no effect on lime water. A solution of E in water (*a*) decolorized alkaline permanganate solution in the cold, (*b*) gave a bright yellow precipitate with potassium iodide solution.

(vi) A colourless crystalline solid F melted on heating and began to evolve ammonia. When heating was continued, the product in the test-tube resolidified. This solid was shaken with aqueous sodium hydroxide; when a drop of copper sulphate solution was added to the resulting solution, a pink colour appeared. A concentrated aqueous solution of F was mixed with a little concentrated nitric acid; a white precipitate appeared.

(vii) A colourless crystalline solid G was readily soluble in water to give a neutral solution, which effervesced gently with sodium carbonate solution, and briskly when warmed with nitrous acid. When G was heated with soda-lime a gas was evolved which had a fishy smell and was alkaline to litmus. Solutions of C and of formalin were both made slightly alkaline to phenolphthalein and then mixed; the mixture was acid to phenol-phthalein and remained so after the addition of several drops of aqueous sodium hydroxide.

(viii) A white crystalline solid H had a slight odour and was moderately soluble in water to give an acidic solution. On shaking H with aqueous ammonia, a white precipitate appeared. When H was warmed with con-centrated sulphuric acid, the gaseous products burned with a blue flame and gave a white precipitate with lime water.

(ix) A white crystalline solid I was sparingly soluble in water, the suspension being acidic to litmus. I was, however, readily soluble in sodium hydroxide solution. A solution of I in alkali was carefully made neutral to litmus by the dropwise addition of dilute acid; the product gave an intense reddish-purple colour with a few drops of ferric chloride solution. When hydrochloric acid was then added in excess, the colour disappeared, and a white precipitate was formed. When I was warmed with methanol and a few drops of concentrated sulphuric acid, a volatile product with a pro-nounced 'aromatic plant' smell was obtained. On heating I with soda-lime, a smell of 'carbolic' was noticeable.

(x) A crystalline solid J was moderately soluble in water to give an acidic solution. When hydrochloric acid, followed by sodium nitrite solution, was added to a cooled solution of J, and the product was added to a solution of β-naphthol in alkali, a bright red precipitate was formed. A solution of J with bromine water gave an immediate precipitate. A solution of J with barium chloride solution gave a white precipitate insoluble in dilute hydrochloric acid.

(xi) A crystalline solid K was sparingly soluble in water; the suspension was acid to litmus. K was, however, readily soluble in aqueous alkali and in dilute hydrochloric acid. A solution of K in excess of the latter was cooled, and a solution of sodium nitrite was added. The resulting solution was added to β-naphthol in aqueous alkali; a bright red precipitate appeared. When K was heated with soda-lime, an oily distillate with a characteristic smell was obtained. This distillate was insoluble in aqueous alkali, but readily soluble in dilute hydrochloric acid.

(xii) L was a solid with a pronounced smell, melting at about room temperature. L was immiscible with water, and burnt on a crucible lid with a smoky flame, leaving no incombustible residue. L gave an orange precipitate with 2,4-dinitrophenylhydrazine reagent. L reacted with iodine in aqueous potassium iodide and aqueous alkali; the layer of L slowly disappeared and a pale yellow precipitate was formed. This was filtered off; the filtrate on acidification gave a white precipitate.

32. On ozonolysis a hydrocarbon, A, of molecular formula $C_{10}H_{20}$, gives two isomeric products, B, and C, $C_5H_{10}O$. Oxidation of B leads to an optically active acid, D, $C_5H_{10}O_2$, whereas oxidation of C leads to an acid, E, $C_4H_8O_2$, which cannot be resolved into optically active forms. Reduction of C gives F, $C_5H_{12}O$, dehydration of which, followed by ozonolysis, gives acetone as one of the products. Deduce the structure of A and elucidate the reaction sequence.   (*Cambridge Schol.* Group I, 1961)

Answers to the exercises

Chapter 3

3. $C_4H_8O_2$.
4. M.W. $= 135$; one nitrogen.
5. $C_6H_4Br_2O$.
6. $C_3H_7NO_2$ (alanine).

Chapter 4

4. C_3H_8.
5. 60% CH_4; 40% C_2H_6.

Chapter 5

7. 72% hexane; 28% hexene.

Chapter 10

7. One hydroxyl group per molecule.

Chapter 12

4. 2MeO groups;

Chapter 13

10. A is $CH_3CONHC_4H_9$.
11. P is acetophenone oxime.

Chapter 14

18. U is o-cresol.
19. A is $CH_3CH(CH_2Br)CH_2CHO$.

Chapter 15

13. X is propionic acid.

Chapter 16

5. U is $CH_3CH=CHCN$.

Chapter 20

13. A is chloroacetyl chloride.

14. A is alanine methyl ester hydrochloride.

$$(CH_3CH(N^{\oplus}H_3Cl^{\ominus})CO_2CH_3).$$

15. A is

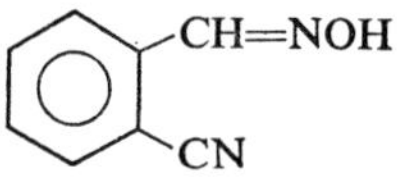

16. A is cyclohexene,

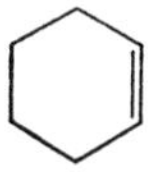

Miscellaneous exercises

16. A is $C_6H_4{\displaystyle <{CN \atop NH_2}}$, orientation *m* or *p*.

17. A is $CH_3CHOHCH_2CH_3$; B is $o—C_6H_4{\displaystyle <{CH_2CH_3 \atop CO_2H}}$; Z is the ester of A and B.

18. A is $o—C_6H_4{\displaystyle <{C\equiv CH \atop OCH_3}}$

19. A is $C_6H_5—CH=CH—CN$ or o-, m- or p- $C_6H_4{\displaystyle <{CH=CH_2 \atop CN}}$

20. W is $CH_3C_6H_4Cl$, orientation unknown.

21. A is $NCCH_2CH_2CN$.

22. A is ${CH_3 \atop CH_3}{>}C{<}{OH \atop CN}$ acetone cyanohydrin.

23. A is 'Perspex'—polymethylmethacrylate.

24. A is ${CH_3 \atop HOCH_2}{>}C{<}{CO_2H. \atop CO_2H}$

25. A is m- or p- $CH_3.C_6H_4.CHOHCH_3$.

26. A is toluene.

27. A is ethylbenzene $C_6H_5.C_2H_5$.

28. A is aldol, $CH_3CHOHCH_2CHO$.

31. (i) A is $C_2H_4Br_2$, either isomer, or a low homologue $RC_2H_3Br_2$.

(ii) B is a bisulphite compound of acetone or other low $CH_3CO—$ ketone.

(iii) C is chloral hydrate.

    (iv) D is calcium acetate.

    (v) E is lead formate.

   (vi) F is urea.

  (vii) G is glycine or a similar amino-acid.

(viii) H is methyl oxalate.

   (ix) I is salicylic acid.

    (x) J is anilinium sulphate.

   (xi) K is anthranilic acid or a similar aromatic amino-acid.

  (xii) L is acetophenone.

32. A is $CH_3CH_2CH(CH)_3CH{=}C(CH_3)CH(CH_3)_2$.

Index

Note: Entries are alphabetized 'letter by letter', e.g.

ethyl cyanide
ethylene
ethyl glycollate

The prefixes α-, β-, m-, N-, n-, o-, p-, s-, t-, are neglected in indexing, but compounds beginning cyclo- and iso- are indexed as such.